MINUTES OF THE RAINBOW CIRCLE,
1894–1924

MINUTES OF THE RAINBOW CIRCLE, 1894–1924

Edited by

MICHAEL FREEDEN

CAMDEN FOURTH SERIES
VOLUME 38

LONDON

OFFICES OF THE ROYAL HISTORICAL SOCIETY
UNIVERSITY COLLEGE LONDON
GOWER STREET WC1E 6BT
1989

British Library Cataloguing Publication Data

Camden, Fourth Series, Vol. 38
'The Minutes of the Rainbow Circle, 1894–1924',
ed. M. Freeden
ISBN 0–86193–120–3

Printed and bound in Great Britain by
Butler & Tanner Ltd, Frome and London

CONTENTS

PREFACE

Some abbreviations used in the Minutes of the Rainbow Circle have been retained, but others have been spelt out in full for the sake of readability. In Appendix II, which contains short biographies of members, I have expanded on information regarding the lesser-known members, as other sources on the more famous are readily available.

Many individuals have generously assisted me in collating information for the annotations and the biographical entries. In particular I would like to thank Mr. S.S. Wilson, the last secretary of the Rainbow Circle, for his invaluable advice and comments and for his support for the project of publication. Dr Angela Raspin, the archivist of the British Library of Political and Economic Science—where the Minutes are deposited—as well as Ms. Fiona Maccoll, were unsparing with their time and greatly facilitated the process of transcribing the Minutes. Dr. Colin Matthew, as Literary Director of the Royal Historical Society, provided constant encouragement as well as exemplary editorial nous and patience. I wish also to record my appreciation of the very helpful communications from Lord Roskill, from Mr. J.G. Dewes, Secretary of the Sir Richard Stapley Educational Trust, and from Mr. D. Pegg, Archivist of Pearl Assurance plc. My thanks are also due to the staff of the following institutions for their courteous assistance: The House of Lords Record Office, the Public Record Office, the Bodleian Library, Oxford, and the British Library; as well as the librarians of the following Oxford colleges: Balliol, Mansfield, Nuffield, Pembroke, St. John's, Wadham. There are others, too numerous to mention, whose indulgence I request for a general expression of gratitude.

Michael Freeden
Mansfield College, Oxford

LIST OF RAINBOW CIRCLE MEETINGS

First Session 1894–1895: The Old Manchesterism and The New Radicalism

1. J.A.M. Macdonald	The Ethical Deficiencies of the Old Radicalism
2. J.A. Hobson	Economic Deficiencies of the Manchester School
3. W. Clarke	Political defects of the Old Radicalism
4. S. Olivier	The Literary Revolt against Manchesterism
5. H. Shuttleworth	The Religious Revolt against the Manchester School
6. H. Burrows	Trade Unionism as a revolt against the Manchester School
7. C. Edwards	The Revolt of the Co-operator against Manchesterism
8. J.R. MacDonald	Summary of the discussions of the Session

Second Session 1895–1896: The New Radicalism

9. G.H. Perris	The Evolutionary Standpoint in Social Theory
10. H. Samuel	The New Liberalism
11. H. Burrows	The Position of the Socialist Societies
12. H. Burrows	Reply to the Discussion
13. A.L. Lilley	The Religious Societies
14. B. Costelloe	The Individual & the State
15. General Conversation	
16. J.A. Hobson	Individual and State Property
17. J.R. MacDonald	The State & Education

Third Session 1896–1897: Democracy

18. H. Samuel	The Democratic Franchise
19. J.R. MacDonald	The Referendum
20. H. Burrows	Democracy
20a. H. Burrows	Democracy (continued)
21. C.P. Trevelyan	The Organization of the Representative Chamber

x   MINUTES OF THE RAINBOW CIRCLE, 1894-1924

Ninth Session 1902–1903: The Political and Economic Situation in France, Germany, and the United States

73. A.L. Lilley — Church & State & Education in France
74. W.M. Crook — The Constitutional Problem in France
75. J.M. Robertson — The Economic Situation in France
76. J.H. Harley — Socialism in Germany
77. G.H. Perris — Militarism in Germany
78. D. Morrison — Industry & Education in Germany
79. W.P. Reeves — Race Problem in U.S.A.
80. J.R. MacDonald — Democracy & Imperialism in U.S.A.
81. J.A. Hobson — Capitalism in U.S.A.

Tenth Session 1903–1904: Problems of India and the British Colonies

82. J.M. Robertson — India
83. J.A. Hobson — South Africa
84. G.H. Perris — Egypt
85. J.R. MacDonald — Canada
86. W.P. Reeves — Australia
87. H. de R. Walker — New Zealand
88. J. McKillop — The Tropical Belt
89. J.H. Harley — The Fiscal Question
90. J.A.M. Macdonald — The Constitutional Question of Imperial Federation

Eleventh Session 1904–1905: The Newer Demands of the Political Left Wing

91. J.A. Hobson — The Referendum
92. J.A.M. Macdonald — Home Rule All Round
93. J.R. MacDonald — Relations of L.R.C. and other Progressive Parties
94. J.H. Harley — Compulsory Arbitration
95. J.M. Robertson — Old Age Pensions
96. J. McKillop — Municipal Financial Problems & Readjustment
97. G.H. Perris — National Finance
98. A. Parsons — The Transport Question
99. F.J. Matheson — Housing and Land Tenure
100. Informal Meeting

Twelfth Session 1905–1906: To What Type of Organisation Society Corresponds; Applications to Current Problems

101. J.A. Hobson	To What Type of Organisation does Society Correspond? (1)
102. J.H. Harley	To What Type of Organisation does Society Correspond? (2)
103. J.R. MacDonald	The Organisation of Industry
104. J.M. Robertson	The State in Relation to Property
105. S. Olivier	Racial Problems
106. G.H. Perris	International Relationships
107. W.M. Crook	Organisation of National Politics
108. A.L. Lilley	The State in Relation to Religion & Education

Thirteenth Session 1906–1907: English Statesmen of the Nineteenth Century

109. J. Bullock, W.M. Crook	Earl Grey
110. J.H. Harley	Lord Melbourne
111. G.F. Millin	Sir Robert Peel
112. J.O. Herdman	Lord Aberdeen
113. A.L. Lilley	Lord Palmerston
114. W.P. Byles	Lord John Russell
115. J.M. Robertson	Beaconsfield
116. W.M. Crook	Gladstone
117. R. Rea	Lord Salisbury
118. Circle Dinner	

Fourteenth Session 1907–1908: Socialism—following the Lines of Émile Faguet's book 'La Socialisme en 1907'

119. J.M. Robertson	The Social, Political & Economic Facts which have given Birth to Socialism
120. J.H. Harley	Historical Sketch of the Development of Socialism
121. F.J. Matheson	The Chief Constitutive Ideas & Aims of Socialism
122. H. Burrows	Anarchism
123. P. Alden	Democratic Redistribution of Property: Peasant Proprietary & Small Co-operative Production

	Acts etc.) possessed, but not sufficiently used
147. H. Burrows	The Future Scope of Local Government and the Future Relations between the Municipality & the National State
148. Rainbow Circle Dinner	

Seventeenth Session 1910–1911: Modern Legislative Systems, with Special reference to Second Chambers

149. J.H. Harley	The Second Chamber in France and Switzerland and the Referendum
150. H. de R. Walker	The Second Chamber in Canada, South Africa and Australasia
151. G.P. Gooch	The Second Chamber in Germany & in Austria-Hungary
152. F.J. Matheson	The Second Chamber in the U.S.A.
153. J.M. Robertson	Bicameral versus Unicameral Legislative Systems considered in the light of the four preceding papers
154. G.H. Perris	The British Cabinet & Executive in Relation to Parliament
155. M.A. Cloudesley Brereton	Motherhood, the Home & Medical Inspection of Schools
156. J.R. MacDonald	The British Parliament in Relation to Suggestions for the Future
157. J.A.M. Macdonald	The British Parliament in Relation to Proposals for Home Rule All Round
158. J.O. Herdman	Representative Government
159. Rainbow Circle Dinner	

Eighteenth Session 1911–1912: Modern Thinkers and the Movements with which they are Associated

160. W.M. Crook	Tolstoi
161. H.J. Golding	Bergson
162. M. Adams	William James
163. R.P. Farley	Sorel & Syndicalism
163a. G.H. Perris	Hervé & the Peace Movement
164. J.A. Hobson	Olive Schreiner, Ellen Key and Feminism
165. C.I.S. Smith	Women in Sweated and Dangerous Trades
166. J.M. Robertson	Ferrer & the Anti-Clerical Movement in Spain

Twenty-Fifth Session 1918–1919: Post-War Issues

227. S. Olivier	The British Bureaucracy
228. G.P. Gooch	Extension of Self Government for India
229. J.H. Harley	The Future of Poland
230. G. Paish	The effect of the War on the Finance of the belligerent countries
231. A. Wigglesworth	State control of Trade after the War
232. H. de R. Walker	Housing & Town-Planning after the War
233. J. McKillop	The future of Trade Unionism
234. J.O. Herdman	The Passing of the Judiciary

Twenty-Sixth Session 1919–1920: The Peace; Problems for Britain at Home and Abroad

235. G.P. Gooch	The Peace Terms as they affect the conquered nations
236. S. Olivier	The Mandatory System of the League of Nations
237. C. Hurcomb	The Limits of Goverment control in times of peace
238. A. Wigglesworth	The New Industrialism
239. R. Lynd	Sinn Fein
240. J.M. Robertson	Egyptian Unrest
241. B. Basu	Indian Unrest
242. W.M. Crook	The League of Nations

Twenty-Seventh Session 1920–1921: The Present Political Situation

243. G.P. Gooch	The present political situation in Germany
244. J.A. Hobson	The present political situation in the United States
245. A. Wigglesworth	The present political situation in Italy
246. J.H. Harley	The present political situation in Poland
247. R.W. Seton-Watson	The present political situation in Austria
248. M. Andra	The present political situation in France
249. N. Buxton	The present political situation in the Balkan States
250. H.B. Usher	The present political situation in Mesopotamia
251. Meeting abandoned due to illness of lecturer	

INTRODUCTION

1893 was a watershed in the development of progressive thought in Britain. The failure of the Liberal party, under Gladstone's increasingly tired leadership, to rise to the challenge posed by the 1891 Newcastle Programme exacerbated the tendency of various radical groups to press for their inclination, practical or programmatic, towards a more collectivist social reform. The most famous of these were the Fabians, rallying to the cause of political activism under the cry 'To Your Tents, Oh Israel'.[1] Many progressives deserted the Liberals, thus hastening the formation of the Labour party. Other advanced liberals continued to fight to battle from within. A number of the more reflective representatives of those coteries, 'interested in the study of social questions', decided in that same year to get together and proceeded to hold a series of meetings in the National Liberal Club. They included William Clarke, one of the Fabian Essayists, J.A. Murray Macdonald, the Liberal M.P., and the journalist W.M. Crook.[2] Thus began one of the most remarkable discussion groups of modern times in Britain, the Rainbow Circle. Spanning close to forty years, incorporating some of the most influential and original social and political thinkers and activists from the liberal and moderate socialist camps, it served as a testing ground and melting pot for their ideologies and policies.

The aims of the Rainbow Circle were initially highly structured and remained so for some years. The discussions were intended 'to provide a rational and comprehensive view of political and social progress, leading up to a consistent body of political and economic doctrine which could be ultimately formulated in a programme for action, and in that form provide a rallying point for social reformers.'[3] The Circle's members saw themselves as true inheritors of the mantle of philosophic radicalism, now recast in a clearly collectivist or, as it could better be described, communitarian mould. The debates of the first year were thus devoted to an attack on the old Manchester School of economics. Significantly setting the tone for the future, the Circle began to work towards an appreciation of the interconnections

---

[1] 'To Your Tents, Oh Israel', *Fortnightly Review*, vol. liv (1893), 569–89.

[2] See *Second Chambers in Practice* (London, 1911), introduction by Ambrose Parsons, p. v; J.A. Hobson, *Confessions of an Economic Heretic* (London, 1938), pp 94–5. Other N.L.C. members who helped to formalize the Circle were Herbert Burrows, J.A. Hobson, Richard Stapley and Ramsay MacDonald.

[3] Herbert Samuel Papers, A/10/1, House of Lords Record Office.

between ethics, economics and politics.[4] The brand of social and political thought it produced was hence both methodologically and ideologically nearest in spirit to the rising new liberalism, with its organicist proclivities, its balance between individual and social needs, and the benevolently interventionist role accorded to the state. Despite occasional disagreements and disclaimers to the contrary, it maintained a remarkable cohesion of purpose and outlook at least until the first world war.

No record remains of the Circle's activities inside the National Liberal Club, though we know that it heard a paper read by Canon Shuttleworth.[5] In November 1894 the group began convening regularly at the Rainbow Tavern in Fleet Street—from whence the name—but the paucity of the food[6] or, according to another version, a 'shortcoming of the more profitable forms of drink' occasioned a move shortly thereafter to the premises of Richard Stapley, a prosperous merchant whose house at 33 Bloomsbury Square offered the Circle hospitality and 'post-prandial amenities.'[7] In 1929 it was demolished, and the Circle repaired to Percy Alden's offices at 32, Gordon Square. None of these premises survives, nor do the insignia of office—the chairman's chair and the rosebowl that stood before him. In contradistinction, the preservation of four out of five of the Circle's minute books—the first in Ramsay MacDonald's handsomely rounded script, the fifth unfortunately vanished when a second world war German bomb destroyed the house at Gordon Square—provides a continuous glimpse into the unfolding concerns and debates of progressive social reformers who worked unceasingly to help fashion the thinking at the basis of the British welfare state.

The Circle was a small, cohesive and relatively close-knit group. It included many exceptional and some colourful individuals, as the appendix on members attempts to show. At the same time, the very length of its existence must have assisted in fomenting friendships and in defining its homogeneity. But it is of great importance to note that the Circle itself was not the initial forum nor the fulcrum of the activities of its members. Rather, it was created at the interstices of a number of important London social and political associations and thus held together a remarkable network of interlocking relationships. Indeed, the small number of London progressives, whose imprint on the new intellectual and political movements of their times was so considerable, moved in overlapping and reinforcing circles. Many of

[4] Ibid.
[5] *Second Chambers in Practice*, p. v.
[6] See meeting 275 (1924).
[7] Hobson, *Confessions*, p. 95.

the Rainbow Circle's members belonged to the Liberal party as aspiring politicians or fervent reformers (and a minority joined the Labour Representation Committee when it was formed in 1900). Over the years Alden, Buxton, Byles, Gooch, Murray Macdonald, Rea, Robertson, Samuel, Trevelyan, and Walker were returned to Westminster as Liberal M.P.s, and after the war Alden, Buxton and Trevelyan joined Ramsay MacDonald as Labour M.P.s. Many others were unsuccessful parliamentary candidates: Burrows, Cooke, Costelloe, Hobson (as an independent), Keay, Lane Fox-Pitt, Raphael, Roskill, Rylett, Stapley and Usher. In addition, a number of Circle members were on the L.C.C., on Borough Councils or School Boards.

The University settlement movement provided further fertile ground for future members. Alden was the first Warden of Mansfield House settlement. John Bullock introduced to the Circle his fellow resident from Toynbee Hall, Trevor Walsh, and other former residents came as guests or as speakers. Beyond that, intellectual and political life was in a state of great fermentation through the Fabian and ethical societies. J.A. Hobson, for example, was not atypical in devoting his career to writing and lecturing, and contributed not only to most of the leading radical organs at the turn of the century, but lectured ceaselessly for the Extension Movement, the Ethical Movement, and occasionally the Fabians and the London School of Economics (this latter institution affording a link with the most imperialistically-minded of the Rainbow Circle members, W. Pember Reeves, as well as a further sphere of association with Wallas, Oakeshott, McKillop and Burns).

However, though membership of the Fabian Society was rife among Circle participants, not too much should be read into this circumstance. Outside the hard-core of Fabian activists who were committed to some version of socialist gradualism, the other Fabian 'Mitläufer' were a motley sort. The only dedicated and central Fabians were Maurice Adams, co-founder of the Fellowship of the New Life; Clarke, one of the original Fabian Essayists; and, in the early years, Ramsay MacDonald. For the rest, Fabian membership did not imply subscription to a creed antagonistic to liberalism. Some of the socialists, or Christian Socialists, such as Belcher, Dearmer and Oakeshott, no doubt found the Rainbow Circle too tame or irrelevant for their purposes and left at an early stage, though Burrows remained loyal to the end, and Sydney Olivier and Graham Wallas—two further Fabian Essayists—maintained strong links with the Circle and returned to it in later years. But many joined the Fabians simply for the obvious reason that the Society provided an organized stimulus to their interest in social questions. Some Rainbow Circle members, such as Bullock,[8] Frederick James Matheson, John McKillop[9] and Ambrose Parsons, allowed their membership to lapse long before they parted company with the Circle; Henry Golding, R.P. Farley and J.H. Harley—who did not—were relatively inactive in the Fabian Society.[10]

Far more important to understanding the mentality and ends of the Rainbow Circle was the Ethical Movement. The South Place Ethical Society, the London Ethical Society and the West London Ethical Society (the Ethical Church, Bayswater),[11] all products of the 1880s and 1890s—though South Place had its origins in a non-conformist liberal-humanist tradition[12]—provided centres of involvement for some Circle members. The ethical societies were concurrently concerned with facets of the social question and with the secular and humanist moral instruction of the middle classes, and served on the whole as foci for progressive causes.[13] In particular, South Place Ethical Society became a centre of radical intellectual thinking through providing a vital podium for the reflections of Herbert Burrows, Hobson, John M. Robertson and, later, Cecil Delisle Burns. All four became 'Appointed Lecturers' for South Place, the first three alternating for the Sunday lecture from the early part of this century. As Hobson later wrote, 'My close connection with this liberal platform, lasting continuously for thirty-six years, was of great help to me in clarifying my thought and enlarging my range of interests in matters of social conduct. Addressing audiences consisting for the most part of men and women of the business and professional classes, with a scattering of educated clerks and manual workers, I found myself driven to put ethical significance into a variety of current topics and events, many of which belonged to the fields of politics and economics.'[14] Graham Wallas, though not a member, was a supporter and frequent lecturer.[15]

[8] Bullock was primarily responsible for *Old Age Pensions*, Fabian Tract No. 89. See Fabian Society Papers, Nuffield College, Oxford, E 3, varied correspondence in 1899.

[9] McKillop conducted a few classes for the Fabian Society (see ibid., C 7, Fabian Society Executive Committee Minutes, 19.3.1897, 22.4.1898; and *Fabian News*, Sept. 1896). He also lectured occasionally (ibid., C 39, 11.2.1898 on 'Socialism and Race'), though his proposal to write a Fabian Tract on Education was allowed to lapse following a report by G.B. Shaw. (Ibid., E 3, 23.11.1899).

[10] Fabian Society Papers, C 7, 22.9.1905 records the dropping of Samuel and W.P. Byles from the list of Fabian members, though there is no record of their activities, if any.

[11] See G. Spiller, *The Ethical Movement in Great Britain: A Documentary History* (London, 1934).

[12] Cp. S.K. Ratcliffe, *The Story of South Place* (London, 1955).

[13] Cp. I.D. MacKillop, *The British Ethical Societies* (Cambridge, 1986).

[14] Hobson, *Confessions*, pp. 57-8.

[15] Ratcliffe, *The Story of South Place*, p. 67.

Other ethical societies also gave sustenance to Circle participants. Murray Macdonald was one of the earliest members of the London Ethical Society, in which the philosophers Bernard Bosanquet and J.H. Muirhead were central figures. Clarke was another member. T.F. Husband was connected with it through the activities of his wife, Mary Gilliland Husband, the main organizer of the L.E.S. The L.E.S., interestingly, began its Sunday evening lectures at Toynbee Hall in 1886—further evidence of the complex of liaisons. Russell Rea and Corrie Grant (who never played an active part in the Circle but was an early member) were officers of the West London Ethical Society, and G.P. Gooch was a member.[16] Adams was in charge of the Croydon Ethical and Religious Fellowship. Ramsay MacDonald, G.H. Perris and Golding were regular speakers for the Union of Ethical Societies.[17] MacDonald, Perris and Hobson were frequent contributors to its weekly, *Ethical World*,[18] as were Robertson and Gooch. The Union of Ethical Societies was also instrumental in founding the Moral Instruction (later Education) League, aimed at improving school curricula, and St. George Lane Fox-Pitt—a member of the Circle for a short period—was at one time its vice-president and treasurer.[19] It is worth noting also that due to the close relations among the ethical societies and the ploughed furrow of the lecture circuit, most of the above-mentioned met and heard each other frequently.

Another group of Rainbow Circle participants was united through an alternative focal point, though of a less encompassing and significant nature. They were members of a small organization founded in 1904, the British Institute of Social Service, the forerunner of the National Council of Social Service. Here again practical and ethical ends merged. The Institute's objectives included the collection, registration and dissemination of information relating to social service and industrial betterment, in order to improve and elevate national life. While trying to 'avoid the pitfall of party controversy',[20] it was clearly an attempt to organize and co-ordinate the forces of social reform, to eliminate 'muddling through' and to bring a semblance of a scientific rational spirit to practical social effort.[21] To which ideological effect this fact-finding was put can be surmised from its membership. Matheson was its secretary from 1906–9 and 'during his term of office the

---

[16] Spiller, *The Ethical Movement*, pp. 67, 91.
[17] MacKillop, *The British Ethical Societies*, pp. 107–10; H.J. Golding in *The Fiftieth Anniversary of the Ethical Movement* (New York, 1926), pp. 177–81; *South Place Ethical Record*, March 1931, 2-3; Spiller, pp. 99–109.
[18] Spiller, pp. 109–11; MacKillop, pp. 147–62.
[19] Cp. Spiller, pp. 124–56; *The Times*, 7.4.1932.
[20] Fabian Society Records, B7/1.
[21] Cp. F.J. Matheson, 'A Clearing House for Social Reform', *Progress*, vol. xi (1916), 53–63.

whole work of the Institute was established, built up, and systema-
tised.'[22] Among the first officers of the executive committee of the
B.I.S.S. were the following Circle members: Hobson, Murray Macdonald, the social reformer Percy Alden, the librarian of the London
School of Economics John McKillop, and the historian G.P. Gooch.
Later Samuel and Richard Stapley, the Circle's chairman, joined its
council, the latter becoming chairman of the executive committee in
1915. The industrialist F.W. Goodenough became treasurer of the
B.I.S.S. in 1922, and Parsons joined the executive committee in 1928.
The Liberal H. de R. Walker volunteered help in its library just before
the war. In 1906 the B.I.S.S. began to publish a journal, *Progress*,
edited by the Rev. A.H. Byles, a brother of the Circle member W.H.
Byles, and later by Matheson, while another Circle participant—R.P.
Farley, the writer on social affairs—was an occasional contributor.
When Stapley died in 1920 he left a large sum of money to the
establishment of the Sir Richard Stapley Educational Trust. Alden
directed the Trust, and the secretary of the B.I.S.S., Joyce Brown,
also became the Trust's secretary. Moreover, *Progress* was converted
in 1922 to the organ of the Stapley Educational Trust.

There was of course one further major domain in which the paths
of Circle members crossed: the press. Joint work on the Liberal daily
Echo appears to have been the basis for mutual acquaintance. Crook
was its editor from 1898–1900, to be succeeded by Alden from 1901–
2. Harley was a staff member, and Ramsay MacDonald became chief
leader-writer in 1901.[23] The *Daily News* provided employment for its
editor, Gardiner, and for G.F. Millin and Perris, and Harley and
Clarke were on the staff of the *Daily Chronicle*. Other Circle members,
such as Hobson, obtained occasional income from these papers. Perris,
Rylett and Hobson worked on the short-lived *Tribune*, when the
eminent liberal theorist and sociologist L.T. Hobhouse was political
editor. Hobson had been a long-standing staff member of the illustrious liberal weekly the *Nation*, to which other Circle members
occasionally contributed. When the *Contemporary Review* came under
Gooch's co-editorship in 1911, the Rainbow Circle found an obvious
outlet not only for members' articles in general, but specifically for
talks given under its auspices. The editorial policy of the *Contemporary
Review* began to correspond closely with the causes, national and
international, espoused by the Rainbow Circle.[24]

Evidently, the Rainbow Circle contained a number of cohesive
and overlapping sub-groups, including individuals who were at the

[22] *Progress*, vol. iv (1909), 7.
[23] Cp. S. Koss, *The Rise and Fall of the Political Press in Britain*, vol. i (London, 1981),
p. 388.
[24] Cp. F. Eyck, *G.P. Gooch: A Study in History and Politics* (London, 1982), pp. 231–6.

forefront of their professions and well-integrated into the chief forms of radical expression and action available in turn-of-the-century London. Its activities and debates cannot therefore be understood in isolation from these formative progressive forums. As for the general background of its participants, not only was the field of journalism well-represented, but also the civil service, the legal profession and religious office-holders, whether nonconformists, catholics or anglican christian socialists.

Although the Rainbow Circle saw itself as a private discussion group and consequently felt able to engage in free and open debate, its minutes indeed attesting to the range and occasional audacity permitted by its relaxed and compact ambience, it did embark on a small number of journalistic ventures itself. Twice it considered publication of the minutes; twice this was eventually turned down, until in 1911 the Circle published the full version of talks and discussions that had taken place over the previous year on second chambers[25]—plainly a topical reaction to the 1909–11 House of Lords crisis. Some speakers, of course, replicated their talks in separate publications, or used them as raw drafts of future articles and chapters. That aside, the main publishing venture of the Circle was the launching of the *Progressive Review*. Notwithstanding the Circle's variegated background, here was further evidence that it had developed its own distinctive style and interests that were neither Fabian nor socialist; not even, on the whole, akin to Liberal party positions. 'Finding that we were more or less at one in many things', recalled Samuel, 'the Rainbow Circle decided, in 1896, to publish a review to propagate those doctrines that were held in common.'[26] Commenting on the *Progressive Review*, Hobson observed that 'The term 'New Liberalism' was adopted by Samuel and others as rightly descriptive of its aims'.[27] And Golding had occasion to record that 'membership of the Rainbow Circle, to which I was very undeservingly admitted in 1911, gave me chastening intercourse with some of the strongest minds in the liberal movement in thought and politics . . . leading progressives were of the company'[28]

The *Progressive Review*, as the minutes bear out, occupied much of the energies of the Circle in 1895–6. Most of its capital was raised by Samuel, Stapley, Hobson and Trevelyan. Clarke became editor, with Hobson as second editor. The monthly saw first light in October 1896

---

[25] *Second Chambers in Practice*, op. cit. Matheson, one of the contributors, was working at the time for the publisher P.S. King who, during a short period of time published not only this volume, but books by Hobson and Harley.

[26] H. Samuel, *Memoirs* (London, 1945), p. 24.

[27] Hobson, *Confessions*, p. 52.

[28] Golding, *op. cit.*, p. 180.

and, although some of its writers were Circle members, shielded by anonymity, it aspired to a wider spread of contributors from across the radical and socialist fields. The failure to achieve that end was one of the reasons for its floundering a year later;[29] more important were the altercations, both ideological and personal, among its central figures. The ideological discord related to the rising political menace of rampant British imperialism, among others against the backdrop of the 1896 Jameson raid in South Africa, thought to have been masterminded by Joseph Chamberlain at the Colonial Office. It is interesting that the most serious divisions the Rainbow Circle exhibited were not on domestic social affairs but, through Samuel and Pember Reeves, on attitudes towards (Liberal) imperialism—opposed in particular by Hobson and Clarke[30]—and, later on, in connection with its stance towards the first world war.[31] The personal friction arose largely between Clarke and Ramsay MacDonald, the latter acting as secretary. Clarke resented the call of other activities on MacDonald's time and regarded this as an additional burden upon his uncertain health,[32] whereas MacDonald was upset by what he conceived to be plotting against him behind his back by the directors. By the time the two were ready for reconciliation the economic circumstances of the *Review* had doomed it.[33]

The *Review* was designed 'to do for the public generally what the Circle discussions are intended to do for the members.' It identified a gap left by the existing reactionary or too open monthlies, leaving 'the modern collectivist movements ... without an organ which attempts to give them rational expression.'[34] It saw itself as a self-appointed mouthpiece of the progressive movement.[35] In the introduction to its opening number—the best general statement of the Rainbow Circle credo—it lamented the paralysis of the Liberal party and indicated a

[29] The problem beset the *Review* from the start. See Clarke to MacDonald, 30.1.1896, Ramsay MacDonald Papers, P.R.O. 30/69/1200.

[30] Clarke was alarmed about the possibility of the Liberal Imperialism of Samuel and R.B. Haldane ('that little band of men on the make ... promot[ing] a bastard Liberalism & a lot of imperialist bosh') penetrating the *Review* and infusing it with 'all the everlasting humbug of the 'New Liberalism'.' (Clarke to MacDonald, 2.2.1896, Ramsay MacDonald Papers, P.R.O. 30/69/1200).

[31] See Hobson, *Confessions*, pp. 95–6, commenting on the breach between Robertson and Reeves, supporters of the war, and MacDonald, Burrows and (presumably) himself, seekers of an end to the hostilities.

[32] Cp. also the difficulties hinted at in the R.C. minutes, P.R. Committee meeting (undated) following meeting on 8 January 1896.

[33] Cp. Samuel papers, A/10/6–25; Samuel, *Memoirs*, p. 24. The *Fabian News* (Sept. 1897) commented: 'It is unfortunate that the public has not adequately supported the promoters of this excellent enterprise.'

[34] Samuel papers, A/10/2, circular from R. MacDonald dated 27.2.1895.

[35] Ibid, A/10/5. Circular from R. MacDonald dated August 1896.

key theme of the early years of the Circle: the endeavour to synthesize, realign and unify, across party lines, a plethora of advanced political ideas relating to the social question. 'At no time has so large a body of thoughtful opinion, scattered over the length and breadth of the land, been so powerfully impressed by the need of a genuine policy of drastic reform in the social, economic, and moral conditions of life ... Liberal thought and the enthusiasm of social reform are sprouting from a thousand seeds sown by education in a thousand separate spots.'[36]

In a forceful exposition of the social radicalism of new liberal ideology, the *Review* called for a new progressive party (while leaving the door open for the Liberal party to assume that mantle) needed 'to carry to completion the task of securing genuine economic freedom, ... [and] to undertake the onerous and multifarious duties which devolve upon a modern state in contributing, by legislative and administrative acts, to secure the material and moral welfare of the people ... If it shall still be considered the chief business of the State to secure liberty, this term must carry an enlarged and enlightened conception of the functions of the State which shall be limited only by the power of the conscious organisation of society to assist in securing for its members the fullest opportunities of life.'[37] It stressed in particular the antithesis of riches and poverty, the advantages of public control of monopolies while retaining the stimulus of private enterprise, the need for reformulated principles of social justice, and the democratization of the machinery of government. On the international arena it was predictably and significantly bland, referring simply to 'right and abiding principles of international intercourse and some just policy for the adaptation of the outwardly conflicting claims of racial development throughout the world.'[38]

The first five years of the Rainbow Circle were devoted to a detailed examination of the political and social theory of progressivism. Following the first year's session on Manchesterism, a number of talks stand out. Samuel introduced his view of the new liberalism, intending both to delineate that perspective unequivocally from socialism and to explore paths of ideological agreement among progressives.[39] Despite a confused reiteration of Benthamite principles, it gave vent to the

[36] 'Introductory', *Progressive Review*, vol. 1 (1896), 1-2.
[37] Ibid., 4.
[38] Ibid., 8.
[39] Witness C.P. Trevelyan's account to his mother immediately after his close friend Samuel had given his talk on the new liberalism: 'Samuel and I have been trying to thrash out difficulties at the Rainbow Circle with the thinking Socialists. I think we make them come down a little from their ideal eminence—certainly we get our own minds clearer as to what we want.' (Quoted in A.J.A. Morris, *C.P. Trevelyan 1870–1958* [Belfast, 1977]).

growing sense of social unity and the prospective role of the state that
pervaded the Circle's analyses. The previous month Samuel had just
heard G.P. Perris expounding on the organic analogy, the employment of which now became increasingly salient in Circle debates, and
was shared by a range of speakers encompassing Perris, Burrows,
Hobson, Harley, Ramsay MacDonald, Crook and Adams.[40] Socialist
views such as those of Burrows were now perceived as similar to those
of the new liberals; what worried many members was that no party
could serve as a practicable vessel of either. Hence the road was paved
towards broaching the idea of a progressive party on lines similar to
those already tested in the London context[41]—the forging of a political
structure to encompass the accord in social analysis as well as to
express the organic conception of society itself.

As the *Progressive Review* episode demonstrated, issues of empire—
and race—were another sphere not easily assimilated to progressive
outlooks. The abandonment of Empire was not on the agenda, but
the abyss separating the position of Reeves from those of Hobson,
Robertson and Clarke was unbridgeable. Reeves' unmistakable racist
views, with their reference to the dangers of the multiplication of
native, 'dark' races had to wait quite a few years for a direct rebuttal
within the Circle by Olivier.[42] Not that those views were generally
shared ones, but the anti-imperialists were too preoccupied with the
larger social, economic and moral issues to take issue with Reeves'
fulminations. Deep divisions persisted among members with respect
to the question: did imperialism advance civilization or undermine
democracy?—if indeed any such assessment was possible.[43] The entire
session of 1899–1900, against the back-drop of the Boer war, was
devoted to imperialism, with Hobson adumbrating his favourite theme
of the grave dangers imperialism constituted to the imperial state and
Clarke reinforcing that position, identifying the militarist/capitalist
combination that sapped the moral freedom of the colonizing country.
Douglas Morrison came under heavy attack—at a meeting in which
Reeves was absent and the anti-imperialists abundantly represented—
for suggesting that some races were incapable of receiving civilization.[44] Samuel rallied the imperialist forces the following month,
decrying the little Englandism that damaged social reform and prais-

---

[40] See meetings 9 (1895), 61 (1902), 101, 102, 103 (1905), 107 (1906) and 130 (1908).
Cp. M. Freeden, 'The New Liberalism and its Aftermath' in R. Bellamy (ed.), *Victorian
Liberalism* (London, 1989).

[41] Cp. P. Thompson, *Socialists, Liberals, and Labour. The Struggle for London 1885–1914*
(London, 1967).

[42] Meetings 28 (1897), 38 (1898), and 105 (1906).

[43] Meeting 38 (1898). The milder discussion in the follow-up to the debate in meeting
39 may be explained by Hobson's absence.

[44] Meeting 49 (1899).

ing an imperialism that improved trade and protected and uplifted the native.[45] The heat of the imperialist issue dissipated in the following years and its frequency on the Circle programmes declined. Hobson returned to it in a talk on South Africa in 1903[46] and again in 1914 to arraign the spurious socialism of allocating public money and power for private gains.[47] But by then all eyes had turned to Europe.

The question of women merits separate comment. Remarkably, no woman was ever a member of the Rainbow Circle. The presence of two lady guests was first recorded in 1902,[48] and on two occasions only, in 1911 and 1912, did the Circle experiment with a Ladies' Night—less patronizing than it sounds, as the ladies in question came not just as guests or spouses of male members, but addressed the gathering themselves. Though Cloudesley Brereton (whose wife was later to give a talk) had raised the question in 1909 and had rallied more supporters than objectors, 'the majority of the members present shewing a discreditable neutrality',[49] this readiness to invite woman speakers did not however occur until the suffragettes had made their weight felt. It was only in 1924 that a Ladies' Night—this time of the traditional kind—was reinstituted for a special celebratory meeting,[50] and repeated again at the 300th meeting in 1927.[51] The very last Circle meeting significantly excluded lady guests.[52] Despite that, political and social issues pertaining to women frequently appeared on Circle agendas. Samuel's 1896 suggestion that women could be excluded from the suffrage, being as they were on the wrong side of the divide between wise and unwise electors, was singled out for criticism. Burrows, closely associated with the unionization of women, reiterated his wish that they organize to attain higher living standards.[53] In an ambivalent move towards greater social equality, women were positively encouraged to work, with 'foster mothers to look after their children.'[54] Stress was laid on the education of girls.[55] Divorce was an area where it was thought women's equality could be advanced,

[45] Meeting 50 (1900).
[46] See meeting 83 and footnote.
[47] Meeting 192.
[48] Meeting 71 (1902).
[49] Meeting 140. It is unclear whether Parsons considered their neutrality or their coolness towards the attendance of women to be discreditable.
[50] Meeting 275.
[51] Cp. A. Parsons to R. MacDonald, Ramsay MacDonald Papers, P.R.O. 30/69/1436/883, referring to the Rainbow Circle Dinner at Pagani's, Great Portland Street, on the occasion of the 300th meeting on 12.1.1927.
[52] See invitation in British Library of Economic and Political Science, Rainbow Circle, Coll. Misc., 575/6.
[53] Meeting 29 (1897).
[54] Meeting 107 (1906).
[55] Meetings 132 (1908) and 177 (1913).

though the institution of marriage was considered to be under some threat.[56] Political equality was not considered to be an issue; indeed, speakers such as MacDonald doubted that the enfranchisement of women would make any great political difference.[57] The only direct talk on feminism—at the height of the suffragette movement—was sparsely reported, with Hobson emphasizing its twin demands of liberty and equality, and a broad discussion on equality of opportunity ensuing.[58] However, though political rights, education and conditions of labour were areas where women were considered to have equal claims to men, in the fundamental sphere of human nature women were still viewed differently. Of especial interest was a session in which Burrows promoted his radical views on sexual equality, only to run up against a wall of prejudice that did little credit to a progressive Circle, still ensnared by prevailing ideas about female instability and intellectual inferiority side by side with moral and spiritual superiority.[59] Though many members had active and highly successful working wives, it can hardly be suggested that the Circle distinguished itself as a group at the forefront of women's emancipation.

Not surprisingly, the political mechanics of government exerted a fascination on Circle members at a time when the House of Lords cast a dark shadow on effective representation of a popular will and when the franchise was still of a restricted nature. In addition to sporadic meetings, two annual sessions were devoted almost entirely to the workings and reform of democracy. The Circle was unanimous in wanting reform, though differences emerged on details. MacDonald, for example, in opposing referendums as reactionary and a hindrance to legislative work, signalled his attachment to an élitist theory of democracy based on expertise.[60] When Hobson returned to the subject some years later, his advocacy of the referendum as a means of control over representatives as well as an educational encouraging of citizens' responsibility met with a cool reception.[61] On the whole the Circle desired reasonably short Parliaments, preferred a representative to a delegate role for M.P.s, and already in 1898 considered the abolition of the veto to be a preliminary to any further reform of the Lords.[62] The 1910–11 session, devoted entirely to second chambers, examined the experience of other countries and came to the conclusion that a unicameral system might be the most enlightened but, because Britain

[56] Meeting 132.
[57] Meetings 156 (1911) and 211 (1916).
[58] Meeting 164 (1912).
[59] Meeting 133 (1909). Cp. also J.A. Hobson, *A Modern Outlook* (London, 1910), pp. 109–42.
[60] Meeting 19 (1896).
[61] Meeting 91 (1904).
[62] Meetings 21 and 23 (1897), 40 (1898).

was not ready for it, reform of the upper chamber rather than of the electoral system should be the prime objective.

The Edwardian years still saw the Circle hard at work systematically addressing issues of social reform, interspersed with a consideration of Britain's colonies and main international rivals and allies in the economic and political spheres. The earlier radicalism re-emerged twice, once in a detailed examination of the role and nature of the state (twelfth session) and then in a series of talks reflecting the analysis of the French writer and socialist Émile Faguet (fourteenth session), the book being available to members for 2/6. Unfortunately the latter lectures were not recorded by Parsons, there being unfulfilled plans to publish them. He did however revealingly see the series as 'in accord with the early traditions & aims of the Circle'.[63] It was indeed the last to be wholly dedicated to the theoretical exploration of those aims that the Circle had frequently engaged in, even if it attested to a broader range of views than the topic might have elicited in the past. In part, this was explained by a narrowing of the notion of socialism from any movement for the betterment of social life to the removal of material inequality.[64] Significantly, there was still room for the progressivist view that the contrast between liberalism and socialism was beside the point, the real contrast being between socialism and individualism.[65] Three of the four sessions before the war were inspired by specific issues and crises at the centre of the political stage: the Lords, as noted above, the industrial unrest, and Lloyd George's Land Campaign. However, the Circle also excelled in displaying its erudition in spheres somewhat removed from the hurly-burly of contemporary politics. Its sessions on political thinkers, statesmen, philosophers and writers, though rarely without a moral for the present, afford an illuminating insight into the concerns and standards of turn-of-the-century intellectuals; their interest lies not the least in the podium they provided for the bravura performances of that most erudite of late-Victorians, J.M. Robertson.[66] Impressive, too, was the lack of national insularity of the Circle and the wide acquaintance of its members with developments and movements not only in the anglophone world and the British colonies but on the continent as well.

Over the years, the Rainbow Circle developed a set routine, meeting as a rule on the first or second Wednesday of each month after dinner

---

[63] Parsons to MacDonald, 31.5.1907, Ramsay MacDonald Papers, P.R.O. 30/69/1151/133–6.

[64] Meeting 120 (1907).

[65] Meeting 122 (1908).

[66] For a recent assessment of Robertson, see G.A. Wells (ed.), *J.M. Robertson: Liberal, Rationalist, and Scholar* (London, 1987).

at 8 p.m. and usually dispersing at 10 p.m. Experiments with different days or times were quickly abandoned. Its membership was initially restricted to a number fixed at 20. In 1902 it was decided to raise the limit to 30 as it became more difficult to ensure attendance—a natural concomitant of the success and commitments of some of its participants as they grew older.[67] The Circle however found it difficult to recruit to that new level, a number of candidates refusing or, when elected, not turning up, and its membership stabilized round the 25 mark, rising only from 1907,[68] though guests were frequently present. Though Stapley provided the focus for the Circle and was held in high esteem and affection by its members,[69] his imprint on the actual conduct of affairs was minimal; the only paper he ever gave was an embarrassingly mystical account of the hope, engendered by the war, of contact with the world of spirits. The real organizational burden was shouldered by the secretaries: MacDonald, Bullock and Parsons,[70] though the committee was responsible for bringing the annual pro- gramme to the approval of the Circle. Parsons's good humour suffuses the minutes, and as he built up confidence during his long span in office, from 1906 to 1929, he allowed the occasional personal touch of wit or mild reproach to intrude. If his sudden and untimely death[71] was less of a blow then it would otherwise have been, the reason lay in the decease of many a member as the Circle grew older and weaker, individually and collectively.

After the war, the Circle went into noticeable decline, its themes narrowing in scope, and its speakers—with the exception of those old professional lecturers, Hobson and Robertson—thinning out in ability and number. Partly, this reflected the ideological and political paucity of the post-war era; partly, the death or resignation of some of the more spirited members. Hobson recalled the split between supporters and opposers of the war as a major catalyst of the downturn in the

[67] For a rare glimpse of the full selection process see the committee minutes prior to meeting 219 (1917).

[68] Meeting 153 (1911) recorded the largest attendance on record of 24 members out of 29 and four visitors.

[69] See especially meetings 100 (1905), 169 (1912), 200 (1915) and 242 (1920). See also P. Alden, 'British Institute and National Council of Social Service', *Progress*, no. 53 (1920), 43–7, who applauded Stapley's unselfish altruism, his intellectual interests and liberal views and who wrote of Stapley's various interests: 'The Rainbow Circle was perhaps nearest of all to his heart.' (p. 45).

[70] The fourth and last secretary, appointed in 1929, was S.S. Wilson.

[71] The Circle's attitude to Parsons was demonstrated in a gift he received with an accompanying letter. See meeting 180 (1913). See also the letters from MacDonald to Alden ('The prime Minister was terribly shocked to hear of Mr. Parsons' death') and to Mrs. Parsons ('I shall always remember him as the enthusiastic and devoted secretary of the Rainbow Circle'), Ramsay MacDonald Papers, P.R.O. 30/69/751/12, 326, both 9.8.1929.

Circle's fortunes. 'While the Circle was carried on for many years longer,' he wrote, 'it never quite recovered its early equanimity and though fed by much younger blood did not develop the earlier sense of cameraderie.'[72] Clearly, the imagination as well as the chemistry of the Circle had become severely taxed: overarching themes failed to materialize, many talks were mere surveys of current international affairs—with Gooch emerging as the new workhorse, and the general theoretical concerns of the early years notably absent. Even those who had lived by and off the Press now turned against it in sorrow and dismay.[73] In all senses, the Circle had run out of steam. Evidence from the missing post-1924 years reinforces this view.[74]

The end came suddenly, though not entirely unexpectedly. A fire that broke out early in 1931 in the house of the Circle's President, Roskill, killed his wife and resulted in his resignation. Over the summer, a number of the older Circle members met at the Reform Club and decided that the Circle should be allowed to expire gracefully, rather than collapse in ignominy. Alden acted upon this advice, and a note putting the proposal to the whole body was circulated among the remaining members.[75] The replies, as preserved in letters sent in particular from the dwindling old guard, show a mixed response. Brereton and Matheson expressed a somewhat sentimental desire to preserve the Circle; Hobson maintained a tired and indifferent neutrality, shifting the decision to the younger members; and Olivier and Goodenough favoured dissolution. Olivier's retort summed up the sad changes in the Rainbow Circle as well as in the social environment that had nourished it: 'A younger generation ought to be forming its own discussion clubs on the basis of the contemporary stimuli which cause it to take interest in public affairs. What these precisely are for the present generation I am not certain that I even clearly apprehend: but at any rate they do not appear to me to be quite the same as those which inspired the creation of the rainbow.'[76] The formal end came at the 341st meeting on the 14th October 1931, when a last minute appeal for new members failed, though one further informal gathering took place on the first of February 1933.[77] Its subject included the rise of Hitler to power two days earlier. The rainbow had indeed faded from the skies above Europe.

[72] Hobson, *Confessions*, p. 96.
[73] See Hobson in meeting 225 (1918) and Gardiner in meeting 261 (1922).
[74] See Appendix I.
[75] See Appendix I.
[76] For this letter and the others mentioned, see British Library of Political and Economic Science, Coll. Misc. 575/6.
[77] See Appendix I.

THE RAINBOW CIRCLE.

1st Session, Nov. 1894—June 1895

[1] The first meeting of the reconstructed Rainbow Circle was held at the Rainbow Tavern, Fleet St., at 7 p.m. on Wed: 7 November 1894.

Mr William Clarke was in the chair.

After dinner the following business was transacted:

Resolved: That the Committee have power to invite two visitors to the Dinners, provided that the visitors are capable of contributing to the discussion.—Moved by Rev Percy Dearmer, seconded by J.A. Hobson and carried unanimously.

Resolved: That the provisional committee be re-elected as follows: Herbert Burrows, William Clarke, John A. Hobson, J. Murray Macdonald M.P., J.R. Macdonald and Richard Stapley. Moved by Rev Percy Dearmer, seconded by Rev J.H. Belcher, and carried unanimously.

That J. Murray Macdonald M.P. be elected President: Proposed by J.A. Hobson, seconded by Herbert Burrows and carried unanimously.

That J.R. MacDonald be elected Secretary and Treasurer: Proposed by Herbert Burrows, seconded by Richard Stapley and carried unanimously.

Mr. Murray Macdonald then opened the discussion on 'The Ethical Deficiencies of the Old Radicalism'.

He began by saying that he proposed to use the word State in its strictly legal sense as meaning the persons whom the Constitution invests with the supreme power of making the laws. From the Radical point of view the state ought to act on the individual citizen only by way of restraint. There was no ethical sanction for the state compelling one to yield a portion of his annual income to help to educate other people's children and to weaken the sense of parental responsibility. We can agree with the old Radicals in maintaining individual liberty, but we disagree with their ethical theory of rights, they saying man's rights are the direct and immediate inheritance of nature, we that they are won by discipline and after a struggle with forces opposed to them. The Radical theory that rights existed before and independent of society has never been brought into touch with actual facts of life and is disproved by the fact that the very possession of rights implies an existence in a community, the members of which have moral & social relations with one another. But the philosophical mistakes of the old Radical was [sic] due to his political and intellectual position. The true theory of the relation between state & individual seems to be that the individual should hold a free and independent relation towards the state criticising its arrangements and attempting to modify them where they are defective whilst at the same time he finds in the state and in the state alone the conditions of a virtuous and noble life.

In the discussion in which all took part the following were the chief points urged:

1. That the opener should have defined the state as the communal personality not as a formal expression of government. Thus the difference between the old Radicalism and ethical collectivism would be clearer;

2. That at least part of the state's right to take A's property to educate B's children lay in the fact that A had used the state to enable him to acquire his property;

3. That Radicalism was too abstract in its conception and that as a matter of fact its leaders knew nothing about history;

4. That the disability under which the early Radicals laboured inasmuch as they had not been taught the organic relations of individuals falsified their ethics.

J.A. Murray Macdonald   Chairman

* * *

[2] The Rainbow Circle met on Wednesday 5 December 1894 at the Rainbow Tavern, Fleet Street E.C.

Mr. J.A. Murray Macdonald M.P., President, was in the chair and there were 16 members present.

After dinner Mr J.A. Hobson open[ed] the discussion on the 'Economic Deficiencies of the Manchester School'.

The first accusation to be brought against the Manchester School was that it created for its own special purposes an economic man, an embodiment of the selfish motives only. Such a man has no existence and the science based upon his possible actions has an inadequate bearing on human life. In defending this creation, the school further shows its deficiency inasmuch as it maintains that it has regard only [for] those motives which prompt a man to acquire wealth, not those which are exercised in his use of it. Although they recognised the four departments of Economics—Production, Distribution, Exchange and Consumption, they had scarcely anything to say about the last except in so far as it related to further production. This narrow view brought them into difficulties in defining capital and led them to make a false distinction between productive and unproductive consumption.

Besides, their conception of production was quantitative and not qualitative. Expansion of markets and cheap cost of production were the two closely-related instruments of this mercantile policy and so they advocated Laissez Faire as an economic method. This method can be assailed by alleging that it has not resulted in the production of greatest quantities though that is an open question; but its weakness is in its failure to satisfy the consumer in the use of wealth. Finally, the Manchester School completely failed to recognise the part which Society plays in the production of wealth and consequently could not recognise Society's claim as a consumer.

The chief points raised in the discussion were:

1. That the School was right within the strict limits which it at first placed upon itself and that it was the fault of those who came later to give its principles a wider application.

2. That the School did not take into account what Prof. Marshall had called long and short views of the efficiency of labour, & so could not foresee the results that would follow its successful applications.

3. That its economics were simply expressions of the business experiences of the manufacturers and financiers who founded it and that it had therefore a historical justification which does not hold good now under changing social circumstances.

J.A. Murray Macdonald   Chairman

9th January 1895

* * *

[3] The Rainbow Circle met on Wednesday 9th January 1895 at 33 Bloomsbury Square at 8 p.m.

Mr. J. Murray Macdonald, President, was in the chair and there were present 12 members.

Owing to difficulties in making arrangements for the usual dinners of the Circle it was unanimously carried that the Circle thank Mr Stapley for his offer to allow it to meet at his house and accept the same.

Mr William Clarke then opened the discussion on the 'Political defects of the Old Radicalism'. Political Radicalism was an inheritance from Puritanism moulded by the ideas of freedom which had an outcome in the French and American revolutions. Although the party was composed of sections that were frequently in conflict, yet it held its fundamental notions of the nature of government in common and the line of conflict between Paine and Burke is the dividing line between the Radicalism and Toryism of the end of last and the beginning of this century. The main intention of the Radicals was to reconstruct political institutions upon a rational foundation, and in fulfilment of this attempt propagated a belief in the supreme value of impersonal Parliamentary government. The compromise with rational principles which both America and France had to make in forming their government shows the inadequacy of Radical political opinion in the days of Paine; and the general failure of Parliamentary government now shows the same thing. In this respect its weakness lay in its failing to make allowance for the adaptability of old institutions to new needs: e.g. it had not the historical spirit, and both criticised and reconstructed systems of government in the spirit of finality. In its method of government it was curiously enough both strongly individualistic and yet was devoid of the idea of local self government. Although Manchesterism was in no way involved in the ideas of men like Paine, yet the cutting adrift of Chartism from Radicalism left the politicians of the latter school to the mercy of the manufacturers who ultimately involved them in the further mistakes of hard abstract individualism and the politico-economic mistakes of the visionary free-traders.

The chief points raised in the discussion were:

1. That as a matter of fact the representative system is only beginning to show normal results and that it is too soon yet to pass judgment upon it.

2. That the failure of American democracy has not been owing to the inadequacy of its methods or to the shortcomings of its nature, but to the fact that hitherto politics have been neglected in the solution of wealth-production problems.

3. That the failure of the better school of Radical thought was owing to the small backing which it had in the country.

4. That Old Radicalism really consisted of two well marked sections— the working-class or Socialistic party, and the capitalist or individualist party and that the accident of political conditions brought them for a time into cooperative contact.

5. Mr Clarke in his reply laid special stress on the distinction that ought to be observed in such discussions between Parliamentary and Representative government.

William Clarke   Chairman

* * *

[4] The Rainbow Circle met on Wednesday 6 February 1895 at Mr Stapley's 33 Bloomsbury Square w.c.

Mr William Clarke was in the chair and there were 10 members present.

After a preliminary announcement with reference to the proposed publication of a 'Progressive Review':

Mr Sidney[1] Olivier read his paper on 'The Literary Revolt against Manchesterism'. In the historical sense of the term there was no such thing as a 'literary revolt' against Manchesterism. The revolt was rather a continued opposition and resistance to the crude theory of individual and social life which was held by the more extreme individualists of the Manchester School and which had an outcome in the earlier industrial developments of the century. Against such theories and developments the literary artist, whatever be his form of expression, must protest. In that protest Carlyle, Shelley & Coleridge have a common meeting ground. The opposition between materialism, utilitarianism and Manchester Economics on the one hand and the literary spirit on the other is fundamental. Lying upon the practical man is the necessity of living and doing, and in recognizing that, his guide will generally be empirical utilitarianism, and if he enters the field of literature it will be as a propagandist rather than as an artist. The literary artist must on the other continue to assert the existance [sic] of a power in life which refuses to be summed up in economic advantage at one end of the scale or sexual impulse at the other, or by both combined. To this artist the care for practical necessities is the work of weak and erring men. The problem still remains how artist and politician can co-operate in advancing the work of each other.

The discussion largely turned upon the question whether the literary artist was not essentially a revolutionist by nature and would refuse to conform to any coercion; whether for instance the new revolts in literature led by Tolstoi and Ibsen &c. were not really revolts against the growing movements of Socialism.

J.A. Murray Macdonald   Chairman

* * *

Committee

The Committee met on Thursday 21st February at the N.L.C.[2] at 4.30.

Present Wm Clarke, Herbert Burrows & J.R. MacDonald.

A report as to the position of the 'Progressive Review'[3] was made & the Hon Secretary was instructed to issue circulars to the members

[1] Read 'Sydney'.
[2] National Liberal Club.
[3] A radical-collectivist journal established by members of the Rainbow Circle, that lasted for a year in 1896–7. See Introduction.

inviting subscriptions and to approach the Hutchi[n]son Trustees[4] with a view to obtaining a grant from them.

J.A. Murray Macdonald   15th March 1895

* * *

Committee meeting 6 March 1895.

The Committee met at 33 Bloomsbury Square on Wednesday 6 March 1895 at 7.30.

Present: Mr J. Murray Macdonald M.P., President, William Clarke, Richard Stapley and J.R. MacDonald.

Resolved that Mr Oscar Bowen's name be struck off the membership roll owing to his non-attendance at Circle meetings.—Carried unanimously.

Resolved that circulars be sent to the Rev Douglas Morrison and Mr. Gustav Steffen[5] asking them to join the Circle.—Carried unanimously.

It was reported that shares to the value of £385 had been subscribed for in the Progressive Review and it was decided to ask Mr Olivier to approach Mr D'Arcy Reeve[6] and the secretary to write to the Hutchinson Trustees with a view of obtaining financial help. Mr William Clarke was also asked to communicate with the Rev Douglas Morrison and friends in America, and Mr J. Murray Macdonald M.P. undertook to see Mr Hudson Kearley M.P.[7] and Mr Byles M.P.

J.A. Murray Macdonald   Chairman

* * *

[5] The Rainbow Circle met at Mr Stapley's, 33 Bloomsbury Square W.C. on Wed: 6 March at 8 p.m.

Mr J. Murray Macdonald M.P. was in the chair and 11 members were present.

Canon Shuttleworth opened the discussion on the Religious Revolt against the Manchester school. He confined himself exclusively to the Christian Socialist movement. The Chartist movement has been the only real working man's movement, and through that the Christian

[4] This was the bequest of Henry Hutchinson that assisted the Fabian Society, and of which Clarke was a trustee. Cp. P. Pugh, *Educate, Agitate, Organize: 100 Years of Fabian Socialism* (London, 1984), pp. 53–62.

[5] The economist Steffen, a Fabian originating from Sweden, did not join.

[6] D'Arcy Reeve was a benefactor of the Fabians.

[7] Hudson Kearley (1856–1934). Liberal M.P. 1892–1910.

Socialists came into contact with the common people. Maurice[8] was in every way the leader of this revolt and his strength lay in insisting that religion should be cleared of the Commercial spirit and this[9] its principles should be applied to industrial life. Kingsley's[10] place was that of popular interpreter of Maurice. After the collapse of the Chartist movement the Christian Socialists directed their efforts towards a purifying of religious conceptions and the establishment of undertakings on the lines of industrial association. They also materially helped Trade Unionism in its early struggles. It can be claimed for this revolt that it demonstrated the necessity of a union between religious and social affairs and their ideal of such a union still remains the inspiration of the present revival in social interests.

It was maintained in the discussion that:

1. Too great stress had been laid on the influence of the Christian Socialist movement; that its ends had been contributed to by other religious movements;

2. That the Christian Socialists had no social philosophy.

Other detailed points were raised particularly the obligation of the Christian Socialists to the German Transcendentalists.

J.A. Murray Macdonald   Chairman

* * *

Committee Meeting

The Committee met at the National Liberal Club on Friday 15 Mch '95. present Mr Murray Macdonald, Mr Wm Clarke, Mr J.A. Hobson, and Mr J.R. MacDonald (Hon Sec).

The Secretary reported that 397 shares had been subscribed for in the Progressive Review, and it was decided to approach one or two others who might be inclined to subscribe.

J.A. Murray Macdonald   Chairman

* * *

Committee Meeting

The Committee met on Thursday 28th March at 7 p.m. at the National Liberal Club: Present Mr. J. Murray Macdonald M.P., Mr William Clarke, Richard Stapley, and J.R. MacDonald (Hon. Sec.)

---

[8] John Frederick Denison Maurice (1805–1872). Theologian, one of the founders of Christian Socialism.

[9] Read 'that'.

[10] Charles Kingsley (1819–1875). Writer and Christian Socialist.

Mr Clarke reported that he had seen Mr Fletcher[11] and suggested to him the advisability of his becoming editor of the Progressive Review. Mr Fletcher had consented and Mr Clarke desired the Committee's opinion on the matter. After some discussion it was resolved on the motion of Mr Stapley that Mr Clarke and Mr Fletcher be asked to be joint editors. Mr Clarke agreed and was asked to report Mr Fletcher's further decision to the Committee.

J.A. Murray Macdonald   Chairman

* * *

[6] The Rainbow Circle met at Mr Stapley's, 33 Bloomsbury Square W.C. on Wednesday 3rd April, seven members being present.

Mr J. Murray Macdonald M.P. was in the chair.

Mr Herbert Burrows read a paper on 'Trade Unionism as a revolt against the Manchester School'. The whole Trade Union movement is a class struggle between worker & employer; in so far as it affects the relations between workman & workman it is in the coercive direction, because only by moving workingmen in the mass could it hope to succeed. It is therefore not a descendant of the Guilds but a child of modern industrialism—of the class war in production & distribution. It came into sharp conflict with even the early developments in Manchester industry and yet curiously enough the older unions agreed with their capitalist opponents with regard to the evils of State interference. So far, Trade unionism was conducted on lines of political individualism, and not until very late years do we find the antagonism carried into the sphere of social philosophy. The protest of Trade Unionism was therefore one of sheer necessity, and not of intelligent social idea, on the part of men who in order to save themselves from becoming mere commodities to be bought in the cheapest market had to form an *imperium in imperio*. The earliest sign of Trade Union political activity was in 1865 when the unions demonstrated in Hyde Park in favour of the franchise.[12] Still, however, there is much jealousy in unionism of the new political forces that are being marshalled under the general term 'Labour'.

The discussion turned largely upon the impossibility of an extension of the Trade Union movement in numbers of adherents and activity ever solving the social problems of the day.

J.A. Murray Macdonald   Chairman

[11] A.E. Fletcher, previously editor of the Daily Chronicle (1890–94), was editor of the New Age in 1895. The Progressive Review was to share its offices with the New Age.

[12] The reference should have been to May 1866.

[7] The Rainbow Circle met at Mr Stapley's, 33 Bloomsbury Square on Wednesday 1st May. Mr. J. Murray Macdonald M.P. was in the chair and nine members were present.

The paper on the Revolt of the Co-operator against Manchesterism was read by Mr Clem Edwards. Tracing the growth of Industry through the Eighteenth into the Nineteenth Century, he said that it meant the subordination of labour to the power of capital. Not content in these days to control the means of production and to control the worker through them alone, the capitalist had also appropriated the means of distribution and used them in times of industrial peace to filch his workmen and in times of industrial war, to starve them. Against such a condition, the co-operative movement was a protest. The idea was to make the workmen independent of their masters for their food supply. Historically, co-operation in production, however, preceded co-operation in distribution although the latter has outstripped the former in success and bulk. Owenism, Chartism, Christian Socialism and Co-operation had intimate relationships[,] the members of one of these societies being generally members of the other. On its Christian side the movement was based on the idea of brotherhood, but on its economic side, it only meant the elimination of middlemen's profits.

The discussion largely turned upon the present position and prospects of the Co-operative movement.

Richard Stapley   Chairman

* * *

The Executive of the Rainbow Circle met at Mr Stapley's on Wednesday 1st May at 7.30.

Mr Murray Macdonald was in the chair. Further progress with the Progressive Review was reported and a draft circular by Mr Clarke was presented, which after some alterations was ordered to be printed and circulated amongst members.

Chairman

* * *

[8] The Rainbow Circle met at Mr Stapley's 33 Bloomsbury Square on Wednesday 19 June, Mr Stapley in the chair, & 12 members present.

Mr. J.R. MacDonald summarised the discussions of the session. The points of the paper were that Manchesterism was essentially a revolt and not primarily a positive contribution to social philosophy;

that it was a political method and creed rather than a social faith; that it was a necessary stage in the industrial life of the country inasmuch as co-operation could not have preceded it; that its failures, & the inner raison d'être of the revolts made against it, was that it had no very positive idea regarding the meaning & scope of individualism. The general results of the discussion had been an agreement on the following main positions[:] that the conception of the individual as independent of society is false; that economics of the quantitative kind must be supplemented by economics of the qualitative kind; that formal political democracy is not sufficient in itself to secure good government; that Trade Unionism cannot be made the basis of a great political movement; that co-operation is equally narrow; & fundamentally that the politics of the past corresponded to the economic problem of production & in the future that they must correspond to the problem of use.

William Clarke   Chairman

* * *

Committee

The Committee met on Wednesday 2nd October at 33 Bloomsbury Square W.C. at 7.30 p.m. Mr J. Murray Macdonald in the chair & 5 members were present.

Mr. C.P. Trevelyan & Mr. J.F. Oakeshott were added to the membership.

The secretary presented a financial statement showing that the income of the last session had been £2.10.0 and the expenditure £2.13.7½ whilst there were one or two outstanding a/cs. The committee recommended that the subscription for 1895–96 should be 3/- instead of 2/6d.

It was also decided in accordance with the recommendation of the guarantors, to draw up a circular stating the purpose of the Progressive Review, giving a list of promised contributors and appealing for capital; & the secretary was asked to make a preliminary draft.

Chairman

* * *

The committee met at 4.30 p.m. at National Liberal Club present 5 members.

The secretary presented draft circular for Progressive Review which was ordered to be printed as amended.

Chairman

2nd Session. Oct. 1895—June 1896.

[9] The Rainbow Circle met on Wednesday 2nd October 1895 at Mr Stapley's, 33 Bloomsbury Square W.C. at 8 p.m. Mr J. Murray Macdonald was in the chair & 11 members were present.

Mr William Clarke was elected President for the Session & took the chair. Mr J.R. MacDonald was reelected Hon Secretary & Treasurer, and Messrs Stapley, Hobson, Samuel, Murray Macdonald, Burrows and Clarke elected on the committee.

It was decided that the subscription be 3/- for the Session.

Mr Perris read his paper on 'The Evolutionary Standpoint in Social Theory'. The Twentieth Century's chief demand of the sociologist will be that he places his facts in relation to each other & to some whole—to take a dynamic & not a static view of his subject. This is the imperium of the idea of evolution. But that idea requires considerable correction. In the first place, we must come to a new understanding of the process of the law of the survival of the fittest as it applies to man. The purely biological view is incomplete because it has no acquaintance with social forces & hence sees in social and moral conservation the operations of some force strange to itself. The first attempts to apply a crude Darwinism to politics strengthened individualism & the idea of Natural Rights, and influenced economics mainly in giving a new existence to the Malthusian theory. Here again, social facts demand a revision of evolution and evidently the revision must be conducted from the assumption that liberty tends to progress only when it is subject to solidarity. Here we have to lean upon, at least as a utility in thought, the organic analogies in social life. From this, moreover, we not only get a new phraseology and method, but an ideal of man's work & destiny which is an inspiration to the student—a corrective to the man of action.

The discussion turned mainly upon the extent to which the organic likeness of society can be legitimately pushed; & as to how far it was true that man was an end in himself & what cosmic conceptions corresponded to the two extremes of abstract individualism and abstract socialism.

William Clarke   Chairman

* * *

[10] The Rainbow Circle met on Wednesday 6 November 1895 at 33 Bloomsbury Square W.C. Mr William Clarke was in the chair, & 12 members & one visitor were present.

Mr Herbert Samuel read a paper on the New Liberalism to open the series of discussions on the principles & aims of existing societies. The Liberalism based upon Bentham's philosophy & Adam Smith's economics is sapped and riddled & its most successful opponents have been the Socialists. And yet the S.D.F.[13] can only command a limited amount of intelligent support and the Fabians have no complete & self-sufficing theory of government. There seems to be the possibility of a third social philosophy independent of the other two & towards its discovery the New Liberalism moves. Its root idea must be the unity of society—complex in its economic, cooperative, ethical and emotional bonds. At the same time care must be taken to guard the New Liberalism for the error to which it is prone of considering that political action is the only medium of progressive effort. Yet a very positive view of the State as 'a partnership in every virtue & all perfection' must be held. The chief article in the political creed of the New Liberalism [is] a determination to abolish every evil condition from life. An examination of these conditions raises first of all the question of industrial production. Here the New Liberals join issue with the Socialists contending that the Socialist State still wants construction. There is not sufficient data to hand to warrant anything but an agnostic position towards the industrial State. 'Each case must be dealt with on its own merits with but subordinate reference to any general principle'.[14] Another question which has to be faced is the liberty of individuals in a state. Here again old beliefs must be left. To coerce a minority may be to free a majority. The greatest liberty of the greatest number is the motto of the New Liberalism. Above all we must frankly accept democratic methods; & embrace our Imperial opportunities.

The discussion turned on whether there was a sufficiently strong grasp of sociological principle in the paper to bear a comprehensive political construction;

whether the opportunism of the New Liberalism was the moral compromise of men of principle or the immoral yielding of men without principles; & whether apart from some wing of the Socialist party any party would be likely to adopt Mr Samuel's view; & whether the Liberal party would.

William Clarke   Chairman
4. xii. 95

* * *

[13] Social Democratic Federation.
[14] This is loosely paraphrased from W.S. Jevons, *The State in Relation to Labour* (London, 1882), from which Samuel also quoted in his book *Liberalism: An Attempt to State the Principles and Proposals of Contemporary Liberalism in England* (London, 1902).

[11] The Rainbow Circle met at 33 Bloomsbury Square on Wednesday 4 December 1895. Mr William Clarke was in the chair and 12 members were present.

It was decided to hold an extraordinary meeting to discuss future work on Wednesday 18th inst.

Mr Herbert Burrows opened on the position of the Socialist societies. He traced the growth of Socialism through Chartism & Christian Socialism down to the Social Democratic Federation & the peculiar cast which Irish nationalism gave to a certain section of English Radicalism. The relation of the societies to Liberalism is hostile and also to the older Trade Unions. To the older theories of Economics they are also hostile but are benevolently neutral to their more recent expressions. He did not think that the I.L.P. section was permanent. Socialism in its pure sense stands for reconstruction and its raison d'etre is the apparent injustice of existing society in every aspect; its weakness lies in its materialism which makes it attend too exclusively to individual environment. It is differentiated from all political parties by its fundamental ideas of property. The Socialist influence on politics is essentially practical as both history & existing political programmes show. The question of coercion must be faced, but it must not be assumed that Socialists are leaving liberty for coercion, but rather that they are leaving more coercion for less coercion. The imminence of the Socialist ideas of property is evident by the attempts to form a New Liberal party, and steps are being already taken to emphasise the international character of the economic & political change which means socialism. But we must not talk of finality. We can only speak of what the next stage is to be. Everything points to that being Socialism.

The points raised were:

That in so far as Social-Democracy is based on materialism Mr Burrows gave a false idea of it;

That the difficulty of foreign exchanges was not faced;

That it was not clear what was to be the community & how it was to express its will;

That the cleavage between the new Liberalism & Socialism is not to be found in their ideas of property but in the ordinary political possibilities of the two parties;

That there was no guarantee of permanence in the Socialist state;

That the attempted connection between Home Rule & Socialism cannot be made out.

William Clarke   Chairman

* * *

Rainbow Committee met on Wed 18th December at 7.30 p.m. at 33 Bloomsbury Square, Mr Stapley in the chair.

It was announced that Mr Stapley had guaranteed £100, Mr Samuel £100, & Mr Hobson £25 in addition to their previous guarantees, these extra sums to be paid only if the £1500 capital be not subscribed and if the said guarantors deem that the payments are required & that the Review is worthy of support.

Resolved that Mr Samuel & the Secretary be empowered to see a solicitor with reference to the formation of the Limited Liability Company.

The following were suggested as directors Messrs Stapley, Samuel, Hobson with either Mr Kearley M.P., Mr Russell Rea or Mr Howard if one of them would consent.

Resolved that Mr J.R. MacDonald be secretary to the company & that he be asked to obtain contracts for printing &c.

[12] On Rainbow Circle business it was resolved that the scheme proposed by Mr J.R. MacDonald to draft a series of resolutions relating to 1. The relation between the individual & the state; 2. The relation between the state & industry; 3. The nature of democracy; & 4. Forms of democratic machinery, should be adopted as the Circle's subject for discussion when the present arrangements have been finished.

It was resolved that Mr B.F.C. Costelloe be asked to join the Circle & that Mr Samuel convey the resolution to him.

Mr Herbert Burrows then replied to the discussion on his paper read on the 4th inst.

Chairman

* * *

The Committee met at Mr Stapley's, 33 Bloomsbury Square on Thursday 2nd January 1896 at 4.30 p.m. Present Mr William Clarke in the chair Messrs Stapley, Burrows, Samuel, the Secretary, & Mr Russell Rea as a provisional director of the Progressive Review Company.

The minutes of last meeting were read & confirmed after alteration.

The Secretary stated that the Guarantee for the P.R. capital was £1275 with a special conditional guarantee of £235.

The Prospectus & other forms connected with the formation of the Company not having been returned by the solicitor, their consideration was postponed until next meeting.

Resolved that the Westminster Gazette auditor be asked to be auditor to the Company, that the City Bank, Ludgate Hill Branch, be its Bank, & that the Registered Offices be at Temple House, & that Mr Gilbert Samuel[15] be asked to be Solicitor.

Resolved that the 'New Age' office be shared with Mr Fletcher at an inclusive rent of £30 per annum or with the electric light as a possible exception.

Publisher's contract: Resolved that the Secretary try to make better terms than those offered in Messrs Marshall's letter of the 28 Dec: 1895 & refer indemnity form to the solicitor.

Printers' Estimates: These were submitted, 5000 copies being basis of estimate.

Messrs Hazell, Watson & Viney £50; net,

Mr Bonner £43 net;

Messrs Morrison & Gibb £45 less $2\frac{1}{2}\%$ discount on monthly account.

Resolved that the Secretary get further Estimates.

Paper estimates: Dummies of various qualities were submitted with prices from Messrs Spicer—Resolved that the Review be printed on paper similar to that used in the 'Economic Review',[16] but that if possible a somewhat cheaper quotation should be got.

Resolved that the cover be brick red & that dummies be presented at the next meeting.

Advertisers' contracts. Only one from Messrs Hazell, Watson & Viney was presented and it was resolved that the Secretary endeavour to get others for the next meeting.

Resolved that the secretary for the directors & by their order sign the necessary contracts.

Resolved that the editorial fees be fixed at £150 in cash & £100 in shares for the first year, Mr Clarke undertaking to pay for his own assistant.

The secretary intimated that he would charge no fee for his first year's service.

Date of Publication: Resolved that Mr Marshall be consulted as to the best time.

Resolved that circulars be sent to members of progressive associations & others interested in our opinions as the best means of advertising the Review; also that a circular be sent to publishers drawing attention to the review for the purpose of getting books sent for criticism.

Resolved that editorial fee & office rent begin from the 1st January 1896 if the Review be published in the spring; & also in that event that the necessary office furniture be immediately procured.

[15] An elder brother of Herbert Samuel.
[16] The journal of the Oxford University branch of the Christian Social Union from 1891–1914.

Resolved that the Review be anonymous & that the editor have discretion in fixing scales of pay.

The next meeting was fixed for Wednesday 8 January at 4.30 p.m. at 33 Bloomsbury Square, w.c.

Chairman   Richard Stapley

* * *

The Committee met on Wednesday 8th January 1896 at 4.30 at 33 Bloomsbury Square;[17]

Present Mr Richard Stapley in the chair, Messrs Herbert Samuel, Herbert Burrows, William Clarke & the secretary.

The minutes of last meeting were read & signed.

The Secretary stated that the Progressive Review guarantee amounted to £1288 & the special guarantee to £235.

The prospectus & memorandum of association were presented: Resolved that they be referred to Mr Costelloe for an opinion & be then printed with the share forms.

Resolved that all cheques bear the signature of the Secretary & either Mr Richard Stapley or Mr Herbert Samuel, & that all monies be passed through the Company's bankers.

Resolved that Mr Gilbert Samuel be appointed solicitor, subject to confirmation.

Resolved that the Secretary procure a seal for the Company.

Publishers' Estimate: The Secretary reported that the price of 6d to be paid by Messrs Marshall was owing to the low price (8/6d for 13) at which the publishers proposed to invoice the review to the trade. Resolved to accept Messrs Marshall's price on these conditions.

Printer's Estimate: The estimates of Messrs Hazell Watson & Viney and of Mr Bonner were again presented & Mr Bonner interviewed. Resolved that Mr Bonner's Estimate be accepted.

Size: Resolved that the Review be 96 pages instead of 104.

Resolved that Messrs Marshall be asked to proceed with the fixing of the name of the Review on their brass plate & on the office door;

Resolved that Messrs Marshall's agreement that he publish for twelve months specify 'if the Review be published for that time'.

Paper: Resolved that we print on 'Economic Review' paper & that the cover be brighter than that on the dummy supplied.

Advertisement agent: Postponed.

Resolved that the first number appear on the 21st March.

---

[17] The original programme had planned a Circle meeting for that evening, with T.F. Husband talking about 'The Ethical Societies'. That talk never took place. See Herbert Samuel Papers, A/10/4, House of Lords Record Office.

Draft circulars were submitted by the secretary & were passed on to Mr William Clarke & Mr Herbert Samuel for revision.

£12 was voted for office furniture; & One guinea as a subscription to Durrant's cutting agency.

William Clarke

* * *

Progressive Review Committee:

A meeting of the Progressive Review Committee with Mr Russell Rea in attendance was held at the Progressive Review office Temple House, Temple Avenue E.C. Present Mr Herbert Samuel in the chair, Messrs Hobson, Burrows & J.R. MacDonald (Secretary).

The Secretary read a communication from Mr Clarke saying that owing to the interest being taken in foreign politics, our lack of money & his difficulties in getting writers, he was not prepared to go on with the Editorship.

Resolved that Mr Samuel & Mr MacDonald be requested to attempt to get up a good first issue for March & that in the event of their success we proceed to publication as previously arranged.

Resolved that this committee recommends the directors to appoint an editorial committee consisting of Messrs Clarke, Hobson, Webb, Samuel & J.R. MacDonald, which, with the approval of the directors, will nominate its own PR officers.

Russell Rea   Chairman

* * *

Progressive Review Directors:

A meeting of the directors of the Progressive Review Publishing Co was held at the offices of the Review on Saturday 15 February at 11 a.m.

Present Mr Russell Rea (in the chair) Messrs Hobson, Samuel, Stapley & the Secretary.

The secretary reported the arrangements made for issuing the Review in March & after discussion it was resolved on the motion of Mr J.A. Hobson seconded by Mr Richard Stapley: That the directors having regard to the state of the public mind deem it advisable to postpone the publication of the first number of the Progressive Review until the 25th September.

The Secretary was instructed to ascertain the liabilities of the company up to date & the meeting adjourned until Saturday the 22nd inst.

Richard Stapley
Chairman

* * *

Progressive Review Directors:
The directors of the Progressive Review Publishing Co. met at 3 Kensington Palace Gardens on Saturday 22nd February at 6 p.m.

Present Mr Richard Stapley, in the chair, Mr Herbert Samuel & the Secretary.

The minutes of last meeting were read & confirmed.

The Secretary presented accounts as follows: Messrs Marshall £5; Mr A. Bonner £5.8.9; Mr Gilbert Samuel £8.2.2; Messrs Spicer £3.4.4. Other miscellaneous charges amounting to £11.11.7 were reported. Resolved to give the Secretary an honorarium of £15.0.0 for work until September.

Statutory meeting—fixing of date was postponed.

The following papers were presented: (1) Circular to shareholders passed with instructions to print 100; (2) Prospectus,—amended and 200 ordered to be printed with a fly leaf;[18] (3) Circular to Publishers—postponed; (4) Bankers' order for opening account—postponed.

The secretary was instructed to postpone furnishing office until Mr Stapley could ascertain whether a desk he had would be available; to get envelopes for the notices to the public addressed; to order 200 memorandums of association to be printed.

Resolved that the Directors meet again on Saturday 14 March at 6 p.m. at 3 Kensington Palace Gardens.

Herbert Samuel   Chairman

* * *

A meeting of the directors of the Progressive Review Publishing Co. Ld. was held at 3 Kensington Palace Gardens W. on Saturday March 14th at 6 p.m.—Present Mr Herbert Samuel, in the chair, Messrs J.A. Hobson, Richard Stapley & the Secretary.

The minutes of last meeting were read & signed.

The instrument appointing the directors was presented.

The Secretary reported that the Prospectus as passed at the last

[18] See Samuel Papers A/10/5.

meeting was printed & circulated together with the circular to members, & that the Memorandum of Association was also printed.

Office furniture: Mr Stapley's desk not being available, the Secretary was instructed to buy one.

Accounts: The accounts presented at last meeting were ordered to be paid, Mr A. Bonner's being amended to date the sum being £7.18.6 less $2\frac{1}{2}$ discount prompt cash.

*

Lettering of door: It was decided to letter the door as follows: 'Progressive Review' & 'Progressive Review Publishing Co. Ld.'

Agreement with Publisher: The draft as returned by solicitor & altered by directors was presented & initialled by the chairman, the secretary being instructed to forward it to Messrs Marshall for perusal.

The allotment of shares & fixing date of statutory meeting were postponed: also circular to the public & publishers.

Editorial arrangements—postponed.

Resolved that the directors meet again at Temple House at noon on Thursday 19th inst.

Richard Stapley   Chairman

* That the Banking Account of the Progressive Review Publishing Company Limited, be opened with the City Bank Limited, Ludgate Hill subject to the control of Mr Herbert Samuel & Mr Richard Stapley members of this Board, the signature of any one of whom & the counter signature of the Secretary Mr J. Ramsay MacDonald shall be sufficient authority to the City Bank for the payment of all monies & generally for all matters and transactions connected with the said Banking Account.

Chairman

* * *

The Directors of the Progressive Review Publishing Co. Ld. met at Temple House on Tuesday 19th March at noon

Present Mr Richard Stapley in the chair, Mr J.A. Hobson & the Secretary.

The minutes of last meeting were read & signed.

The Secretary reported that 956 shares had been applied for & was instructed to write to the guarantors who had not replied about the end of the month.

The publishers' agreements were discussed & approved as the

initialled drafts. The Secretary was instructed to prepare them for signature.

The arrangements regarding editorial services were discussed & it was Resolved—That Mr William Clarke & Mr John A. Hobson be appointed joint editors[19] of the Progressive Review & that their payment be decided next directors' meeting.

It was also resolved that Mr J. Ramsay MacDonald act as Managing Director & Secretary, & that the payment for his services be fixed at the next Directors' meeting.

Resolved that Mr Wharrier be appointed auditor; & that the secretary be instructed to get what books are necessary after consulting with the auditor.

The next meeting of directors was fixed for Tuesday 31st March at noon.[20]

Chairman   Richard Stapley

* * *

NOTE
[13 & 14] The Rainbow Circle met on Wednesday 6th Febry. at 33 Bloomsbury Square W.C. when Mr Lilley read a paper on the 'Religious Societies'; & again at the same place when Mr Costelloe opened a discussion on the 'Individual & the State'. The Secretary being absent, there were no minutes.

[15] The Rainbow Circle met at 33 Bloomsbury Square W.C. on Wednesday 1st April at 8 p.m. but owing to a small attendance because of the proximity of Easter, Mr Hobson's paper was postponed & only a general conversation engaged in.

William Clarke   Chairman

* * *

[16] The Rainbow Circle met at 33 Bloomsbury Square on Wednesday 6 May at 8 p.m.

Present Mr William Clarke (in the chair) and eleven members with Messrs Douglas Morrison & Young visitors.

Mr John A Hobson read a paper on Individual and State property.

---

[19] In effect Clarke was the chief and Hobson the second editor.

[20] For all further meetings of the Progressive Review committee see Ramsay MacDonald Papers, P.R.O. 30/69/1201, which contains the minute book of the committee from February 1896 to June 1898.

The problem to be discussed was, what are the rights of property from the point of view of social utility? The individual's natural right to property is, to begin with, a subsistence wage because that alone enables him to continue to be an efficient workman. Further, he has claims (which will vary with his personal character and the quality of his work) so that his will may be enlisted to produce more than a bare subsistence value. There can be no claim to property not earned because it enervates; & yet interest may be defended as the price of abstenance[sic]. The social activities which some of the propertied classes indulge in, do not justify their enjoyment of other people's property. But as there is a right to individual property, so there is a right to social property, because every worker uses natural & social forces in his work, & because society has also an existence & efficiency to maintain.[21] This is the real philosophical defence of public income in the shape of rates & taxes & other imposts. To draw lines between the two properties was impossible. With social evolution the lines would contract or expand. What we had to do was to recognise the two properties.

The criticism took the line of pointing out that Mr Hobson had not defined property, that his position was too materialistic, and that he had given the term property so wide a range that it was difficult to apply his principles.

Richard Stapley   Chairman

* * *

[17] The Rainbow Circle met at 33 Bloomsbury Square on Wednesday 3rd June at 8 p.m.

Present 11 members & one visitor.

Mr J.R. MacDonald read a paper on the State & Education. The subject naturally divided itself into two divisions: Why the state should educate, & How it should educate. On the first point, we ought to regard a national system of education not as an unpleasant resort because the dame school had broken down but as part of the proper duty of a state—just like the maintenance of a strong navy. The claim of the child to a sufficient education is not against parents or Churches, but against the community. On the second point we have to decide an awkward preliminary. What are the rights of the parent regarding the kind of education to be given to his child? It is this problem that lies at the bottom of the religious controversy. The only satisfactory position to take up is that the state has no call to interference in the

---

[21] A theme developed in J.A. Hobson, *The Social Problem* (London, 1901).

matter. The child's 'right' is to be protected from a religious bias, & what is commonly called religious education must be regarded by the state as simply a training of character which ought to be one of the main purposes of education. The parent has no 'right' to impose, or have imposed, his dogmas on his child. The need of the time in education is to protect the child from the parent. So far as the development of character is concerned the voluntary schools are pernicious in the extreme, & the introduction of the Bible as a text book is particularly bad as a moral influence. It is the one piece of secular education taught in many schools. The paper concluded with a practical scheme of moral teaching.

The discussion turned mainly upon the rights of parents & the place of the Bible in schools.

William Clarke   Chairman

* * *

3rd Session 1896–97.

[18] The Rainbow Circle met at 33 Bloomsbury Square W.C. on Wednesday 7 October 1896 at 8 p.m.

Mr William Clarke was in the chair & there were thirteen members present.

The subscription was fixed at 3/- for the Session. The Committee was reelected; & Mr William Clarke & J.R. MacDonald reelected President, & Secretary & Treasurer respectively. A vote of thanks to Mr Stapley for his hospitality was unanimously passed.

Mr Samuel read a paper on the Democratic Franchise. The democrat starts with the assumption that an enjoyment of the full privileges of citizenship is necessary to individuality. But that does not quite settle the question of the Democratic franchise, because an universal suffrage may militate against the welfare of the individual in other directions. The wise use of power must be considered as well as the demands of an abstract theory of citizenship, & experience has taught us that these often conflict. The question of the democratic franchise is therefore mixed up with that of who is the wise citizen. An educational test will not detect him. We must really consider the relation between the electorate, the Parliament & the administrative officers from the beginning, & thus we shall see how inadequate fancy franchises, property qualifications, & even representation by taxation are as guides in our enquiry. If we regard, as we ought, the electorate simply as voters & not as legislators we must declare for manhood suffrage with a few minor exceptions, because no important dividing line between wise & unwise electors can be found. The line, however, can be drawn at the present time between men & women & on that ground Mr Samuel opposed female suffrage though not opposed to women members.

The point seized upon most in the discussion was whether the opener was entitled to use the expression 'failure of democracy', & in connection therewith some differences were expressed as to the point of view from which democracy should be studied.

The circle was generally agreed on the programme part of the paper with the exception of the opposition to women's suffrage.

William Clarke   Chairman

* * *

[19] The Circle met on Wednesday 4th November 1896 at the Holborn Restaurant.

Present nine members, Mr William Clarke in the chair.

A resolution of sympathy with Mr & Mrs Stapley on their illness was passed & the Chairman was asked to send it to them.

Mr J.R. MacDonald opened the discussion upon the Referendum. The objections which the advocates of a Referendum took to the Representative system were that it would not do enough work & that it would not obey the constituencies. But taking the Swiss experience of the Referendum it was shown that instead of doing legislative work it mainly blocked it.[22] Nothing else in fact could be done by a right to veto which had any influence. Hence it was that the enlightened support to the Referendum came from reactionaries not from progressives. Nor would the Referendum secure that the people's wish should be the basis of legislation, for there was a wide gulf fixed between a desire & the capacity to fulfil that desire. The people's desire must be paramount in a democracy but the fulfillment[sic] of those desires often being by methods that are too intricate & special for the people to understand must be left to the care of a special class doing the work of a special social organ. It was natural that the idea of the Referendum should have been part of the idea of French Revolution politics. It is out of sympathy with modern organic conceptions of Society, & when it is remembered that these conceptions have been forced upon us from the practical as well as from the theoretical side, we may claim that the Referendum is not entitled to be called a progressive proposal.

---

[22] Articles on the subject were shortly to appear in the *Progressive Review*. See L. Wuarin, 'Genuine Democracy in Switzerland' and L. Tomn, 'The Latest Phase of Direct Legislation', no. 10 (1897).

The discussion which followed turned mainly upon the conception which the members had of a democracy.

William Clarke   Chairman

* * *

[20] The Circle met on Wednesday 2nd December 1896 at 8 p.m. at the Holborn Restaurant.

Present: Messrs W. Clarke (in the chair), Herbert Burrows, G.F. Millin, Herbert Samuel, Hon W.P. Reeves, C.P. Trevelyan, Rev. A.L. Lilley, Richard Stapley, J.R. MacDonald & as visitor R. Rylett.

Mr Rylett was elected member of the circle.[23]

Mr Burrows opened the discussion. His idea of democracy was not a balancing of checks but a social & political state under which the necessity for checks was done away with. That involves the abolition of class interest. Proportional representation had some commendable features but the difficulty of working it was an almost insuperable barrier to its adoption. On the whole though opposed to the cumulative vote in theory he would not altogether oppose it in practise[sic] owing to its value in securing the representation of minorities. He was firmly convinced of the democratic appropriateness of equal electoral districts as making for a human as against a propertied basis for representation. He was for a similar reason in favour of One Vote One Value, & suggested some punishment for those who would not vote at elections. The Second Ballot was also worthy of support. Its alternative was the caucus & the caucus was a machine which by the destruction of a direct responsibility on the part of representatives made for jobbery & corruption. Rival candidates & political groups should fight out their differences at the polls & the second ballot should be established so that in the end the majority would be represented. Mr Burrows concluded by a defence of the theory of natural rights as a basis for democratic thought & organisation.

It was decided to discuss only Proportional Representation & the discussion turned upon the difficulty from a democratic point of view in discovering the real unit of proportion,—the case of Ireland & Scotland being instanced as difficulties.

The meeting was adjourned until the 17th.

[20a] The adjourned meeting was held on the 17th at 33 Bloomsbury Square.

Mr William Clarke in the chair.

---

[23] Rylett was working for the New Age and must have been introduced by Clarke, who was soon to consider him as possible replacement for MacDonald as *Progressive Review* secretary. See Clarke to Samuel, 12.7.1897, Samuel Papers, A/10/10.

Mr Burrows recapitulated his position & the Second Ballot & Caucus System was discussed.

The points urged in favour of the second ballot were that it would secure majority representation & encourage a healthy spirit of political independence. Against it, it was urged that there was at the present time no numerical majority in many constituencies, that it would encourage the growth of groups, that it would destroy the necessary democratic organisation in the constituencies, that what benefits may arise from it under existing conditions are owing to merely temporary circumstances.

William Clarke   Chairman

* * *

[21] The Circle met on Wednesday 13th January 1897 at 33 Bloomsbury Square W.C. at 8 p.m.

Present Mr William Clarke, in the chair, and thirteen members & Dr Herren of Iowa university as visitor.

Mr C.P. Trevelyan opened the discussion on the organization of the Representative Chamber. Beginning with the relation between members & constituencies, Mr Trevelyan pointed out that the controversy between champions of the theories of delegacy & representation was not new. It would be absurd to make the member independent of his constituency. The frequency of elections prevents that from happening altogether, but in addition to that restraint, it might be well to formulate, before elections, a series of important questions upon which members will be pledged to act merely as delegates. Both extreme conceptions of the rights & duties of members are false. A member has, in fact, to be both free & bound. A further aspect of this question is the payment of public service. Some advocate payment of members because it will promote labour representation, but that is a class argument; others, because it will make them servants, but that is only desirable to a certain extent; the true justification lies in the fact that it will widen the field from which legislators may be chosen, so that all the material available for parliamentary work may be at the disposal of the constituencies. It is a grave mistake to attempt to keep up a too close touch between the House of Commons & the constituencies by very frequent elections. A very short parliament will be the opportunity of the rich man & the corporation & from the democratic standpoint would do more harm than good by leading to political unsettlement. A quinquennial period would satisfy every democratic need. As to the election of ministers, the Commons are the real authority. The Cabinet gets more supreme although more obedient to the majority so far as legislative work goes. Its absoluteness is in diplomatic & administrative affairs. With all its logical faults the present method of selection is as good as any. It may not be very democratic in form, but the limits placed upon the Queen in choosing the Prime Minister & upon the Minister in choosing his cabinet, give genuine democratic results whilst obviating many difficulties of methods of selection better in form.

The circle was agreed against the delegate theory of membership, & in favour of shorter parliaments though divided between three, four & five years. The discussion of the appointment of premiers & cabinets was adjourned to another meeting.

William Clarke   Chairman

* * *

[22] The adjourned discussion took place at 33 Bloomsbury Square on Friday 22nd January, Mr William Clarke in the chair.

The discussion was upon the method to be adopted of electing the Prime Minister, a sharp difference of opinion dividing the members. The opener, Mr Murray Macdonald, Mr Crook & Mr Samuel advocated, more or less strongly the present system of final choice by the Sovereign between possible rival claimants. Messrs Hobson & Perris were strongly of opinion that democratic methods alike in form & substance should prevail & that therefore the Premier should be directly elected by the House of Commons. As to the question of Committee methods there was a general approval of the system of committees of the House of Commons in connection with the great spending departments.

It was decided that the next meeting should be on February 10th instead of February 3rd as the former date was inconvenient to many members.

William Clarke   Chairman

* * *

[23] The Circle met on Wednesday 10th February at 8 p.m. at 33 Bloomsbury Square W.C.—Present Mr William Clarke in the chair & nine members.

Mr Murray Macdonald opened the discussion on the Monarchy & a Second Chamber in relation to democracy. In such a discussion we must start with clear ideas as to what the British constitution really is. We know the legal theory, but facts do not support it, for the supreme authority rests with a majority of the House of Commons, although the House of Lords apparently hamper the exercise of that authority by amending its work & interpreting independently the opinion of the electorate. In the constitution the monarchy has no power. Then why retain the form? Why not elect the official head of the nation? So long as present political conditions last, the president would only be a ceremonial functionary & his part in politics would only be that filled now by the hereditary sovereign. A ceremonial functionary had better be hereditary. Moreover a president if elected should be elected for reasons above & beyond party or political. Only to secure moral gains can such a change be justified; but it is very doubtful if anything but party considerations would influence the vote. Monarchy as we know it is not inconsistent with democracy. If a Second Chamber can be justified it must be on the grounds that it is composed of men representative of different interests from the first. And what is to be the standard of that?[24] We can establish no such standard. A second chamber is neither necessary to nor consistent with democracy. In immediate political practise[sic], however, the moral of this is not to join in the cry for the abolition of the House of Lords. The attack should be indirect by increasing the efficiency of the House of Commons & thus increasing the country's respect for it.

In the discussion which followed special emphasis was laid upon the moral argument against a hereditary sovereign, & the failure of Mr Murray Macdonald's conclusion regarding the House of Lords' agitation to meet the requirements of his theoretic conclusions. Various methods of dealing with the present difficulties with the Lords were also discussed, the feeling of the Circle being against both Monarchy & a Second Chamber.

William Clarke   Chairman

* * *

[24] The Circle met on Wednesday 3rd March 1897 at 33 Bloomsbury Square—Present, Mr William Clarke in the Chair & 7 members with Mr Shaw Stewart as visitor.

It was decided to ask Mr W.P. Reeves to open on the relation between the democracy & the Colonies & Mr Bryce on Imperial Affairs—holding an extra meeting on the 26th May.

Mr Perris opened the discussion. He began by discussing the part which national feeling was playing in current European politics, &

[24] The original has been crossed out and reads: 'composed of superior men to the first. And what is to be the standard of superiority?'

whilst admitting the desirability of maintaining national & local colour in politics, he pointed out how strong the tendency of the time was against it. Moreover the practical difficulties are many. It may be preserved by Mr Gladstone's first Home Rule scheme, but that is dead; by Grand National Committees, but that is not very promising; by Home Rule All Round, but that is only yet a formula. Referring to the structure of Federal Parliament, he pointed out that the great difficulty lay in determining their powers against those of the Imperial Assembly. Local affairs of a minor nature could easily be dealt with however, & perhaps the best way to advance was to begin by handing over the control of non-contentious business to bodies, or committees, coloured by national feeling.

The discussion turned mostly upon the possible conflicts between the Imperial & the National bodies; but the Circle was agreed that the less we had of written constitutions the better & that devolution could be justified. 1. If it increased the citizen's sense of responsibility 2. If it increased interest in Imperial affairs.

J.A. Murray Macdonald   Chairman

* * *

[25] The Circle met at 33 Bloomsbury Square W.C. on Wednesday 7th April at 8 p.m.

Present J. Murray Macdonald in the chair & eleven members.

It was decided, in the event of Mr Bryce declining, to invite Mr Spencer Wilkinson to open the May debate on Democracy & the Imperial Idea.

Mr Costelloe opened the discussion on the relation between Local & Central Government. The question might be discussed in three aspects—Home Rule, Local Option & Municipal Government. The first raises the question of what is the political unit, & although rigid definitions are here impossible, this unit must be of some considerable mass. We must reject the communistic theory on the one hand but on the other we shall find it very difficult to set limits beyond which the unit ought not increase. The difficulties peculiar to the second aspect arise from considerations of how far within the unit special local circumstances should be recognised. The third point of view has also its difficulties. It is, for instance, quite impossible to say whether the Poor Law & the Licensing Acts are administered locally or imperially. At this point, Mr Costelloe asked 'Where have we got to?' The historical tendency has been to increase both local & central authorities. Both centralisation & decentralisation have been going on apace. But there is no method in the tendency. Its chaos can be best seen in Local finance. No one has ever attempted to construct the system of Local Taxation in its relation to Imperial aids on its only reasonable basis that it should be determined by Local & Imperial benefit. Nor have we decided who should pay local rates & how they should be paid. There was a good case in favour of making both landlords & tenants bear the burden, & the best method would be to collect from the tenant & give him powers to recover from the landlord as under Schedule A. Failing this, a separate site valuation might be made.

R. Stapley   Chairman

* * *

[26] The Circle met on Wednesday May 5th at 8 p.m. at 33 Bloomsbury Square, when Mr Graham Wallas opened the discussion on the place of the Expert under Democracy.

[27] A special meeting of the Circle was held on Wednesday 26 May at 8 p.m. at 33 Bloomsbury Square

Present Mr Richard Stapley, in the chair, & twelve members with two visitors & Mr Spencer Wilkinson.

Mr Spencer Wilkinson opened the discussion. The problem of Imperial politics is one of the relationships between competing nations. The first law of national life is that a people should be independent. Their struggles are contests of will, & the logic of war is that in their conflicts, nations attempt to destroy the organs by which national will is expressed—the armed forces & ultimately the government. Applying this logic to an insular nation like Great Britain, Mr Wilkinson pointed out that the law of mechanical displacement compelled the construction of a special ship for war purposes, & proceeding to discuss the modifications in warfare made by naval forces, he pointed out that the most important was the rapidity of naval movements compared with those made by land forces. The conclusion was that so long, but only so long, as the insular Empire kept the sea, it was supreme. The Law of Empire is that a victorious naval power can land troops anywhere. Special circumstances connected with the rivalries of European empires determine that it is best for Europe generally & for European nations in particular that England should be the supreme naval power of the world. And yet England cannot maintain that position unless its national policy is determined by moral considerations, & its weight thrown in upon the side of great human causes.

R. Stapley   Chairman

* * *

[28] The Circle met on Wednesday 2nd June at 8 p.m. at Mr Stapley's.

Present Mr Richard Stapley, in the chair, & twelve members with Mr Hill as visitor.

Mr Reeves opened the discussion on Democracy & the Colonies. He would leave the dark peoples under British rule out of sight, contenting himself with the one remark that they should be governed from the Colonial Office & not by Chartered Companies. Regarding the white colonial population, it was united to the mother country by bonds neither so strong on the one hand nor so weak on the other as many people imagined. The difficulties ahead of Colonial government are obvious. The first is that, as the Colonies are not self governing, the crown veto may be exercised & serious trouble may follow. Then the financial relationships between colony & mother country not only bind but drive asunder as we see in the Eastern & Western American States. These are the two main sources of possible danger. In the future, a progressive policy should nurture the idea of federation, although it will not come just yet. The Colonial Agents' General should be allowed to sit &, on occasion, speak in the House of Commons; the Viceroy's staff should always include men versed in colonial ways. Moreover, the Home Government should ease the financial burdens of the Colonies & that could be safely done by passing an Act of Parliament allowing Trust Funds to be invested in Colonial Government Securities & by backing certain Conversion Loans. The zollverein would be a short cut to Federation. But the zollverein is impossible though the Board of Trade should make special efforts to foster commerce between the colonies & the home country. Other points urged by Mr Reeves were the appointment of an Inspector of Imperial Defence, & the admission of Colonial Premiers to the Privy Council.

Chairman

The Committee met at Mr Stapley's on Wednesday 2nd June at 7.30 p.m. to discuss the programme for 1897–98, which was postponed until the 16th inst., when it again was discussed and settled as follows:

[copy of programme included in minutes]

4th Session 1897–98.

[29] The circle met on Wednesday 6th Octr 1897, at 8 p.m., at Mr Stapley's.

Present Mr Stapley in the chair, and 10 members.

Mr Herbert Burrows opened the discussion on 'Should there be special protection for children, young persons, & women?' He commenced by drawing attention to the fact that even those who in some respects were most earnest & advanced in their advocacy of women's rights were not altogether agreed as to the justice or expediency of special regulations for the Labour of Women, their objection being that equal laws for both sexes were the thing to be aimed at. He did not think, however, that anyone now-a-days outside the Anarchists would favour a repeal of the Factory Acts. He traced the growth of these & looked upon them as the outcome of the rising social conscience. Dealing first with the labour of young children he advocated the complete abolition of half-time & the raising of the educational, & consequent factory, age to 16, with—as supplementary— free maintenance for the children in the schools. The limit of the age of young persons should be raised to 21, & the Factory Acts for them & for children considerably strengthened. The difficulty in dealing with women's work arose largely from the low wage, which in many instances was a matter of custom as well as of economics, as women had accustomed themselves to subsist on a lower standard of life than men. The organisation of women in trade-unions should be pushed as much as possible,—married women should be prohibited from working in poisonous & dangerous trades, and, above all, home-work should be abolished.

In the discussion which followed, the main objections taken were to free maintenance and to the complete abolition of home-work, especially to the latter as it was felt it would unduly restrict some forms of work artistic & other which could well be pursued at home.

Richard Stapley   Chairman

* * *

[30] The Circle met on Wed. 3 Nov. '97 at 8 p.m., at Mr. Stapley's.

Present Messrs Burrows, Clarke, Hobson, Husband, Murray Macdonald, Morrison, Reeves, Roskill, Rylett, Samuel, Stapley, & Trevelyan.

Mr. Stapley was elected chairman for the Session. Hon. W.P. Reeves was elected a member of Committee in the place of Mr. Samuel, & the other members of Committee were re-elected viz. Messrs Burrows, Clarke, Hobson, Murray Macdonald, & Stapley.

Mr. J. Ramsay MacDonald was re-elected Hon. Sec.

Mr. W.D. Morrison, of 2, Embankment Gardens, Chelsea, S.W., & Mr. J. Roskill, of 1, Paper Buildings, Temple, E.C., were elected members of the Circle.

Mr. Reeves opened the discussion on 'What state-regulations should apply to men in existing conditions of private employment?' He began by dissociating himself from the dictum of W.S. Jevons that the principle of State-interference is, prima facie, bad; and indicated six respects in which State-control over employment of men was proper & expedient, viz. sanitation, extortion, education, immigration of aliens, unemployment, & compulsory arbitration. Mr. Reeves then sketched the provisions of the New Zealand Industrial Conciliation & Arbitration Act of 1894 which was a scheme for the adjustment of labour disputes between Trade Unions & employers. Of disputes between individual men & their masters, or between employers & bodies of men not legally associated, the Act took no notice. Local Boards of Conciliation were set up, composed of equal numbers of masters & men with an impartial chairman. At the request of any party to an 'industrial dispute', the District Board could call the other parties before it, & hear, examine, & award. The Board was armed with the fullest powers for taking evidence & compelling attendance. Its award, however, was not enforceable by law, but was only a friendly recommendation to disputants. In case these or some of them refused to accept the award, they might appeal to the Court of Arbitration, a tribunal consisting of a judge of the Supreme Court sitting with two assessors, one being selected by Associations of Employers & the other by Federations of Trade-Unions. The award of the Court could be either legally enforceable or not, as it thought advisable. If it was to have legal force, it was filed in the Supreme Court, and then either party could by leave of a judge get an order exacting a penalty for breach of the award. The penalty was not to exceed £500 in the case of any individual employer or Trade-Union. Should the funds of a Union be insufficient, each member was liable to the extent of not more than £10. The right under the Act to elect Conciliation Boards & the Assessors of the Arbitration Court belonged to such unions of masters or workers (men or women) as might register under the Act. Provision was made for the filing, in the Supreme Court, of contracts embodying working conditions agreed on by employers & Union. These documents, called Industrial Agreements, were, when filed, binding for the period mentioned therein provided it did not exceed three years. The greater the use of these agreements the less would be the friction & the more would the Act do in the cause of genuine industrial peace.

The discussion which followed Mr. Reeves's opening turned mainly on the changes which would be necessary in any such enactment before it was applicable to Britain, & on the objections to any scheme of compulsory arbitration. Mr. Reeves in reply to the objection that the Act did not deal with unorganised trades stated that it was sufficient for the purposes of the Act if seven workers organised & registered as an industrial union. He thought that the Act was not likely to perpetuate existing industrial conditions, but that it was likely to level up the conditions of labour, to reduce exorbitant profits, to organise labour more completely, & to hasten the taking over of certain industries by the State. He denied that previous attempts by the State to regulate wages had failed. As to the alleged absence of a basis for the decision of the arbitrator, he maintained that public opinion & the notion of what was decent & right supplied an adequate basis.

Richard Stapley

* * *

[31] The Circle met on Wednesday, December 1st at 8 p.m. at Mr Stapley's. Present Mr Richard Stapley, in the chair, Messrs Husband, Olivier, Perris, Rylett, Millin, Burrows, Reeves, J.R. MacDonald, Lilley, W. Douglas Morrison & Corbett as visitor.

The minutes of last meeting were read & signed.

It was agreed that as the Circle was rich, the question of subscription be deferred, & the accounts were passed.

Mr Perris moved that the proceedings of the Circle be edited & printed & a decision was postponed until the next meeting.

Mr. J.R. MacDonald opened the discussion on What should be the function of the State in case of injuries? For the purposes of the discussion, injuries should be divided into two classes, preventible & non-preventible. So far as the employers were responsible for the former, they should be subject to an Employers' Liability Law; so far as the workmen were responsible some penalising restrictions in compensation should be imposed, but not of a kind or severity to cripple the social efficiency of the workman. Whatever the State did to secure compensation for non preventible accidents must be done in such as way as not to increase the accident total. Prevention is better than compensation. German experience seemed to prove that all accidents could be compensated without any danger of inviting either employer or employed to be careless. That being so, how should these accidents be compensated? Who ought to pay? The possible sources of payment are, the workman (but from the nature of the enquiry, we cannot think of him), the individual employer, the trade, & the State from its ordinary revenue. The Chamberlain Act[25] placed

[25] A reference to the Employer Liability Act (1880) and its extension by the Workmen's Compensation Act (1897), in which Joseph Chamberlain played leading roles.

the responsibility on the first; the German law places it upon the second. The objection to Mr Chamberlain's scheme is that it is incapable of extension. In practise[sic], the German law is much better. But both are subject to two serious objections, the one political & the other economic. The first is that neither is specially adapted to rapidly reduce accident risks. These have already been reduced by Employers' Liability Acts to the point where they do just pay & any further levelling up of industrial conditions must come mainly from State regulations in the shape of more stringent Factory Acts & Departmental regulations. The economic objection is that profits in different trades are not fixed by degrees of trade risks & therefore ought not to be rated in accordance with them. The only rational & fair point of view to adopt is to regard risks inseparable from trade as in reality social risks & attempt to abolish that conveniently-called inseparable risk by State regulation & inspection. The state ought therefore to regard its Exchequer as responsible for the compensation of Act-of-God accidents.

In discussion some objection was taken to the interpretation of German figures by the opener, but the main point at issue was the obligation of profits to pay for accident risks. The one view was Put burdens on & let the burdened escape them as they only can by diminishing the risks of their trades; on the other hand it was argued that that policy rarely worked out, & that greater possibilities lay in its opposite of taking off unreasonable burdens & exacting as a quid pro quo a high standard of safety efficiency.

Richard Stapley   Chairman

* * *

[32] The Circle met at Mr Stapley's on Wednesday 5 January 1898. Present Mr Stapley (in the chair) Mr Rylett, G.H. Perris, W. Clarke, J. Murray Macdonald, Herbert Burrows, Douglas Morrison, J.R. MacDonald & J.C. Kenworthy as visitor.

The publication of the minutes was discussed & the matter was referred to the Committee for consideration & report.

Mr Rylett opened the discussion on the Economic Effect of the Single Tax. The point he desired to prove was that the Single Tax would give to Labour its natural reward, & a series of diagrams was exhibited. The simplest process was Labour & Land producing Wealth which was distributed in the form of Wages & Rent. The second diagram showed land of equal value except in productivity. In that case, Labour would be attracted to the most productive areas

& if rent be charged for land on the margin of cultivation, Labour strives to transfer itself to areas a grade higher in the scale of productivity. But when labour by its own growth in quantity extends the area of cultivation, the area of rent-paying land is also extended & the rent rate is equivalent to the difference in productivity between the non-rent paying & the rent paying land. In other words, rent is paid from natural wages & economic wages remain at the value of the produce of labour working on the margin of cultivation. The fact that landownership was a monopoly had a further evil effect upon wages. By withholding land of a certain value of productivity from labour, labour forces down the margin of cultivation & thus increases rent & lowers wages all round. When the community steps in as owner, two things happen. First, labour is concentrated on the best land as there would then be no speculative holding; & secondly, wages would be raised as the margin of cultivation would be raised. The social & industrial effects might be summarized under three heads: First: The State would own its own wealth & be put in possession of ample resources; secondly: There would be a greater demand for labour consequent upon the opening up of the land; thirdly: There would be a just distribution of wealth owing to Labour being again paid its natural wages. No one would get more or less than he had earned. Mr Rylett concluded with a reference to New Zealand & New South Wales which he said fully bore out his contention.

In the discussion it was evident that the Circle agreed upon the justice of rent nationalisation but disagreed with Mr Rylett on the following main points.

1. He was wrong in distributing Wealth into Rent & Wages, because capital is not analysible into wages & performs a distinct economic function with phenomena special to itself;

2. Wages do not follow the law of diminishing returns. Within the sphere of manufacture, the law of increasing return holds good.

3. The Single Tax does not settle the competition of increasing .population.

4. The Land nationalisation theory does not explain certain well determined movements in politics in the direction of the public ownership of capital.

J.A. Murray Macdonald   Chairman

* * *

The Committee met at Mr Stapley's on Wednesday 2 February, at 7.30 p.m.

Present Mr Murray Macdonald, in the chair, Mr J.A. Hobson & the Secretary.

It was resolved to report against publishing the minutes but to recommend the Circle to consider the advisability of publishing a book of say eight or nine articles dealing systematically with the present political position.

Chairman

* * *

[33] The Circle met at Mr Stapley's on Wednesday 2 February at 8 p.m.

Present, J. Murray Macdonald in the chair, Millin, J.A. Hobson, Lilley, Perris, Samuel, Reeves & the Secretary.

The report of the Committee as above was presented; Resolved that the decision be deferred until the April meeting, Mr Perris & J.R. MacDonald being asked to consider & report on the proposed book, presenting a syllabus of the papers if they think it advisable.

Resolved that the March meeting be held on Wednesday the 9th owing to the London County Council elections being held on the 3rd.

Mr J.A. Hobson opened on the unemployed. It was essential to make his personal position in economics clear. Unemployment was not a local matter, nor could it [be] adequately considered from any sectional point of view, because the great fact needing an explanation is the simultaneous unemployment of capital, land & labour. He wished to lay special stress upon that. He could discover no adequate explanation saving that of the theory of underconsumption. The community can produce more at any given time than it consents to consume, the reason being that savings are put into fixed forms employed to increase the volume of production. At the same time no change has happened to increase correspondingly the effective demand. He supported his opinion that this is actually happening, not by statistics—which are not available—but by the common opinion of commercial men & the periodical glut of loanable capital. The two suggested checks on this process of overproduction & underconsumption is, that interest will fall, which it does not always do. When it does, however, it rather acts as a stimulant on saving & consequently sets up a tendency to intensify the difficulty. The second suggested check is that the overproduction causes a fall in prices & therefore clears the market. But, as income must shrink with prices, saving will not be checked by a general fall of prices. He would suggest as a test of every remedy for unemployment, Will it increase the volume of consumption? He could see no way out of this grand conclusion that there is an economic justification for the right to employment:

1. Because the access to nature under conditions fit for life is not open to all;

2. Because industry as at present conducted gives no guarantee that every willing man can find employment;

3. Because the progress & welfare of Society demand protection against the misery & inefficiency of the unemployed.

The State's ultimate duty is to guarantee work & wages to those willing to work. There are certain practical difficulties in the way of this ideal. The subsidised workers, for instance, must not put their goods on the open markets, & so long as the policy was a palliative, the bounties given should be lower than the wages paid on the open market. Another difficulty was, ought the worker to be employed at his own trade? Three definite proposals, he would now make:

1. The activity of the Poor Law should be extended. Land & raw material might be acquired for the employment of the unemployed;

2. Labour colonies might be tried, but going still further down towards the root of the matter;

3. A further tax upon unearned incomes should be imposed so as to increase the standard of social consumption & the workers['] share in the national product.

The discussion which followed emphasised:

1. That the necessary reorganisation should begin with the cultivation of the land & proceed from that;

2. That the underconsumption theory is not superior to the old one of maldistribution, & that Mr Hobson's reply to the old economists was incomplete;

3. That the practical difficulties in the way of adopting Mr Hobson's proposals make them useless;

4. That the international character of trade so complicates matters that England cannot be studied alone, & suggests the folly of widening our Empire to protect our trade;

5. That expenditure on factories means fresh employment & that therefore Mr Hobson's view of the antagonism between saving & consumption is false;

6. That the problem should be stated in terms of distribution not of consumption.

William Clarke

* * *

[34] The Circle met at Mr Stapley's on Wednesday 9 March, 1898 at 8 p.m.

Present Mr William Clarke, in the chair, Sidney Olivier, J. Murray Macdonald, G. Millin, J.A. Hobson, Herbert Samuel, T.F. Husband, J. Roskill, J.R. MacDonald.

Mr Sidney Olivier opened the discussion on [']How far do existing social conditions necessitate the nationalization of industrial capital'? He began by declaring himself to be a Collectivist. An examination of the economic facts relating to such supplies as railways, trams, milk, &c., shows that they are now conducted at much greater cost & with much greater waste than are necessary. The same conclusion is reached by an examination of what is ordinarily termed 'business'. The first difficulty that Collectivism has to meet is that of vested interests both on the side of labour & of capital. The latter sees itself passing from private hands & resistance is natural; the former considers all sweeping economies as involving at some point a saving of labour, &, again, resistance is natural. Capitalist opposition is well grounded, but the opposition of labour is conducted under a misapprehension for, if Collectivism were fully adopted, labour would be saved quantitatively without suffering a reduction of its aggregate income. Those are, however, but preliminary difficulties. The real task of the Collectivist propagandist is to prove the sanction of social necessity for his opinions. That is a very difficult matter, & is mainly an affair of circumstance & mental attitude. In 1895,[26] for instance, the working people did not see it, but despite some beneficial work by collectivist politicians, were looking elsewhere for salvation. He therefore considered that the sanction of social necessity could not be proved at the moment by the laying down of a programme of nationalization. The task before the Collectivist was to familiarise the popular mind with the general Collectivist outlook & accustom it to think in the general Collectivist groove.

Some members regretted that Mr Olivier had not dealt with the special question of present-day industrial tendency & that he had not regarded the alternatives presented as against the socialist remedies.

Objection was taken to the generalisation that because some forms of industry were being taken over by the community, that consequently an unqualified nationalisation was being evolved. The supply of gas & water was of a special character.

It was urged that Foreign trade would be impossible under Socialism.

On the other hand it was pointed out that the facts of the public management of industry showed that the movement was not confined to any form of supply; that no alternative to Socialism was equally

[26] Referring to the 1895 elections, in which Fabians like Olivier failed to realize their policy of permeation and to become an effective political force.

economical to labour & capital; that already individualism in Foreign trade had broken down & that markets were being opened from the Army & Navy estimates & held by information supplied by Consuls.

It was decided that no meeting should be held in April.

Richard Stapley   Chairman

* * *

[35] The Circle met at Mr Stapley's on Wednesday 4th May at 8 p.m.

Present: Mr Richard Stapley, in the chair, J. Murray Macdonald, Herbert Samuel, T.F. Husband, G.H. Perris, B.F.C. Costelloe, J.R. MacDonald & Rev. John Bullock, visitor.

The Secretary presented the report of the sub-committee appointed to consider the advisability of publishing a volume of essays & it was agreed that the scheme outlined should be sent out to the members & that it should be discussed at the next meeting.

On the motion of Mr J. Murray Macdonald, seconded by Mr Herbert Samuel, the Rev John Bullock was elected a member of the Circle.

Mr J. Murray Macdonald opened the discussion on 'Can the State establish a standard of value'? The answer depended on whether value is objective or subjective. If there is an individual element in value, the State cannot establish its standard. The most distinguished exponent of value as an objective fact is Marx who seeks to explain value ratios in terms of labour—the common element of all produce. The law of value, he lays down, is determined by the quantity of labour of average efficiency in itself & its conditions, necessary for the production of the given produce. His theory of surplus value—unpaid working time—is a deduction from this law. Moreover, capital in productive operation is divided into two parts, the constant & the variable, & only from the latter—e.g. really from labour, is profit derived. Regarding the last point, industries vary considerably in the proportions of the two capitals employed & yet the experience of the business world is altogether against the deduction from Marxian economics that the relative quantities of the latter employed should determine the relative profits. Marx himself had become aware of the inconsistencies between the theories of his first book & the experience of the business world & in his third & concluding volume introduces the amount of constant capital as a co-determinant with labour of value.[27] In tracing all values to labour, Marx confines his search to

[27] The third volume of Capital had in fact been substantially completed by the time the first volume was published in 1867.

products of labour; but even then, labour is not the only common element in them. There is a common scarcity. Nor ought he to have passed over value in use as a determinant of value in exchange. He did indeed allow the influence of competition but regarded it as only an exceptional circumstance moving values slightly up & down—throwing them off equilibrium at the point of labour equivalents. Value was a matter of supply & demand; the State could not therefore establish its standard & that being so the economics and practicability of socialism fell together.

The discussion was taken up in pointing out that even if the State could not establish a permanent standard of value it could establish a temporary & workable one;

That the opposition between economic classes in the community gave the law of supply & demand a validity which was abnormal for the present time;

That socialism did not vitally depend on Marxism.

Richard Stapley   Chairman

* * *

[36] The Circle met at Mr Stapley's on Wednesday 8th June at 8 p.m.

Present Mr Richard Stapley, in the chair, Messrs Millin, Bullock, Burrows, Murray Macdonald, Clarke, Morrison, Lilley, Rylett, Samuel, Hobson, J.R. MacDonald, Hon. Secry. with Messrs Kenworthy & Fuller as visitors.

The question of publishing a book of essays was considered, the discussion at first turning upon whether the Circle should meet again. It was first resolved unanimously that the Circle should meet for another Session.

Mr Hobson then moved that the consideration of the book be postponed until the end of the next Session;[28] that the discussions for 1898–99 should be upon subjects likely to compose a practical programme for a Progressive Party, & that the Committee meet & draft subjects. This was carried, & Mr Samuel was added to the Committee for the purpose of arranging the subjects.

Mr W.M. Crook's name was removed from the list for non-attendance.

Richard Stapley   Chairman

* * *

[28] The possibility of publication of Circle minutes arose again only in 1907.

The Committee met at Mr Stapley's on Wednesday 29th June at 12 o'clock noon.

Present Mr Richard Stapley in the chair, Messrs Hobson, Samuel & J.R. MacDonald, Hon Secretary.

The subjects for the 1898–99 Session were decided & the openers suggested as follows:

[1898–99 programme attached to minutes]

5th Session, Oct. 98-June 99

[37] The Circle met at Mr Stapley's on Wednesday 4th[29] October at 8 p.m.

Present: Mr Richard Stapley, in the chair, Herbert Samuel, Burrows, Millin, Murray Macdonald, Douglas Morrison, Hobson, Bullock, J.R. MacDonald with Messrs Pease, who opened, & Hirst visitors.

The Committee's recommendation that the subscription be fixed at 2/- was adopted.—Resolved that Mr Russell Rea be reinstated member of the Circle.—Resolved that the openers of discussions be asked to formulate a set of propositions raising the main points of their opening statements & send twenty copies to the secretary to be sent out with the monthly notices.

Mr Pease opened the discussion on how the progressive party should deal with the drink traffic. He assumed that we should take for granted that there was need of some regulation of the drink traffic. The most drastic proposal is to prohibit, but Mr Pease showed that except in a few exceptional rural districts prohibition was a failure. The most popular regulation proposal—Local Veto—could be opposed by some serious objections. It was a class measure; it would have to be worked by the public opinion of areas which would be governed as a rule by the private drinker on the one hand or the public drinker on the other. Would the publican get fair treatment in Clapham or just treatment in Whitechapel? The plan would, moreover, give unstable results. But his objection to it was even more fundamental. To reduce public houses is not to regulate the drink traffic. No mere mechanical method of changing the number of houses will touch the evil to any great extent. Mr Pease then proceeded to explain the systems known as the Gothenburgh, the three-fold option, & municipal management,[30] & then detailed his own proposals. He proposed

1.- to fix a maximum & minimum number of houses according to a

[29] Read '5th October'.

[30] The Gothenburg system was a Scandinavian experiment in handing over licensing powers to a non-political, non-profitable public company. Alternative systems related to forms of local option.

population scale; 2.- to adopt high licences; 3.- to vest licencing authority in a representative body which he thought might be the town councils & corresponding authorities; & 4. to empower munici- palities to establish & conduct their own public houses. Subject to a general law regulating the possible extreme numbers of public houses in a governing area, he would give the proper authority full liberty to adopt whichever of these expedients it thought best suited to its circumstances. Finally, he thought that the publican was fairly entitled to some form of compensation. He thought the best form was a period of notice during which holders should be guaranteed possession of their licences during good behaviour.

There was a pretty general agreement in the circle in favour of high licences & a maximum number of houses;

That parish councils should not hold licences or be licencing auth- ority;

That to make Town Councils the licencing authorities would lead to the subordination of municipal politics to contests between tem- perance societies & the public house;

That the way out of the difficulty might be to leave the admin- istration of the trade (within certain general limits such as a maximum number of houses) to the private individual, but increase the inspect- ing powers of local authorities.

The circle was not very favourable to municipalisation.

Richard Stapley   Chairman

* * *

[38] The Circle met at Mr Stapley's on Wednesday 9th November 1898 at 8 p.m.

Present: Messrs Stapley (in the chair) H. Samuel, J. Bullock, Russell Rea, J.A. Hobson, J. Roskill, G.H. Perris, W. Clarke, H. Rylett, W.P. Reeves, A.L. Lilley, G.F. Millin, J. Murray Macdonald, Douglas Morrison & J.R. MacDonald (Hon: Sec:) with Messrs Bunting, Donald, Bonar & Alden, visitors.

Mr Pember Reeves opened the discussion on the Progressive Party & the Empire. The great problem of Empire is the treatment of native races. It is a mistake to suppose that they die off when brought into contact with whites. Some minor races do, but the chief native races— the African Negro, the Hindu, the Chinese—multiply rapidly under our rule. This problem we have never faced. We have, in the first place, been too careless in selecting governors & in staffing our Col- onial Office at home, &, in the second place, we have made no intelligent attempt to educate the people. The population problem was really one of the standard of living & until we adopt means to raise that, our difficulties with the numbers of these people will increase. That is the problem of our dependencies; the colonies, which are on a totally different footing, naturally raise the question of imperial defence. To some extent they do contribute to their own defence & the complaints made against them at home are therefore not altogether correct. On the other hand, the colonies will not contribute liberally to imperial defence until & unless they have some voice in our foreign policy. Mr Reeves thought that it would be a good thing for the democracy of this country if the colonies did have a voice in imperial matters.

In the discussion the points emphasised were chiefly:

1. That the fact of Empire 'has been given to us' & we cannot shirk its responsibility: & it was urged that this fatalist notion was absurd & pernicious.

2. That education should be in the methods of trade & of military drill: & that it should be determined by a careful investigation of the religious beliefs & social customs of the people.

3. That our dependencies should be governed by civilians & not by military men.

4. That imperialism advances civilization as can be proved by the record of British rule in Egypt: & that it is impossible to make any such claim because there are different types of civilization.

5. That it broadens the outlook of democracy: & that it destroys democratic institutions as seen in the influence of retired Indian officials.

The discussion was adjourned & the Circle resolved to meet again to resume it on Thursday 17th inst.

Richard Stapley   Chairman

* * *

[39] The adjourned meeting of the Circle was held at Mr Stapley's on Thursday November 17th 1898.

Present: Mr Richard Stapley (in the chair) W.P. Reeves, G.F. Millin, Russell Rea, W. Clarke, G.H. Perris, J. Murray Macdonald, Bullock, H. Rylett, with W.P. Byles, R.W. Corbet & C. Spooner visitors.

The minutes of the previous meeting were read & confirmed.

The Hon W.P. Reeves again opened the debate. He thought there was a consensus of opinion last meeting that philanthropy plus ten per cent had actuated us in building up the Empire. In criticising the present imperialist movement we must remember that the spirit of the times has changed since Cobden lived, that for instance it was now firmly believed by the upper & middle classes that trade follows the flag & that in consequence we should own as much of the earth as possible. Our great duty is to see that what we have is well governed. The policy of the Colonial Office at the present time is to know as little as possible. It would be going too far to say that our rule had brought no benefit to our tropical dependencies, but it certainly has not done so much as it might. The present loose bond between our white colonies & the mother country could not continue. The colonists were not on an equal footing with the people of the mother country; the royal veto was real though not much used. Yet a crisis might arise at any moment which would compel constitutional revision. Foreign complications might occasion such a crisis. The colonies will not submit to be made mere recruiting grounds for the army & navy. If we reduced the cost of armaments we should overcome one of the greatest obstacles to Federation and lay Britain open to the civilizing influence of her colonies.

The discussion which followed revealed substantial agreement with the opener, but emphasis was laid on

1. That it was the first duty of England to look after its home affairs;

2. That abroad the policy of the Open Door was to be preferred to that of annexation;

3. That especially regarding the tropics we should discourage further acquisition

4. That for the maintenance of happy relations with the colonies, as distinguished from the tropical dependencies, reliance should be placed on a healthy moral sentiment;

5. That this might be encouraged by permitting representatives of the Colonies to address the House of Commons on special occasions regarding matters of special colonial interest.

Whilst there was a general condemnation of the methods by which the Empire has been built, no one proposed that it should now be abandoned.

Richard Stapley   Chairman

* * *

[40] The Circle met at Mr Stapley's on Wednesday 7 December at 8 p.m. Present Mr Stapley (in the chair) Clarke, Burrows, Bullock, Olivier, Perris, Douglas Morrison, Rylett, Murray Macdonald, Husband, Millin, Samuel, Rea, Lilley, J.R. MacDonald with Messrs Benson & Byles as visitors.

Mr Clarke opened the discussion on the House of Lords. He had two difficulties in dealing with the subject. In the first place, so long as this jingo spirit lasted there would be no collision with the House of Lords & until that came the subject of discussion was purely academic; in the second place the English people are not democrats & will remain under any circumstances an oligarchy. The aristocracy have made the most of their opportunities. They have arrested their economic decline, they are interesting themselves in popular questions; on the other hand the influence of the Commons is declining. The Liberal attack is insincere. Their threats mean nothing; the interests of leading Liberals are well served by the Lords; the spirit of Liberalism is as adverse to equality as that of Conservatism. The House of Lords will stand & it is unnecessary therefore to discuss whether we ought to have one or two chambers. Regarding its reform, the shoemaker idea would not work. The Crown would not accept them & you cannot trust even a shoemaker peer. Two possible methods are that peers should elect representatives as the Scottish peers now do,[31] & the second that life peerages should be created. We accept or reject these in accordance with what our idea is of what the House of Lords should do. Neither of these reforms, for instance would make the Lords pass Liberal bills. But it is to secure that that the Liberals are thinking of the question at all. A second elected chamber would not do because its power would be coordinate with that of the House of Commons, nor is it practical to try & select the peers that are to be summoned as Professor Thorold Rogers suggested.[32] If Mr Morley's[33] proposal were adopted that a peer would be able to select whether he should sit in the Lords or try to sit in the Commons, the Lords would be hopelessly stupid & the reactionary forces considerably strengthened in the Commons. The most practical of all the proposals for dealing with the House of Lords is the abolition of its veto. But even to do this requires a leader more determined & honest than any whom we now have & a public opinion more robust than what we can now draw upon. Our treatment of the House of Lords, however, must depend upon what we conceive to be the future in store for England. We were doomed to decline as an industrial nation, & we shall become the leisured resting place of the world. In such a country there is no room for democracy.

The chief points urged in the discussion were:

1. That England could not sink to the social state described in his

---

[31] I.e., electing sixteen of their number for the duration of each parliament.

[32] James Edwin Thorold Rogers (1823–1890). Economic historian, Drummond Professor of Political Economy at the University of Oxford. For the proposal see J.E. Thorold Rogers, 'The House of Lords', *Fortnightly Review*, vol. xlii (1884), 257–270.

[33] John Morley (1838–1923). Liberal M.P. and politician, who agitated for reform of the House of Lords from the 1880s onwards.

conclusion by Mr Clarke, because of the dogged nature of the Anglo-Saxon character & the establishment of English colonies; & because even now the north & the midlands were robust at heart.

2. The feeling was unanimous that the House of Lords ought not to be improved, at least until deprived of its power of veto;

3. It was also generally agreed that an attack on the Lords would be futile unless it were made in connection with the mutilation or rejection of a popular measure; & that then it would not succeed unless there were unanimity & determination in the attacking party.

4. On the whole the abolition of the veto was approved as being the best method of attack but opinions were expressed:

1. That this would be an anticlimax to the statement & agitation of any grievance which stirred up public feeling against the Lords;

2. That it presented nearly as many practical difficulties as a much more drastic treatment;

3. And that it was an imperfect settlement of a problem in democratic government which raised a whole group of questions relating to local self government, the reform of the House of Commons & so on, & which could be settled only as the whole group was settled.

It was decided that the January meeting should be postponed from the 4th to the 18th of that month.

Richard Stapley   Chairman

* * *

[41] The Circle met at Mr. Stapley's on Wed. 18 Jan. '99 at 8 p.m. Present Mr. Stapley (in the chair), Messrs. Murray Macdonald, Morrison, Lilley, Millin, J.R. MacDonald, Bullock, Samuel, Husband, Trevelyan, Rea, Hobson, Burrows, & Clarke.

The minutes of the previous meeting were read & confirmed.

Mr. Douglas Morrison opened the discussion on Church & State, beginning with an historical sketch of the relations between the Roman State & the Christian Church. According to the Byzantine theory state & church were one & the Supreme power in both was united in one person who was at once a sacred & secular dignitary. But the theory which gained dominance in the West after the fall of the Western Empire was the ecclesiastico-political theory that the church was a divinely established universal state, whose head was the only source on earth from which legitimate power proceeded. This latter theory was supplanted by what is practically the modern doctrine of the sovereignty of the state within its own dominions, under which the head of the state became an ecclesiastical as well as a civil personage, as was the case under the old Roman civil law. The modern state repudiates the doctrine of the co-ordinate authority of church & state, &, while allowing the church complete liberty within its own sphere, determines the limits of that sphere.

The relations between state & church may be loosened, but they cannot be severed altogether. Not even in the U.S.A. is there complete separation, & neither there nor in France can Britain find a complete guide in this matter. As for the plea of religious equality, the attitude of the state cannot be the same to different religious communities, but must be determined by their respective characters, numbers, power, & wealth. Churches are not private societies but public institutions existing for public objects of supreme importance. The State has the same right over the property of an obscure Nonconformist sect as over the revenues of the See of Canterbury. Disestablishment without disendowment is a step which will never be taken, & if there is to be disendowment there must be disendowment all round.

In the discussion which followed, & which was of a hostile nature, exception was taken to the historical part of the paper in one or two respects. The chief points taken against the remainder of the paper were as follows:

1. That each church need not have a special organisation.

2. That the social utility of the church, if proved, was the only valid argument for the[34] establishment.

3. That the church was an anti-democratic organisation & had been one of the greatest obstacles during the present century to progressive legislation.

4. That the paper dealt with expediencies & avoided fundamentals.

5. That both Church & State derive their authority from the same source but must have separate organisations.

6. That disestablishment as a claim for free expression would be accelerated more from within the church than from without.

Richard Stapley   Chairman

* * *

[42] The Circle met at Mr. Stapley's on Wed. 1 Feb. '99 at 8 p.m. Present: Mr. Stapley (in the chair), Messrs. Hobson, Bullock, Husband, Rylett, Millin, Clarke, & Mr. Gwyther[35] as guest.

The minutes of the previous meeting were read & confirmed.

Apologies for absence were intimated from Messrs. Murray Mac-

---

[34] Read 'its'.
[35] Presumably James Gwyther, friend of Ramsay MacDonald's.

donald, Ramsay MacDonald, Douglas Morrison, Perris, Rea, & Samuel.

Mr. Millin opened the discussion on 'The Land.' He said that as a temporary expedient we must support any well-devised scheme for taxing ground values, but the ultimate aim was public ownership of land; which beyond all question belongs primarily to the whole nation. The state should buy up land from time to time as opportunity arose. Free trade in land was not what was wanted, but the only trading in land should be between the individual & the state.

In the informal conversation which followed, the suggestion was made that in the taxation of land values the local authority should have the option of taxation or purchase, on the landowner's valuation; also that the state-provision of capital was necessary, in addition to land nationalisation, in any radical land reform. It was further pointed out that in practical politics the housing question might be separated from other aspects of the land question; & that for purposes of housing, sanitation, & civic structure, the city should have its own city land, the town its own town land, & the village its own village-land.

Richard Stapley

* * *

[43] The Circle met at Mr. Stapley's on Wedn: March 1st 1899, at 8 p.m. Present, Mr. Stapley in the chair; and Messrs. Russell Rea, Perris, Rylett, Samuel, Hobson, Olivier, Clarke, Roskill, Murray Macdonald, Millin, Morrison, and Bullock, and a visitor Mr. Parsons.

The minutes of the previous meeting were read and confirmed.

It was decided that the next meeting be held on April 12th.

Mr. Perris opened the discussion on 'The Weak,' cursorily describing the problems, which the subject suggested, under the following headings:

The protection of Infants, Infant Insurance, Illigimates [sic][36], Education of children, Conditions of School life, Child labor, Women, Home labor, Factory work, Sweating, Prostitution, Old age, Displacement of the elderly, Pensions, the Blind, the Maimed. State Doctors, the position of Hospitals, Thrift and Insurance, Sickness, Dangerous industries, Statistics of Death Rates, Lunatic Asylums, the care of persons mentally deficient, the Criminal law, Inequity of present punishments, Prison life, Reforms needed. The Residuum, the unsuccessful, the present poor law, Alterations required, Reformative colonies, their objects, the possibility or otherwise of their financial

---

[36] Presumably 'Illegitimates'.

success. The Slums, their cause, condition, remedies, the Building Acts.

The discussion which followed was of a very discursive character. Elementary School teachers were sharply criticised, and were defended. The need for smaller classes & for prolonged education was agreed on.

State Hospitals were approved.

Over-inspection was deprecated.

The comparative advantages of scattered homes for pauper children, & of boarding-out were discussed.

Old Age pensions were approved.

It was urged that the State must take increased responsibility for children, and for sanitary matters.

Sympathy was expressed for fallen women, and for breakfastless school children.

It was generally agreed that palliatives for many evils are immediately necessary, but that care must be taken lest these block the way against real remedies.

Richard Stapley[37]

* * *

[44] The Circle met at Mr Stapley's on Wednesday 12th April at 8 p.m.

Present: Mr Richard Stapley, in the chair, Messrs. Millin, Husband, Trevelyan, Rylett, Hobson, Samuel, Bullock, Morrison, J.R. Mac-Donald; with Mr John M. Robertson, & Mr Llewellyn Davies as visitors.

The Circle congratulated Mr C.P. Trevelyan M.P. on his election to the House of Commons.[38]

Mr Trevelyan opened the discussion on Home Rule. He was as firmly persuaded as ever in the wisdom of Mr Gladstone's Irish policy. None of the great determining factors in Irish & English politics have materially altered under a Unionist Government. But, on the other hand, we have to confess that even Mr Gladstone failed in the sweeping method which he adopted. Political circumstances are less favourable for the Gladstone method now than in 1886. In the first place Ireland is to be reformed only as a reforming enthusiasm is imparted to English political thought. The Bloomsbury Square Committee of Public Safety must begin its consideration of the Home Rule question with that in

---

[37] Crossed out after the chairman's signature: 'The Circle thought that the field covered was too wide'.

[38] In a by-election for the Elland division of Yorkshire.

view. Then, the matter is not merely an Irish question. Parliament is overworked; the private member is nowhere; the separate interests of Scotland & Wales are neglected or inefficiently attended to; imperial matters occupy a lessening portion of Parliamentary time. The opinion of the opener was in consequence tending towards national legislatures having control at least of justice & Police & of Local & Private legislation. Ecclesiastical & educational matters might be added. Matters relating to Trade & Industry should be dealt with by the Imperial Parliament.

The discussion turned largely upon the relations that should exist between the Imperial & the Local Parliaments. The in & out relationship proposed in Mr Gladstone's second Bill found no support & the Circle seemed to consider that an exclusion of any part of the country from the Imperial Parliament as proposed in Mr Gladstone's first bill, was out of the question. The possible alternatives considered were Home Rule all round with a proper imperial Parliament, & national committees with considerable powers consisting of all the members elected by the separate nationalities sitting for national business during the recess. Upon these alternatives, the Circle was pretty evenly divided. It was generally agreed that Irish Home Rule roused no great interest even in Liberal meetings, & yet that the matter could not be dropped by progressives first of all for expediency's sake, & secondly for the sake of principle & justice.

Richard Stapley   Chairman

* * *

[45] The Circle met at Mr Stapley's on Wednesday 3 May 1899 at 8 p.m.

Present: Mr Richard Stapley, in the chair, Messrs Samuel, Bullock, Millin, Murray Macdonald, Hobson, Husband, Rylett, Douglas Morrison, Lilley & J.R. MacDonald with Mr Benson as visitor.

It was decided that the Committee should meet & present to the next meeting of the Circle a proposal for the discussions of next Session.

Mr Samuel opened the discussion on the Progressive Party. Although the specific achievements of progressive politics since 1885 are few the permanent forces making for progress are strong & the problem is how are they to be utilised. Those forces are: the self-interest of the suffering classes, & of the classes deprived of the pressing desirable things of life such as ample leisure, the convictions of the mass of men sensitive to a public conscience. On the other side are those moved by a narrow self interest threatened by the legitimate demands of the dispossessed, including as classes landlords, abnormally rich men, church clergymen, & also those who hold the imperialist opinions of the Jingo. The latter classes & sections are numerically insignificant. Why, then, is progress slow & scanty? There is a want of definite leading on labour questions; the Socialists alone have inspired of late the masses of the people with a sense of the reality of their professions [but] their proposals are too visionary to serve the purposes of practical politics; the genuine forces of Progress are beset with the inefficiency of Whiggery on the one hand & with the intolerance of Socialism on the other; the progressive labour policy must be inspired by full knowledge & sympathy with labour demands & must at the same time conciliate the employer by proving to him that the changes which it contemplates will not injure him if indeed they do not benefit him. This party would moreover conciliate the commercial classes generally. Again the progressive party must not close its doors upon the man who believes in the high calling of this country amongst nations & who, nevertheless, is not a Jingo. The party must, therefore, have a policy of rational patriotism. The Tory provides for both of those classes &, in addition, he passes an occasional factory [Act] & puts into operation his vast social influence. That is why the reactionary few triumph over the progressive many, & only when Progressive leaders recognise those facts & adopt policies & programmes accordingly, will there be a vigorous & flourishing Progressive party.

In the debate it was urged that the distinctive characteristic of Liberalism was constitutional reform & that it should still rally Progressive forces round that work.

The point that Liberalism could promote the desires of the labour movement & secure the consent of capital to that work was specially contested on the ground that those desires no longer challenged merely the methods of capitalism but some of its essential results.

It was also argued that the progressive value of the principles upon which Liberalism rested was exhausted & that the problems of modern progress appealed in different ways to those who had been united on Liberalism as it was, & that consequently one of the greatest impediments in the way of reform was the attempt made to keep the Liberal party together. Some of the members also felt that Mr Samuel's references to patriotism were too vague to form a foundation for any new departure. No one disputed the truth of the general terms but their application would raise dissension rather than make harmony at the present time.

Richard Stapley

* * *

[46] The Circle met at Mr Stapley's on Wednesday June 7th 1899 at 8 p.m.

Present. Mr Richard Stapley (in the chair), Messrs Husband, Trevelyan, Douglas Morrison, Hobson, Millin, Rylett, Perris, Lilley, Olivier, Burrows, Bullock, Russell Rea, Samuel, & J.R. MacDonald; with Messrs W.P. Byles & S. Bland visitors.

The recommendation of the Committee that Imperialism should be the subject of the discussions of next session was adopted & referred back to the Committee to make the ordinary arrangements & issue the syllabus.

The following members were unanimously elected:

Mr Graham Wallas, proposed by Mr Herbert Samuel & seconded by Mr Harold Rylett;

Mr W.P. Byles proposed by Mr Perris & seconded by Mr Hobson

Mr. J.M. Robertson proposed by Mr Hobson & seconded by Mr Russell Rea.

Mr Hobson opened the discussion on a Progressive Party. The principles upon which such a party must be based are already in existence in the form of widely held intellectual affinities which as a matter of fact place the leaders of the Radical, the Socialist & the Labour groups much nearer to each other than their followers imagine. The issue of intellectual affinity in political cooperation depends upon the application of the principles of that affinity to democratic government, social reform & imperial affairs. Under the first head we must advance in the direction of the total extirpation of heredity in government & the full development of local self government; under the second fall such attempts to vindicate humane sentiment like Old Age Pensions, & to secure economic justice, like Taxation of Ground Rents. The danger attending such reforms is that they appear to settle more than they do, & consequently by giving a premature sense of security hamper the Progressive Party in its more organic ideals. But it should be emphasised that we want the land and not merely the rent & special emphasis should be laid on railway nationalisation. Under the third heading we must decide what our attitude to Imperialism & expansion is to be. The opener laid down some guiding propositions. The present temper & ideals of the country made reform in democratic machinery impossible & blocked the way of social reform; they tended to concentrate autocratic power in the hands of a few completely removed from democratic control, but as completely under the thumb of certain pernicious social influences. The yielding of certain progressives to imperialism is one of the worst features of present day politics. The public morality is being degraded by crooked appeals to false ideals of right & wrong; & an unscientific & harmful political method of judging every expansive step on 'its own merits' is being upheld. So long as the present spirit lasts there can be no robust progressive party.

Regret was expressed that Mr Hobson was not more constructive. A vigorous party could be built up only on specific proposals of a practical kind.

It was urged that Mr Hobson had exaggerated the part played by Imperialism; & as we had an empire & could not get rid of it, the profitable thing to discuss was not whether we should have any Imperialism but what the characteristics of a good kind of Imperialism are.

The fundamental objection to Imperialism was stated to be a reintroduction of aristocratic thought & assumptions in politics & that its influence should be estimated from that starting point, & this was restated thus: that a democratic justice was imposed from within whilst an imperialistic justice was imposed from without. On the other hand it was replied that imperial responsibilities improved the character of our citizens & that it was as much our duty to improve the world where we could as to improve ourselves.

At the conclusion of the discussion a cordial vote of thanks was carried most heartily to Mr Stapley for his generous hospitality to the Circle.

Richard Stapley   Chairman

* * *

6th Session 1899–1900

[47] The Circle met at Mr Stapley's on Wednesday, 4th October 1899.

Present: Mr Richard Stapley, in the chair, Douglas Morrison, J. Bullock, A.L. Lilley, G.H. Perris, H. Burrows, Graham Wallas, W.P. Byles, H. Rylett, J.M. Robertson, C.P. Trevelyan M.P., G.F. Millin, H. Samuel, J. Murray Macdonald & J.R. MacDonald Hon: Sec:

The officers for the Session were appointed as follows: Chairman: Mr Richard Stapley; Secretary: Mr J.R. MacDonald; Committee: Messrs Herbert Burrows, Herbert Samuel, G.F. Millin, A.L. Lilley, J. Bullock & C.P. Trevelyan M.P.

The accounts showing a balance of 7/2d due to the Hon: Secretary were presented & adopted, and a subscription of 2/- was fixed for 1899–1900.

Agreed that in future all nominations for membership should be handed to the secretary & placed before the committee prior to election.

Agreed to ask Mr H.R. Fox Bourne to open the discussion on May 2nd.

The discussion was opened by Mr J.M. Robertson. For the purposes of this discussion he restricted the meaning of Empire to the rule of a state over a subject aggregate. Such a rule is the beginning of a united people but only on condition that assimilation takes place between conqueror & conquered, & historical experience shows the instability of empires. Assyria & Egypt grew slothful & incompetent on the military side; Athens grew while making enemies; Sparta depended upon a special kind of military organisation; the Empire of Alexander had no centre; Carthage was a trading, commercialist empire & as such was bound to fall to the attack of a military people like the Romans; Rome, imperially wise in many ways, decayed when militarism produced an imperator, when the agricultural competition of fruitful provinces ruined the Roman husbandman, & when the economic centre of empire moved to Constantinople; the barbaric Empire of Denmark had no adequate centre; the Germanic Empire maintained anarchy & led to the Thirty Years' War; the Spanish Empire bred autocracy in church & state; the Dutch commercial empire was met with the rivalry of England; Napoleon's conquests were as Alexander's. The British Empire is a commercial product, & when we had to fight for it, first to gain it & then to retain it, we fought with allies against nations weak from a military point of view by reason of their imperial territories & responsibilities. Today we are burdened with risk of attack & cannot shield ourselves except by compelling rival nations to menace us all the more. On the other hand we are assuming further risks by the further extension of territory on the false assumption that our dependencies must offer a certain market for our produce. Moreover, as our economic strength is sapped by the exhaustion of our mineral supplies our danger must enormously increase, even if the colonies come closer to us, for when the economic centre shifts, the imperial equilibrium is disturbed.

In the discussion which was prolonged the following were the main points put forward[:]

That we had established between ourselves & our subject peoples a bond of moral responsibility—a kind of imperial strength which no other empire has enjoyed;

That our empire is the expression not of commercial enterprise & force of arms merely but of a racial nation-producing quality; & that the foundations of our empire are the self-governing sections of it.

Stress was laid on the operation of causes of internal decay, especially the moving of the economic centre from this country, & the growing dominance of colonial opinion upon imperial policy.

Sydney Olivier   1.11.99 Chairman

* * *

[48] The Circle met at Mr Stapley's on Wednesday 1st November at 8 p.m.

Present: Mr Sydney Olivier, in the chair, Messrs Douglas Morrison, J.M. Robertson, Russell Rea, A.L. Lilley, Herbert Samuel, G.H. Perris, Herbert Burrows, William Clarke, J. Bullock & J.R. Mac-Donald (Hon: Sec:) with Mr Pyddoke[39], visitor.

Mr William Clarke opened the discussion on Imperialism & Democracy. Rome was the great type of an Imperial State & after a full historical examination, Mr Clarke maintained that the Roman imperial policy led to militarism & Caesarism, to slaughterings & conquests, to centralisation & officialdom, to an economic parasitism & exploitation, to the separation of economic classes at home—just to those conditions which no democracy could survive. The reason for the incompatibility of imperialism with democracy lies in the nature of the state which is built up of these elements: man's social nature, his environment & his convenience. An empire won & held by the sword & composed of different races must deteriorate social morality in the imperial people; an empire containing lands in which the imperial people cannot live but which have to be cultivated by slave labour & inhabited by races permanently subject cannot provide a suitable environment for the governing race's progress; nor can such an empire be convenient to its rulers since it can neither be a field for emigration nor a market for trade. The imperialist spirit throughout the century has been accompanied by the military spirit & this is seen not so much in the actual increase of armaments as in the increasing bureaucracy of our government & the secrecy with which public affairs are conducted. Democratic forms are not being threatened but democratic power is declining as is instanced in the growth of Cabinet authority & the inability of the private member to do anything in Parliament. But from the democratic point of view the most serious argument against imperialism is that it saps that moral freedom which gives sanction to political freedom. It is a mere delusion to believe that it is our love of freedom & uprightness which makes us an imperial people. We are suffering from a combination of the capitalist & the

---

[39] H. W. Pyddoke became a resident at Toynbee Hall in 1901, and was presumably the guest of J. Bullock, himself a resident and lecturer there.

soldier which in the course of a generation or two will kill democracy in this country.

In the course of the discussion it was urged:

That there was a law of decay which was operating upon us as it has operated upon other races & that whatever system of government we pursued ruin would overtake us.

That it was quite possible for a people to govern themselves on one set of political principles & other races upon another set, & that therefore the rules of a self governing state did not apply to empire. The progress of democratic authority alongside of imperial expansion was cited to prove this. But it was pointed out that reform had been granted in times of reaction against war.

That the colonies were even more democratic than ourselves & even more imperialist.

Richard Stapley   Chairman

* * *

[49] The Circle met at Mr Stapley's on Wednesday 6th December 1899 at 8 p.m.

Present: Mr Richard Stapley—in the chair—Messrs G.H. Perris, Douglas Morrison, J.A. Hobson, J. Bullock, H. Rylett, J.M. Robertson, W. Clarke, A.L. Lilley, J.R. MacDonald; with Messrs W.M. Crook, Roskill & Atkin as visitors.

Agreed to accept the hospitable offer of Mr Stapley to entertain, on behalf of the circle, Mr Sydney Olivier, on his departure for Jamaica,[40] the members of the circle being invited as guests. The 20th December was provisionally fixed upon as being a convenient date.

The Rev. Douglas Morrison opened the discussion on Race & Empire. There have been Empires like the Turkish which destroyed & Empires like the Roman which promoted civilization. From our historical experience we arrive at some such laws as follows: Some races are incapable of receiving civilization & die out, others are capable of receiving it to an extent which depends upon whether their attainments in civilization are of a kind with the civilization of the imperial people. If we justify empire because it extends the area of possessions of a civilized people, we are met with the question How far is it right to exterminate the native races in order to extend the field of civilization? If we say there is no such right we must condemn the existence of the United States, Canada, &c, if we admit the right, how far are we to carry it? Another kind of empire is that which

---

[40] To become Colonial Secretary.

establishes political authority over a subject people & establishes peace & security & justice. It widens the outlook of the subject peoples, & in all these respects it promotes civilization. The danger is that this may tend to the establishment of a dead level, but this would be obviated if the imperial agents knew their business, which is to develop the capacity of self government in the subject peoples. The only defence of Empire is that it promotes liberty.

Mr Morrison's use of the expression 'empire' was challenged. It was pointed out how unsatisfactory & dangerous the assumption that occupation gave a right to the soil of a country was, & how impossible it was to argue upon the rights of previous settlers. It was urged that it was not so much a formal law & order as an interbreeding which promoted progress & that in this respect the English occupation of countries failed. It was emphasised that 'lower' races should be divided into 'lower in kind' & 'lower in degree' in order to ascertain the civilizing effect of an Imperialist policy; & it was also urged that from the nature of civilization & the civilizing process, the nation could not be the civilizing unit but rather the individual, & that a politically imposed 'law & order' crushes out civilizing possibilities.

Richard Stapley   Chairman

* * *

[50] The circle met at Mr. Stapley's on Wednesday, the 17th of January 1900 at 8 p.m.

Present: Mr. Richard Stapley—in the chair—Messrs. Harold Rylett, J.M. Robertson, Graham Wallas, G.F. Millin, C.P. Trevelyan, Herbert Samuel, J. Bullock & W.P. Reeves: with Messrs. F.G. Thomas & W.M. Crook as visitors.

It was proposed that Messrs. J. Roskill & W.M. Crook be reinstated as members. The question was referred to the Committee.

Mr Herbert Samuel opened the discussion on 'Imperialism in relation to Social Reform'.[41] Does Imperialism divert energy and ability from Social Reform? A great Empire must absorb much governing force; armaments must absorb a large part of the revenue, but in the case of England a large navy would be necessary without the Empire. The Empire, however, does divert large sums that would be better spent on education, poor relief, etc. Such is the indictment against the Empire. But we must judge it, not only by what it is, but by what it is in process of becoming. If it has faults, amputation is not the only cure. The average elector wants men who will maintain the

---

[41] Samuel's paper replaced one announced in the programme by G.H. Perris on 'Imperialism in relation to Trade and Finance.'

Empire without neglecting Social Reform. The 'Little Englandism' of many Progressives stands in the way of Social Reform. If such men are driven from power, the Empire is not to blame, but the social reformer. London, as evidenced by the Parliamentary, School Board & County Council elections, desires social reform & strong government of the Empire. Progressive Imperialists would relieve the House of Commons by delegating business; & they would preserve peace. The diffusion of men of administrative capacity over the Empire is not a serious objection. We have competent men enough; education will supply more; opportunities develop men. So far in answer to the indictment. But in two ways the Empire is the most valuable ally of Social Reform. Social Reform can be achieved by the State; by Trades Unionism; by propaganda; by industrial progress & by the growth of trade. Poverty can best be fought where riches are most accumulated. The Colonial expansion of other powers improves England's trade & the condition of her people; her own expansion does this in the highest degree. To whom do we wish our social reforms to apply? Free Trade & the labour movement are cosmopolitan. Our Empire subserves the welfare of other peoples. We can protect small nations from attack or govern them, giving them the fruits of our own experience, according as they are on the same level of civilisation as ourselves or on a lower. In the white colonies the Empire serves the cause of social reform by protecting them; in other cases, as in Egypt, it uplifts the native. Progressives who are sensitive to ignorance at home should not be conservative of it in Africa. Empire, therefore, contributes to social reform at home by enriching the people; in the colonies, by protecting them; in the dependencies, by the excellence of its administration.

In the discussion it was pointed out that Empire produced pride & contempt; materialised the Imperial people; increased the volume of trade without increasing the organisation of industry; that the test of the advantages of Empire was how far the subject populations were educated up; that further expansion ought to be avoided & the responsibilities of Empire studied.

Richard Stapley   Chairman

* * *

The Committee met on Wednesday 7 March 1900 at 7.45 and elected Messrs Crook & Roskill.

The Secretary asked to be relieved of his duties owing to pressure of work & the Committee asked him to reconsider the matter & bring it up at the Circle meeting.

Chairman

* * *

[51] The Circle met at Mr Stapley's on Wednesday 7 March at 8 p.m.

Present: Mr Richard Stapley (in the chair) J. Murray Macdonald, Graham Wallas, Douglas Morrison, Rev. A.L. Lilley, G.F. Millin, J. Bullock, W.P. Byles, C.P. Trevelyan, Herbert Samuel, Russell Rea, J.R. MacDonald—with Mr Kenworthy as visitor.

The question of the secretaryship was discussed & Mr Douglas Morrison moved that Mr J.R. MacDonald be asked to retain the minute secretaryship & that the Circle elect a secretary to issue notices of meetings &c. Mr MacDonald agreed to continue the secretaryship under that condition. Mr Morrison's motion was carried & Mr Bullock consented to act as corresponding secretary.

Mr C.P. Trevelyan opened the discussion. In discussing Internationalism we may take it to mean, in the main, the spirit which tends towards international peace. At the present time that spirit is without form though it exists. The old facts separating the nations exist still despite steam & education & especially is this the case with the larger nations. And yet any movement which tends to hinder Internationalism would be condemned by that very fact. Is Imperialism such a movement? The Empire is very conscious of its own strength & that makes it rather careless of foreign opinion. In so far as this keeps us clear of alliances it is for our good, but it goes further sometimes & makes us presumptious. The militarism which is supposed to follow Empire is not serious for the purposes of the present discussion as the smallest states arm. The serious question is, does Empire make our people jingo? It must be remembered that the jingo was not born with Disraeli, & though his age does not endow him with virtue it clothes him with a comparative amount of innocence. The exuberant energy of our people should be controlled but not crushed. Its exercise no doubt creates some jealousy in Europe but this we must face taking care not to give undue irritation. But Internationalism involves more than our relations with Europe. We should so govern our Empire that war within its borders will be a thing of the past; & we should attempt to effect an 'Internationalism with America', with which we are of one kindred.

The following were the chief points of the discussion:

That although Empire appears to secure a large area for peace it also offers an extended border for trouble;

That international friendship was not to be won by a constant reference to the feelings of other peoples, but by a steady & consistent pursuit of our own moral way; & that, when listening to European attacks we should not forget that behind them, there is a good deal of respect.

That whilst on the surface America appears to be a natural ally of

ours, the American national character is, on the whole, repellant to
ours.

Richard Stapley   Chairman

* * *

[52] The Circle met at Mr Stapley's on Wednesday, 11th April,
1900 at 8 p.m.

Present: Mr Richard Stapley (in the chair) W.P. Reeves, J.A.
Hobson, G.F. Millin, J. Bullock, H. Samuel, Russell Rea, Rev.
Douglas Morrison, J.R. MacDonald with the Rev. Mr Corbett as
visitor.

Mr Reeves opened the discussion on Imperialism in relation to the
Colonies. We should be careful to use the term colony only to those
parts of the empire which are self governing and are peopled by white
races. With reference to the topical question of South Africa, Mr
Reeves thought that a control of the Transvaal from London, or a
military occupation, should be provisional. The South African ideal
form of government would be a mixture of the autonomous colony
and a loose federation with common customs tariff &c. It might be
advantageous to establish two large Dutch provinces for which
purpose part of northern Cape Colony would be separated from the
Cape Town government; the governor of Cape Colony should cease
to be High Commissioner; reserves should be established for natives.
The present war had given an opportunity, unfortunate in its circumstances, to the colonies for showing their affection to the Home
Country. How far this demonstration of feeling may lead to a claim
to have a voice in the decision of Imperial affairs, is an open question,
but those who thought that recent resolutions from the Colonies
[were] declaring for a certain kind of settlement of the South African
situation, should remember that in sending them, the Colonies thought
they were only reiterating the opinions of the people over here.
Regarding schemes of Imperial Federation, if the colonies came into
an Imperial Council a burden of 16/- per head would be imposed
upon their people as their share of Imperial expenses. Half measures
are more likely to be adopted as for instance an advisory council
composed of colonial representatives to advise the Colonial Secretary.
Another scheme, which Mr Reeves preferred, would be to give colonial
representatives e.g. Agents General a seat in the House of Commons
with speaking but not voting powers. Mr Reeves then dealt with the
Australian Federation Bill[42] & thought it would be the death blow to

---

[42] 1900, the basis for the Commonwealth of Australia.

Federalism because it threw off the bond of the Privy Council upon which the legal fabric of the Empire rested.

It was pointed out in the discussion that the present colonial rally to the Empire was not a matter of reason but of sentiment & was therefore not only not permanent but not very assuring; & that until the Colonies decide to bear their proper part in the financial burdens of Imperialism little can be said in favour of their loyalty. It was also argued that Imperial Federation did not make for unity, but for a formal union of independent states without an Imperial centre of gravity; and that however tentative the first steps of Federation they *would* only be *first* steps and the Colonies would advance further & fuller claims to their just share in deciding Imperial policy. The practical difficulties of establishing a genuinely Imperial Parliament were pointed out, & the merging of the Privy Council in the House of Lords was suggested.

Richard Stapley   Chairman

* * *

[53] The Circle met at Mr Stapley's on Wednesday 2 May at 8 p.m. Present: Mr Stapley (in the chair) Perris, Millin, Burrows, Russell Rea, Hobson, Robertson, Lilley, & J.R. MacDonald with Mr H.R. Fox Bourne as visitor.

Mr Fox Bourne opened the discussion on Imperialism & the government of dependencies. A dependency is a state which we have acquired, but which we cannot stock with our own people. It has to be ruled despotically, the sovereignty being in Downing Street. The nature of the despotism is determined in the main by the objects we have in view in retaining the dependency. British dependencies are held for two purposes chiefly—for trade & for defence. India is an example of the former. The good we have done to India has been in protecting one Indian race from another. We have not advanced civilization there; our rule has been a long series of blunders. The way we face famine & plague today shows how far short our government of India falls of excellence. Yet on the whole, we have tried to be gentle and just. Our administration should be directed more strenuously than it has been hitherto by the idea that there can be no sanction for dependencies unless they can be shown to be for the good of the subject as well as for the governing people. The development of the qualities of self-government should be the aim of Indian statesmen. The time might come when India would be no longer a dependency but a self governing ally of ours. The problem of the African races is different though the justification for our governing them must be the same. Our main purpose in Africa at present is to make money out of it and we ought not to deceive ourselves by saying that we are there for civilizing purposes. He favoured the establishment of reserves like Basutoland but was afraid that they would not be permanent as the trader in South Africa has always managed to get round the government. He thought that the trader should be strictly excluded from those reserves, but he would admit the genuine missionary.

It was pointed out in the debate that the reservation idea was a negation of the Imperial idea; that one of the conditions of progress was mixture of race, & that opportunity should be taken to give effect to it regarding the apparently stagnant African races; that self-government, used in the political sense only, is misleading as a policy for the dependencies because the native must receive protection from some of the economic & moral conditions which have followed our political rule; that the establishment of law & order is no justification for Imperialism. Imperialist government must show that it makes progress possible.

The next meeting was fixed for the 30 May as the usual date fell in Whit week.

Some conversation followed upon the work of next Session and it was decided to discuss the contribution of certain national entities & epochs to civilization, & the following division was suggested: Pre-Greek Egypt, Jews, Greece, Rome, Islam, Feudal Europe, Italian Republics, Spain, China, India. Openers were also suggested & the scheme was left in the hands of the secretary to have printed & circulated.

Richard Stapley   Chairman

* * *

Committee meeting
The Committee met at Mr Stapley's 33 Bloomsbury Square on Wednesday 30 May 1900 at 7.30 p.m.
Present Mr Stapley, Mr Samuel & J.R. MacDonald.
It was decided to recommend that the October meeting should be dropped & that the circle open the session in November. It was also decided to recommend 'Literature & Politics' as the subject of next Session's discussions.

Richard Stapley   Chairman

* * *

[54] The Circle met at Mr Stapley's on Wednesday 30 May at 8 p.m.

Present: Mr Richard Stapley, in the chair, Samuel, Perris, Hobson, Lilley, Millin, Rylett, Russell Rea, Bullock, J.R. MacDonald.

The recommendations of the Committee were reported and accepted.

Mr J.A. Hobson opened the discussion on Imperialism & reviewed the question generally. He disputed, by references to African & Asiatic policy, the assumption of the Imperialist that the partition of the world is practically settled already; on the contrary, Imperialism still involves further territorial acquisition. It also involves more & more interference on the part of Downing Street & consequently a greater consumption of our own political energy. A detailed statement of the most praiseworthy arguments used by an Imperialist followed. But these are disposed of when we examine our rule in India, Egypt or South Africa. As a matter of fact civilization grows, it is not imposed, & the English political character is less fitted than that of some other nations to educate a people in the ways of civilization. One of the fundamental mistakes which the Englishman makes is that a law & order upheld by coercion is civilization; and his constitutional lack of sympathy blinds him to the great evils wrought by his benevolent intentions. The dangers of Imperialism to the Imperialist state are many. Revolt, envy, stagnation at home are the most important. Regarding the plea of inevitibility [sic], a vicious policy & motive must of course lead to a vicious end, & in this respect we should be very careful how we offer unconditional protection to missionaries & traders abroad, & how far we should permit international politics to be guided by international financiers.

The usual discussion followed.

Richard Stapley   Chairman

* * *

7th Session, 1900–1901.

[55] The Circle met at Mr Stapley's on Wedn: Nov. 7 1900 at 8 p.m.

Present—Mr Stapley, in the chair, Messrs. Byles, Burrows, Clarke, Crook, Lilley, Millin, Morrison, Perris, Rea, Samuel, Bullock, and Mr. Temple, visitor.

Mr. J.R. MacDonald's resignation of the Secretaryship, owing to the pressure of his other work, was accepted with great regret and with a unanimous vote of cordial thanks for his past services.

Mr. Bullock was elected Hon: Sec:

Mr. Stapley was re-elected Chairman

Mr. Crook was elected on to the Committee in place of Mr. J.R. MacDonald.

The accounts for the previous Session were submitted to the Meeting.

Mr. F. Temple was proposed for membership by Mr. Clarke. The matter was referred to the Committee.

It was decided to ask Mr. A.J. Butler, of Weybridge, to undertake the paper on Dante.

Mr. Clarke opened the discussion on Aristotle with a paper of which the following were some of the chief points:[43]

The philosophy of Aristotle was his explanation of Greek political life as he actually knew it when it was passing from ripeness to decay.

The ideal state is a small city—not an amorphous mass like London, still less a monarchy or empire—the citizens must know and care for one another: they must have leisure, hence slavery is accepted as a fact, and they must individually participate in government.

The state exists that citizens may live well: it aims at cultivating the perfection of virtue on a basis of material well-being, not on the basis of the existence of the extremes of wealth & poverty. Stasis, or faction, is fatal to the unity of the state, & arises from inequality of condition.

The State is regulative, not communist, nor 'laissez faire.' The rich are more dangerous than the poor: an educated middle-class are the strength of the State. Conquest is ruinous because it leads to riches.

The successful state is peaceful, unaggressive, with an army only for defence: contrast this with modern Imperialism.

The best rule is that of 'αριστοι—of course not hereditary—limited by wide suffrage & equality of opportunity: no ruler must make the least gain or traffic from government.

The people must never be allowed to sink into poverty.

After a quotation from Prof: Dunning the paper concluded by comparing Aristotle's view with modern views of the contents of the State, especially in the matter of religion.

In discussion the following points were insisted on

Intercourse with neighbours is necessary to the growth of virtue: among modern states Montenegro is nearest to a Greek state: the French have always been more influenced by Greek thought than

---

[43] For Clarke's talk in full, see H. Burrows and J.A. Hobson, eds., *William Clarke. A collection of his writings* (1908), p. 159 ff.

other nations: our crude ideas of Empire are Roman, not Greek: the motive at the bottom of trusts is condemned by Aristotle.

Richard Stapley   Chairman

* * *

On Wedn: Dec: 5th 1900 the Committee met at 7.45 p.m. at Mr. Stapley's to consider the proposal of Mr. Temple for membership, but Mr. Clarke withdrew his nomination and the meeting was closed.

Chairman

* * *

[56] The Circle met at Mr. Stapley's on Wedn: Dec: 5th at 8 p.m.

Present. Mr. Stapley in the chair, Burrows, Clarke, Crook, Lilley, Millin, Rylett, Robertson, Samuel, Bullock, and Rev. A. Fortescue, visitor.

The minutes were read and confirmed.

The Hon: Sec: reported that Mr. A.J. Butler had consented to open the discussion on 'Dante' on Jan: 2nd. It was resolved that he be asked to meet the Circle at dinner on that evening at 6.15 and that the arrangements be left in Mr. Stapley's hands.

It was resolved to hold a special meeting on Dec: 19th to hear & discuss Mr. Robertson's impressions of S. Africa.

Mr. Lilley read his paper on the contributions of St. Augustine to political thought:

Augustine, a Roman to the core, looked on Rome's Empire as a trust and duty delegated by God, and not as a natural right.

He anticipated the re-establishment of the Empire, and the setting-up of ecclesiastical authority, each animated by the same spirit of justice and righteousness, thus realising the ideal 'City of God' on earth.

This City of God was the Catholic Church, organised as a hierarchy, as we know it in mediaeval history, the civil subordinated to the ecclesiastical power, each distinct from the other, & each a delegation from God. While in pagan Rome the Emperor had been the irres-ponsible Guardian of a justice founded on expediency, and law had been deified, now law must be conformed to equity, i.e. to Divine Justice.

'My Country right or wrong' had been the spirit of pagan Rome, but now patriotism must be limited to supporting the State as long as it does not violate the Divine Justice.

Among Augustine's limitations were that he could not conceive the abolition of slavery, that he fell below the pagan standard of religious liberty & toleration, & that he had almost a hatred of republican government.

His great work was to make the Catholic Church self-conscious of its own organic life & of its mission to establish Divine Justice as well as Divine truth.

In the discussion which followed it was contended: that St. Augustine undermined slavery more effectually than if he had attacked it directly, and that standing for righteousness and justice he inevitably looked towards freedom:

that though he latinized the Church and entrusted Roman law to its care, he did not found the Papacy in its modern sense but that this was left to St. Leo or St. Gregory.

Richard Stapley   Chairman

* * *

[57] On Dec: 19th 1900, Wedn:, a special Meeting was held at Mr. Stapley's at 8 p.m.

Present. Mr. Stapley, in the chair, Crook, Lilley, Hobson, R. MacDonald, Robertson, Rylett, Bullock, and one visitor.

Mr. Robertson did not give a formal address, but invited questions, and in replying to them he gave in detail the experiences and opinions of himself, and many Dutchmen & Englishmen whom he had encountered in S. Africa.

The discussion continued until 11 o'clock.

Richard Stapley   Chairman

* * *

[58] On Wednesday, Jan: 2nd, 1901 the Rainbow Circle entertained Mr. A.J. Butler at dinner, at 6.30 p.m. at the Russell Hotel, Russell Square, and afterwards adjourned to 33, Bloomsbury Square for the first meeting of the Twentieth Century.

Present: Mr. Stapley in the chair, Messrs. Burrows, Clarke, Crook, Hobson, Lilley, Millin, Robertson, Roskill, Rylett, Samuel, Bullock (Hon: Sec:) and Butler, Adams, Spooner (Visitors).

The minutes of the last ordinary meeting, and of the special meeting of Dec: 19th 1900, were read & confirmed.

The thanks of the meeting were expressed to Mr. Stapley for his arrangements in connexion with the dinner at the Russell Hotel.

Mr. A.J. Butler opened the discussion on Dante—

The Guelfs in 1266 represented local self-government against feudalism.

In the course of the next 30 years a new aristocracy grew up—the Parte Guelfa.

The Blacks represented this party, while the Whites represented the Commons, and, incidentally, the opposition to Pope Boniface.

Dante, standing for the Commons against the Grandees, was gradually brought to the conclusion that only under a monarch can justice be secured.

Imperial Majesty is founded upon the needs of the body corporate of mankind, and this body is ordered to an end—viz: the happy life of the individual, for Dante never regards a nation as a homogeneous unit.

Hence the necessity for a Monarch or Emperor, who, having nothing more to acquire, may keep the peace among kings, as kings among cities, cities among households, households among their own individual members.

This may be compared with Aristotle's view, in the Politics, of the citizens as a crew of a ship.

The three books of the De Monarchia are—

1. on the necessity for a single Head to repress 'cupiditas', Aristotle's πλεονεξία.

2. a scholastic argument to prove that none but the Roman Emperor is such a Head, de jure.

3. a discussion whether the right of the Roman Emperor is derived directly from God, as Dante thought, or mediately from the Pope as the supposed successor of Peter, who was the supposed Vicar of Christ.

Dante hoped that the Emperor Henry would realise this dream, but he expired baffled & broken hearted in 1313, & Dante lived and died in exile.

'Let us be thankful we live in the 20th century, not in the 14th.'

The following points were insisted on in the discussion. While Dante's aim of a moral & political unity is a permanent one, the means he suggests represent a temporary phase of thought.

Napoleon tried to realise this Utopia of the De Monarchia—universal Empire & subject kings.

Dante is an instance of the Artist being generally supremely mistaken in politics.

The Roman Church, to promote its ideal of universal domination, destroyed for centuries the ideal of Italian national life, & would willingly do so again today.

Perhaps the permanent elements in Dante's thought are—

1. Empire must rely on a moral basis as well as on force.

2. Society is a living organism, on wh: the individual depends, & in wh: only he can fully realise himself.

Mr. Butler was warmly thanked for his kindness in coming & opening the discussion.

Richard Stapley   Chairman

[N.B. The Committee for Session, 1900–1901, consists of—Messrs. Stapley, Burrows, Lilley, Millin, Samuel, Trevelyan, Crook, & Bullock.]

* * *

[59] On Wednesday, Feb: 6th, 1901, the Rainbow Circle met at 33 Bloomsbury Square.

Present: Mr. Stapley, in the chair, Messrs. Hobson, Lilley, Clarke, Burrows, Rylett, Perris, Morrison, Rea, Robertson, Bullock, & Mr. Pomeroy, visitor.

The minutes of the last meeting were read & confirmed.

Mr. Robertson read a paper on Machiavelli—Machiavelli's work has passed into the great intellectual life of Europe, though his writings are not so complete & comprehensive as the little known Defensor Pacis of Marsiglio dei Raimondini pub. 1324.

He is the first of a line of great modern writers on political theory.

Florence, after going through all vicissitudes of government, had flourished for 3 generations under the capitalist family of the Medici.

In the Discourses on Livy Machiavelli had considered how a Republic might maintain itself. In the Prince he has submitted to fate & schemed for his country by way of a new Monarchy.

Macaulay, Hallam, & Lord Acton, & almost all continental critics of the 19th century acquit him of being simply a devil incarnate, the inciter to treachery & tyranny, but his works are still honored by inclusion in the Index Expurg[atorius] as the Papacy has never forgiven his dispassionate presentment of the principles on wh: it has habitually acted, or of its damaging influence on morals—nor his advocacy of Italian unity against the intrusion of the foreigner.

In the Prince he does not transcend his times, but simply deals with practical politics in the spirit of science, and as Republicanism is no longer possible in Florence he shows the Florentine prince how to maintain & extend his dominion.

His true ideal appears to have been the paramountcy of the old Roman Republic, & he loses sight of the fatal consequences of Rome's choice of paramountcy instead of confederation, wh: lead to imperial autocracy with all its well known results.

Like Savonarola & every other Florentine he planned constantly for the subjection of Pisa, though he confesses that 'conquests are the ruin of weak Republics'.

He did not love violence for its own sake, but shewed how men must proceed if they seek to prosper in a violent age.

In discussion the following points were urged:

On the one hand—that Machiavelli severed between politics & ethics, that he was a traitor to his higher convictions & wrote the Prince to please the ruler of his day, that his contributions to political thought though apparently great are really only tricky, that his political principles only amount to the sophism of a ruler having a public as well as a private conscience, that he ignored the ideal elements in human nature & threw his weight into the scale of utter selfishness, or at best ignored the individual in view of the material interests of the state:

on the other hand—that in his time the condottierri were threatening the very existence of all the Italian states, & that Republicanism being dead it was comparatively unimportant who was ruler so long as the State was preserved: that the old Roman idea dazzled him— of the patria overriding all duties—that his social Psychology was wonderfully acute—that statesmen still ought to act, as they confessedly do act, on his principles—that though his message was opportunist, & his philosophy is disputed, his methods are still followed today.

Richard Stapley   Chairman

* * *

[60] On Wednesday, March 6th 1901, the Rainbow Circle met at 33 Bloomsbury Sq: at 8 p.m.

Present: Mr. Stapley in the chair; Messrs. Morrison, Crook, Burrows, Perris, Lilley, Rylett, Millin, & Bullock.

Minutes of last meeting were read & confirmed.

Mr. Bullock read a paper on 'Hobbes'—He considered that Hobbes' defence of Despotism, & his attitude towards Romanism & Puritanism, were mainly due to his environment—& that Hobbes' chief services were his appeal to reason in preference to Scripture, & his pointing out that allegiance ceases when the Sovereign's protection is withdrawn.

It was contended that Hobbes' political thinking flows from his conception of man, not as a social, but as a solitary animal at war with all others: that his view is that society is mechanical, not organic: that his force & lucidity are admirable, but his fundamental premises are untrue.

His freedom from interested motives was discussed. It was argued that royal absolutism was an accident of his time, but State absolutism is now a living idea. In a sense he was a father of modern democracy though not of Liberalism. He aimed at basing the State on reason, & emancipating it from ecclesiastical control.

Richard Stapley   Chairman

* * *

[61] On Wednesday, March 27 1901, the Circle met at 33 Bloomsbury Sq: at 8 p.m.

Present: Mr. Stapley in the chair, Messrs. Crook, Lilley, Millin, Perris, Clarke, Hobson, Murray Macdonald, Morrison, & Bullock, & Adams, a visitor.

The minutes of the last meeting were read & confirmed. Letters of regret were received from Messrs. Samuel, Russell Rea, Byles, Rylett.

Mr. Burrows read a paper on 'Rousseau'. Rousseau is more human & modern than our previous writers. Some of his principles are the foundations of the newer economic & social philosophy of our time.

Corruption & distress were abounding.

Rousseau advocates in his Discourses a return to nature. His vanity arises from weakness of character & the absence of the reticence of a strong spirit.

He first gave a piercing & sympathetic voice to some of the principles & emotions which are eternal in the human heart.

He was the father of modern Democracy, not as it is, but as it ought to be, the Social Democracy of the Future.

In the Social Contract of 1761,[44] Rousseau goes down to natural facts & makes himself the mouthpiece of the suffering & the wronged.

The Social contract never had an actual existence, but it has an implied & unconscious existence in all natural society.

Laws are but the expressed will of the community against antisocial acts or conditions. The 'general will' & the principle of 'give & take' must be at the root of the true social organism of the future.

Rousseau contends that each man ought to have as much right as anybody else.

His idea of all men's natural rights needs to be complemented with the ethical idea of all men's duties to each, & of each to all.

In the discussion it was contended that Rousseau was a reaction against mere rationalism, in that he insisted on man as a creature of emotion as well as of reason.

[44] Should be 1762.

That morality is not given to us but is obtained by struggle.

That Rousseau did not intend to say that there had been really a contract, but that the Sovereign People might decide what liberty each individual might keep.

That the general will is not always the same as the will of all.

That Rousseau discerned the germ of the idea that Society is an organism, & saw the immorality of the extremes of wealth & poverty.

Rousseau is a reaction against Machiavelli's doctrine of a powerful State disregarding the welfare of individuals. He is more poetic than rational, & with regard to his personal character he is a sort of Jekell [*sic*] & Hyde.

Intellectually at least he was sincere, & the modern love of nature can be traced to him, as part of the great debt wh: the modern world owes him.

Richard Stapley   Chairman

* * *

On Mon: May 1st 1901 the Committee of the Rainbow Circle met at 33 Bloomsbury Sq: at 7.30 p.m.

Present Mr. Stapley in the chair, Mr. Samuel, & Mr. Bullock, Hon: Sec:

It was decided to recommend to the Circle that Mr. G. Wallas should be removed from the list of members in consequence of his continued absence, without explanation, from our meetings, and non payment of subscription.

It was also decided to suggest to the Circle that the next Session should be devoted to the consideration of a second series of great political thinkers viz: Marsiglio, More, Bodin, Locke, Burke, Kant, Mill, Maine, Spencer.

Richard Stapley   Chairman

* * *

[62] On Wedn: May 1st 1901, the Circle met at 33 Bloomsbury Sq: at 8 p.m.

Present, Mr. Stapley in the chair, Messrs. Robertson, Samuel, Byles, M. Macdonald, Morrison, Bullock. Letters of apology for absence were read from Messrs. Millin, Clarke, & R. MacDonald.

Minutes of last meeting were read & confirmed.

The recommendations of the Committee were considered. Mr. G. Wallas' name was removed from the list of members. It was agreed to devote the next Session to a second series of great political thinkers. The list suggested by the Committee was considered & amended, & was finally fixed as follows: Vico, Locke, Hume, Burke, Paine, Hegel, Mill, Marx, Spencer.

Mr. Samuel read a paper on Bentham:

Bentham was in his day the teacher of teachers: he provided the arguments for reforms, & the enthusiasm wh: set them in motion: he taught men to question all existing institutions, to submit them to the test of reason, & to accept nothing on faith. To him we largely owe the peaceful English Revolution of 1828–74.

His works are now so little studied chiefly because of the completeness of their practical success. He was first of all a law-reformer.

From law reform he was lead to frame a system of political science founded on the Utilitarian principles of Hume & Beccaria, in 1789.[45]

Afterwards realising at last that the rulers of England were animated chiefly by selfishness, & had little real care for the welfare & improvement of the people, he became an ardent Reformer & Democrat.

Pleasure & pain, Bentham taught, are the ultimate facts, & to increase pleasure & to diminish pain is to promote happiness. Government exists for the good of the governed, & its aim must therefore be to secure the greatest happiness of the greatest number.

Bentham was a republican & supported annual elections, the ballot, equal electoral districts, household franchise & women's suffrage; freedom of religion & of the press.

Though an Individualist he advocated state provision of schools, hospitals, & institutions for the able-bodied unemployed. He was strongly anti-Imperialist, & a free-trader.

He coined the term 'international law', advocated reduction of armaments, & a court of international judicature for arbitration.

Now a day we have gone back from Bentham to Aristotle & say that the State exists to promote the best life of its members rather than their happiness, if by 'happiness' we mean their pleasure as judged at the moment by themselves.

Bentham's anti-socialist bias is accounted for by the corrupt & selfish government of his time—ill-directed, meddlesome, & wasteful. His style, except in the Fragment on Government [and in his pamphlet—R.S.] is tedious & involved. His permanent value is the boldness of his thought, his resolute search for truth, & his passionate love of justice: also in his successful attack on the superstition that the English constitution was necessarily perfect & above criticism.

Throughout his long & laborious life he had no other aim or reward but that of promoting the happiness of mankind.

---

[45] A reference to the *Introduction to the Principles of Morals and Legislation.*

In the discussion it was argued—on the one hand that Bentham gave the Liberals their creed, & that his principle of the greatest happiness of the greatest number is being revived in Germany today: on the other hand that Bentham dealt too much with abstractions, that his teaching was mainly destructive, liberating individuals from the trammels of the State.

Again—that though Bentham did not go to the bottom of moral problems, his teaching is too systematic & thoughtful for the modern opportunists of today. As a freethinker he was ostracized by the Universities, & by all the dogmatists of his time.

He fought for the freedom wh: must precede economic reconstruction.

Richard Stapley   Chairman

* * *

On Wednesday, June 5th 1901, the Committee met at 33 Bloomsbury Sq. at 7.45 p.m.

Present, Mr. Stapley (in the chair), Mr. Millin, Mr. Samuel, Mr. Burrows & Mr. Bullock, Hon: Sec:

The names of writers were suggested for the subjects for the next session.

Richard Stapley   Chairman

* * *

[63] On Wedn: June 5th 1901 the Circle met at 33 Bloomsbury Square, at 8 p.m.

Present. Mr. Stapley in the chair, Messrs. Burrows, Lilley, Millin, Perris, Samuel, & Bullock—also three visitors, Messrs. Adams, Barratt, & Rev. T. Perris.

Letters of apology for absence were received from Messrs. Hobson, Byles, Rylett, M. Macdonald, R. MacDonald, Robertson-

The following members were absent, from whom no letters had been received, Messrs. Crook, Morrison, Reeves, Rea, Roskill, Trevelyan.

The minutes of the last meeting were read and confirmed.

Mr. Burrows & Mr. Lilley gave an account of the circumstances attending the death of our late member Mr. Clarke, at Mostar;[46] and of the proposals for memorials to him.

---

[46] In Hercegovina, during a tour of the Balkans.

It was unanimously resolved that the Chairman be asked to write a letter of condolence to Miss Clarke, on behalf of the Circle.

The Rev. Harley was proposed for membership by Mr. Burrows with the request that his name should not be considered by the Committee until he had attended a meeting of the Circle.

The recommendations of the Committee for readers for the next Session were agreed to.

In the absence of Mr. Hobson, through illness, the subject of 'Comte' was not discussed.

Richard Stapley   Chairman

* * *

8th Session—Oct., 1901-June, 1902.

[64] On Wednesday, Oct. 2nd 1901 the Circle met at 33 Bloomsbury Square, at 8 p.m.

Present, Mr. Stapley in the chair, Messrs. Crook, Lilley, Hobson, R. MacDonald, Millin, Morrison, Reeves, Rylett, Samuel, Bullock, & Rev. Atkinson, visitor.

Messrs. Burrows Robertson & Rea wrote regretting their absence— Messrs. Byles, M. Macdonald & Perris, Roskill & Trevelyan were also absent.

The minutes of the last meeting were read and confirmed.

The accounts for the past session were submitted and accepted.

Mr. Stapley was unanimously re-elected as Chairman; & Mr. Bullock as Hon: Sec:

Messrs. Burrows, Crook, Lilley, Millin, & Samuel were re-elected, and Mr. J.R. MacDonald was elected, in place of Mr. Trevelyan, as members of Committee.

The list of the attendance of members during the past Session was read, as follows.

8. Chairman, & Hon: Sec:

7. Mr. Lilley.

6. Messrs. Burrows & Millin.

5. Messrs. Crook, Morrison, Perris, Samuel.

4. Messrs. Robertson & Rylett.

3. Mr. Hobson.

2. Messrs. Byles, M. Macdonald, & Rea.

1. Mr. Roskill.

0. Messrs R. MacDonald, Reeves & Trevelyan.

Messrs. R. MacDonald & Reeves intimated their hope of being able to attend more frequently in future.

The Sec: was directed to write to Messrs. Roskill & Trevelyan & to report at the next meeting.

Mr. Samuel read his paper on Vico:

Vico , 1668–1744, son of a bookseller at Naples, a scholar, barrister, prof: of rhetoric, of great perseverance & self-esteem in spite of poverty & ill-health. In the Nuova Scienza, 1725, he seeks to set forth the evolution of human history from the earliest records, & to deduce from it certain eternal principles; viz:

All societies or nations pass through a cycle of three stages, divine, heroic, human, & then begin again.

In the divine or theocratic stage a nation is dominated by religion & is barbarous & cruel.

In the heroic or aristocratic it is dominated by chivalry, force tempered by religion: marriage, the family & cities are instituted.

In the human or democratic stage, after a revolt against aristocratic tyranny, laws are made equal & rest on reason. This happy stage leads to prosperity, effeminacy, apathy & discord, the nation either decays or is conquered, & thus returns to the divine stage of religion & barbarity.

Mankind, except the Jews, have passed through this cycle once, from Noah's Ark to the fall of the Western Empire, & are now passing through the third stage of the second cycle.

Vico was the precursor of Niebuhr[47] & Mommsen,[48] but his conclusions are very faulty owing to the limitation of his materials, & his orthodoxy as a Catholic.

His glory is that he was the first to attempt to found historical philosophy upon accurate historical research, but he overlooked the following considerations—that human nature is always being modified—that no nation is let alone for ages without conquest or amalgamation, that new institutions like representative government, & new scientific weapons, greatly modify our inferences from past to future history; and that therefore the science of politics can only classify & explain, but cannot predict.

In the discussion which followed it was contended that Vico ought not have been included in our list, because he failed to establish any principle for our guidance. It was also imputed to him as a fault that he overlooked providential control.

On the other hand Vico was praised for shewing that even in Naples in century 17th a man might dare to consider history in a scientific

[47] Barthold Georg Niebuhr (1776–1831). Historian of Rome and Prussian civil servant.
[48] Theodor Mommsen (1817–1903). German historian.

spirit, & with original thought: that he was a pioneer, & shewed that there might be a philosophy of history, and that he was possibly more nearly right than the reader of the paper as to the permanence of human nature.

Richard Stapley   Chairman

* * *

[65] On Wedn: Nov: 6th 1901 the Circle met at 33 Bloomsbury Square, at 8 p.m.

Present. Mr. Stapley in the chair, Messrs. Byles, Crook, Hobson, Lilley, Morrison, Perris, Robertson, and Bullock—also three Visitors, Rev. J.H. Harley, Rev. S. Stephen, & Mr. Mead.

Messrs. R. MacDonald, Millin, Rea, & Rylett wrote regretting their absence.

Messrs. Burrows, M. Macdonald, Reeves, & Samuel were also absent.

The minutes of the last meeting were read & confirmed.

Letters were read from Messrs. Roskill & Trevelyan regretting their inability to attend regularly at the meetings of the Circle in future, and the Honorary Secretary was directed to remove their names from the list of members, & to express to them the hope of the Circle that they would attend at any time as Visitors.

The Rev. J.H. Harley undertook to read a paper on 'Burke' in Jan: in place of Mr. J.A. M. Macdonald.

Mr. Lilley then read his paper on 'Locke'.

Locke, 1632–1704, as a writer on government lifted the Revolution settlement out of its position as a temporary expedient into an atmosphere of universal reasonableness. He gave it self consciousness & self confidence, & reconciled it to the Revolutionary forces of political speculation, & through Montesquieu & Rousseau he recommended it as a model to France & the world.

He was the characteristic writer of the spirit of William III's reign in its moderation & common sense, its suspicion of mysticism in theology & politics, its practical & rational compromise. In these principles he had an honest faith, & he justified them reasonably.

In his first treatise on Government he demolishes Filmer, & his scriptural arguments. In his second he justifies King William & the people of England, basing his argument on his view of man's natural rights, & on the law of nature as a law of reason & not of mere force.

Civil society was based on the consent of its members for the sake of expediency.

The five great principles he lays down are

1. Government exists for the good of the governed:

2. Positive laws must be tested by reason:

3. Government is a trust from the people, wh: they may resume if the trust is misused:

4. The legislative is the highest function of government, & must be under the immediate control of the people.

5. The consent of the legislature is necessary for annexing a man's property against his will.

Locke's defects are those of his age—extravagant individualism, & a theory of sheer human atomism. His law of nature as a law of reason is a late product & not an antecedent of human evolution.

In the discussion wh: followed, surprise was expressed that Locke's Essay on Toleration was not alluded to: his views on toleration & on individual liberty were wider than those of Milton & Elliott[49] who had partially anticipated him.

His view of the law of nature was that of the moral thinker or idealist, & should be contrasted with that of Hobbes who anticipated modern natural science in describing the law of nature as a law of force. Locke's principles of economic distribution, of the rights of property, & his theory of value as based on labor were sound.

He had helped to get theology out of politics, & putting liberty into a philosophy, he had taught the people to restrict the sphere of government.

His idea of individual liberty is needed in Socialistic thought today.

Richard Stapley   Chairman

* * *

[66] On Wedn: Dec. 4th 1901 the Circle met at 33 Bloomsbury Square, at 8 p.m.

Present. Mr. Stapley in the chair, Messrs. Harley, Hobson, Lilley, Ramsay MacDonald, Millin, Morrison, Perris, & Bullock, also Mr. Mead, visitor. Messrs. Burrows, Byles, Crook, Murray Macdonald, Rea, Rylett, Samuel, wrote regretting their absence.

Messrs. Reeves & Robertson were also absent.

The minutes of the last meeting were read and confirmed.

The date of the next meeting was altered to January 15th.

Mr. Morrison read his paper upon 'Hume':

English thought, with the exception of Herbert Spencer, has been

---

[49] Presumably Sir John Eliot (1592–1632). Writer and campaigner for parliamentary rights against Charles I.

critical, while continental thought, with the exception of Kant & his school, has been generally speculative & constructive.

Like Berkeley & Locke before him, Hume, b.1711 examines the origin & range of our mental faculties, in his Treatise on Human nature, published 1738.[50]

In 1761[51] appeared his Enquiry concerning the Principles of Morals, wh: is an exposition of the principles of Utilitarian Ethics.

Hume died with unclouded serenity at the age of 65. He considers that the test of the excellence of a government is the extent of its utility.

The institutions of a government are the products of a nation's permanent character. Reason is the only guide of life, & fanaticism is to be abhorred.

Public opinion, not force, is the ultimate foundation of all government.

A perfect commonwealth ought to establish a fundamental law against conquest, wh: is the ruin of free governments.

But, said Dr. Morrison, 'We are not to look for the realisation of the ideas of individual justice in nations any more than we should look for it in nature, wh: is simply non-moral.'

In the brief discussion wh: followed it was contended on the one hand that Hume was an arid thinker, on the other that his utilitarianism was based on social sympathy, & benevolence, & that he did not support the idea of 'The Great Man': that England has converted faction, as Hume desired, into party government, & that his defence of the party system is not seriously affected by the events of the French Revolution. His reliance on public opinion justifies the modern referendum.

Richard Stapley   Chairman

* * *

[67] On Wednesday, Jan: 15th 1902, the Circle met at 33 Bloomsbury Square at 8 p.m.

Present. Mr. Stapley in the chair, and Messrs. Byles, Harley, Hobson, Lilley, R. MacDonald, Robertson, Rylett, Samuel, & Bullock, also two visitors.

Messrs. Burrows & Millin wrote regretting their absence.

Messrs. Crook, M. Macdonald, Morrison, Perris, Reeves, and Rea were absent.

---

[50] Should be 1739–40.
[51] Should be 1751.

The minutes of the last meeting were read and confirmed.

Mr. Harley then read his paper upon 'Burke'[52]:

Burke was many sided, he 'struck ile' in many departments, though he was master of none of them.

Born in 1730,[53] the son of an Irish attorney, he was educated at Trinity College Dublin. He came to London, & in 1756 published his treatise on 'The Sublime & the Beautiful.'

He made many friends, impressed them with his ability, & quarrelled with most of them.

In 1765 he became Secretary to Rockingham, & soon after entered the House of Commons.

In the controversy with the American colonies he tried to steer a middle course, but while desiring to avoid coercion, he aimed in reality at supporting the Status Quo, even by force if necessary.

His speech on American conciliation is his greatest work. In it he seems by instinct to anticipate the Imperialism of a later century where in Mr. Harley's opinion 'there is peace.'

When the French Revolution came he took a more simply Conservative attitude of entire hostility towards it, and he underestimated, if he did not altogether deny, the capacity in every social organisation for change & growth.

Burke thought & said nothing original, for, says Mr. Harley, no one really does so except in a lunatic asylum.

At the Chairman's request Mr. Robertson opened the discussion with a short speech:

Burke had no intellectual probity, and no principles. He was led by his emotions & his interests. It was so with regard to Catholic Emancipation & to the American Colonies. He had no sympathy for the sufferings of the French people or for the peoples of India as distinct from their princes. While he saw the sufferings of the poor he made himself the tool of his rich patrons. He is a pathological case, though a great literary man. He had no real prescience or original thought.

In the subsequent discussion it was contended that he did at first think of society as a growth, though afterwards he came to regard it as a form, cast in a mould, & that we must remember that the organic view of Politics & life had not yet been discovered, & that each department of life had then to be considered separately:

that he was neither consistent nor honest, and that he defended his section of the Whigs, & their ideas of expediency, with genius, & that

---

[52] A more detailed account appeared in J.H. Harley, *The New Social Democracy* (London, 1911), chapter II.

[53] Should read '1729'.

he was original only in his forceful way of stating what others had said before him:

that he shewed no apparent knowledge of the real state of the French people, in spite of writings of Chesterfield[54] & Arthur Young:[55]

that his life & work were a disappointment, leaving behind him no permanent contribution to political thought: that he was a representative of the Irish character, 'which first attaches itself to something by its emotions & then seeks for principles to justify its attachment.'

Richard Stapley   Chairman

* * *

[68] On Wednesday, Feb. 12th, 1902, the Circle met at 33 Bloomsbury Sq. at 8 p.m.

Present. Mr. Stapley in the chair, Messrs. Burrows, Hobson, Lilley, Millin, Morrison, Reeves, Robertson, and Bullock.

Messrs. R. MacDonald & Rylett wrote regretting their absence.

Messrs. Byles, Crook, Harley, M. Macdonald, Perris, Rea, & Samuel were absent.

The minutes of the last meeting were read & confirmed.

Mr. Harley was unanimously elected a member.

Mr. Robertson read his paper on 'Paine:'

Tom Paine was born at Thetford in 1737. Privateer's man, staymaker, & for several year's [sic] excise man at Lewes, he lost his first wife soon after marriage, & was separated from his second wife by consent, no blame resting on him, and at the age of 37 he was homeless & penniless.

By the advice of Benjamin Franklin he emigrated to Philadelphia in 1774 & started the Pennsylvania Magazine with wh: his career as a writer commences.

His master-bias appears in his appeal to reason as implicit in the moral judgments of men, &, within a year of his separation from an unsuitable wife, he is pleading for the rights of women, for international copyright, for arbitration, against cruelty to animals, & against negro slavery.

In the corrupt & semifeudal England of the 18th century whose politics he described in the one word 'jockeyship', he had found no means of self expression such as he now found in America. He was the

---

[54] 4th Earl of Chesterfield (1694–1773). Close to literary circles in Paris, including Voltaire. In 1753 predicted the French Revolution.

[55] Arthur Young (1741–1820). Farmer and writer, author of travelogue through France just prior to the Revolution.

first man there to advocate independence, coupling it with the abolition of negro slavery and by his famous pamphlet 'Commonsense' he converted George Washington from royalism to republicanism. He anticipates Gibbon in shewing the inherent absurdity of that 'useful prejudice' hereditary monarchy.

His political ideas were probably derived implicitly from the Ethics of his Quaker ancestry. He planned & carried out the mission wh: obtained help from France for the struggling United States, he shewed conspicuous courage in battle, and devoted all the proceeds of his writings—exceeding £50,000, to the cause of American freedom.

After the peace of 1783 he returned to England, & devoted some years to scientific work, making the first tubular bridge, & suggesting the application of steam to navigation by means of paddle wheels. Presently came the French Revolution: & in the earlier of his two great books—'The Rights of Man'—Paine answered Burke's 'Reflections on the French Revolution' and pulverised Burke's denial of the right of a nation to choose its own rulers.

The ethical gist of Paine's book is that we ought to do as we would be done by. It was of course condemned as seditious & libellous: the real answer to it being that the England of George III was not good enough or sane enough to exist under a moral & reasonable constitution instead of the one wh: was actually resting on force, brutality, & superstition.   Paine signally failed to anticipate the excesses into wh: the French Revolution was goaded by the hostility of England Prussia & Austria, & by the plots & attacks of the French emigrant nobility & clergy.

In Paris during the Revolution he advocated a Republic but pleaded for the life of Louis XVI, & was therefore suspected, arrested, & sentenced to death.

He remained in prison nearly a year, writing his second great book—'The Age of Reason' and on his release he retired finally to America where his Deistic opinions exposed him to much obloquay. [*sic*]

Had America listened to his plea against negro slavery, she would have been spared the horrors of the Great Civil War of 1861: and here in England after a century of 'progress' we are still asking for the Old Age Pensions wh: Paine planned, still baffled by normal brutality when we strive for peace & arbitration; still sunk in the snobbery of royalism & aristocratism, still unprovided with true representative government or a just system of taxation, on all of wh: points Paine's teaching was clear & outspoken.

In the discussion wh: followed it was generally agreed that Paine was far too optimistic as to the pace of rational progress, and that this was due to his judging of the progress of backward, aristocratic, military nations like England & France by the standard of a progressive democratic comparatively rational nation like the United States.

His forecast of free trade & old age pensions was commented on, and the connexion between the Quaker doctrine of the Inner Light, & Paine's belief in a God of perfect Reason & goodness.

It was contended that, above & beyond mere politics, Paine's greatest aim was to foster the moral betterment of the social life of the mass of the people.

Richard Stapley   Chairman

* * *

[69] On Wedn: March 5th 1902 the Circle met at 33 Bloomsbury Square, at 8 p.m.

Present. Mr. Stapley in the chair, Messrs. Burrows, Harley, Lilley, Ramsay MacDonald, Morrison, Perris, Reeves, Robertson, Rylett, Bullock: also Visitors, Messrs. Haldane, Pyddoke, Corbett, Buckland, Hopkyns.

Messrs. Byles & Millin wrote regretting absence.

Messrs. Crook, Hobson, M. Macdonald, Rea, & Samuel were absent.

The minutes of the last meeting were read & confirmed.

It was agreed that Mr. Hobson should read his paper on Marx on Ap: 9th, and Mr. Reeves on 'Mill' on May 14th.

Mr. Haldane then gave a very full address on 'Hegel', which was almost exclusively concerned with his philosophy.

At its conclusion Mr. Haldane was asked to state what were, in his opinion, Hegel's contributions, if any, to Political Thought & Science. In his replies, & in the discussion wh: followed the following opinions were expressed as deducible from Hegel:

That Liberty is not [to] be obtained apart from the State, but only through the State,

that Hegel is a foe to philosophic Anarchism, and to the Static idea in Politics.

that Land Nationalisation & even Communism might be found implicitly in Hegel, but that as soon as he comes to practical politics he is simply the Prussian Junker.

that theoretically he taught that no political doctrine is fixed & final—consequently no Hegelian can be an enthusiast in politics.

Richard Stapley   Chairman

* * *

[70] On Wedn: Ap: 9th 1902 the Circle met at 33 Bloomsbury Sq. at 8 p.m.

Present Mr. Stapley in the chair, Messrs. Byles, Crook, Harley, Hobson, Lilley, Ramsay Macdonald, Perris, Rylett, Bullock; also Mr. Barratt, visitor.

Absent. Messrs. Burrows, Murray Macdonald, Millin, Morrison, Reeves, Rea, Robertson, Samuel.

The minutes of the last meeting were read & confirmed.

It was agreed that the next meeting should begin at 7.30 with the consideration of subjects for next Session.

Mr Hobson then read his paper on 'Karl Marx.' To Karl Marx chiefly we owe Democratic Socialism, a popular policy of progress with intellectual foundations, a systematic shape, & practical ends.

His intellectual penetration, persistency & honesty were wonderful.

Born at Trier in 1818, the son of Jewish parents, he devoted himself to history & philosophy at the German Universities.

In Paris, in 1843, he became the friend of Frederic Engels. In 1848, at Brussels he drew up the manifesto of the Communist League. After sundry adventures, arrests, & expulsions, he came in 1849 to London, where he died in 1883, after struggling at first with the direst poverty.

He consistently taught the need for the proletariat to rely on itself & to establish by force the international social revolution. Above all he urges the abolition of private capitalism.

During these years he wrote 'Das Kapital', a new philosophic interpretation of history, & a radical revision of the foundations of economic theory.

He saw in England great masses of workmen helpless in the grip of industrial private capitalism.

His foundation doctrine is that all value is the result of labor, and from this his whole system is logically deducible. But the question remains: Must not utility as well as cost, or labor, be taken into account in estimating value?

Also is there not an economic explanation of the necessity of interest in view of capital resulting, at least in part, from abstinence, though the bulk of private capital has been extorted by superior force in buying labor-power?

Marx has tried unduly to simplify the nature of surplus value by making it emerge exclusively from labor power instead of from the joint action of all the factors in production.

The real indictment against private capital is the mode by wh: the bulk of it is acquired.

In the subsequent discussion the following were some of the points insisted on:

That Marx recognised the supreme importance of the land, at least, not remaining in private hands:

That whether his theory of surplus value be true or not his real contribution to politics is his proof that progress can only come by class war:

That Marxianism is as much a temperament as a theory, & is impervious to mere nationalist considerations:

that Marx shewed how the aspirations of humanity act through economic forces:

that he was an economic rather than a political thinker, but that he shewed, above all, how everywhere the workers are always being robbed.

Richard Stapley   Chairman

* * *

[71] On Wednesday, May 14th 1902, the Circle met at 33 Bloomsbury Square at 7.30 p.m.

Present. Mr. Stapley in the chair, Messrs. Burrows, Crook, Lilley, Ramsay MacDonald, Perris, Reeves, Robertson, Samuel, & Bullock— also Mr. Hopkyns, visitor, and two ladies.

Messrs. Byles, Hobson, M. Macdonald, & Millin wrote regretting their absence.

Messrs. Harley, Morrison, Rea, & Rylett were also absent.

The minutes of the last meeting were read & confirmed.

The nine subjects to be discussed during the next Session were decided on.

Mr. Reeves then read his paper on 'John Stuart Mill.'

J.S. Mill was a great teacher who went on learning to the last, & had the courage to recant towards the end of his life some of his earlier views.

His latest opinions on Capital & Labor must be sought in his last articles & in his autobiography. After a mental crisis at 20 he realised that the happiness of self can best be found in seeking the good of others. He saw that morality, like truth, is neither revealed nor intuitive, but is the result of reasoning & experience.

He discriminated between higher & lower pleasures shewing the former to be really preferable, and refined Utility into Altruism & humanised Bentham.

When he was born men were sent to Botany Bay for political opinions, & 20 years later were prosecuted for religious ones: so he was naturally a radical & a champion of individual liberty, but not of laissez-faire, nor of anarchy.

He saw the dangers of over centralisation, but he knew that these were not then to be feared in England, where there was an excessive jealousy of governmental & legislative interference which he thought selfish local mismanagement often needed.

He recanted the old Wage Fund Theory, & his chapter on the Future of the Industrial Classes opens a new vista of economic speculation.

He urged the checking of reckless increase of children. He did not foresee the present mighty combinations of capital.

Though he was strangely ignorant of German & English Socialism he looks forward in his Autobiography to a condition practically Socialistic, & says that equal remuneration of labor appeals to a higher standard of justice, while at present remuneration is almost in inverse ratio to labor.

In the discussion wh: followed it was suggested:

That J.S. Mill was on the whole one of the sanest & best of our public men in his honesty & love of truth & justice, & in his philanthropy. He had a healthy suspicion of government by experts wh: is really fatal to democracy & he insisted on the distribution of wealth being no less important than its creation. His work on the subjection of women was also of great value. He was mistaken in insisting on an educational franchise & in resisting the cession of India to the Crown.

Richard Stapley   Chairman

* * *

[72] On Wednesday, June 4th the Circle met at 33 Bloomsbury Sq: at 8 p.m.

Present. Mr Stapley in the chair, Messrs. Burrows, Crook, Harley, Hobson, Lilley, Millin, Morrison, R. MacDonald, Reeves, Robertson, & Bullock—also two Visitors, Messrs. McKillop & Adams.

Absent. Messrs. Byles, M. Macdonald, Perris, Rea, Rylett, & Samuel.

The minutes of the last meeting were read & confirmed.

It was decided to hold the meetings of the next session on the second Wedn: in the month, except in April.

The readers of the papers were finally fixed.

Mr. Crook read his paper on 'Herbert Spencer':

At the age of 40 in poverty & with health broken by insomnia & dyspepsia he devoted his life to serious thought. He studied the Kosmos in the light of Evolution, & politics are but a small part of this study.

He ignores the Unknown & Unknowable Final Cause, & deals only with phenomena.

Knowledge of the lowest kind is un-unified knowledge.

Science is partly-unified knowledge.

Philosophy is completely-unified knowledge.

Starting with the persistence of force he lays down the law of the instability of the homogeneous, the law of the multiplication of effects, & the law of segregation.

Barbarous tribes are almost homogeneous collections of individuals well nigh independent of each other. He notes striking differences between societies & individual organism.

The state is maintained solely for the benefit of the citizens.

He does not advocate simple 'Laissez Faire'. In the maintenance of equitable relations among citizens governmental action should be extended & elaborated.

Militarism, like State Socialism, tends to stereotype everything. Its watchword is obedience not liberty.

He is the preacher of the immaterial; the prophet of infinite & eternal energy; and the apostle of a system of Ethics higher than that wh: is taught in Christian Churches.

The discussion, wh: followed, range[d] over a very wide field, & the following were some of the criticisms wh: were offered:

That Spencer was deficient in recognising consciousness in the lowest forms of life, & the conscious efforts in evolution.

That he was a scientific mind gone astray into Philosophy, that he did not do justice to the constructive side of the state's work, & that he was deficient in foresight.

That he was ignorant of what State Socialism really means, & that he confused it with Communism, & sometimes with Anarchism from wh: he shrank.

That his great co-ordinating power as a thinker, and his great ethical service, arose from his being the first to apply evolution universally.

That he is the pioneer of the revival of the inductive method.

On the other hand that his influence has been for harm in our time in politics on account of his alleged atomic individualism.

Richard Stapley   Chairman

* * *

Ninth Session: October, 1902–June, 1903

On Wedn: Oct 8th, 1902, the Committee met at 33 Bloomsbury Sq: at 7.50 p.m.

Present. Mr. Stapley in the chair, Mr. Lilley, and the Hon: Sec:— The minutes of the last Committee meeting, June 5. 1901, were read & confirmed.

Mr. J. McKillop was unanimously recommended for election.

Richard Stapley   Chairman

* * *

[73] On Wedn: Oct. 8. 1902, the Circle met at 33, Bloomsbury Square at 8 p.m.

Present. Mr. Stapley in the chair, Messrs. Lilley, Morrison, Rea, Samuel, Bullock, and Mr. Walsh, visitor.

Letters, or messages, were sent by Messrs. Crook, Burrows, Hobson, & Robertson.

The following were also absent—Messrs Byles, M. Macdonald, R. MacDonald, Millin, Perris, Reeves, Harley, Rylett.

Minutes of the last meeting were read & confirmed.

Accounts for last session were submitted & accepted.

The list of attendances of members for the past session was read— as follows:

9. Messrs. Stapley, Lilley, & Bullock.
7.   "   Hobson, & R. MacDonald.
6. Messrs. Harley, Morrison, Robertson.
5.   "   Crook, Perris, Reeves.
4.   "   Burrows, Millin, Rylett.
3.   "   Byles, & Samuel.
0.   "   M. Macdonald, Rea.

Mr. Stapley and Mr. Bullock were unanimously re-elected Chairman & Hon: Sec: respectively.

The other members of Committee were elected as follows: Messrs. Crook, Lilley, R. MacDonald, Millin, Morrison, Samuel.

Mr. J. McKillop, and, subject to his consent, Mr. Maurice Adams were elected members of the Circle.

Mr. Samuel gave notice that at the next meeting he would propose the alteration of the limit of numbers from 20 to 30.

Mr. Lilley read his paper on 'Church & State & Education in France':

In all Roman Catholic countries the Church has always made herself the formidable rival of the State, & is now a menace to the peace of France.

Charlemagne & St. Louis both tried to curb its turbulence. The Concordat of Francis I & Leo X, 1516, settled their relations till 1789. The Edict of 1749 gave the king power over monasteries equal to Henry VIII's.

In 1789 the State resumed Church property & paid salaries to the Clergy. The Civil Constitution, 1790–1801 made the clergy really national & subordinate to civil power. The Concordat of Napoleon & Pius VII: 1801, lasts still. The Organic Articles[56] further curb & regulate the clergy. Unauthorised orders, or unauthorised houses of authorised orders have always since 1749 been liable to suppression & confiscation.

In 1806 all education was made a State monopoly under the University of Paris. Bishops obtained leave to found seminaries for training clergy, staffed them with Jesuits, & allured into them the young of the upper & middle classes who had no intention of becoming clergy.

In 1850 the Loi Falloux threw open the teaching profession.

In 1880, Jules Ferry[57] made elementary education: universal, gratuitous, & lay.

The Concordat giving the State the nomination of Bishops is the last remaining national check on ultra-montanism. The religious orders & the diocesan priests have long waged a relentless campaign of calumny & hatred against the Republic: & have used their schools for this purpose, specially the Assumptionists & Jesuits: therefore the State enforces the existing laws against unauthorised congregations & houses, & the working class centres are earnestly anticlerical.

In the discussion wh: followed Mr. Walsh, visitor, described the French Schools of today in detail—In the elementary schools the teachers are devoted to their pupils, & they open the schools on Sundays for readings &c. The Higher Primary Schools are very good & do not unfit children for manual work. The Ecole Professionelle, 14–18, prepares boys for trades &c—The first 3 hours daily are given to general education, the last 5 to technical.

It was observed that as the clergy become more devoted to Rome the people became less Christian. The action of the present French Government was fully justified & compared favourably with that of the present English Ministry.

Richard Stapley   Chairman.

* * *

[56] The Organic Articles unofficially supplemented the Concordat.

[57] Jules Ferry (1832–1893). French politician and premier. Attempted to expel the Jesuits from the schools.

On Wedn: Nov. 12th 1902, the Committee met at 33 Bloomsbury Sq: at 7.50 p.m.

Present. Mr. Stapley in the chair, Mr. Crook, & the Hon: Sec:

The minutes of the last Committee meeting, Oct: 8 1902, were read & confirmed. Mr. W.T.H. Walsh was unanimously recommended for election.

Richard Stapley   Chairman

* * *

[74] On Wedn: Nov: 12th 1902 the Circle met at 33 Bloomsbury Square at 8 p.m.

Present. Mr. Stapley in the chair, Messrs. Crook, Harley, Lilley, R. MacDonald, Samuel, & Bullock.

Letters or messages explanatory of absence were received from Messrs. Adams, Burrows, Morrison, Millin, & Mackillop [sic], & Robertson.

The following were also absent: Messrs. Byles, Hobson, M. Macdonald, Perris, Reeves, Rea, & Rylett.

Minutes of last meeting were read & confirmed.

Mr. Adams' letter was read & his election ratified.

Mr. Burrows' letter offering resignation was read, & it was resolved that he be asked to suspend his resignation for this Session.

Mr. W.T.H. Walsh was unanimously elected.

Mr. Samuel's motion altering the limit of the number of members from 20 to 30 was carried unanimously:-

Mr. Crook read his paper on the 'Constitutional Problem in France:'-

There is no Constitutional Problem in France, because there is no Constitution, as the term is understood in England & U.S.A.

This difference is not due to race. The political problems in France are quite different to those in England. This difference is due to history, & the history has been largely made by geography.

French development has been sometimes violently checked with consequent explosions. The Republic is the most stable government wh: France has enjoyed for a century, & the lapse of time strengthens it.

The 300 members of the Senate are elected by 43,000 senatorial electors, themselves chosen by local councils & municipalities. The Senate is growing more Republican & reflects the real permanent feeling of France.

Most Senators have been trained in local gov: & are steady Liberals.

The Senate is a check on Reaction as in the case of Boulanger[58] but not of Drefus [sic], while our House of Lords is nothing but a check on Progress.

The Chamber of 600 Deputies represents Paris & the big towns wh: are more decadent & hysterical than the country. Elected by manhood suffrage. Ten million electors over 21. One man, one vote. Two years' imprisonment for plural voting. All pollings on one Sunday. Election expenses paid by locality. Second ballot. Corrupt practises [sic] mainly confined to clergy.

Members paid £360 p.a. Any minister can speak in either House. Experts who are not members can be called to address the Chamber.

The Chamber is composed of several groups, of wh: the Buon-apartists & Monarchists are disloyal to Rep. but the really dangerous enemy is the Roman Church wh: has long been tampering with the army by means of Church Schools: hence the enforcement of existing laws to protect the present liberty of France wh: the Church hates.

France is as well fitted for Parliamentary government as any other nation. The word is French & Simon de Montfort was a Frenchman.

Mr. Lilley spoke on the present proposals of French political reformers. He said that the Dreyfus affair drove many Liberals into the Socialist party. He pointed out that there was great abuse of the right of interpellation, & that the extravagance of the budgets was caused by their being made by individuals in the Chamber. He described the proposals for an executive separate from Parliament & for more power for the President.

Richard Stapley   Chairman

* * *

[75] On Wednesd: Dec: 10th 1902 the Circle met at 33 Bloomsbury Sq: at 8 p.m.

Present. Mr. Stapley in the chair, Messrs. Adams, Byles, Crook, Harley, Lilley, Mackillop, Robertson, Rylett, Walsh, Bullock; also Mr. Parsons & another visitor.

Apologies for absence were received from Messrs. Burrows, J.R. Macdonald, & Morrison.

Also Absent. Messrs. Hobson, M. Macdonald, Millin, Perris, Reeves, Rea, Samuel.

Minutes of last meeting were read & confirmed.

Mr. Harold Cox'[59] letter was read declining election.

[58] Georges Boulanger (1837–1891). French general and Royalist.
[59] Harold Cox (1859–1936). Economist and journalist. Secretary of the Cobden Club 1899–1904. Liberal M.P. 1906–9.

Mr. Robertson read his paper on the 'Economic Situation in France.'

France is mainly agricultural. It is manufacturing & mining in a far less, though increasing, degree. England's output of coal is more than 7 fold that of France and of iron more than 3 fold.

France comes much nearer to feeding herself than does England especially in cereals.

F: debt, 12 hundred mill: E: 7 hundred mill:

F: charge on debt 50 mill. E: about 22 mill.

F: navy 12 mill: E: 30 mill:

F: army 28 mill: E:—

F: is increasing her mineral output. E: is not.

F: is arresting growth of military & naval expenditure, while E: is greatly increasing hers.

French industrial life is on the whole more stable than English. Official corruption is as well repressed as in any other European state, & the proletariat is as widely awake as any to the standing phenomenon of unearned wealth resting on toiling poverty.

The debt charge of 50 mill: & the national defence charge of 42 mill: are met by taxation wh:—as yet—hardly touches incomes directly, or unearned increment at all. The opposition to taxes on income & rent comes mainly from moneyed classes, clergy, economists, & middle class rentiers.

In 1895 Leon Bourgeois'[60] proposal failed for a progressive death duty, wh: would have prepared the way for a progressive income tax.

The burden of Militarism greatly needs reducing.

Old Age Pensions, too, are needed to check present excessive thrift,[61] but to meet this expense a progressive tax on income & land values is first needful. With all their burdens the French people exhibit a higher average of material well being then the English thanks mainly to their prudence in the matter of their birth rate.

State monopolies already produce 20 p.c. of the revenue. Tobacco alone produces 16 mill:

Besides paying the war indemnity to Germany, France has added 400 mill: to her debt in the past 30 years.

In the discussion, stress was laid on the wonderful parsimony of French peasants. Their prosperity was ascribed by one speaker to the expulsion of kings, by another to the multiplication of small holdings in land. On the other hand it was suggested that the wide spread of agriculture in France was a source of weakness, & that old age pensions

---

[60] Leon Bourgeois (1851–1925). French socialist; prime minister 1895–6.

[61] Robertson shared with Hobson an adherence to unorthodox underconsumptionist views.

would form no substitute for the 'dot'[62] —also that thrift in N. France was more than balanced by increasing alcoholism. It was also stated that the stationariness of population was an evil, & that free-trade would prove a great benefit, if accepted, by France.

Richard Stapley   Chairman

* * *

[76] On Wed: Jan: 14th 1903 the Circle met at 33 Bloomsbury Sq., at 8. p.m.

Present: Mr. Stapley in the chair, Messrs. Crook, Harley, Lilley, MacKillop, Millin, Morrison, Perris, Robertson, Rylett, and Bullock, also Messrs Alden & Maynard, Visitors.

Apologies for absence were received from Messrs. Byles, M. Macdonald, R. MacDonald, and Walsh.

Also absent. Messrs Adams, Burrows, Hobson, Reeves, Rea, & Samuel.

Minutes of last meeting were read & confirmed.

Mr. Percy Alden was unanimously elected.

Mr. Harley read his paper on 'Socialism in Germany:'-

In 1877 there were 9 Socialist members among the 397 members of the Reichstag, now there are 59, with probability of increase at the next election, & this without having compromised with any other party.

In 1891 the Coercion Acts against Socialism were repealed, & the Conference published the Erfurt Program.[63] Bebel[64] was the leader, a bonâ fide workman, originally a R[oman] C[atholic] apprentice, & a born diplomat.

Followers of Lasalle[65] desired gradual parliamentary action. Those of Marx despised it, & awaited the inevitable evolution of Capitalism. Bebel leaned to the former policy. Von Vollmar,[66] the Bavarian Socialist, advocated opportunist co-operation with the Gov: to better the lot of the workman. In the Erfurt Program the first or theoretical part was Marxian, the second was parliamentary reform & legislation: in this combination lies the strength of German Socialism.

Kautsky[67] & Bernstein[68] lead the opposite wings of the party—

[62] The marriage dowry.

[63] In which the German Socialist party committed itself to an internationalist Marxist line.

[64] August Bebel (1840–1913). Co-founder of the German Socialist party.

[65] Ferdinand Lassalle (1825–1864). German socialist.

[66] Georg von Vollmar (1850–1922). Leader of the Bavarian Social Democrats.

[67] Karl Kautsky (1854–1938). German Marxist theorist and politician.

[68] Eduard Bernstein (1850–1932). German evolutionary socialist and politician.

Bernstein having moved away from pure Marxianism. The present weakening of Trades Unionism in England, & the protective German Tariff Bill tend to strengthen the Socialist party, & to convert the Roman Catholic workmen, & the smaller agrarians.

In the discussion the following opinions were expressed:

The recognition of Evolution must alter the course of evolution, & pure Marxianism is consequently losing its hold. The result will be that the party will gain more benefits for the people in the future.

Mommsen's[69] letter is an indication of the possibilities of a modified Socialist party.

Germany is now where England was before Free Trade: and Socialism is a protest against despotism of one man.

Socialism in Germany is in strong contrast to that in Russia, wh: started at the agrarian end owing to the existing community in land.

Bernstein's attitude of compromise on Imperialism is a serious danger.

Richard Stapley   Chairman

* * *

[77] On Wedn: Feb. 11. 1903 the Circle met at 33 Bloomsbury Square at 8. p.m.

Present. Mr. Stapley in the chair, Messrs. Adams, Alden, Crook, Lilley, MacKillop, Millin, Perris, Robertson, and Bullock, also visitors Mr. Stels, & Mr. J. Kettle.

Apologies for absence were received from Messrs. Byles, M. Macdonald, R. MacDonald, & Walsh.

The following members were also absent. Messrs. Burrows, Harley, Hobson, Morrison, Rea, Reeves, Rylett, Samuel.

Minutes of last meeting were read & confirmed.

Mr. Perris read his paper on 'Militarism in Germany'. Out of a population of about 60 mill:, on a peace footing there are about 600,000 soldiers—on a war footing there are also 3 mill: fully trained reservists, and 4 mill: less trained or ageing reservists under 45.

The cost of the army in peace is £34 mill: besides the loss of all that the 600,000 men would produce: the average German spends $2\frac{1}{2}$ years of life in barracks, a loss of national production of about £45 mill: a year.

Since 1870 Germany & other nations have aimed at increasing

---

[69] In 1902 Mommsen published a letter in *Die Nation* (p. 163ff.) warning against the Kaiser's absolutist tendencies and expressing surprising sympathy with, and admiration for, the Social Democrats [cp. L. Wickert, *Theodor Mommsen: Eine Biographie*. vol. iv (Frankfurt a. M., 1980), pp. 79–81].

their reserves. Germany could now put 3 times as many men in the field as she did in 1870.

Continental conscription has the advantage in justice over a mercenary army like the British.

The crowning aim of militarism is the unconditional obedience of the soldier.

About 400,000 become liable each year for military service, of whom about 100,000 escape it for various reasons.

The military Staff of 200 officers is the brain of the army, by wh: many men of talent are made to equal one man of genius.

For $2\frac{1}{2}$ years the average German is a slave, his moral & intellectual faculties are in abeyance, he is employed in no productive labor, but in learning the art of homicide.

Militarism means corruption, perversion of mind, breach of natural relations, arrest of all higher work, licence for petty tyranny, extinction of will & intelligence, creation of a dominant caste reactionary & antidemocratic, the brutality of wh: is illustrated by the survival of duelling.

Both Gladstone & Bismar[c]k were men of pure family life, disinterested, patriotic, professedly Christians—but contrasted in B's scorn of democracy, abuse of Kaiser Frederic[k], & unscrupulous foreign policy.

German Militarism has accomplished German Unity, such as it is, but this might have been gained by other means, & the burdens of the European armed peace might have been avoided.

Militarism is doomed to sterility, & Imperialism always fails.

In the discussion it was contended that the geographical conditions of Germany laid her peculiarly open to attack from France & Russia; that, in the past, this cause, & the bigotted & unpatriotic leadership of Austria, & the ceaseless intrigues of the Papacy, had subjected Germany to invasions, civil wars, & the arrest of material welfare & industrial development, that nothing had been found to give security from foreign aggression & internal war except military unity under a strong non-Catholic power, that military drill raises the half savage rustics morally & physically, that universal conscription makes Germany & France serious, as contrasted with England, & averse to a great war.

On the other hand it was urged that conscription has made Germany stupid, & has lowered its morality.

From a third point of view it was suggested that neither the unity nor the alleged intellectual sterility of Germany is due to military strength, but that small states always tend to promote brilliant & original thought, while large states & empires are adverse to it.

It was also suggested that the weakness of the Liberal party in

Germany was partly due to its failing to recognise in the past that unity & military strength were necessary to provide security against foreign aggression.

Richard Stapley   Chairman

* * *

[78] On Wedn: March 11th 1903, the Circle met at 33 Bloomsbury Sq: at 8. p.m.

Present. 13 members out of 22, viz: Mr. Stapley in the chair, Messrs. Adams, Alden, Crook, Harley, M. MacDonald, MacKillop, Millin, Morrison, Perris, Reeves, Robertson, & Bullock, also 3 Visitors.

Apologies for absence received from Messrs. Byles, R. MacDonald, & Walsh.

Also absent: Messrs. Burrows, Hobson, Lilley, Rea, Rylett, & Samuel.

Minutes of the last meeting read & confirmed.

Dr. Morrison read his paper on 'Industry & Education in Germany'.

In 1830 about 80 p.c. of the population were engaged in agriculture, now about 33 p.c. out of population $56\frac{1}{2}$ mill: & Germany has to import an increasing part of her food supply. There are 33 towns over 100,000. 300,000 holdings above 50 acres, but $3\frac{1}{4}$ mill: of holdings below 5 acres, & 2 mill: between 5 & 50. These maintain the physical stamina of the population. In wine, tobacco, sugar, fruit, & forestry, Germany makes the most of her opportunities.

Her mineral industry has quadrupled in last 20 years, & imports & exports have greatly increased.

Among the causes of this—since 1870, free trade within the German Empire, nationalisation of railways, common postal system, growing sense of national unity, as well as excellent educational system, which aims at & attains completeness, moral, mental, & intellectual, & thoroughness. Both the commercial & agricultural training are specially good.

The discussion was mainly concerned with the effects of German education. It was contended that this does not produce soundness of judgement or largeness of view in thought & scholarship, nor encourage practical efficiency & personal initiative in commerce & manufacture. This last criticism was however disputed.

It was also said that while Protection has stimulated manufactures, & enriched the landlords, it has not increased the material comfort of the poor. Education, & especially technical education was admitted to be probably one of the chief causes of German industrial success.

The encyclopedic knowledge of German scholars, & the success of German specialists were fully admitted.

Richard Stapley   Chairman

* * *

[79] On Wednesd: Ap: 1. 1903, the Circle met at 33, Bloomsbury Sq., at 8. p.m.

Present. 11 members out of 22—viz: Mr. Stapley in the Chair, Messrs. Adams, Alden, Crook, Lilley, R. MacDonald, MacKillop, Millin, Samuel, Walsh, Bullock.

Apologies for absence, received from Messrs. Byles & Robertson, & Reeves.

Absent: Messrs. Burrows, Harley, Hobson, M. Macdonald, Morrison, Perris, Rea, Rylett.

Minutes of last meeting read & confirmed.

A discussion took place on the subjects for consideration next Session. The following were suggested:

1. A continuation of the present course, to deal with Italy, Russia, Austria, & Japan.

2. Federal Home Rule—specially Switzerland & U.S.A.

3. Evolution & fate of Empires.

4. National & municipal finance & taxation.

5. To leave each reader to choose his own subject.

6. Problems of India & the British Colonies.

The last named subject was decided on by a large majority, 8 to 3, & was referred to the Committee.

Mr. Reeves' paper on Race Problem in U.S.A. was read by the Hon: Sec:

The white population of U.S.A. was composed in the first place of English, Scotch, Dutch, & Huguenots, later there came Spaniards, & French Canadians; since 1846, Irish and Germans in large numbers, and now Italians & Slavs.

The chief causes of almost complete assimilation have been—Vast area, Rapid Transport, complete Toleration, Gift of citizenship, Common language learnt by all children, Common schools, Aloofness from European entanglements.

The Negroes are the one real race problem: 1/9 of population. They have doubled since Emancipation but rate of increase is diminishing. Most of the 8 mill: have more or less white blood & are superior intellectually to pure negroes. The northern states are too cold for the negro. Everywhere political & social antipathy is very strong. They swarm in the 'Black Belt,' & do most of the agricultural work in the South at lower wages than whites, & much unskilled work in the towns. All whites are against them, & despise & dislike them, while they are as yet submissive & peaceable under it.

It was contended, in the discussion, that negro criminality was exaggerated, that education & that intermarriage might help to solve the problem, that negroes were capable of becoming skilled workers— on the other hand that a lower race cannot develop a real civilization in face of a superior race.

Richard Stapley

* * *

[80] On Wedn: May 13, 1903, the Circle met at 33 Bloomsbury Sq. at 8. p.m.

Present. 12 members out of 22. Mr. Stapley in the chair, Messrs. Harley, Lilley, M. Macdonald, R. MacDonald, MacKillop, Perris, Reeves, Robertson, Rylett, Samuel, Bullock, and 4 visitors.

Apologies for absence were received from Messrs. Byles, Crook.

Also absent—Messrs. Adams, Alden, Burrows, Hobson, Millin, Morrison, Rea, Walsh.

Minutes of last meeting were read & confirmed.

It was decided to adhere to the 2nd Wedn: in the month.

The nine subjects & seven of the readers were decided on: readers on South Africa & New Zealand were left for arrangement.

Mr. J.R. MacDonald read his paper on 'Democracy & Imperialism in U.S.A.'

The industrial position in U.S.A. favors Imperialism. Expanding manufactures were menaced by European appropriations of Asian & African markets. The Western States hoped for East Asian commerce.

The American is restless, aggressive, & without communal conscience. Atomic individualism & worship of the flag prevail. Misrule in Cuba & destruction of the Maine converted U.S.A. into a world power. U.S.A. has long resented contempt of European States. It now in turn despises them & is confident of its power to enforce the Monroe doctrine. Its rapid exploitation of natural wealth, & its boundless territory have encouraged self assertion.

Blatant patriotism & flag worship have been used to assimilate foreign elements. U.S.A believe they can solve every problem & benefit the globe by bossing it. Industrial problems & the rise of Socialism may mitigate & chasten this temper in the future.

In the discussion it was urged that the present prevalent American temper will not be permanent, that saner elements exist & will prevail, that there is already division of opinion on the retention of the Phillipines, that Cuba, Mexico, & S. America have not been annexed, & that American diplomacy shows a tendency to become pacific:

that equality is the keynote of American democracy:

that though torture has been wholesale in the Phillipines, it is only the brutality inseparable everywhere from Imperialism, & that power over others always makes men cruel, as in modern capitalism:

that revenge for the Maine was the motive for war with Spain on the part of a majority of Americans, & that the greatest imperialistic danger to U.S.A. is the temptation to intervene in China.

Richard Stapley

* * *

[81] On Wednesday, July 1st the Circle met at 33 Bloomsbury Sq. at 8. p.m.

Present. 13 members out of 22. Mr. Stapley in the chair, Messrs. Adams, Harley, Hobson, Lilley, M. Macdonald, R. MacDonald, Morrison, Perris , Rea, Robertson, Rylett, Bullock; also 3 visitors.

Apologies from Messrs. Byles, Crook, McKillop.

There were also absent: Messrs. Alden, Burrows, Millin, Reeves, Samuel, Walsh.

Minutes of last meeting read & confirmed.

Mr. H. de B. Walker was unanimously elected a member.

Mr. Hobson read his paper on 'Capitalism in U.S.A.'

Manufactures occupy 24 p.c. of the workers, agriculture 36 p.c. in wh: Capitalism is no longer advancing. The formidable aspect of trusts is that they are strongest in the supply of necessaries & of requisite services, railroads, mines, finance, oil, sugar, steel &c. The progressive substitution of mechanical for human power increases the part played by capital as against labor.

Machinery has developed faster in U.S.A. than anywhere else. Protection has aided this.

Municipal services, specially electric, & excepting water, are generally in the hands of trusts.

The Railroad, rather than the Tariffs, has been the parent of Trusts, as in Standard Oil Co: & Carnegie Steel Co:—Railway concentration is bringing the control of the financier over transport & industry.

This control is further advanced in U.S.A. than in any other country. The financier provides capital for new undertakings, & holds stocks

& shares, & too often manipulates them to make huge profits from forced oscillations of values.

Moderate reformers propose to check the Trusts by abolishing tariffs & enforcing existing laws against illegal combinations.

More drastic reformers would strengthen the power of the Central Gov: & tax monopoly profits. If these measures fail attempts will probably be made to nationalise rails & mines.

In the discussion it was asked if workmen are taking shares in the Trusts, & so becoming supporters. The absence of State control, & the weakness of Federal control over the Railways was emphasised. The written constitution is an obstacle to improvement, & the Senate is undemocratic. Factory system so exhausting that it destroys strength for thought. There are so many openings for careers that Socialist thought is backward.

Richard Stapley

* * *

Tenth Session. 1903–1904.

[82] On Wednesd: Oct: 14. 1903 the Circle met at 33 Bloomsbury Sq., at 8. p.m.

Present. 10 members out of 22. Mr. Stapley in the chair, Messrs. Alden, Harley, Hobson, Lilley, M: Macdonald, R. MacDonald, Robertson, Rylett, Bullock, and Mr. Mead, Visitor.

Apologies for absence: Messrs. Byles, & McKillop.

Also absent: Messrs. Adams, Crook, Millin, Morrison, Perris, Rea, Reeves, Samuel, Walker, Walsh.

Minutes of last meeting were read & confirmed.

Accounts for past session read & accepted.

Subs: for current session reduced to 1/-.

Attendances of members for past session were read:—as follows.

9 out of 9. Messrs. Stapley & Bullock.
8 out of 9. Mr. Lilley.
6   ”   Messrs. Crook, Harley, McKillop, Robertson.
5   ”   Messrs. Adams & Perris.
4   ”   Messrs. Alden, R. MacDonald, Millin, Morrison, Rylett, Samuel.
3   ”   Mr. Murray Macdonald.
2   ”   Messrs. Rea, Reeves, Walsh.
1   ”   Messrs. Byles & Hobson.
0   ”   Mr. Burrows.

Mr. Stapley & Mr. Bullock were unanimously re-elected Chairman & Hon: Sec: respectively.

The other members of the Committee were elected as follows. Messrs. Crook, Hobson, Lilley, R: MacDonald, Morrison, Samuel.

Mr. A.A. Parsons was unanimously elected a Member.

Mr. Burrows' name was erased for non-attendance.

Mr. Robertson read his paper on India.

In England it is an axiom that no statesman or party can be trusted to govern without constant criticism & constitutional opposition, but in dealing with the subject & voteless races of India & Egypt our national self esteem makes the opposite assumption.

The commonest vice of all absolute governments is overtaxation. India's debt has increased from 137 m: in 1889 to 211 m: in 1901. Expenditure, apart from interest on debt: from 53 m: to 73 m: of wh: nearly 16 m: is military.

The main source of income is land tax—over 18 m: Compare this with England where land owners have largely controlled the incidence of taxation.

Salt tax, $5\frac{1}{2}$ m: is a government monopoly & this revenue is wrung from the very poorest: the amount of salt used does not increase with the population thus shewing a lowering of the standard of life.

Proportion of literates—about 5 p.c. has been stationary for past 10 years.

Imports are 72 m: Exports 90 m: Balance 18 m: might be thought to be pensions, interests, & dividends.

Chief exports, rice & wheat of wh: the people have not enough for themselves. Tea, jute, indigo, seeds, hides, raw cotton—The ill-paid labor is Indian—Capital & profits British.

The one hopeful work is the extension of profitable irrigation—the best of wh: was begun before British rule, & in wh: we have wasted large sums by mismanagement.

The livestock has been frightfully reduced by famine. In 1850 the average daily income was officially estimated at 2d, in 1882 at $1\frac{1}{2}$d, in 1900 by Mr. Wigby at 3/4d. Sir C. Elliott,[70] conservative, ex-governor, says—'Half our agricultural population never know, from year's end to year's end, what it is to have their hunger fully satisfied.'

Roads, & rails, & often canals, have been made for British purposes, mainly military: at India's expense. We may judge of the severity of the land tax by the proposal of officials to limit it to 50 p.c. of the produce. The result bankruptcy of the peasants, & enforced sale of their land, much of wh: cannot find purchasers.

---

[70] Charles Alfred Elliott (1835–1911). Lieutenant-governor of Bengal 1890–95.

Experienced native Indians in Civil Service are in the main as just & more experienced than young Englishmen.

Pax Britannica & Justice are dear at the cost of progressive improvement & consequent moral degradation.

India needs the diminution of the burdens wh: are destroying her, & especially the increased employment of natives instead of English.

In the discussion it was suggested that English rule breaks down the curse of caste—on the other hand that the English form a marked caste of their own:—that India is the crowning failure of our Empire, & that we have enervated native Indian political life: that while taxation ought to be elastic, we have helped the money lender, & have broken up the old village communities: that we deride the Baloos[71] whom we have created, & have not kept faith with the Hindoos who desire to enter Gov: service:—that while China is the best managed & happiest large population in the world, India is the worst managed & most miserable. Returned Indian officials are the most consistent opponents of democracy in England.

Richard Stapley

* * *

[83] On Wednesday, Nov. 11. 1903, the Circle met at 33 Bloomsbury Sq: at 8. p.m.

Present. 15 members. Mr. Stapley in the chair, Messrs. Adams, Alden, Crook, Harley, Hobson, Lilley, Millin, Morrison, Parsons, Perris, Rea, Rylett, Walker, Bullock.

Apologies for non attendance, from Messrs. Byles, M: Macdonald, R. MacDonald, Robertson, Samuel.

Also absent: Messrs. McKillop, Reeves, Walsh.

The strongest sympathy was expressed with Mr. Robertson in connection with the miscarriage of justice wh: it was felt he had suffered with reference to a libel circulated against him at Newcastle.[72]

Mr. Hobson read his paper on South Africa:

South Africa is the least selfgoverning of British selfgoverning colonies. 3/4 mill: of whites in population of $5\frac{1}{2}$ m:

There is no intention of really enfranchising the colored population. Lord Milner has just forced Customs Law of Preferential Tariffs on

---

[71] Possibly the Baluchis.

[72] On 2nd November 1903 Robertson lost an action for libel he had brought against the proprietors and publishers of the *Leeds and Yorkshire Mercury*. An article had been published accusing him not only of being a rabid little Englander but of dealing with 'matters unmentionable in polite society' when editor of the *Free Review*, and he was pronounced unsuitable to represent Tynesiders as their prospective Liberal candidate. Cp. *Daily News*, 3.11.1903.

Cape Colony, against the views of the responsible government. Taxes are being levied by Governor's warrant. War office forbids officers to give evidence in enquiries into Court Martial sentences.

The larger part of South Africa has climate & political & economic conditions of a tropical crown colony.

A barren soil, incapable of irrigation, sparsely populated. Concentration of mineral wealth in a comparatively small tract producing diamonds & gold.

A little ring of capitalists, chiefly Jews[73] & British aristocrats, controls the chief industry & wealth of the country. The war they contrived has freed them from all real restraint or fear of competition.

They can now choose between forced native labor & importation of Asiatics. They will probably prefer the latter wh: will bring increased evils in its train.

The future appears to be one of unrest, internal divisions, & possible loss of South Africa.

In 1898, last normal year, South Africa exported nearly 20 mill: of gold & diamonds, & only 4 m: of other things.

Mr. Chamberlain's proposals[74] will increase the already high cost of commodities in South Africa & will not benefit a single industry.

To keep South Africa in the Empire we shall have either to grant complete autonomy & to allow the financial ring & the Boers to keep the black majority in practical slavery, & deprived of justice & equality before the law—or else we shall have to keep a large army in South Africa to support the rule of the monopolist ring against Boers, blacks, & a considerable section of the British settlers.

In the discussion wh: followed it was suggested that the irrigation needed for agriculture can only be paid for by taxing gold—

that the Boer is as tyrannical to the native, as the Briton is, & wishes to increase the hut tax—

that the immediate welfare of the natives is best helped by refusal of self-government—but that only self government will enable the whites to deal with the ring, that we are pledged to grant it, & must leave the natives to its tender mercies:—

that the South African press is entirely controlled by the ring, is quite untrustworthy, & seeks to manufacture opinion in South Africa & England.

Richard Stapley

* * *

[73] Despite previous criticism of Hobson's Boer War Judenhetze and a subsequent toning down of his comments in 1900 (Cp. H. Mitchell, 'Hobson Revisited', *Journal of the History of Ideas*, vol. xxvi (1965), 397–416; and B. Porter, *Critics of Empire* (London, 1968), pp. 201–2), he clearly had not abandoned his original views.

[74] On tariff reform.

[84] On Wednesd: Dec: 9th 1903, the Circle met at 33, Bloomsbury Sq. at 8.p.m.

Present. 10 members, Mr. Stapley in the chair; Messrs Adams, Crook, Hobson, Lilley, M. Macdonald, McKillop, Parsons, Perris, Bullock.

Apologies for absence. 5 members, Messrs. Byles, Morrison, Rea, Robertson, Walker.

Also absent. 8. Messrs. Alden, Harley, R. MacDonald, Millin, Reeves, Rylett, Samuel, Walsh.

Minutes of last meeting read & confirmed.

Mr. F.J. Matheson. prop. Mr. Perris, unanimously elected.

Mr. L.T. Hobhouse, prop. Mr. Hobson, unanimously elected.

Mr. Perris read his paper on Egypt:

In the discussion it was urged that Egypt is the best instance of British Imperial sway, but that good results to the serfs are no justification for the seizure:

that Arabi's[75] movement gave promise of national self-government: that no elements of self-government existed in Egypt, & that therefore some European power was bound to intervene when Arabi arose:

that it was still too soon to say whether our interference will help the progress of the world: that Egypt, thanks to our irrigation works, may again become a granary for the world:

on the other hand that the Suez Canal is the most important thing in connexion with Egypt: that England has preponderating interests in the Canal, & that the mercantile world is satisfied with England's management of it.

Richard Stapley

* * *

[85] On Wednesday, Jan: 13th 1904 the Circle met at 33 Bloomsbury Sq. at 8. p.m.

Present: 15 members. Mr. Stapley in the chair, Messrs. Alden, Harley, Hobson, Lilley, R. MacDonald, Millin, Parsons, Rea, Roberston, Rylett, Samuel, Walker, Matheson, & Bullock, and Mr. Hughes, Visitor.

Apologies for absence (3): Messrs. Byles, Crook, McKillop.

Also absent. (7.) Messrs. Adams, M. Macdonald, Morrison, Perris, Reeves, Walsh, Hobhouse.

Minutes of last meeting read & confirmed.

[75] Arabi Pasha (c.1840–1911). Egyptian leader whose nationalist reforming movement against the Khedive led to the British conquest of Egypt in 1882.

Mr. R. MacDonald read his paper on Canada:

When Free Trade was established in 1846 Lord G Bentinck foretold that Canada would seek annexation with U.S.A. while a deputation of Canadian merchants prophesied ruin & rapid decay. There is still a sense of hostility between Canada & U.S.A. & the Canadian feeling some dependence on G.B. remains backward & Conservative.

Since 1891. the drift of Canadian feeling has been against annexation & latterly she has become more self reliant, though Imperialist talk is still common. Canada will continue to protect her own manufactures by tariffs & bounties against G.B. & with a still higher tariff against other countries.

Woollen, Iron, & Machinery industries are all complaining that even now they are not protected highly enough against G.B.

Canada imports 9 m. worth of goods yearly from G.B. & hardly any raw material, for wh: she partly depends on U.S.A. from whom her imports are 23. m:

Canada exports to G.B. 23 m:—nearly all being cattle corn meat & wood.

Canada's trade relations with G.B. are less important to her or to G.B. than is the case with any other of our colonies.

Canada's loyalty to the Empire is founded on sentiment. Substitute commercial bargaining as the basis, & it will lead to friction on both sides & the loyalty will perish.

Special friendship between G.B. & her colonies can only continue as long as they remain practically independent, self-governing & self developing.

The sordid attempt to put the Empire on a business footing will break it up.

In the discussion it was suggested:

that a 2/- duty on corn would mean a gift of 1 m: from the poor of England to comparatively rich Canada:

that the economic bond is becoming stronger between U.S.A. & Canada, that settlers & capital are coming in from U.S.A. especial[ly] into districts north of Lake Superior wh: are rich in minerals.

that Canadian farmers & organised laborers are free-traders, rent, clothes, &c being higher for protection: that the present obstacle to reciprocity between U.S.A. & Canada is the Senate of U.S.A.:

that Goldwin Smith's[76] present opinion is that U.S.A. does not desire to annex Canada but expects to see it independent.

that the foreign immigrants to Canada no longer regard England as the friend of freedom, and that the French Canadian element wh:

---

[76] Goldwin Smith (1823–1910). Regius professor of modern history at Oxford, 1858–66. Moved to Canada, 1871, became a writer and journalist and advocate of unpopular causes.

numbered 70,000 in 1791 is already 2,000,000: & that the consequent increasing sinister influence of the Roman Church will have to be reckoned with.

Richard Stapley

* * *

[86] On Wednesday, Feb: 10th 1904 the Circle met at 33 Bloomsbury Square at 8. p.m.

Present: 12 members out of 25. Mr. Stapley in the chair, Messrs. Byles, Crook, Harley, Hobson, Lilley, R. MacDonald, McKillop, Reeves, Walsh, Matheson, & Bullock.

Apologies for absence: Messrs. Morrison, Parsons, Samuel, Walker.

Also absent: Messrs. Adams, Alden, M. Macdonald, Millin, Perris, Rea, Robertson, Rylett, Hobhouse.

Minutes of last meeting read & confirmed.

Mr. Reeves gave an address on Australia:

The price of food there has fallen 33 p.c. in 40 years: their protection is mainly for revenue, to support governmental enterprise.

If G.B. gave 5 p.c. preference Australia would not reduce her tariff much if at all. Empire does not depend on commercial treaties.

Importation of Chinese labor disgusts Australia. Australia's federal system is the most democratic in the world. Governor General is good, but the appointment of the six lieutenant governors should be elective, & not by crown. Bi-cameral legislatures should be made unicameral.

In the discussion it was contended:

That the Labor Party ought to share in the responsibilities of government:

That the colonies wish to appoint their own lieutenant governors:

That secondary education is weak, as yet, in Australian towns, but that the efforts of the Bible party, & of Romans & Anglican[s] to upset secular elementary education have always failed.

That directly the coastline is left behind, life is one long fight against drought:

That the level of food & comfort is higher than in England.

Richard Stapley

* * *

[87] On Wednesday, March 9th 1904, the Circle met at 33 Bloomsbury Sq: at 8. p.m.

Present. 10 members out of 25. Mr. Stapley in the chair. Messrs. Adams, Crook, Hobson, Lilley, McKillop, Parsons, Walker, Matheson, and Bullock.

An apology for absence was received from Mr. Byles.

Also absent (14), Messrs. Alden, Harley, M. Macdonald, R. MacDonald, Millin, Morrison, Perris, Rea, Reeves, Robertson, Rylett, Samuel, Walsh, Hobhouse.

Minutes of last meeting were read & confirmed.

A letter was received from Mr. Hobhouse thanking the Circle for his election in December 1903, and giving his address.

Mr. Walker read his paper on New Zealand:

New Zealand being an island, with but little gold mining, & with a climate similar to G.B. the sentiments of the people are more like our own than is the case in Canada, Australia, or South Africa.

27 p.c. of its inhabitants were born in G.B. and 97 p.c. within the Empire.

New Zealand agreed more readily than Australia to contribute to the British Navy.

It has given a preference to British goods, not by lowering its import duties, but by increasing them 20 to 50 p.c. on non-British goods: but there is reason to fear that this was done under pressure from the home Government & with an implied promise of reciprocity.

Almost the whole opposition press in New Zealand supported Mr. Seddon's[77] protest against introduction of Chinese labor into Transvaal.

New Zealand is unlikely to seek admission into the Australian Commonwealth, but might have to do so if it ceased to be part of the Empire.

It has the best record of all selfgoverning colonies for treatment of native races: there are Maoris in both Houses of Parliament & a half caste in the Ministry.

It was the first British state to introduce Old Age Pensions & Parliamentary Franchise for women: During past 13 years Trades Unionists & Labor Party have co-operated with Liberals, & have shared responsibility of Govt:

Conversational discussion followed, mainly on Education, & on the Native Question.

Richard Stapley

* * *

[77] Richard John Seddon (1845–1906). Premier of New Zealand 1893–1906. State socialist, had just condemned Chinese labour.

[88] On Wednesd: Apr: 13th 1904, the Circle met at 33 Bloomsbury Sq: at 8. p.m.

Present: 13 members out of 25. Mr Stapley in the chair. Messrs. Crook, Harley, M. Macdonald, R. MacDonald, MacKillop, Parsons, Robertson, Rylett, Samuel, Walker, Walsh, & Bullock, also two visitors.

Apologies for absence received from Messrs. Alden, Byles, Hobson, Millin, Matheson.

Also absent. 7 members Messrs. Adams, Lilley, Morrison, Perris, Rea, Reeves, Hobhouse.

Minutes of last meeting read & confirmed.

It was decided that the next Session should be devoted to the consideration of some of the newer demands of the political 'Left Wing'.

Mr. Harley undertook the May paper in place of Mr. Samuel.

Mr. McKillop read his paper on the Tropical Belt:[78]

Our Malayan settlements best illustrate this subject: we must regulate & utilise the immense vital energy wh: is running to waste in the Tropics: In temperate regions we struggle against Nature's niggardliness, in the tropics against her prodigality: Rice & bananas require little labor, & Java is the only really cultivated tropical land: Mineral resources, like vegetable, are hardly touched, & the jungle is King.

There is difficulty of obtaining labor, where whites cannot work, & blacks need not, owing to the fertility of the soil.

Tidal energy, too, in West Indies & Malaya, is as great as that now wasted around Great Britain.

In temperate autonomous colonies capital tends to be locally owned, but in tropical it must be either owned by the State or externally, or as in Malaya by Chinese immigrants, where roads, rails, & harbours have been made out of superfluous revenue, & state capital tends to oust private.

The Governments of our crown colonies vary, but do not tend towards democratic self-government wh: is unsuitable for tropical races, indolent & not self reliant.

No one fiscal system is possible for all our colonies & protected states: our eastern tropical possessions might contribute a naval contingent of men for Imperial defence.

It is doubtful if we are really benefitting [*sic*] the tropical races whom we govern. Colonial governors & officials are doing their best,

[78] For similar views by McKillop see his review of J.A. Hobson, *Imperialism: A Study* (*Fabian News*, Feb. 1903) where, despite some differences of opinion, he stated prophetically: 'Fifty years hence it will certainly be studied as the best exposition of the cult of anti-Imperialism'.

but education is very unsatisfactory. The strategic importance of the tropical belt to our scattered Empire ought to be better appreciated.

In the discussion, the following points were suggested:

That Education has not been given a chance, incompetent men being sent, & technical education neglected:

That the returned crown colony official is an increasing danger to free public life at home, & that though our moral standard may not degenerate moral conduct is upset by the circumstances of Imperialism:

That the attempt to govern another race against its will does more than climate to degrade the governing race: & that the best help is that given without political authority:

That our Mission is to break down oriental subservience to custom & tradition, & to teach a free attitude towards Nature.

Richard Stapley

* * *

[89] On Wednesday, May 11th 1904 the Circle met at 33 Bloomsbury Sq: at 8. p.m.

Present: 12 members out of 25. Mr. Stapley in the chair. Messrs. Harley, Hobson, Lilley, M. Macdonald, McKillop, Parsons, Perris, Robertson, Rylett, Matheson, & Bullock. also one Visitor.

Apologies for absence (4): from Messrs. Alden, Byles, Crook, & R. MacDonald.

Also absent: (9). Messrs. Adams, Millin, Morrison, Rea, Reeves, Samuel, Walker, Walsh, & Hobhouse.

Minutes of last meeting read & confirmed.

Nine subjects for discussion were selected by shew of hands out of 13 wh: were suggested, & nine members consented to read papers on them.

Mr. Harley read his paper on 'The Fiscal Question'

The Canadian Dominion Parliament is silent on the Fiscal Question: Australasia is less interested in it, than in opposing the importation of Chinese labor: & South Africa is absorbed in the latter subject.

Joseph Chamberlain being determined to alter our Fiscal Policy, & finding no real colonial demand for a change now declares that the change is necessary in the interests of Great Britain on three pretexts.

1. Greater relative growth of exports from Germany & U.S.A.
2. Displacements of skilled labor:
3. Disorganisation of production due to dumping.

The relatively slow growth of British exports of late is really due partly to our starved consular service & partly to the unaccommodating methods of British manufacturers & commercial travellers, as well as to other causes.

J.C.'s proposed Protection is no adequate remedy, as the comparison of N[ew] S[outh] W[ales] with Victoria shews.

In spite of its relative greater increase of exports Germany's condition is unsatisfactory & unsound.

If our colonies are alienated it is not by British Free Trade but by the ignorance, inefficiency, & haughtiness of those who represent G.B. specially army officers.

In the discussion it was contended:

That the Fiscal Proposals are J.C.'s 2nd dodge for getting larger income to meet Tory extravagance, after the Colonial premiers refused to share English military & naval expenses: that Free Trade, a non-aggressive policy & a lowered military expenditure are needed, & that the laborers will insist on sharing the fruits & profits of machinery: that land monopoly must be broken down: that if J.C. were honest he would tax foreign dividends, not the home consumer: that the experience of all foreign countries using protection shews that it disguises the taxation wh: is due to military expenditure, & raises the cost of living while it lowers wages: & that dumping is not continuous, but only occasional, & that we do it to other countries.

The Chairman suggested that an import duty on foreign flour would not raise the price of bread.

Richard Stapley

* * *

[90] On Wedn: June 8th 1904 the Circle met at 33 Bloomsbury Sq: at 8. p.m.

Present: (13 out of 25). Mr. Stapley in the chair, Messrs. Adams, Byles, Harley, Hobson, Lilley, M. Macdonald, McKillop, Perris, Robertson, Walker, Matheson, & Bullock; also 3 Visitors.

Apologies for absence: (4) Messrs. Crook, J.R. MacDonald, Parsons, Rylett.

Also absent: (8)- Messrs. Alden, Millin, Morrison, Rea, Reeves, Samuel, Walsh, Hobhouse.

Minutes of the last meeting read & confirmed.

The erasure of Mr. Hobhouse's name for non-attendance & non payment of subscriptions was deferred in order that Mr. Hobson might have an interview with him.

It was decided that the meetings next Session should be on the 1st Wedn: in the month except in Jan:

e

Mr. Murray Macdonald read his paper on 'The Constitutional Question of Imperial Federation: '

Only in Great Britain does the principle of self government operate at all fully. How can we extend to partially self governing colonies such fulness as we have?

Is the change needed? Is it desirable? What readjustment does it involve?

At present the self governing Colonies have no voice in making peace or war. They will rightly refuse ere long to be deprived of this.

If they are not to become independent States the Tariff Problem & Free Trade Question must lie at the root of any proposal for federation. But at present the Colonies are Protectionist, & G.B. free trade.

At first Joseph Chamberlain proposed that Colonies should lower their Tariff for G.B.; & G.B. should raise her Tariff against foreign nations.

Now he proposes that G.B. should adopt Protection, & unite with Colonies to exploit foreign States.

It rests on that false view of Commerce—that the gain of one State means the loss of others.

Commerce is really mutually advantageous.

Federation must be based on a higher morality of peace & goodwill towards the outside world, & on the self government of the component states.

It will be defensive externally, & will regulate justice internally.

The Imperial Federation Defence Committee[79] proposes that the Colonies shall share the burdens of army & navy, but not share in foreign policy. Thus we lost U.S.A.

The Federal Union Committee proposes an Imperial Parliament & Executive for Imperial concerns, & each of the nations in the U.K. to have its own Parliament for its internal & domestic concerns—i.e. Home Rule all round—& the Colonies to be invited to send representatives to Imperial Parliament & share its burdens.

In the discussion it was contended by some speakers that Federation was impractical & undesirable: the burden of our unfree Empire in India was cited: the growing class-consciousness of capitalists is opposed to federation with democratic Colonies: on the other hand—Home Rule all round was supported as exploding House of Lords & solving the Irish Problem.   Richard Stapley

* * *

[79] The Imperial Federation (Defence) Committee was formed in 1894 by members of the defunct Imperial Federation League and was instrumental in encouraging the formation of the Committee of Imperial Defence in 1904.

Eleventh Session, 1904–5.

[91] On Wedn: Oct: 5, 1904 the Circle met at 33 Bloomsbury Sq: at 8. p.m.

Present—(10 members out of 24) Mr. Stapley in the chair, Messrs. Adams, Harley, Hobson, R. MacDonald, Matheson, Parsons, Rylett, Walker, and Bullock. also Mr. Roskill, Visitor.

Apologies for absence: Messrs. Alden, M: Macdonald, McKillop, & Samuel.

Also absent: Messrs. Byles, Crook, Lilley, Millin, Morrison, Perris, Rea, Reeves, Robertson, Walsh.

Minutes of last meeting read & confirmed.

Accounts for past Session were read & accepted.

Attendance of members for past Session read as follows:

9 out of 9	Messrs	Stapley, Bullock.
8	”	Hobson, Lilley.
7	”	Harley.
6	”	McKillop, Parsons.
5	”	Crook, M: Macdonald, Robertson, Rylett, Walker.
		Matheson, 5 out of 6.
4	”	Adams, R. MacDonald, Perris.
3	”	Alden.
2	”	Byles, Millin, Rea, Samuel, Walsh.
1	”	Morrison, Reeves.
0	”	Hobhouse.

Mr. Stapley, & Mr. Bullock were unanimously reelected Chairman & Hon: Sec: respectively.

Six other members of Committee were elected as follows: Messrs. Crook, Harley, Hobson, Lilley, R. MacDonald, McKillop.

Mr. H. Burrows was re-elected a Member.

Mr. Hobson read his paper on 'The Referendum.'

The Referendum is an adjunct to, or a substitute for Representative Government—& a check on its abuse.

In Switzerland the Referendum & Initiative trace from the Landsgemeinde, the assembly of all citizens of the Canton; when these gave place to Representative Government certain reservations were made, & since 1834 direct popular control has been strengthened.

50,000 citizens can demand the Referendum on the revision of the constitution of the Federal Republic. If carried, a general election follows, a bill is drafted & submitted to a 2nd Referendum. 30,000 citizens can make the same demand in the case of any federal law. Federal budget & treaties are excluded.

The procedure in the Cantons is similar but very various.

In U.S.A. the compulsory Referendum exists in every State except Delaware for constitutional amendments. A movement is on foot to apply Referendum & Initiative to almost all State legislation. The Referendum & Initiative have been already obtained by several towns. They are a counter-move to the despotism of the industrial & political bosses, who have collared the machine of representative government for corrupt purposes. They would also make each citizen feel his responsibility for self-gov: Great Britain is in danger of the same corruption, i.e. the Spoils System, as U.S.A.

The machine of our Gov: is falling into the hands of a capitalist gang—thus Education Act[80] & Drink Act[81] have been passed by a majority elected on the War Question in 1900.

If it be objected that the average citizen is ignorant, we may answer that he is at least more impartial than the average M.P.: & the absence of the power of veto is a ludicrous excess of our confidence in our elected representatives.

The Referendum would be a political education, would check party spirit, & would deepen that sense of individual responsibility in each citizen, on wh: Democracy must ultimately depend.

In the discussion: difficulties were suggested of applying the Referendum to technical questions, such as Education was alleged to be, or Companies' Bills, or Trades Union Bills. It was denounced as individualistic, & as likely to promote political dishonesty. Shorter Parliaments were preferable: or waiting, at least, until people were better educated.

It was generally agreed that Home Rule All Round must precede Referendum & Initiative.

Richard Stapley

* * *

[92] On Wedn: Nov. 2nd 1904, the Circle met at 33 Bloomsbury Square at 8. p.m.

Present. (13 out of 25.) Mr. Stapley, in the chair, Messrs. Alden, Crook, Hobson, M: Macdonald, R: MacDonald, Parsons, Perris, Rea, Robertson, Rylett, Walker, & Bullock—also 2 Visitors.

Apologies for absence—(6) Messrs. Burrows, Lilley, Millin. McKillop, Matheson, & Samuel.

Also absent: (6). Messrs Adams, Byles, Harley, Morrison, Reeves, Walsh.

---

[80] Enacted in 1902.
[81] The Licensing Act (1904).

Minutes of the last meeting read & confirmed.

Mr. Hobhouse's name was erased from membership.

Mr. M: Macdonald read his paper on 'Home Rule All Round':

The Liberals are appealing to the country on Social Reforms: but in 1886, & 1892 the Liberal majority was powerless to effect these because of the House of Lords, & Irish Nationalists.

Lord Rosebery has said that if the House of Lords be not dealt with drastically it will wreck Liberal reforms in the future, as it has in the past.

In 1885, & 1892 the Irish Nationalists have held the balance between Conservatives & Liberals, and it may probably do so again.

If the next Liberal majority ignores the difficulties of House of Lords & of Ireland it courts disaster.

House of Lords has opposed or mutilated English & Scottish social legislation, as much as Irish Self-Gov:

Subordinate national legislatures for other than imperial matters would solve the problem for England & Scotland as well as for Ireland, and the constitutional difficulties, involved in giving a legislature to Ireland only, would be avoided.

The congestion of business in House of Commons increases. The laws of the 3 nations are not even now identical.

The mingling of Imperialism with local questions in House of Commons does harm to both, & confuses the issue at elections.

Federal Home Rule would facilitate the Federation of the Empire, for our colonies have Home Rule but no representation in House of Commons as yet.

It would remove domestic social reform in each country from the purview of House of Lords -

In the event of such devolution, questions about taxation will be the most difficult.

In the discussion, it was urged that Wales is a nation & ought to have Home Rule.

that the Labor party, & the Plutocrats are as dangerous to Liberalism as the Irish & House of Lords

that the Jingoism of House of Commons would be increased by the removal of social reformers:

that logical measures do not appeal to Englishmen & that therefore this reform is impossible:

also that it would do as well if powers of legislation were given to County Councils.

Richard Stapley

* * *

[93] On Wednesd: Dec. 7th 1904, the Circle met at 33 Bloomsbury Sq: at 8. p.m.

Present (14 out of 25). Mr. Stapley in the chair, Messrs. Adams, Alden, Crook, Harley, Hobson, M: Macdonald, R. MacDonald, McKillop, Matheson, Morrison, Parsons, Perris, & Bullock, also Mr. Pyddoke, Visitor.

Apologies for absence (6) were received from Messrs. Byles, Burrows, Rea, Robertson, Samuel, Walker.

Also absent: (5) Messrs. Lilley, Millin, Reeves, Rylett & Walsh. Minutes of last Meeting read & confirmed.

Mr. J.R. MacDonald read his paper on
'Relations of L.R.C.[82] and other Progressive Parties.'

The L.R.C. was the result of an attempt in Feb: 1900 to unite Socialists, Co-operators, & Trades Unionists into a political party. Subsequently the independence of this party was made absolute as against the Liberal & Tory parties. Two L.R.C. candidates—Keir Hardie & Bell[83]—were elected in 1900, & since then the foundations of future labor representation have been laid in many constituencies.

Liberal papers especially mis-represent L.R.C. After next general election there will be a real Labour group, for L.R.C. men will draw many votes from both Tory & Liberal—Four fifths of L.R.C. candidates are fighting only one opponent each.

We aim at a new social order dealing justice to those classes wh: contribute most to the social good. Towards land, unemployed, feeding of school-children, & probably towards capital our attitude is Socialistic. The L.R.C. aims at a national, not sectional, platform & policy; & will not bargain with sections, or particular interests.

In the discussion wh: followed it was suggested that:—The Labor Party is not a national party, but the party of a class or section, and without a policy on such national questions as India, the Navy, Education &c—that it is exclusive & will not accept the membership of individuals: for this reason it fails to draw to itself the advancing Liberals. It has arisen only because the Liberal party has neglected the needs of the Labouring classes in the past.

It was objected that the Labor Party, representing a class interest & not a principle, would tend to ally itself with Imperialism; also that it is an attempt to catch voters for Socialism without their knowing it.

On the other hand Liberals were blamed for trying to capture the

---

[82] Labour Representation Committee.

[83] James Keir Hardie (1856–1915). Labour leader and socialist. Richard Bell (1859–1930). General secretary of the Amalgamated Society of Railway Servants, Labour M.P. 1900–1910.

Labor Party, wh: was praised as consciously feeling its way towards a better social order.

It was suggested that in England the two old parties are disintegrating into groups, while in France the groups shew signs for re-integrating into two great parties.

Richard Stapley

* * *

[94] On Wedn: Jan: 11th 1905 the 94th Meeting of the Circle took place at 33 Bloomsbury Square, at 8. p.m.

Present: (10). Mr. Stapley in the chair, Messrs. Alden, Byles, Crook, Harley, Parsons, Rylett, Samuel, Walker, and Bullock.

Apologies for absence (3). Messrs. M: Macdonald, Matheson, Burrows.

Also absent: (12) Messrs. Adams. Hobson, Lilley, R. MacDonald, McKillop, Millin, Morrison, Perris, Rea, Reeves, Robertson, Walsh.

Minutes of last meeting were read & confirmed.

Mr. V. Bamford[84], & Mr. G.P. Gooch were proposed for membership.

Mr. J.H. Harley read his paper on Compulsory Arbitration.

International Arbitration concerns past facts—Arbitration between capitalists & workers concerns future rights.

In New South Wales the miners are refusing to work for the lowered wages ordered by the Compulsory Arbitration Board. There is no compulsory arbitration in U.S.A. or in Europe except in canton of Geneva.

In France the proposal of compulsion for 6 months has been suggested by M. Millerand.[85]

Compulsory arbitration became law in New Zealand in 1894, later in N.S.W. Commonwealth of Australia proposes a Court of 5— President a judge. 2 representatives of each side.

In New Zealand Court of 3. 1 judge, & 1 representative on each side.

The Australian Bill recognises unions of workers, but threatens to penalise them if they take part in politics: hence Australian Labor organs disapprove the Bill.

In England the law has been strained against Labor in the Taff Vale decision.[86]

---

[84] Read 'Branford'.

[85] Alexandre Millerand (1859–1943). French socialist, later prime minister and president.

[86] A decision by the Lords in 1901 to recognize trade unions as legal entities capable of being sued for damages over strike action.

These Compulsory Arbitration Courts will practically fix a minimum wage, with possible exceptions.

The proposed preference for Union over non-Union Labor is objected to by many people: the Act has succeeded in New Zealand where Capitalism is weak & has been kept down. In U.S.A. the Socialist vote has greatly increased, & a big Labor struggle seems imminent.

In the discussion it was suggested that Compulsory Arbitration was only a part of a larger question—viz: the fairer distribution of the fruits of labor. Trusts are the enemies of small employers as well as of labor. Such courts must have compulsory power, & judges must sit for life.

The discussion then turned to New Zealand, & it was agreed that the Act has succeeded there, because capitalists & landowners had previously had their wings clipped, & Labor had been thoroughly organised.

Richard Stapley

* * *

[95] On Wedn: Feb. 1st 1905 the 95th Meeting of the Circle was held at 33 Bloomsb: Sq: at 8. p.m.

Present. (12) Mr. Stapley, in the chair. Messrs. Harley, Hobson, Lilley, McKillop, Matheson, Morrison, Parsons, Rea, Robertson, Walsh & Bullock. also 2 Visitors Messrs. Waldegrave & Geddes.

Apologies for absence: (5) Messrs. Byles, Burrows, Millin, M: Macdonald, & Samuel.

Absent (8) Messrs. Adams, Alden, Crook, R. MacDonald, Perris, Reeves, Rylett, Walker.

Minutes of last Meeting read & confirmed.

Mr. V. Branford was elected a member.

Mr. G.P. Gooch was elected, subject to his expressing his wish to join. (South Villa, Campden Hill Road, W.)

Mr. Robertson read his paper on Old Age Pensions. The arguments for O.A.P. are ethical & economic. Industrial producers are as much entitled to O.A.P. as soldiers, sailors, or civil servants. In the case of these latter the Pensions are due to collectivist humanity, & are an addition to their living wage.

The wages of agriculture & town laborers do not leave margin enough to provide for O.A.P., being barely a living wage & often below it, & skilled mechanics would have to diminish their own & their children's efficiency—not to mention unemployment & sickness.

The minimal sum needed is less than half of that wh: has been added recently to the national expenditure. The State already gives pensions to its highly paid servants whose employment is steadiest,—at the cost largely of the poor, whose pay is low & whose work is irregular.

Thrift ought to mean abstinence from work, & a wise distribution of expenditure, & ought to [be] distinguished from mere saving of money credits to be invested at interest.

Saving advantages the individual as against others, & is at present the only way of providing comfort for old age, but it injures the community for it curtails consumption & leads to glut & depression of trade. It encourages workers who are still employed to lessen the total of consumption & so of employment for themselves & others. Steady employment demands steady consumption wh: O.A.P. would greatly increase.

The worker should be encouraged not to save but to spend with security of O.A.P. & the increased employment & production would provide fields for taxation to pay their O.A.P.—Thus the process of equalising distribution—the Socialist ideal—would be assisted.

The richer classes & traders already save more than is needed for working capital.

Economic rent, railways, & banking, & insurance ought to be nationalised to raise revenue. O.A.P. would be the beginning of systematic Socialism.

Rigid limit of 65 will have to be relaxed, & superannuation substituted.

O.A.P. will have an opposite tendency to the old Poor Laws, & will not encourage reckless propagation as the present chaos does.

In the discussion wh: followed the following points were suggested:

That to ask for O.A.P. would be an indignity, specially if any enquiry were made into character.

That the country is ripe for them, & that they would stimulate savings—That pensions, like insurance can be done better by the State than by groups: that the age of 60 would be better than 65: that the wastrel class might be led by O.A.P. to look forward: that in France the proposed age is 55: that between 25 & 40 a man ought to spend freely on his children: that naval & military officers are not degraded by O.A.P.

Several speakers dwelt on the fallacy of saving from the point of view of the welfare of the community.

Richard Stapley

* * *

[96] On Wedn: March 1st 1905 the 96th Meeting of the Circle was held at 33 Bloomsb: Sq: at 8. p.m.

Present. (6) Mr. Stapley in the chair, Messrs. Crook, Harley, Hobson, McKillop, & Bullock.

Apologies for absence (7) Messrs. Alden, Byles, Matheson, Morrison, Parsons, Robertson, Walker.

Also absent. (13) Messrs. Adams, Lilley, M. Macdonald, R. Mac-Donald, Millin, Perris, Rea, Reeves, Rylett, Samuel, Walsh, Burrows, Branford.

The Minutes of last Meeting read & confirmed.

A letter was read from Mr. Reeves proposing to resign membership on account of health—The Secretary's reply asking him to retain his membership was approved.

Mr. McKillop read his paper on Municipal Financial Problems & Readjustment:

Taxation may be according to benefit received, as Rates for Electricity, Trams, Water, Gas &c—or according to ability to pay, as Income Tax &c.

The Income of a local authority is derived from

1. Rates on immovable property.
2. Grants in aid, from State.
3. Contributions from other local authorities.

The system of taxation should be simple & easily understood.

1. The rate on immovable property can be computed with certainty, & can be easily & economically collected. It is neither unjust nor inequitable.

2. Grants in aid, from State, are licence duties, portion of estate duties, & certain custom & excise duties. In these there is gratuitous complication & slovenly distribution.

3. Contributions from other local authorities are complicated & absurd: & in distribution the wealthier areas get most.

The total revenue of all local authorities is about 110 millions. All services are either—(1) purely national, as the army, navy &c wh: should be paid for by taxes: or (2) purely local as gas, water &c: wh: should be paid for by rates. or (3) partly national & partly local, as education, poor relief, police, roads, health &c: wh: should be paid partly by taxes & partly by rates: a permanent Commission should arrange the division of their expenses, the State should pay more than at present, & the locality less: & the locality should know how much it has to spend, & should keep within that amount.

The total rates in 58 county Boroughs vary to an astonishing degree. Norwich 82d in the £, Oldham 28d.

In the details there is an even greater difference:

Sewage, at Wigan 25d in £, Brighton 1d

Streets, at Stockport 21d in £, Bootle 4d
Police, at Liverpool 11d in £, Hastings 3d
Schools, at Halifax 20d in £, S. Helens 0d
  If judged by population, the differences are great:
Rates in Hastings are 25/- per head—Walsall 6/10 -
  The discussion wh: followed was of a conversational character.

Richard Stapley

* * *

[97] On Wedn: Ap: 5th 1905, the 97th Meeting of the Circle was held at 33 Bloomsbury Sq:, at 8 p.m.
  Present (14.) Mr. Stapley in the chair, Messrs. Adams, Crook, Hobson, Lilley, R. MacDonald, Matheson, Millin, Morrison, Perris, Rylett, Samuel, Walsh, and Bullock, also 3 Visitors.
  Apologies for absence (6.) Messrs. Alden, Byles, M: Macdonald, McKillop, Parsons, Walker -
  Also absent: (6.) Messrs. Harley, Rea, Reeves, Robertson, Burrows, Branford.
  Minutes of the last Meeting were read & confirmed.
  It was decided that the discussions of the next session should 'proceed on theoretical lines', and should deal with
  'Ethical principles underlying some political questions'.
  Mr. Hobson & Mr. R. MacDonald undertook to draft nine headings for discussion, & to submit them to the meeting on May 3rd.
  It was unanimously agreed to celebrate the 100th Meeting of the Circle, by holding a special social meeting in the latter half of June.
  Messrs. Stapley, Hobson, Crook, & Samuel consented to act as a Sub-Committee to arrange details. The suggestion of a Saturday to Monday Week-End in the country, June 24–26, was received with approval.
  Mr. Perris read his paper on National Finance. The first requisite is an honest, simple, & comprehensive statement of total revenue, expenditure, & indebtedness: the second is complete Parliamentary control, by means of a Committee, over every item of revenue as well as expenditure. This will be the more necessary if the State enters on constructive work by taking into its own hands manufactures, railways &c -
  Taxation should be simple, & imposed according to ability to bear it. Taxes on food press most heavily on the poor. Death duties were the first move in the right direction. Increased Income Tax on rich will be the second, & on monopolies, specially Public House licences.
  Improfitable, unproductive expenditure has increased under

Imperialism along with inefficiency waste & corruption. Army & Navy expenditure has more than doubled in 10 years, & is now 79 m:—The result—army scandals, army schemes, chaos, & threat of conscription. Greatest prodigality of all has been on the Navy: witness present 3 Power standard, & ships costing 36 m: sent to the scrapheap.

Public debt enormously increased by unproductive expenditure, & consols fallen from 114 to 88.

We need economy, & expenditure on a policy of construction & amelioration, instead of on unprofitable engines of destruction.

In the discussion it was urged that net Retrenchment was not desirable, but that expenditure should be wiser & more productive, and that indirect taxes should be reduced, & heavier taxes should be levied on large incomes, socially earned incomes & on land. The poorest are least able to shift taxation. 1/12 of a working class income goes to taxation.

Richard Stapley

* * *

[98] On Wednesday, May 3rd, 1905 the 98th Meeting of the Circle was held at 33 Bloomsbury Sq. at 8. p.m.

Present (11 Members) Mr. Stapley in the chair, Messrs. Alden, Crook, Harley, Hobson, McKillop, Matheson, Millin, Morrison, Walsh, Bullock, & two visitors.

Apologies for absence (7.) Messrs. Byles, M: Macdonald, R. Mac-Donald, Robertson, & Perris, Parsons, Burrows.

Also absent (8) Messrs. Adams, Lilley, Rea, Reeves, Rylett, Samuel, Walker, Branford.

Minutes of last Meeting read & confirmed.

Mr. J.O. Herdman, proposed by Mr. Crook, elected.

Discussion of subjects for next Session, deferred.

On the invitation of the chairman it was decided to hold the 100th Meeting of the Circle at his country residence on Sund: July 2nd.

In the absence of Mr. Parsons, through illness, the Sec: read his paper on 'The Transport Question'.

The Transport Question is really connected with the Fiscal Question. The Fabian Society has suggested a national Trading Fleet, a nationalization of Canals & Rails as a constructive counter-policy to 'Tariff Reform'.[87]

As regards Roads the Motor might be used as an adjunct to the Rail to convey goods to a[nd] from outlying villages.

[87] See Fabian Tract no. 116, *Fabianism and the Fiscal Question: An Alternative Policy* [by G. Bernard Shaw].

Great Britain is the only country, excluding Canada & U.S.A., wh: does not own or control part of its rails—& its rates for goods & passengers are highest in the world except Transvaal. In Belgium a great increase of traffic has followed the reduction of rates & fares. The import trade to England is well organised, but our internal trade, particularly in agriculture, is not. Collecting & packing small parcels is expensive, & railways in private hands have to make dividends every year, & cannot afford experiments.

Railway Act of 1844[88] witnesses to the possibility of the State purchasing the Rails: if the State does so, it will have value for its money, & profits enough to pay interest on the capital expended.

The increased expense of fair wages & hours for the real workers would be met by the abolishing of 3000 Directors, of 3000 clerks in the Clearing House & of wasteful competition. The State could afford to reduce rates to stimulate trade.

Canals might be nationalised first. This would lead to the greater cheapness & efficiency of rails. At present the Railway Interest is too powerful in Parliament.

In discussion the following points were suggested:

That the Great Central spent 12 m: with the aim of serving the public even at the cost of losing dividends—doubt was expressed by subsequent speakers on the chivalrous disinterestedness of the Great Central—that though the State ought to own the Rails, the present time is not opportune for purchase, as Electric traction is imminent.— that existing canals could certainly be improved & made more useful.

— that State control of rails is already carried far, & ought to be carried farther, in preference to purchase, except in case of Ireland.

— that railway rates are not really less in U.S.A. than in England — that free travel would help the housing question: that French roads are better than English—but English rails better than foreign: that railway nationalisation is no good unless land be nationalised as profits would go into landlord's pocket: that there should be one charge for freight regardless of distance, as penny post: that rails may become antiquated by increasing speed on roads & canals.

Richard Stapley

* * *

[99] On Wedn: June 7th 1905 the 99th Meeting of the Circle was held at 33 Bloomsbury Sq. at 8 p.m.

[88] Introduced by W.E. Gladstone to standardize railway legislation; the provision for state ownership was never taken up under the Act.

Present (13 members) Mr. Stapley in the chair, Messrs. Crook, Harley, Hobson, Lilley, M: Macdonald, R. MacDonald, McKillop, Matheson, Millin, Perris, Walker, Bullock.

Apologies for absence (3) Messrs. Morrison, Parsons, Samuel.

Also absent (10) Messrs. Alden, Adams, Byles, Rea, Reeves, Robertson, Walsh, Burrows, Branford, Herdman.

The resignation of Mr. Rylett was received with much regret.

In view of the absence of Mr. Burrows from all the meetings of the Circle it was resolved that it is desirable to transfer his name from the list of members to that of Visitors, & that he be written to accordingly. The list of subjects and readers for next Session was arranged.

Mr. Matheson read his paper on 'Housing and Land Tenure,' wh: he had kindly undertaken at short notice in the place of Mr. Rylett.

The evils of our present land system are
(1) Private ownership representing private theft.
(2) The rights of primogeniture.
(3) The evasion of fair contributions to public expenses along with exclusive enjoyment of advantages created by communal action.

There are many palliatives, but only one remedy: land nationalisation. Land differs from all other commodities in being indispensable & incapable of increase. Private property in land must be bought out. The basis should be the owner's valuation for taxation or purchase.— the price, perhaps 25 years purchase—i.e. 25 times the amount of the present net rental. This net rental is perhaps 100 mill: £ for 77 mill: acres. Land bonds might be issued for 2,500 mill £, the interest on wh: would be provided by the rents. Land should be revalued periodically, & would continue to increase in value about 2 p.c. per annum, & the land bonds would be wiped out in less than 50 years.

The present law enables bad landlord to rob good tenant, & bad tenant to rob good landlord.

Housing problem would be mitigated & rapid transit facilitated, & the unearned increment would go to the community. The caste system would be broken up, under wh: at present 1/200 of the people own 10/11 of the land.

With reference to palliatives: all the more moderate reforms would be equally opposed, and if carried would be mere tinkering: they may be grouped under the following:
(1) ownership of land.
(2) Land transfer.
(3) Relations of landlord & tenant.
(4) Power of local authorities to acquire land.
(5) Taxation of land values, mining rents & royalties.

Saving existing contracts all owners of land values mining rents &

royalties ought to pay rates, and all future increment in land values ought to accrue to the public.

In the discussion wh: followed, and wh: was unfortunately of a conversational character, the subject of the paper was soon overlooked, & an animated argument took place on whether the term capital could legitimately be applied to land.

Richard Stapley

* * *

[100] On Sunday, July 2. 1905, the 100th Meeting of the Circle was held, informally, at Mr. Stapley's country house in Sussex. A large number of members were present, & some ex-members & visitors. A silver bowl, subscribed for by the members, was presented to Mr. Stapley.

Richard Stapley

Note by H. Samuel, M.P.[89]

The Circle having been invited by Mr. Stapley to his country-house, The Farm, Horeham Road Sussex, from July 1st to 3rd 1905, the hundredth meeting was held there on Sunday July 2nd. There were present—(19 Members) Mr. Stapley, in the chair, and Messrs. Adams, Alden, Byles, Crook, Harley, Hobson, Lilley, Murray Macdonald, Ramsay MacDonald, McKillop, Millin, Parsons, Perris, Russell Rea, Robertson, Samuel, Walker, Walsh; also Messrs. Burrows and Hammond (visitors).

After a few words from the Chairman, Mr. Burrows expressed on behalf of the Circle their gratitude to Mr. Stapley for a most delightful visit, and the esteem, friendship and affection with which all the members regarded him. He associated Mrs. Stapley also with this expression of their goodwill. In celebration of the 100th meeting, he presented to Mr. Stapley, on behalf of the Circle, a silver bowl suitably inscribed.

Mr. Stapley responded.

Subsequently, Mr. Murray Macdonald moved and Mr. Samuel seconded, a resolution that each paper read during the ensuing session should conclude with a resolution embodying the principle on which the writer had proceeded. After some discussion this was carried by 8 to 3.

---

[89] With some corrections in Bullock's handwriting.

The Circle also passed a vote of sympathy to Mr. Matheson in his illness.

There being no further business, the Circle adjourned.

* * *

Twelfth Session, 1905–6.

[101] On Wedn: Oct: 4th 1905 the 101st Meeting of the Circle was held at 33 Bloomsbury Sq. w.c.

Present (17 members out of 24) Mr. Stapley in the chair, Messrs. Adams, Byles, Crook, Harley, Herdman, Lilley, M. Macdonald, R. MacDonald, McKillop, Matheson, Millin, Parsons, Perris, Samuel, Walker, and Bullock. also 1 Visitor & Mr. Burrows.

Apologies for absence (2) Messrs. Hobson & Robertson.

Also absent. (5) Messrs. Alden, Morrison, Rea, Reeves, and Walsh.

Minutes of the two last meetings read & confirmed. Mr. Samuel was asked to add a descriptive note on the 100th Meeting.

Accounts for past Session read & accepted.

The Secretary reported that the largest attendances had been 14 in Dec: & Apr: the least 6 in March. Average—11.

The attendances of members were as follows.

9 out of 9 meetings. Messrs. Stapley & Bullock.

8	”	Mr. Hobson.
7	”	Messrs. Crook & Harley.
6	”	Mr. Matheson.
5	”	Messrs. R. MacDonald, McKillop & Parsons.
4	”	Messrs, Alden, Morrison, Perris, & Walker.
3	”	Messrs. Adams, Lilley, Macdonald, Millin, Walsh
2	”	Messrs. Rea, Robertson, & Samuel.
1	”	Mr. Byles.
0	”	Mr. Reeves, who had been ill. Mr.

Herdman, elected in May, & Mr. Branford.

Mr. Stapley & Mr. Bullock were unanimously reelected Chairman & Hon: Sec:

Messrs. Crook, Harley, Hobson, Lilley, R. MacDonald, & McKillop, were unanimously reelected to the Committee.

Mr. Branford's resignation was received.

It was decided that the paper on Racial Problems should be read by Mr. Olivier, Mr. Reeves or Mr. Samuel.

Mr. Hobson's paper[90] was read by the Hon: Sec:

Many analogies or metaphors are used in describing the political constitution, as a building, a machine, or a tree, so the social constitution can be pictured as a sea, a machine, a crystal, or a chemical compound as by Huxley, or better as a biological organism.

Society is a structure, the relations between whose parts are determined by an internal principle of growth. Is this structure physical, psychical, or both?

The human body is a Society of living cells.

Anthills & Beehives may be called organisms. As a physical organism Society is of a low grade like the Protozoa.

Those who regard Society as psychical speak of it sometimes as an organism, i.e. having an end of its own, sometimes only as organised, i.e. subserving the ends of its members. This latter view seems inadequate.

There is no reason why the term organism may not be applied in a spiritual as well as in a material sense.

The evolution of Society is a psycho-physical process. Society is certainly organic, but can we rightly also call it an organism?

If so, each of us is a cell in a number of different organisms, a church, a party, a school of thought, a nation, or humanity at large.

The recognition of the organic nature of Society is impaired by the gross mal adjustment of its parts. In this it is far below the hive or anthill.

The economic solidarity of human society is better developed than its political solidarity; & its moral or conscious solidarity is least developed of all. Human Society is of low structure & defective functioning.

The subsequent discussion equally ignored the resolution, wh: was to have been the subject of both paper & debate.[91] The following were some of the views maintained:

That Society is not an organism:

That changes of organisation change the ends of individuals:

That man undoubtedly differs much from a cell:

That someday Humanity will be an organism, & nations will be organs:

That Justice is alterable by the individual:

That Society is a living thing:

---

[90] 'To What Type of Organisation does Society Correspond?'

[91] The resolution, as printed in the programme, was: 'That the formulation and the attainment of the individual end involves the prior formulation and attainment of the social end'.

On the other hand that Society is more like a chemical or mechanical organism:

Again that Society not only is an organism, but is something more: but again that Society is a communism of individuals & not a mere aggregation:

and, lastly, that the subject is impractical and unprofitable.

Richard Stapley

* * *

[102] On Wedn: Nov: 1st 1905 the 102nd Meeting of the Circle was held at 33 Bloomsbury Sq. at 8. p.m.

Present (14 members out of 25) Mr. Stapley in the chair, Messrs. Crook, Harley, Herdman, Lilley, R: MacDonald, McKillop, Matheson, Millin, Parsons, Robertson, Walker, Burrows, Bullock. Also 2. Visitors.

Apologies for absence. (3) Messrs. Byles M: Macdonald, Walsh.

Also absent (8) Adams, Alden, Hobson, Morrison, Perris, Rea, Reeves, & Samuel.

The Minutes of the last meeting read & confirmed.

Mr. Burrows was elected a member for the third time. (Note— erased for non-attendance Oct: 14. 1903, elected 2nd time, Oct: 5. 1904, erased for non attendance June 7. 1905).

Mr. Olivier's consent was announced to read a paper on 'Racial Problems' on March 7th 1906.

Mr. Harley read his paper on 'To what type of organisation does Society correspond?'

Sociologists may be classed as—(1) Biological:

(2) Dualistic, Psychological, & Metaphysical:

(3) Classificatory.

Class I traces from Menenius Agrippa,[92] & deduces Society from a primitive horde.

There is much in the psychological view to supplement the Biological. The Classificatory is the most suggestive school of sociologists.

At the summit of the sociological scale stand the political institutions & the tissues of ethical ideas.

What then is Sociology? It is mainly a question about names. Once

---

[92] (Fictitious) Roman consul who in 494 B.C. became renowned for appeasing the plebians through the parable of 'the belly and the limbs'—an early organic analogy— and who features in Shakespeare's *Coriolanus* with that analogy.

begin to classify & it is seen that Sociology is not formless or disconnected.

In the Social organism growth is less limited, changes are more various, & interdependence is closer, than in a biological organism.

Society is a super organism.

Mr. Harley concluded by stating that he agreed with the resolution which was formally before the Circle.

In the discussion it was contended:

That organism is a useful metaphor, but not true in strict scientific sense: that persons can truthfully be called parasitic, but not absolutely parasites: that Sociology ought to be regarded historically.

That in the resolution the word 'prior' does refer to time, & that the ideas of 'Ends' is a fallacy.

On the other hand that 'prior' is logical, & not temporal in this case; that the individual end is always part of a larger social end, & that one individual is greater than others in proportion as he forefeels the needs of society.

That a deeper intent ought to be given to the term 'organism'. That if Society is the highest organism, it is in a low state of development or evolution.

Richard Stapley

* * *

[103] On Wed: Dec: 6th 1905 the 103rd Meeting of the Circle was held at 33 Bloomsbury Sq. at 8. p.m.

Present. 15 members out of 25. Mr. Stapley in the chair, Messrs. Byles, Crook, Harley, Herdman, Lilley, R. MacDonald, Matheson, Millin, Morrison, Parsons, Walker, Walsh, Burrows, Bullock.

Apologies for absence. 3. Messrs. McKillop, M: Macdonald, Perris.

Also absent. 7. Messrs. Adams, Alden, Hobson, Rea, Reeves, Robertson, Samuel.

Minutes of last Meeting, read & confirmed.

The January meeting was cancelled.

With Mr. Crook's approval it was decided to ask Mr. Robertson to read his paper on Feb: 7.

Mr. J.R. MacDonald then read his paper on 'The Organisation of Industry':

Production, exchange, & consumption are operations of the social function. To some small degree, even now, each works for all & all for each: even the capitalist seeks to discover & satisfy the needs of men in general.

Unemployment & unequal distribution of wealth result from this social function of industry being managed for private profit. It is the consuming community wh: employs both capital & labor.

Land, capital, & labor are the three factors of production. The owner of each exacts from the owners of the others a toll, measured not by the value of his service, but by the intensity of the need wh: the others have of what he can supply:

Land is a complete natural monopoly:

Capital is often almost an economic monopoly:

Labor is as plentiful as blackberries:

Hence the present condition of high rents, high profits & interest, low intermittent subsistence wages. These three factors are dissociated by private ownership, instead of being co-ordinated as are the tissues in a biological organism.

The present mal distribution of wealth can never be corrected until the community controls the three factors of production, in the interests of all: at least as regards the great industries wh: supply the common needs.

At present the artistic workshop supplies the individual needs of a few, but even this will become more social in the future when the State will employ the artistic craftsman, & will not compel him, as now, to haggle over his creations in order to obtain his sustenance.

In the discussion wh: followed it was urged—

That the idea of socialism crushing individuality is a mere bogey, as regimentation will give greater freedom:

again, that if material life be socialised, ideas & artistic creation will be free as they are not now:

that individuality sacrificed for the benefit of the community is not lost, but saved & ennobled.

that the achievements of any great individual are largely the result of numerous activities of others wh: the State, or Society, has placed at his disposal.

On the other hand it was objected that the biological conception leads us only into a morass: & that all progress is the work of individuals, & never of societies.

Richard Stapley

* * *

[104] On Wedn: Feb: 7th 1906, the 104th Meeting of the Circle was held at 33 Bloomsbury Sq: at 8. p.m.

Present: (14 members out of 25.) Mr. Stapley in the chair, Messrs. Adams, Alden, Harley, Herdman, Hobson, Lilley, McKillop, Matheson, Millin, Parsons, Robertson, Walker, Bullock—also 5 Visitors.

Apologies for absence (6). Messrs. Byles, Crook, M: Macdonald, R. MacDonald, Morrison, Burrows.

Also absent (5.) Messrs Perris, Rea, Reeves, Samuel, Walsh.

Minutes of last meeting read & confirmed.

A letter was read from Mr. Samuel, asking to be released from reading a paper in May.[93]

It was resolved to ask Mr. Crook to take the vacant date.

The following Resolution was unanimously adopted.

'The Rainbow Circle heartily congratulates its Eight members on their success in obtaining seats in the House of Commons at the recent General Election, while it earnestly hopes that they will still be mindful to give—& perhaps occasionally to receive—inspiration on the first Wedn: in each month at the Meetings of the Circle.'

The Chairman invited the members of the Circle to dine with him at the N[ational] L[iberal] C[lub] on the 7th of March to celebrate the above return.

Mr. Robertson read his paper on 'The State in relation to Property':

Even under Socialism the State would recognise private property. Conditions under wh: the State may appropriate part of the property of any of its members to its collective use:

1. That the *purpose* is the good of the community.
2. That the *extent* is, in theory, as far as the purpose is served, but, in practise [*sic*], as far only as the patience of citizens will extend.
3. That the *rules* of taxation accord with the current political ethic.

Taxation must be in proportion to ability to pay, & must minimise friction, wh: is social loss.

J.S. Mill objected to graduated income tax, as discouraging work & saving, & preferred death duties & legacy duties: but it may be replied that the miser should not be encouraged, & that taxes ought to promote consumption, because consumption more than anything else promotes production.

A theoretic minimum income, representing what is necessary to sustain life, should not be taxed: Luxuries should be, as tobacco & alcohol. Customs wh: raise the price of necessaries are harmful.

Income Tax cannot be differentiated as between Bachelors & Parents, but is rightly differentiated between small incomes & larger, & should be more so. It should also discriminate in favour of earned as against unearned incomes.

With regard to Land Values—as the State has always permitted

---

[93] The programme listed Samuel's paper as 'The State and the Family.'

investment in land it should not attempt to confiscate past unearned increment, but may rightly confiscate from a present or future point. The 'Tax & Buy' proposal is fair & wise.

Taxation can, at best, but roughly equalise burdens: there are bound to be inequalities.

Beyond this, the progress will be towards Socialism, all means of production for economic ends being socialised. Already we have seen that, in industry, the State has first regulated private employment, & has then afterwards extended public employment.

The discussion wh: followed shewed an almost entire agreement with the paper: a few points were suggested:

That capital might be accumulated by the State, & lent to private enterprise:

That where anyone creates value society co-operates in this creating, & may claim to take its share: whatever portion of income is due to the individual factor should of course be left to him:

That in the 'Tax & Buy' proposal, there will be need to have a Public Valuer.

The idea that the tenant eventually pays the taxes on a property was affirmed & denied.

Richard Stapley

* * *

[105] On Wedn: March 7th 1906 the 105th Meeting of the Circle was held at the National Liberal Club.

It was preceded by a dinner at the N.L.C. to which Mr. Stapley, the Chairman, invited all the members of the Circle, to commemorate the election of Eight of their number to seats in the House of Commons—namely Messrs. Alden, Byles, Murray Macdonald, R: MacDonald, Rea, Robertson, Samuel, & Walker.[94] 23 out of 25 members of the Circle were present. Mr. Adams sent a telegram of apology on account of illness. Mr. Burrows was absent.

5 guests ex members of the Circle were also present—Messrs. Grant, Hills, Olivier, Roskill & Trevelyan.[95]

The Chairman proposed the health of the Eight Members of Parliament & Mr. R. MacDonald responded, and proposed the Chairman's health wh: was received with acclamation.

---

[94] Although Gooch was also returned to Parliament, he did not take up the Rainbow Circle place to which he had been elected in February 1905 until re-elected in 1909.

[95] C.P. Trevelyan was also (re)elected M.P. in 1906, though he had resigned his Circle place in November 1901.

Mr. Olivier read his paper on 'Racial Problems'.[96]

Is it not an assumption to speak of the 'function of race differences in the growth of humanity,' as though this growth were a final cause: again, has not the so-called 'Right to satisfy appetite' been the chief motive in almost all interferences, rather than any ethical idea? Race is simply a method in wh: life & energy have manifested themselves. There is no evidence of design in race differences.

All men have fundamental identity: their distinctions have been caused by the conditions into wh: life has forced them. Conquered races are sometimes more spiritual & artistic than their conquerors, and savage races have sometimes a higher code of conduct in certain departments than civilized proletariats.

If one man has command over the services of another of the same race he often abuses it, & the dangers are enhanced by racial differences.

Color-prejudice has increased of late in the southern States of U.S.A. & in S. Africa, simultaneously with the development of capitalist manufacturing industry. The lower race is often said to be only fit for slavery wh: is disguised under the name of discipline. In Nigeria, where there is no such industry, Great Britain is abolishing slavery. The economic intercourse of higher and lower races has lead, & must always lead, to the destruction of much that is good in each race.

Mr. Walker was invited to speak of his experience in Africa & West Indies: He contended that Mohamedanism was better suited to West Africa than Christianity as it accepts polygamy: that the Jamaican constitution is unsatisfactory & hybrid: Barbados is a white oligarchy: the negroes often will not vote: the elective system is unsuitable to colored races. All laws relating to colored races, in the self-gov: colonies, should be reserved for the Crown.

Mr. McKillop mentioned that formerly the Chinese in the Straits Settlements used to be regarded with good humoured toleration: now that their wealth is increasing & that an economic struggle seems beginning between whites & yellows they are regarded with strong hostility. In the general discussion it was suggested that the worst crimes of dominant white minorities are caused by the fear of the numerical preponderance of the lower race: that imperialism really means the claim of an advanced nation to exploit the land or resources of less advanced nations, that in South Africa & south of U.S.A. the exploiting white minority is parasitic, & that intermarriage is the only solution:

on behalf of our colonists it was urged that their morality varies as in England & is not lower on the whole: that native races ought to be

[96] The views in this talk were developed by Olivier in his book published later in the year (S. Olivier, *White Capital and Coloured Labour* [London, 1906]).

debarred from drink & gunpowder, & have land-reservations & education—that patriarchal government is best for them, as they are not yet fit for democracy: that they should be under the protection of a High Commissioner, & not under the Colonial Government.

Richard Stapley

* * *

[106] The 106th Meeting of the Circle was held at 33 Bloomsbury Sq. on Apr: 4th 1906, at 8. p.m.

Present. (14 out of 25) Mr. Stapley in the chair, Messrs. Adams, Byles, Crook, Harley, Herdman, Lilley, McKillop, Matheson, Millin, Perris, Robertson, Walker, Walsh, & one Visitor.

Apologies for absence. (3) Messrs. Bullock, M. Macdonald, R: MacDonald.

Also absent: (8) Messrs. Alden, Hobson, Morrison, Parsons, Rea, Reeves, Samuel, Burrows.

Minutes of last Meeting read & confirmed.

The question of subjects for next Session was discussed, & Mr. Robertson was asked to bring up a scheme at the next Meeting for the discussion of English Statesmen of 19th century—their development, career, & character.

No conclusion was come to on a proposal to change the evening for meeting to Friday:

Mr. Perris' paper on 'International Relationship[s]' was read:

Discussion:

Armed peace has its uses. It operates not in favor of but against war. It is in favor of international force. Life is the release in the conflict of opposing ideals, as seen, for instance, in the reaction against Individualism, exemplified in Socialism, High Churchism, Imperialism &c. Armed peace is a standing example of the horrors of war in embryo. We are really approximating to internationalism, e.g. the Postal Union. A thorough revision of the principles of evolution is necessary.

The idea that force must persist is in the main due to a fundamentally wrong view of evolution. The fatality of life is the struggle for the means of livelihood. The governing fact of life is the pressure of life or environment. There is an absolute contrast between Empire & democratic development.

Armed peace is absolutely different from perpetual peace. The Hague Conference ought to be political, & periodic. Education leads to the accentuation, & not to the removal of differences. Internationalism cannot lead to the abolition of War.

All energy arises out of conflict—Energy does not arise out of conflict, but expends itself in conflict.

Economic pressure now makes for peace, as does militarism, by its economic pressure. As a result of this pressure, Socialism will develope first in Europe, & of European countries first in France. It was alike asserted that force is, & that it is not at the back of all treaties.

It was affirmed & denied that nationalism is opposed to internationalism. Nowaday teachers of modern language attack their duties in a new way—children do not learn grammar, but sing the 'Marseillaise.'

Richard Stapley

* * *

[107] The 107th Meeting of the Circle was held on May 2nd 1906, at 33 Bloomsbury Sq: at 8. p.m.

Present. (13 Members out of 25.) Mr. Stapley in the chair, Messrs. Byles, Crook, Harley, Herdman, Lilley, M: Macdonald, McKillop, Matheson, Millin, Parsons, Walsh, & Bullock, & 3. Visitors.

Apologies for absence (5) Alden, Burrows, R. MacDonald, Robertson, & Walker.

Also absent (7.) Adams, Hobson, Morrison, Perris, Rea, Reeves, Samuel.

Minutes of last Meeting were read & confirmed. 1st Friday in the month was chosen for meetings next session. Date of next meeting changed to May 30.

List of nine Prime Ministers was settled for discussion next Session. Names of readers were suggested, & Sec: empowered to make arrangements.

Mr. Crook read his paper on Organisation of National Politics:

The Republic of Plato sketches a would-be perfect commonwealth, regardless of practicability. Guardian class to govern, auxiliary to fight, the rest producers of material commodities. Justice would flourish by each class minding its own business. His Ideal was aristocratic, & completely socialistic. His Society, a nest of human ants. Contrast, with this, Herbert Spencer's forecast. If wars can be permanently prevented social amelioration & equitable institutions will follow whether by public regulation or voluntary co-operation.[97]

The English State, like Topsy, 'growed', & is an organism. In home industries our present tendency is towards increased State regulation. So, too, as regards Property, Army, & Police. But in legislative &

[97] See, e.g., H. Spencer, *The Study of Sociology* (London, 1907 edn.), pp. 192–5.

executive work the modern tendency is towards individualism. Specially so in the domain of the family. The lunatic, diseased, deformed, & degenerate are carefully preserved, & generally allowed to propagate. State infliction of euthanasia for the unfit; or even segregation is almost unthought of. Modern humanitarianism nullifies the result of that law of survival of the fittest, wh: works so mercilessly for the individual & so mercifully for the race, in all the organic world below the human species.

In education we are becoming more socialistic, in religion more individualistic. Industry ought to be organised by the State, & unearned increment taken by it. All men & women, perhaps children, ought to have votes. Segregation of unfit is desirable. Let us have Socialism for all that concerns the organic side of human nature, & individualism for the supra organic. In the political world it is a question whether the apparent leaders control the movements, or whether the movements control the leaders.

In the discussion it was suggested:
That in view of the development of women's work many women might go on working, & have foster mothers to look after their children:
That representation ought to be of classes, & not territorial: that children's votes might be limited to those who work: that modern Socialism aims at developing the individual, & so differs from Platonic Socialism: that it is important to organise moderate thinkers.

The possibility of the public conscience differing from the private conscience specially in the matter of dealing with imbeciles & degenerates was affirmed as beyond question & denied as novel & immoral.

Richard Stapley

* * *

[108] The 108th Meeting of the Circle was held on Wed: May 30th 1906, at 8. p.m. at 33 Bloomsbury Sq:
Present. (14 Members out of 25) Mr. Stapley, in the chair, Messrs. Alden, Crook, Harley, Herdman, Hobson, Lilley, McKillop, Matheson, Millin, Parsons, Walsh, Burrows, & Bullock, also 4. Visitors.

Apologies for absence (2) from Messrs. M: Macdonald & Robertson.

Also absent (9) Messrs. Adams, Byles, R: MacDonald, Morrison, Perris, Rea, Reeves, Samuel, Walker.

Minutes of last Meeting read & confirmed.

Mr. Cloudesley Brereton was proposed for membership by Mr. Walsh. His election was deferred to the Oct: meeting.

The Syllabus for next Session was completed.

Mr. Lilley read his paper on 'The State in relation to Religion & Education.'

As long as Socialism endeavoured to connect itself with Christianity it remained nebulous & a mere sentiment. Marx gave concreteness to the Socialist ideal. Thought, including religion, must be free from forced control. Religion lives in a region of feeling & aspiration wh: must be profoundly individual if it is to be real at all. Yet religion & thought are social things for they witness to realities wh:, if they exist at all, exist for all men.

This explains all dogmatism. Theology is practically dead, because thought about the content & conditions of religious experience has been unduly organised from without.

The less complex is the object of knowledge, the more complete will be the statement of truth about it. The individual machine needs direction & organisation from without. The State ought to furnish to all children every opportunity of approach to the accumulated stores of knowledge.

The growing separation of actual religious societies from the State is good.

The agreement of the majority of laymen to the simple Bible teaching, wh: has worked well for 35 years, is a step towards the socialisation of Religion.

In the discussion it was suggested that it is outside the State's sphere to instruct in art, or maintain a national theatre: that Socialists are religious at heart, desiring to set free man's higher nature: that all citizens, & not the parent only, are concerned about a child's religion: that the essence of education is formation of character: that in the spiritual sphere any organisation is fatal.

Richard Stapley

* * *

Thirteenth Session 1906–07

[109] The 109th Meeting of the Circle was held on Friday 5th October 1906 at 8. p.m. at 33 Bloomsbury Square.

Present (12 Members out of 25). Mr. Stapley in the chair, Messrs: Alden, Bullock, Burrows, Crook, Herdman, Lilley, McKillop, Matheson, Millin, Parsons & Walsh.

Apologies for absence (2) Messrs: Byles & Murray Macdonald.

Also absent Messrs: Adams, Harley, Hobson, Ramsay MacDonald, Morrison, Perris, Rea, Reeves, Robertson, Samuel and Walker.

Minutes of the last meeting were read & confirmed.

Accounts for the past session were read & accepted.

The Secretary reported that the attendance of members had been as follows:

8 out of 8 Messrs:	Stapley, Harley, Herdman, Lilley, Matheson & Millin.
7 out of 8 Messrs:	Bullock, Crook, McKillop & Parsons
6 out of 8	Mr. Walker
5 out of 8 Messrs:	Byles & Walsh
4 out of 8 Messrs:	Ramsay MacDonald, Robertson & Burrows
3 out of 8 Messrs:	Adams, Alden, Hobson, Murray Macdonald & Perris
2 out of 8 Messrs:	Morrison & Samuel
1 out of 8 Messrs:	Rea & Reeves.

Mr. Bullock who had held the Secretaryship for six years tendered his resignation with firm insistence. A cordial vote of thanks for his past services was carried unanimously.

Mr. Stapley was re-elected Chairman

Mr. Parsons was elected Secretary

Mr. Bullock was elected on to the Committee in place of Mr. Ramsay MacDonald. The Committee thus consists of Messrs: Crook, Harley, Hobson, Lilley, McKillop & Bullock and the Chairman & Secretary ex officio.

Mr. Cloudesley Brereton, proposed for membership by Mr. Walsh, was unanimously elected.

Mr. Alden, having been unable owing to pressure of work to prepare his promised paper on Earl Grey Mr. Bullock & Mr. Crook kindly opened the discussion.

Mr. Bullock said that Grey[98] marked the introduction of democratic reform of national representation & freedom of speech. He was the last great Whig orator & represented a Whiggism that was tinged with popular sympathies. He opposed the war with France, & indeed Pitt's war policy generally. When in due time he took his place in the House of Lords his attitude was one of consistent, though not exactly enthusiastic, protest against reaction. His dignity, moderation, personal integrity & high-mindedness gained him confidence and enabled him at last to carry through the Reform Bill of 1832 with wh his name will always be associated. That Bill was carried in spite of the violent opposition of the Lords & the Crown. Grey will be remembered not

---

[98] Charles Grey, 2nd Earl (1764–1845). Whig statesman and prime minister 1830–34.

only for the Reform Act itself, but for the fact that in his conduct of it he insisted on the principle now recognised as constitutional, that the Crown must give way to the will of the Commons. The second principle, namely, that the Lords must similarly give way is unfortunately not so well established even now, but Grey did much towards paving the way for its acceptance.

Mr. Crook expressed the hope that the Statesmen who form the subjects of the present session's discussions will be considered not personally but rather from the point of view of the great unconscious forces of wh they were the exponents. The Reform Act was supposed to be the life work of Grey, but it must be remembered also that he bodied forth the first great protest against the reactionary principles of Pitt, who left to English politics two very evil legacies, namely, the suggestion of an alliance with decadent Turkey, and the opposition to Irish aspirations. Grey was by no means a republican, but he was not shocked at the French people's setting up a republic. His firm belief in Freedom is his greatest claim to fame.

In the general discussion wh followed it was suggested that Grey's moderation was one of his best points: that the result of the influence of the French Revolution on the younger spirits in England was to create a new kind of Whiggism, with, as its fine[st] flower Grey: that this Whiggism was effectual by reason of the popular feeling behind it & that the Crown, the House of Lords & the Church were stronger now than at any time during the last century: and that there is an analogy between the attitude of the Lords towards the Reform Act and their present attitude towards the Education Bill.

Richard Stapley   Chairman

2nd Nov 1906

* * *

[110] The 110th Meeting of the Circle was held on Friday 2nd Nov. 1906 at 8 p.m. at 33 Bloomsbury Square

Present. (12 members out of 25) Mr. Stapley in the chair, Messrs: Brereton, Bullock, Burrows, Byles, Crook, Harley, Herdman, Lilley, Matheson, Millin, & Parsons.

Apologies for absence (3) Murray Macdonald, McKillop & Robertson.

Also absent (10) Messrs: Adams, Alden, Hobson, Ramsay MacDonald, Morrison, Perris, Rea, Reeves, Samuel & Walsh.

Minutes of the last meeting were read & confirmed.

A letter from Mr. Walker announcing his resignation was read.

Mr. Harley read his paper on 'Lord Melbourne'.

Lord Melbourne[99] the son of Sir Peniston Lamb, later created Viscount Melbourne was the 'quintessential extract of mediocrity'. Politics in his days being a matter of nice family arrangement, he went into Parliament as member for Leominster in 1805 and sided with the Whigs, but gradually drifted in the direction of Canning who with his friends had made a compact cave among the tories. When Canning became Prime Minister, Melbourne took office as Chief Secretary to the Lord Lieutenant of Ireland. This position, wh he filled with some success, he continued to hold under Lord Goderich & for a time under Wellington: but finally in 1831 he returned to the Whig fold, taking office as Home Secretary under Earl Grey. When Grey resigned Melbourne became Prime Minister. In this capacity his great experience of men, coupled with the fact that he had few opinions of his own, stood him in good stead. He bowed to the inevitable, reformed municipal corporations, abolished the tax on knowledge, & faced the question of secularising the surplus property of the Irish Church. It was the strength of Melbourne that to him all policies might be equally true as all might be equally false.

In the discussion wh followed it was suggested that Melbourne by his opportunism & acquiescence laid the foundations of sound legislation by stronger men: that the successful way in wh he played the forces of Radicalism wh suspected him & of Toryism wh detested him was quite inspiring as a piece of political jugglery: but that his best work was to be found in his remarkable training of Queen Victoria in sound constitutional principles. On the other hand it was asserted that his good influence with Victoria had been greatly exaggerated— and even that that influence might be regarded as not good at all, in that it tended to the strengthening of the Crown and retarded the Republican movement.

Richard Stapley   Chairman

7th Dec 1906

* * *

[111] The 111th Meeting of the Circle was held on Friday 7th Dec 1906 at 8 p.m. at 33 Bloomsbury Sq. wc.

Present (10 members out of 25). Mr. Stapley in the chair, Messrs: Bullock, Burrows, Crook, Harley, Herdman, Lilley, Millin, Parsons & Walsh—Also one visitor—Mr. Hammond.

[99] William Lamb, 2nd Viscount Melbourne (1779–1848). Whig statesman and prime minister 1834, 1835–41.

Apologies for absence (5) from Messrs: Byles, McKillop, Matheson, Morrison & Robertson.

Also absent. Messrs: Adams, Alden, Brereton, Hobson, Murray Macdonald, Ramsay MacDonald, Perris, Rea, & Samuel.

Minutes of the last meeting were read & confirmed.

Mr. Rylett, proposed by Mr. Bullock, was unanimously re-elected to membership of the Circle.

It was proposed by Mr. Bullock & carried unanimously that in future the time of meeting should be 8.15 instead of 8.0.

Mr. Millin read his paper on Sir Robert Peel.[100] He said that Sir Robert Peel's apparent abandonment of the principles wh he had professed & on wh he had built up a great party, must be regarded in the light of his high & upright character. He was an exceedingly clever & able man brought up in Tory surroundings, on Tory principles & with Tory prejudices, & was launched on his political career at a very early age. He was made Chief Secretary for Ireland at the age of 24 & was from the first an opponent to Catholic claims. Yet it was on the question of Catholic emancipation that he first gave grave offence to his party by his bill of 1829.[101] He was even then opposed, though less bigotedly to the principles of his own bill, but he was statesman enough to recognise that the measure was absolutely necessary. His next tergiversation was in connection with his Bank Charter Act,[102] but this was a case of genuine conversion. As soon as he was compelled to study the financial question he saw the error of his early prejudices. His conversion to the Repeal of the Corn Laws was brought about very similarly. He became convinced of the economic necessity for cheap food from abroad, & he sacrificed his political position in order to pass his bill of 1842.[103] Mr. Millin concluded his paper by a consideration of the liberalising influence of Peel's policy on Toryism & of the reverse effect it had on Liberalism. He also suggested that if Peel cd have introduced Co-operation as applied to agriculture he wd have gone down to posterity as the most daring & original reformer of modern times.

In the discussion it was suggested

1. That the great statesmanship of Peel, legislating honestly & fearlessly for the needs of the moment was in part due to his lack of political foresight, but that as he sacrificed peace & power for the good of the nation his opportunism was very different from that of Melbourne.

[100] Sir Robert Peel (1788–1850). Tory statesman, prime minister 1834, 1841–46.
[101] The Catholic Emancipation Act of 1829.
[102] Enacted in 1844, which attempted to regulate currency and credit, especially paper money.
[103] A new Corn Law, also reducing duties on 769 imported articles.

2. That the Bank Charter Act was an absurd & futile measure, instituting an unjust monopoly in the Bank of England.
3. That the Bank Charter Act had put our finances on a comparatively sound basis
4. That Co-operation was not a panacea, & would be quite inadequate to deal with the spread of Trusts & Corporations
5. That the later prosperity of England was largely due to Peel's sound economics, developed by his greatest disciple—Gladstone.

Richard Stapley   Chairman

4 Jan. 1907

* * *

[112] The 112th Meeting of the Circle was held on Friday 4th Jan. 1907 at 33 Bloomsbury Sq:

Present. (12 members out of 26) Mr Stapley in the chair, Messrs: Bullock, Crook, Harley, Herdman, Hobson, Lilley, Matheson, Millin, Parsons, Rea, & Rylett: also Mr. Roskill an old member.

Apologies for absence (8) from Messrs: Alden, Byles, Murray Macdonald, Ramsay MacDonald, McKillop, Robertson, Samuel & Walsh.

Also absent. Messrs: Adams, Brereton, Burrows, Morrison, Perris & Reeves.

Minutes of the previous meeting were read & confirmed.

It was resolved that the Circle should have a Dinner on the 21st June 1907, at the National Liberal Club and that a circular should be sent at an early date giving notice of the event to all members & to those former members who took an active interest in the Circle.

It was announced that Mr. Byles had promised to read the paper on Russell on 1st March.

Mr. Herdman read his paper on Lord Aberdeen.[104] He gave a biographical sketch of Lord Aberdeen's career, laying special stress on his wise & tactful statesmanship as Minister for Foreign Affairs— a post for wh his prolonged travels on the Continent & his personal acquaintance with Foreign Governments specially fitted him. Lord Aberdeen was the greatest advocate for peace that had held high office for 150 years. His qualities were particularly shewn in that he not only prevented war with France over the Tahiti affair,[105] but later established the 'entente cordiale' with that country, Guizot[106] being

[104] George Hamilton Gordon, 4th Earl of Aberdeen (1784–1860). Statesman, foreign secretary, prime minister 1852–5.

[105] Of 1844, in connection with French attempts to establish a protectorate in Tahiti.

[106] François Guizot (1787–1874). French statesman and historian.

foreign minister there: also in that he successfully arranged the Treaty of Washington 1842[107] & the Oregon Treaty 1845.[108] The ministry wh he formed, against his will, in 1852 was unfortunate in that it was responsible for the Crimean War. In all his political ideals Lord Aberdeen was a true liberal.

Mr. Herdman went on to contrast the liberalism of Lord Aberdeen's time with that of the present day to the disparagement of the latter. He also briefly surveyed the relative positions of the Great Powers at the time of Lord Aberdeen's birth & death respectively, & reviewed the British Legislation of that period. He also contrasted the ideals of individualism & collectivism & touched upon many questions including the Law of Periodicity as applied to Sociology, & the Freedom of the will.

In the discussion wh followed it was suggested that a brilliant man is not required at the Foreign Office; that Lord Aberdeen's chance of living in history was in connection with the wicked & disastrous Crimean war: and that Lord Aberdeen had a most beneficial quieting effect upon the country, disturbed as it was by the events of 1848.

One member was understood to criticise Lord Aberdeen's amiability on the score of a like quality displayed by his descendant towards that member on a certain Pleasant Sunday Afternoon. Another member objected that the amiability of the present Lord Aberdeen could hardly be counted as a fault against his illustrious predecessor.

Richard Stapley   Chairman

1st Feby 1907

* * *

[113] The 113th Meeting of the Circle was held on Friday 1st Feb. 1907 at 33 Bloomsbury Sq.

Present (10 members out of 26) Mr. Stapley in the chair, Messrs: Bullock, Byles, Crook, Herdman, Lilley, Matheson, Morrison, Parsons & Rylett: also 2 visitors Messrs: Elder & Hammond.

Apologies for absence (7) from Messrs: Brereton, Burrows, Murray Macdonald, Ramsay MacDonald, Millin, Robertson & Walsh.

Also absent. Messrs: Adams, Alden, Harley, Hobson, McKillop, Perris, Rea, Reeves & Samuel.

Minutes of the previous meeting were read & confirmed.

[107] On the North-Eastern boundary with Canada.
[108] Should be 1846. On the North-Western boundary with Canada.

The Chairman, Mr. Crook, & the Secretary, were elected as a Sub-Committee to make arrangements for the dinner.

Mr. Lilley read his paper on Lord Palmerston.[109] Lord Palmerston began his career as a sharer in England's attempt to stem the Napoleonic power. In 1809, at the age of 25 he was made Secretary at War (with a seat in the cabinet)—a post wh he held for 20 years. In 1830 he was Minister for Foreign Affairs under Earl Grey, & this office he held almost uninterruptedly for 11 years. In 1846 he was again Foreign Minister under Lord Russell, but was dismissed from office in 1851, at the time of the coup d'état, for conducting important negotiations too much on his own responsibility—without reference to the Crown or the Prime Minister. He became prime minister in 1855, and from that time till his death in 1865, save from Feb. '58 to June '59 he directed the destinies of England in that capacity.

In his long political career he played an important part in all the problems caused by the sudden dissolution of the Napoleonic power, & helped more than any other man in England in the reconstruction of Belgium, Spain, Portugal, Italy, Germany & Greece. But for his action with regard to Egypt in 1840,[110] France wd now be master there & the route to India endangered.

For 30 years Palmerston was recognised in Europe as the foster-mother of free nationalities.

In the discussion that followed mention was made of Palmerston's respect for property as the basis of civil rights, of his apparent inconsistency with regard to the freedom of the Danubian Provinces, of his great personal popularity both with the nation & with his subordinates, & of the strength & daring of his statesmanship as shown for example in the Trent affair.[111]

Harold Rylett   Chairman

1st March 1907.

* * *

[114] The 114th Meeting of the Circle was held on Friday 1st March 1907 at 33 Bloomsbury Square w.c.

Present. (6 members out of 26) Mr Rylett in the chair, Messrs:

[109] Henry John Temple, 3rd Viscount Palmerston (1784–1865). Statesman, foreign secretary, and prime minister 1855–8, 1859–65.

[110] Palmerston signed a treaty with Russia in order to contain Egyptian expansion and weaken the latter's indebtedness to France.

[111] In which, during the American civil war in 1861, two confederate passengers were seized aboard a British mail-steamer. Palmerston secured their release through a display of military force.

Bullock, Byles, Herdman, Millin and Parsons—also two visitors Mr. C. Byles & Mr. Hammond.

Apologies for absence (6) Messrs: Burrows, Crook, Matheson, Perris, Stapley & Walsh.

Mr. Byles read his paper on Lord John Russell.[112] -

One of the most striking features of Russell's public life was its duration, as he was for 65 years a member of Parliament and all this time was in the midst of every scrimmage. He stood throughout his life as the special champion of Parliamentary Reform and of Civil & Religious Liberties. He it was who piloted Earl Grey's great Reform Bill[113] through the House of Commons & he it was who kept the subject of Reform alive for another 30 years or so, though he did not succeed in passing his subsequent Bills. He repealed the Test & Corporation Acts[114] & by his Act of 1858 removed the political disabilities of the Jews.

Russell was a sound free-trader, & when he first became prime minister in 1847 he made the Repeal of the Corn Laws complete & immediate, and abolished the protection on sugar, thus completing the work wh Peel had begun.

His Irish policy of coercion & emigration was open to criticism, but the difficulties were very great owing to the Famine. He certainly had ideas in advance of his time & wished to institute a judicial authority between the landlord & the tenant & to give the tenant compensation for his improvements—thus anticipating Mr. Gladstone's legislation.

In ecclesiastical matters, Russell's Durham letter is generally counted as his monster indiscretion.

Mr. Byles dealt at some length with Russell's foreign policy more particularly in connection with the Crimean War, the Italian struggle for unity, the Schleswig-Holstein question, the American Civil War, the Alabama incident,[115] & the Chinese war arising out of the Arrow incident.[116]

He also touched on Russell's achievements in the domain of Literature.

In the discussion it was suggested that Russell showed up very well in his Italian policy—particularly in giving official recognition to the revolution of the Kingdoms of Naples & the 2 Sicilies: that the Durham

---

[112] John, 1st Earl Russell (1792–1878). Whig statesman, reformer and prime minister 1846–52.

[113] The Reform Act of 1832.

[114] The Test Acts, preventing catholics and protestant nonconformists from holding public office, were repealed in 1828.

[115] In 1862 Russell failed to prevent the sailing of the Alabama, a ship supplied to the American South that caused much damage to the North.

[116] Russell protested against the arrest of British crewmen aboard the British ship Arrow, in Chinese waters in 1856.

letter was not merely an attack on the Oxford movement, but was directed against Papal aggression: that there was much to be said for Russell's attitude towards the American War & the Alabama claim, & also for his Irish emigration policy. The last point was debated at some length.

Richard Stapley   Chairman

12th April 1907.

* * *

[115] The 115th Meeting of the Circle was held on Friday April 12th 1907 at 33 Bloomsbury Sq. w.c.

Present (14 members out of 26) Mr. Stapley, in the chair, Messrs: Alden, Bullock, Byles, Crook, Harley, Herdman, Lilley, Matheson, Millin, Parsons, Perris, Robertson & Walsh. Also 5 Visitors Messrs: Barratt, Brooks, Stand[r]ing,[117] Roskill & Dr Sélincourt.

Apologies for absence (4) from Messrs: Burrows, Ramsay Mac-Donald, Murray Macdonald, & Samuel.

Also absent. (8) Messrs: Adams, Hobson, McKillop, Morrison, Rea, Reeves, Rylett & Brereton.

Minutes of the last meeting were read & confirmed.

Some suggestions for the subjects for next session were referred to the Committee.

On the question of altering the day of meeting from Friday to Wednesday next session the feeling of the meeting was taken provisionally. Result 7 to 1 in favour of the alteration.

It was unanimously resolved that a congratulatory letter shd be sent on behalf of the Circle to Sydney Olivier, a former member, on the occasion of his appointment as Governor of Jamaica.

Mr. Robertson read his paper on Beaconsfield.[118]

Disraeli, the most notable egoist of his generation, entered public life to push his own fortunes. His talk, like his dress, was an act of self-obtrusion, a flaunting of his cleverness. He had no political ideals or convictions, and never cared for any cause as such. He stood for Parliament twice as a radical, and then on the advice of Lord Lyndhurst, joined the tory party as a matter of sheer calculating self-interest. He turned against his leader Peel, after 9 years of fruitless subservience, because he was denied office. He was ready to turn Free-trader with Peel while he had hopes of office under him, but he

---

[117] George Standring, twice a guest of the Circle, was an active member of the Fabian Society.

[118] Benjamin Disraeli, 1st Earl of Beaconsfield (1804–1881). Tory statesman and prime minister 1868, 1874–80.

attacked him in the cause of Protection when he found that only as a leader of the protectionist rump he could attain front-bench status. Of all the party chiefs of his age, Disraeli alone became a faction leader pure & simple. When opposing Peel in 1844 he put forth an eminently sane view of the Irish problem, but when he came to power he took no steps to realise those views. He always found that the most profitable line for him was to exploit the resentments set up by the active legislation of his opponents. The secret of his ultimate popular success was his appeal to the passions of racial enmity & belligerence— as witnessed for example in his antagonism to Russia. All that he did was to create jingoism. Tried by the standards of moral character & moral aim, Disraeli has no aspect of greatness. He was a man of abnormal pertinacity & determination, a strong-willed & self-assertive eccentric, but as a statesman & as a politician, he was outclassed by his opponents in his own country & in his own day.

In the discussion general agreement was expressed with Mr. Robertson's views, but it was suggested that Disraeli was great in that he captured the great tory party, that his Irish policy was sincere, that the democratic idea that permeates the tory party at the present day was due in some measure to him, & that there was a certain amount of elevating ideas beneath all his eccentricity & egoism. Some stress was laid upon his essentially Asiatic temperament, character & outlook.

Richard Stapley   Chairman

3rd May 1907.

* * *

[116] The 116th meeting of the Circle was held at 33 Bloomsbury Square on the 3rd May 1907.

Present. (15 members out of 16) Mr. Stapley in the chair, Messrs: Alden, Bullock, Burrows, Byles, Crook, Harley, Herdman, Lilley, McKillop, Millin, Parsons, Robertson, Rylett & Walsh: also 6 visitors—Messrs: Buckland, Evans, Gridley, Hammond, Higgins, & Roskill.

Apologies for absence (2) from Messrs: J.R. Macdonald & Matheson.

Also absent (9) Messrs: Adams, Brereton, Hobson, Murray Macdonald, Morrison, Perris, Rea, Reeves & Samuel.

The minutes of the previous meeting were read & confirmed.

Mr. Sydney Olivier's reply to the Circle's letter of congratulation was read.

The discussion on the subjects for next session was resumed. Of the subjects proposed the Committee recommended either
(i) Bi-cameral legislatures & their working
or
(ii) A series of papers on the history, the ideas, the aims & the latest phases of Socialism—following the lines of Émile Faguet's book 'Le Socialisme en 1907'.[119]

in either case the papers to be written with a view to publication as a book.

The second proposal was carried by a majority of 7 to 6, and the Chairman, Mr. Lilley & the Secretary were appointed as a sub-committee to elaborate the scheme.

It was decided to hold the meetings next session on the first Wednesday in the month instead of the first Friday.

Mr. Crook read his paper on Gladstone:[120]

The life-work of a man should be tried in the light of evolution— in the light of the contributions he makes to human progress. In Foreign politics, Mr. Gladstone so tried, appears as the champion of nationality as against Imperialism, that is to say as the worker for heterogeneity as against homogeneity. He was the life-long champion of the freedom & unity of Italy: a defender of the S.E. European & S.W. Asiatic peoples against the tyranny of Turkey: an opponent of the Opium War with China: and he restored the independence of the Transvaal. He did more for the world's peace than any man in his generation. Within the British Empire, Mr. Gladstone tried by the same touchstone of evolution, appears as the champion of local independence as against centralisation—of variety as against uniformity. The principles of self-government & freedom wh all his life he supported in regard to the colonies he rightly attempted to apply to Ireland. In the domain of religion he was genuinely tolerant—with the tolerance not of apathy but of deep conviction. He, as a High Churchman, belonged to a school of religious thought wh desired uniformity: but nevertheless he seems to have been dimly aware that religion if it is to be kept alive must progress from homogeneity to heterogeneity. Hence he became the champion of Disestablishment, of Nonconformity, of the Jews & of the Roman Catholics. In his financial, economic, & peace policy he was a champion of the change from the militant to the industrial type of society. His whole financial thought & action was devoted to the breaking down of the barriers that hinder international trade.

[119] Émile Faguet (1847–1916). French Academician, writer, literary critic and essayist.
[120] William Ewart Gladstone (1809–98). Liberal statesman, chancellor of the Exchequer, and prime minister 1868–74, 1880–85, 1886, 1892–4.

In the discussion it was suggested

(i) that since the Universe has no moral law the scientific formula used as a touchstone was out of place.

(ii) that the Home-rule bills were thoroughly bad & unworkable.

(iii) that Mr. Gladstone seemed strangely oblivious to the necessities for social reform.

(iv) that Mr. Gladstone's Armenian policy was due more to his religious prejudices than to a deep instinct of justice.

The imagination of the Circle was also actively engaged in speculations as to what would have happened had Mr. Gladstone become a clergyman instead of a politician.

Richard Stapley   Chairman

7th June 1907.

* * *

[117] The 117th meeting of the Circle was held on 7th June 1907 at 33 Bloomsbury Square.

Present (15 members out of 26) Mr. Stapley in the chair, Messrs: Bullock, Byles, Harley, Herdman, Hobson, Lilley, Murray Macdonald, Millin, Morrison, Parsons, Rea, Robertson, Rylett, & Walsh.

Apologies for absence (5) from Messrs: Alden, Crook, Ramsay MacDonald, Matheson & Reeves.

Also absent. Messrs: Adams, Burrows, McKillop, Brereton, Perris & Samuel.

Mr. A.R. Gridley, proposed by Mr. Bullock & seconded by Mr. Walsh, was unanimously elected a member.

Mr. Russell Rea read his paper on Lord Salisbury:

Lord Salisbury[121] was not remarkable for any particular thing he ever did, but he was nevertheless one of the most potent influences of his time. He was the incarnation of the anti-democratic sentiment, but nevertheless he was respected & even liked by the people who recognised his honesty & sincerity. He stood always for aristocracy & privilege, but his ideals postulated for his class a high vocation, duty & responsibility which he himself never shirked. His belief in the right of the ruling classes to rule was illustrated by his appointments to the high offices of state. Everything he did was subordinated to stemming the tide of democracy both here & abroad. He was not specially scrupulous in the methods he adopted for obtaining his political ends: witness for example the circumstances attending his acceptance of the

---

[121] Robert Arthur Talbot Gascoyne Cecil, 3rd Marquis of Salisbury (1830–1903). Conservative statesman and prime minister 1885–6, 1886–92, 1895–1902.

Foreign Secretaryship in 1878. During the period 1885 to 1902, he was prime minister for 13 years and for nearly the whole of that time he held also the Foreign Secretaryship. In all he personally controlled the foreign policy of this country for nearly 20 years, his policy being primarily pacific, and very secondarily pro-Germanic. England has great reason to be thankful to him for his steady pursuit of peace. One after another he removed those things which might in the future make for war. In the Venezuelan incident[122] he acted as a Christian saint— though actuated by a spirit of superb aristocratic insolence!

Lord Salisbury was an imposing personality in the House of Lords wh was quite a respectable & influential body while inspired & controlled by him.

The discussion turned mainly on Lord Salisbury's foreign policy— particularly in regard to the Venezuelan incident, the Fashoda incident,[123] & the South African war. It was generally agreed that his services to the cause of peace were great, though opinion differed as to the extent to wh these services were due to his principles or character. His popularity was attributed (1) to his general sincerity & (2) to the fact that the animus of partisans was drawn away from him to Gladstone on the one hand & to Chamberlain on the other.

Richard Stapley   Chairman

2nd Octr 1907.

* * *

[118] At the Rainbow Circle Dinner held at the N.L.C. on 21st June 1907, the following members were present: Mr. Stapley (in the chair) Messrs: Brereton, Burrows, Bullock, Crook, Herdman, Hobson, Lilley, Matheson, Millin, Morrison, Parsons, Robertson & Walsh: and the following old members: Messrs: Corrie Grant, Hill, Husband, Trevelyan, Graham Wallas & Walker. [menu attached].

* * *

Fourteenth Session 1907–1908

[119] The 119th Meeting of the Circle was held on Wednesday 2nd Oct. 1907 at 33 Bloomsbury Square.

---

[122] Salisbury had refused to agree to arbitration over the boundary between British Guiana and Venezuela, and the U.S.A. considered this to be an assault on the Monroe Doctrine.

[123] The British general, Kitchener, had dislodged a French flag planted on the upper Nile in 1898, in connection with claims in the Sudan.

Present 16 members out of 28 & 2 visitors. Mr. Stapley in the chair.

Apologies for absence (5) from Messrs: Burrows, Byles, Murray Macdonald, Walsh & Ramsay MacDonald.

Also absent. Messrs: Gridley, Morrison, Perris, Rea, Reeves, Rylett & Samuel.

Minutes of the last meeting were read & confirmed.

Accounts for the past session were presented and accepted. As the past session started with a balance in hand of £1–3- and ended with a balance of 4s/4d, the Secretary suggested that the subscription shd be raised from 1/- to 2/-. The Secretary reported that the attendance for the past session had been as follows:

9 out of 9. Messrs: Bullock, Herdman & Parsons.
8   ”   ”   Lilley, Millin, & Stapley
7   ”   Mr. Crook
6   ”   Messrs: Byles & Harley
5   ”   ”   Matheson, Rylett & Walsh
4   ”   Mr. Burrows
3   ”   Messrs: Alden & Robertson
2   ”   ”   Hobson & McKillop.
1   ”   ”   Brereton, Murray Macdonald & Perris
0 out of 9 Messrs: Adams, Ramsay MacDonald, Reeves & Samuel.
Average attendance 11.6

Mr. Stapley was re-elected Chairman

Mr. Parsons was re-elected Secretary

Messrs: Crook, Harley, Hobson, Bullock, Lilley & McKillop were re-elected as the Committee.

Messrs: T.F. Husband & H. de R. Walker, proposed by the Secretary for membership, were unanimously re-elected.

The raising of the subscription to 2/- was discussed & unanimously agreed to.

A letter of resignation from Mr. Murray Macdonald was read. It was unanimously agreed that he shd be informed that the Circle was very loth to accept his resignation & that he shd be asked to keep his name on the books & to come when he could.

Mr. Robertson read his paper on 'the Social, Political & Economic Facts wh have given birth to Socialism.'

As the papers are eventually to be printed[124] it was suggested that it wd not be necessary to give a summary of them in the minutes, & that a brief report of the individual criticisms might be made instead— these criticisms being, perhaps, printed in the book after the respective papers. After some discussion it was agreed to try, as an experiment, a brief collective summary of the criticisms, the question of their

---

[124] They were not published.

publication being left, of course, to an editorial committee to be appointed later on.

In the discussion on Mr. Robertson's paper the following points were raised:

1. That Faguet's definition of Socialism as 'every tendency having for its object real equality among men' was inadequate—that indeed this might be said of the individualism of certain types of individualists. That what we have to consider under the name of socialism is the play of social forces (a) objectively, as affecting the actual structure of Society: (b) subjectively, in the thoughts & feelings of men. Taking (a) first. Society has in modern times been revolutionised industrially. Formerly we had a large number of small business units each operating in a limited area. Now the number of small units is much diminished, the tendency being to socialise capital in companies & generally to develope the capitalistic system for the more effective exploitation of industry. And the area of the operation of these larger business units is enormously extended. Similarly whereas formerly the workman made his own bargain with his employer, now we have Trade Unionism, (wh is a sort of socialising of Labour) and Co-operative Movements. At the same time it wd be a mistake to suppose that there is a *general* evolution in the direction of large industries ripening for ultimate capitalisation. There are quite a number of industries the units of which shew no tendency to amalgamate, & whose effectiveness wd lose rather than gain by such amalgamation. (b) Subjectively we see the beginnings of a conscious use of social power for social good[,] the protests against class tyranny, & the desire to improve the social conditions of the people.

2. That there is a use & scope for 'Utopias'. They serve to test the consistency of abstract ideas, & consciously to direct the energies of reformers to definite aims.

3. That the introduction of machinery is perhaps *the* 'generative fact' par excellence. By means of the telegraph & telephone capital may be transported immediately from one country or continent to another, and its power is immensely increased thereby.

4. That the unemployed question is a very important 'generative fact'.

5. That if Christianity had not permeated thought, socialists wd not have been able to formulate their socialism. To this it was objected that the socialistic ideas themselves are pre-christian.

6. That later 19th Century & 20th Century socialism has little to do practically with earlier communistic conceptions.

7. That Karl Marx's real & valuable contribution to socialistic thought was his introduction of the historic method in socialistic propaganda.

8. That whereas Marxianism was essentially fatalistic, relying on world-movements that were supposed to be imminent, but that as a matter of fact have not taken place, modern socialism desiderates conscious human action as its most important factor. The impetus given to socialism as a religion is due to the fact that all our attention is concentrated on the scheme of things as we know it here & now, action and action alone being regarded as the determining element in human evolution.

Richard Stapley   Chairman

6th Novr 1907.

* * *

[120] The 120th meeting of the Circle was held on Wednesday 6th Novr 1907 at 33 Bloomsbury Square.

Present. 21 members out of 29 and 2 visitors.

Apologies for absence (2) from Messrs: Robertson & Ramsay MacDonald

Also absent. Messrs: Brereton, McKillop, Morrison, Rea, Reeves, & Samuel.

Minutes of the last meeting were read & confirmed.

It was announced that Mr. Murray Macdonald had agreed to retain his membership.

Mr. Harley read his 'Historical Sketch of the Development of Socialism'.

In the discussion Mr. Harley was subjected to some criticism for having given a history of the equalitarian movement rather than a history of socialism in its more modern manifestations. It was suggested that what we should be mainly concerned with is the great vague unconscious movement of the 4th Estate, & the unconscious & compromising socialism going on at the present day quite apart from organised socialist parties: that socialism as it is understood today really begins with the 19th Century & the development of the capitalistic system: that we ought to have a rapid survey of the development of socialism in the British Empire and America, & that in this connection special reference might with advantage be made to New Zealand where the practical effect of socialistic legislation is seen in a striking way.

On the other hand it was contended that Mr. Harley was being criticised for doing, in a very brilliant & lucid way, precisely what the Circle had asked him to do.

The question of the meaning of 'equality' was raised and of whether the sense of individual responsibility ought to be deepened or sub-stituted by a state responsibility.

Reference was made to the wider meaning attached to the term 'socialism' in earlier days, Proudhon's definition of socialism as 'every movement for the betterment of social life' being contrasted with a recent definition as 'a movement for the removal of material inequality by the abolition of riches.'

It was also suggested that Socialism is the Church of the future, that it is now at the pre-Nicene Council stage, & that in time it will be as coercive as any Church has been in the past.

Richard Stapley   Chairman

4th Decr 1907.

* * *

[121] The 121st meeting of the Circle was held on the 4th December 1907 at 33 Bloomsbury Square.

Present. 17 members out of 29.

Apologies for absence. (5) from Messrs: Alden, Brereton, Ramsay MacDonald, McKillop & Walker.

Also absent. Messrs: Hobson, Morrison, Rea, Reeves, Robertson, Perris and Samuel.

Minutes of the last meeting were read & confirmed.

Mr. Matheson read his paper on 'The Chief constitutive Ideas & Aims of Socialism.'

In the discussion the following opinions were expressed:

1. That we shall not get to close quarters with Socialism until we realise that it is a living movement which aims at reducing material life to habitual or instinctive actions. When this has been achieved it will be time enough to adumbrate what the higher life of Socialism will be. The first duty of Socialism is to imbue the workers with a sense of the injustice of their conditions.

2. That the writer had not explained what Socialism is. The battle against private interests & injustice, the ideals of the unity of the human race, of fraternity, & equality of opportunity are not dis-tinctively socialistic, whilst on the other hand apparently little weight is attached by Socialism to Liberty, the greatest ideal & the greatest asset of humanity.

3. That the writer had not given any clear indication as to how his admittedly beautiful dream was to be attained. While we are all equally anxious that injustice shd be done away with and inequalities levelled up it is doubtful whether these desirable ends can be attained

by putting our docks, newspapers, industries &c: in the hands of Departments of State or of Town Halls—and indeed the paper gave no hint as to why or how we should proceed to nationalise any particular industry.

4. On the other hand it was urged that just as tramways had been to a large extent municipalised with advantage not only to the public but to the employees, so other things (e.g. the milk supply) might be municipalised or nationalised, and that by gradually increasing public control of what are really public needs, the ideal state of things pictured by the writer would step by step be brought about.

5. That if Socialism is to be a living force in the next generation it will be as a religion inspired by a golden dream of the future & by a vital sense of present injustice & wrong. Although that dream is no doubt to a large extent illusory, some such illusion has played its part in all historic movements and has had its effect in making great & vigorous souls.

6. That *no* thinking Socialist nowadays accepts the Marxian theory of value, yet no socialistic scheme has been worked out on any other theory. On the Jevonian theory of value[125] it wd be impossible to give the worker the fruits of his own labour.

7. That *every* socialist of repute nowadays accepts the Marxian theory of value.

Richard Stapley   Chairman

8th January 1908.

* * *

[122] The 122nd meeting of the Circle was held on the 8th Jan. 1908 at 33 Bloomsbury Square.

Present 17 members out of 29 and 2 visitors

Apologies for absence (6) from Messrs: Alden, Brereton, Byles, Murray Macdonald, Parsons & Robertson

Also absent Messrs: Adams, Hobson, Perris, Rea, Reeves and Samuel.

Minutes of the last meeting were read & confirmed.

Mr. Burrows read his paper on 'Anarchism'.

In the discussion the following opinions were expressed:

1. Socialism & Anarchism are merely dogmas, and the writer of the paper had dogmatised on every point—including the future. Progress must be based on experience not on theories & dreams. Non-

---

[125] The assertion that value depends principally on utility rather than on labour. Cp. W.S. Jevons, *The Theory of Political Economy* (1st. edn. London, 1871).

socialists are just as conscious of social evils as socialists are and the bureaucracy of socialism would be as hard & cruel as men are today. Liberalism on the other hand has an ideal of liberty & justice.

2. Evolution is opposed to Socialism wh presupposes a sudden immense improvement of human nature

3. Both Liberalism & Socialism desire justice, but differ as to the means & conditions of justice.

4. The contrast between Liberalism & Socialism is beside the mark: the real contrast is between Socialism & Individualism.

Richard Stapley   Chairman

5.2.1908

* * *

[123] The 123rd meeting of the Circle was held on the 5th Feb 1908 at 33 Bloomsbury Square.

Present. 13 members out of 29 and 3 visitors.

Apologies for absence (5) from Messrs: Bullock, Burrows, Byles, Rylett & Walsh

Also absent. (11) Messrs: Harley, Hobson, Murray Macdonald, Ramsay MacDonald, McKillop, Morrison, Perris, Rea, Reeves, Samuel & Walker. Minutes of last meeting read & confirmed.

Mr. Alden read his paper on 'Democratic Redistribution of Property: Peasant Proprietary & Small Co-operative Production'.

In the discussion the following opinions were expressed:

1. That wherever the people get property in land, they get so absorbed in it that they become anti-socialistic.

2. That the natural & practical way in which Socialism is likely to develope is by the increasing development of co-operative movements wh will call forth increasing intervention, protection & legislation by the Government.

3. That up to a certain point co-operation visibly increases the total production, elicits energy & makes life easier for those in the movement, but there is a certain suspicion on the part of cooperators lest the residuum outside the movement shd come in & get its benefits—lest the industrious shd be loaded by the incompetent. The progress to absolute socialism must be very slow, & it will not be realised until sympathy has evolved to the point at wh people are prepared to live up to the formula 'from each according to his capacity: to each according to his needs'—until in fact the co-operator's feeling of sympathy towards the incompetent residuum outweighs the feeling of self interest.

4. That this residuum is to a large extent the result of modern life

in great cities, & constitutes one of our most difficult problems. No appeal to generous instincts will affect it: coercion, & legislation to prevent the production of the unfit are perhaps the only means. On the other hand it was suggested that the residuum comprises a large number of people who *ought* not to be in it & who *need* not be in it because they are capable of being saved: that at present competent people are being made incompetent by hard conditions & avoidable distress: that with a cure of our industrial anarchy, with better education, sanitation & housing the number of the incompetent will be decreased

5. That we are already bearing the weight of the residuum & socialism offers a better means of bearing it. That the higher ideal of Socialism will probably make more headway than the lower ideal of co-operators wh appeals specially to self-interest.

Richard Stapley   Chairman

4th March 1908.

* * *

[124] The 124th meeting of the Circle was held on the 4th March 1908 at 33 Bloomsbury Square.

Present 17 members out of 29 & one visitor, (Mr. Stapley in the chair.)

Apologies for absence (4) from Messrs: Alden, Burrows, Crook & Murray Macdonald.

Also absent. (8) Messrs: Byles, Brereton, Morrison, Rea, Reeves, Samuel, Robertson & Walker.

Minutes of the last meeting were read & confirmed.

Mr. Hobson read his first paper on 'Collectivism'.

The discussion turned largely on the motives for effort, if any, that would be operative under Socialism. It was urged that as Socialism evolves society will 'select' the motives that will 'survive', & that we cannot dogmatise now as to what those motives will be: that even now the person of ability prefers for his own satisfaction to exercise his ability—quite apart from any question of payment; that inventors for instance are under the present system the most robbed of men and their stimulus is not primarily a monetary one[;] that one motive that wd probably persist is the wholesome desire for social recognition: that the value of the stimulus of public-spirited competition between different towns or areas of the country must not be depreciated—the competition for the best municipalised gas or tramways &c:

On the point that the socialisation of industrial concerns would probably result in some reduction of their efficiency, it was urged that Society would be recompensed by greater efficiency on its physical, moral, intellectual & artistic side: that much effort now spent in futile & unproductive ways (such as advertising) would cease[:] that the public officer has improved, & is improving & that the present public opinion on his efficiency & his capabilities of development cannot be relied upon.

The Post Office came in for a good deal of notice, being held up as a model by some members, and to scorn by one who said he would like to see it denationalised.

Richard Stapley   Chairman

18th March 1908

* * *

[125] The 125th meeting of the Circle was held on the 18th March 1908 at 33 Bloomsbury Square.

Present. 15 members out of 28—Mr. Stapley, in the chair, Messrs: Adams, Alden, Byles, Brereton, Crook, Herdman, Hobson, Husband, Lilley, McKillop, Millin, Parsons, Robertson & Walsh—also 3 visitors, Mr. Bowley, Dr. Lawson Dodd,[126] & Mr. Standring.

Apologies for absence (4) from Messrs: Bullock, Burrows, Ramsay MacDonald & Rylett.

Also absent (9) Messrs: Gridley, Harley, Murray Macdonald, Matheson, Morrison, Perris, Rea, Samuel & Walker.

Minutes of the last meeting were read & confirmed.

A letter was read from the Hon. W. Pember Reeves announcing his resignation.

The question was raised as to the steps to be taken to get the present series of papers into shape for publication, and it was agreed that the matter be left over for consideration by the Sub- Committee at the end of the session.

Mr. Hobson read his second paper on 'Collectivism'.

The discussion turned mainly on the evils of bureaucracy. It was stated that at present a strong government desirous of carrying out social reforms in many directions is practically paralysed by a permanent reactionary bureaucracy, and that the country must find some means of freeing itself from its bureaucratic fetters: that the power of organisation of public servants—or of any class that has vested interests—frequently stands in the way of progress: that too

---

[126] Frank Lawson Dodd was an active member of the Fabian Society.

much pressure is brought to bear upon candidates for parliament by public servants & special interests. On the other hand it was contended that rational socialists must face the fact that the community will always have to cope with moral obliquity in some form, and that as every state of society has to meet its own difficulties so socialism will have to meet the peculiar difficulties arising from bureaucracy: that if groups of government employees should exercise undesirable political influence that fact wd carry with it the seed of its own reform, because workers in non-nationalised industries wd then strive to get their work nationalised, & that if all the services were nationalised or municipalised corruption wd be practically impossible.

Reference was also made to the question of disfranchising certain people on matters in wh they have personal interest, and to the idea of substituting parliamentary representation of interests for territorial representation. The balance of opinion seemed to be that this wd be a retrograde step.

Richard Stapley   Chairman

1st April 1908.

* * *

[126] The 126th meeting of the Circle was held on the 1st April 1908 at 33 Bloomsbury Square.

Present. 15 members out of 28. Mr. Stapley in the chair. One visitor.

Apology for absence. from Mr. Brereton

Also absent. Messrs: Adams, Alden, Byles, Murray Macdonald, Ramsay MacDonald, Morrison, Perris, Rea, Robertson, Rylett, Samuel & Walker.

Mr. McKillop read his paper on 'How far is what is called Social Legislation likely to promote the Socialist Ideal'.

The discussion turned largely on the relative merits of Liberalism & Socialism, but suffered from the fact that the definitely socialist members & the definitely liberal members did not seem to be agreed upon what Liberalism & Socialism were. The chief items of social legislation considered were Workmen's Compensation, the Administration of Education, the Free feeding of poor children, & the Wages Board scheme.[127] It was urged that if social legislation contained the germ of the great principle of control by the com-

---

[127] Soon to be established under the Trade Boards Act (1909), which set minimum rates of wages.

munity of its own life, so far it tended to the realisation of the socialist ideal.

Richard Stapley   Chairman

6th May 1908.

* * *

[127] The 127th meeting of the Circle was held on 6th May 1908 at 33 Bloomsbury Square.

Present. 19 members out of 28. Mr. Stapley in the chair. 5 visitors.

Apologies for absence (5) from Messrs: Alden, Brereton, Matheson, Robertson & Rylett.

Also absent (4) Messrs: Murray Macdonald, Morrison, Perris & Samuel

The Minutes of the last meeting were read & confirmed.

The Programme for the next session was discussed and referred for settlement to a special committee, consisting of Messrs: Adams, Hobson, Walsh, Robertson & the Secretary.

Mr. Ramsay MacDonald gave an address on the question 'How far is the Socialist Ideal likely to be promoted by the practical proposals of present Labour Parties (political) and Labour Organisations (industrial)?'

In the discussion some doubt was thrown on the view that the formation of the Labour Party is due to conscious acceptance of socialistic conceptions and that all the initiative of the Labour Party emanates from the definitely & consciously socialist wing. On the other hand it was asserted that the growth of the Labour Party is directly due to the permeation of the Trade Union ranks by socialist propaganda all over the country, and that the power of conscious socialism in the Trade Union movement is much greater than is generally appreciated. It was stated that the Labouring classes have practically nothing to gain from either the Liberal or Conservative party, that Socialism will gradually displace Individualism as the basis of national life and that the Labour Party will get what it wants by bringing more & more pressure to bear on the two regular parties & inducing them to bid one against the other. Attention was also devoted to the point that while undoubtedly the best practical means of realising socialism is to grasp & to concentrate all socialistic (as distinguished from definitely *socialist*) tendencies, nevertheless these tendencies do not necessarily make for socialism; & if they are not controlled & directed by high ideals may sometimes lead to results which Socialism would by no means own.

Richard Stapley   Chairman

3rd June 1908.

[128] The 128th meeting of the Circle was held on 3rd June 1908 at 33 Bloomsbury Square

Present. 14 members out of 28. Sir Richard Stapley in the chair. 3 Visitors.

Apologies for absence (5) from Messrs: Alden, Brereton, Ramsay MacDonald, Perris & Rylett.

Also absent. Messrs: Gridley, Harley, Hobson, Murray Macdonald, Millin, Morrison, Rea, Samuel & Walker.

Minutes of the previous meeting were read & confirmed.

A letter from Mr. Faguet was read, declining the Circle's invitation to the Dinner on the ground of ill-health.

The deliberations of the special committee on the programme for next session were reported & discussed and, with a few modifications, adopted.

Mr. Lilley read his paper 'Conclusions on Socialism'.

In the discussion the notion that Socialism could be regarded as a religion met with some criticism. It was urged that the nucleus of socialism at the present time was its fundamental economic doctrine, and that, until the effects of socialism on everything were realised, it was nothing more than an intellectual exercise to discuss ideal and moral changes & possibilities. It was also urged that socialists shd free themselves from the tendency to boast—not by any means that they held the monopoly in that direction, but that if they could not enter into the spirit of their ideal sufficiently to transcend the error of boastfulness, if they could not rid themselves of a sense of superiority (wh implied lack of self-criticism) they could not hope for much real development.

Chairman

7th October 1908

* * *

[129] At the Rainbow Circle Dinner held on 17th June 1908, the following members were present. Sir Richard Stapley (in the chair), Messrs: Alden, Burrows, Byles, Crook, Hobson, Husband, Lilley, Murray Macdonald, Matheson, Parsons, Perris, Robertson, Samuel & Walsh—and the following old members: Messrs: Roskill & Trevelyan.

It was decided to give up the idea of publishing the papers read during the session. [menu attached]

Richard Stapley   Chairman

7th October 1908.

* * *

Fifteenth Session 1908-9.

[130] The 130th meeting of the Rainbow Circle was held on 7th Ocbr 1908 at 33 Bloomsbury Square

Present 13 members out of 28, Sir Richard Stapley in the chair, 3 visitors.

Apologies for absence (4) from Messrs: Alden, Hobson, Robertson & Rylett

Also absent. (11) Messrs: Byles, Gridley, Harley, Lilley, Murray Macdonald, Ramsay MacDonald, McKillop, Morrison, Rea, Perris & Samuel.

Minutes of the last meeting were read & confirmed.

Accounts for the past session were presented & accepted. The Secretary recommended a reduction of 25 per cent in the subscription.

A record of the attendance during the past session was read, as follows:

Out of a possible 10 meetings (not including the Dinner)

Messrs:		
Herdman, Husband, Lilley & Stapley attended	"	10
" Crook, Millin & Parson	"	9
" Adams, Bullock, Matheson & Walsh	"	8
" Gridley, Harley & McKillop	"	7
" Burrows & Hobson	"	6
" Mr.Byles	"	5
" Alden Robertson & Rylett	"	4
" Brereton, Ramsay MacDonald & Walker	"	3
" Murray Macdonald & Perris	"	2
" Dr. Morrison & Mr. Russell Rea attended		1
" Mr. Samuel	"	0

Average attendance 16.4 as against 11.6 in the previous session—an increase of over 40 per cent.

Sir Richard Stapley was re-elected Chairman

Mr. Parsons was re-elected Secretary

Messrs: Bullock, Crook, Harley, Hobson, Lilley & McKillop were re-elected as the Committee.

Mr. Adams read his paper on 'the Basis of Ethics'.

He said that Ethics was the science of conduct: that conduct was a part of life, & that ethics must therefore find their justification in the law of self-preservation. He then traced this law (a) as expressing the sole activity of the unicellular amoeba (b) as applied to the whole organism in higher forms of life (c) as applied to the herd or family in still higher forms, and reasoned that the impulse to preserve life was directed more & more to the preservation of ever larger & more complex wholes. That human society was rightly to be conceived as an organism & had the unity in variety characteristic of organisms,

& that hence the individual could only realise himself by performing his function in the life of the whole & sacrificing himself to that larger life when necessary. Thus the Common Good was the fundamental ethical principle. But unfortunately the state of present day societies closely resembled that of a diseased body, suffering from parasitism, wh resulted in the degeneration both of the parasites & those whom they starved or poisoned. Our first endeavour shd be to abolish privilege & monopoly & to bring about just conditions. It was true that in all we do we must be self-regarding, but if our centre of interest became the welfare of others, the full realisation of self might be indistinguishable from self-sacrifice. The true & only basis of Ethics was to be found in the conception of society as perfectly unified life.

In the discussion the following opinions were expressed:

1. That the whole basis of life & thought was the Unity of the Universe. For the full realisation of self that harmony was required wh presupposed interdependence & intercommunication with our fellows. That the aim of ethics was happiness, & that our self-realisation could not be attained without striving for the happiness of others.

2. That the question of greatest interest was the sanction for ethics & that at present it was not clear what the stimulus or motive for right conduct would be when the old sanctions had disappeared.

3. That the law of association & sympathy was as important as the law of self-preservation.

4. That the theory of evolution as applied to material things was most convincing, but that the assumption that it was applicable to immaterial things—to wh sphere ethics belonged—was not justified.

5. That the true morality resulted from a compromise between individual & social ideals.

Richard Stapley   Chairman

4th Novr 1908.

* * *

[131] The 131st meeting of the Rainbow Circle was held on the 4th Novr 1908 at 33 Bloomsbury Square.

Present. 17 members out of 29, Sir Richard Stapley in the chair, 2 visitors.

Apologies for absence (4) from Messrs: Alden, Crook, Robertson & Rylett.

Also absent. (7) Messrs: Gridley, Lilley, Ramsay MacDonald, Morrison, Perris, Rea & Samuel.

Minutes of the last meeting were read & confirmed.

Mr. Hobson read his paper on 'National versus Individual Standards of Morality'.

There is a tendency to regard each nation's narrow self-interest as its supreme law, a tendency wh is supported by those political philosophers who insist that there is no 'consciousness of kind', no adequate community of experience, needs & interests outside the national area.

If it be admitted that a strong nation has some obligation to help a weaker nation, the right of the latter to claim such assistance must equally be admitted. At present if assistance be given it is presumed to be given in order to secure some balance of power or other interest.

The history of treaty obligations indicates that a nation as a moral personality is on a lower level than an individual. Treaties recognise indeed a duty to carry out certain defined undertakings, but they are not based on ethical considerations and are repudiated or neglected, without sense of shame, when they are considered inconvenient or disadvantageous.

The invasion of a weaker nation by a stronger is unjustifiable among states on the same level of civilisation, but may be justifiable where the weaker state is a backward or barbarous state wh might benefit by the civilisation forced upon it & whose development might be for the good of the world at large. But the moral defect of imperialism is due to lack of any true sanction, from a society of nations, to the interference of an imperialist nation with the life of a lower people.

The wide divergence between the ethics of individuals & that of nations does not imply essential differences in ideals but only feebler development of moral personality in the Nation & feebler structure of international society.

The discussion turned largely on the rights & wrongs of the British occupation of Egypt & Rule in India. Apart from this, the following opinions were expressed:

1. That there is rather more international solidarity than Mr. Hobson seemed to give credit for & that arbitration & other treaties, & international congresses & conventions are promising tokens of a growing solidarity.

2. That until there is some supreme protective force over the nations of the world, no nation can be blamed for regarding its own preservation & interest as its paramount duty.

Richard Stapley   Chairman

2 Decr 1908

* * *

[132] The 132nd meeting of the Circle was held on the 2nd Decr. '08 at 33 Bloomsbury Square.

Present. 11 members, 3 visitors, Sir Richard Stapley in the chair.

Apologies for absence (8) from Messrs: Adams, Burrows, Byles, Matheson, Perris, Robertson, Rylett & Walsh.

Also absent. Messrs: Alden, Gridley, Harley, Murray Macdonald, Ramsay MacDonald, Morrison, Rea, Samuel & Walker.

Mr. Lane Fox-Pitt, proposed by Mr. Brereton was unanimously elected a member of the Circle.

Minutes of the previous meeting were read & confirmed.

The Secretary read his paper on 'Marriage & Divorce'.

For reasons drawn from anthropology & social history, marriage in civilised societies must be monogamic & life-long as a rule. It wd be accompanied by a system of prostitution wh was an admitted evil. Certain moderate reforms of the marriage laws of this country might be introduced at once, such as divorce on equal terms for men & women, divorce under certain qualifications for drunkenness, lunacy, felony & transmissible diseases, divorce proceedings to be heard *in camera*. More debatable points were whether the magistrates powers under the Act of 1895[128] shd be increased & whether divorce shd be granted for incompatibility of temper & by mutual consent. The latter might lead to grave abuse unless closely restricted: certain possible restrictions were suggested. Prostitution was not, as often stated, mainly dependent upon economic conditions of women, though economic conditions constituted one factor. It might be reduced by lowering the average marriage age by certain means wh were suggested.

Boys & girls shd be instructed individually respecting the natural functions of their bodies & their responsibilities as prospective parents, & speaking generally every effort shd be made to induce a healthier & cleaner public opinion on the whole subject.

In the discussion some divergence of opinion was expressed as to the desirability of granting divorce for incompatibility or by mutual consent & as to whether any fresh legislation was necessary at all, the difficulty of divorce acting as a great safeguard to the general permanence of marriage. It was also suggested that: neo-malthusianism by separating the original two-fold purpose of marriage has changed the whole situation: and that the operation of the married women's property act[129] has given rise to a large number of independent women who voluntarily remain unmarried though many

---

[128] Summary Jurisdiction [Married Women] Act (1895).
[129] Enacted in 1882.

enter into irregular relationships wh are having considerable effect on the institution of marriage.

Richard Stapley   Chairman

6th Jany. 1909.

* * *

[133] The 133rd meeting of the Circle was held on the 6th January at 33 Bloomsbury Sq.

Present. 11 members out of 29, 2 visitors, Sir Richard Stapley in the chair.

Apologies for absence (6) from Messrs: Brereton, Byles, Matheson, Ramsay MacDonald, Robertson & Rylett.

Also absent. Messrs: Adams, Alden, Gridley, Hobson, Murray Macdonald, McKillop, Millin, Morrison, Perris, Rea, Samuel & Walker

Minutes of the previous meeting were read and confirmed.

Mr. Burrows read his paper on the political and economic status of woman with special reference to the bearing of the former upon the latter. The aim of the woman's movement was the complete freedom of woman—political, economic and social, and this freedom was bound to come. On the theories of Lewis Morgan's book 'Ancient Society',[130] the proper evolution of woman had been retarded and this in large measure accounted for the inferior position she now occupied. The difference between man and woman except as regards actual physiology was mainly artificial and would disappear. Mr. Burrows dealt with the usual objections to giving women the vote, and his own disagreement with the limited scope of the present demand, and expressed the opinion that married women needed the vote most. Sexual and economic freedom could never be obtained until social conditions were transformed root and branch. With economic freedom under the new co-operative commonwealth, woman would demand her own sexual freedom not in opposition to man and not through that sex antagonism preached by the suffragettes. It was in that idea of an equal and harmonious action that the progress and development of man and woman would be eventually assured.

In the discussion, the following opinions were expressed:

(1) That woman is inherently inferior to man and less capable of acting steadily and continuously under the guide of reason.

(2) That woman is physically and mentally inferior to man but morally and spiritually superior.

(3) That woman is inferior to man at present but that much may be hoped of her in the future!

[130] Lewis Henry Morgan (1818–1881). American ethnologist. *Ancient Society* published 1877.

(4) That the differences between the sexes ought not to weigh for a moment as regards political liberties.

(5) That the political, economic and sexual liberation of woman is much to be desired as it would indirectly have the effect of reducing the birth rate.

Richard Stapley   Chairman

3rd Feb. 1909

* * *

[134] The 134th Meeting of the Circle was held on the 3rd Feb: 1909 at 33 Bloomsbury Square.

Present. 21 members out of 29. Sir Richard Stapley and Mr. Hobson in the Chair. 4 visitors.

Apologies for absence. (4) from Messrs: Murray Macdonald, Morrison, Samuel & Walker.

Also absent—(4) Messrs: Adams, Gridley, Harley & McKillop.

Minutes of the previous meeting were read & confirmed.

Mr. Robertson read his paper on 'The Population Question: the Malthusian position: Eugenics: Control of Birth-rate: State Subsidies for Maternity'.

The 'Social Problem' was conceived by Plato as the question of the right breeding & rearing of men. Independently of Plato practical men in modern times have contrasted our indifference in this matter with our care in the breeding of animals. Eugenics for mankind is intimately connected with the population question & so with Malthusianism. British ideas of propriety have prevented free discussion of the population question, & economists like Marshall have evaded it. Neo-malthusians must & do insist that control of population is the foundation of eugenics, & they face the question of the quality of offspring & the moral questions involved.

The law of Malthus stripped of its mathematical presentment is still unassailable. In civilised countries prudential checks are now taking the place of vice, famine, disease, infanticide &c: Malthus advocated late marriage rather than the prudential limitation of family wh is now a *conditio sine qua non* of social reform. The prevention of too frequent conception is a gain to the health of wives. If it were the case that prevention increased sexual incontinence among the unmarried this might be a less evil than the infanticide & illegitimacy wh it prevented. Large families cannot be well bred except with such a great strain as few fathers & mothers can bear. Endowment of maternity is now proposed[131]—partly to obviate the supposed danger of a declining birth-rate. Procreation is however in no need of encouragement—rather the reverse.

The discussion seemed to indicate a fairly general agreement with Mr. Robertson, but nevertheless its distinguishing feature was that there was hardly a statement he had made wh was not flatly contradicted, or an opinion he had expressed wh was not vehemently opposed, by one or other of the Circle.

Out of many opinions—far too many to record—the following received considerable attention:

1. That neo-malthusianism is probably going beyond the present necessities of the case

2. That though the advantage of prudential checks is clear from the point of view of individual families it is less clear from a national point of view (a) because these checks may extend so as to become a national danger (b) because they facilitate vice.

Richard Stapley   Chairman

3rd March 1909.

* * *

[135] The 135th meeting of the Circle was held on the 3rd March at 33 Bloomsbury Square.

Present. 13 members out of 29, 1 visitor, Sir Richard Stapley in the chair.

Apologies for absence (4) from Messrs: Burrows, Robertson, Rylett & Walker.

Also absent. Messrs: Adams, Alden, Bullock, Gridley, Harley, Lilley, Murray Macdonald, Ramsay MacDonald, Morrison, Perris, Rea, & Walsh.

Minutes of the previous meeting were read & confirmed.

Mr. Herbert Samuel gave his address on 'Public Responsibility for children: state-feeding &c: the Children Act: possible future developments'.

There are 8 factors necessary to the proper bringing up of a child, vizt: general education, industrial education, moral education, food, clothing, shelter, health, & sympathy & affection. It has long been recognised that general education has come from the State, and it is now beginning to be recognised that industrial & moral education must also come from the State. The other five factors are properly the

---

[131] The endowment of motherhood was pursued in particular by the Fabians. See e.g. Fabian Tract 149, *The Endowment of Motherhood* (London, 1910).

province of the parent & of voluntary organisations. The State shd work hand in hand with the voluntary organisations wh constitute a most valuable national asset. The 'Industrial Revolution' and facilities for travel tend to the breaking up of the family unit. Social reformers must emphasize more & more the importance of the family, & must beware of weakening the family tie. In so far as state-feeding takes away from the family idea it is a real evil. The business of the State shd be to assist the parent to perform his functions & not to substitute the parent. The provisions of recent legislation, including the Children Act,[132] are designed to emphasize the responsibility of the normal parent for the normal child, whilst at the same time they enable the State to go much further where normal conditions do not prevail. It has been suggested that there shd be a Children's Department of State. There is no case for this & it wd be impracticable—but there is much room for better co-ordination.

In the discussion it was suggested that a distinction might be drawn between the principles & the refinements both of general & moral education: the State might instil the principles but hardly the refinements. It was also suggested that the State has a special sphere in physical education, & the point was raised as to the extent to wh this is related to School-feeding.

Richard Stapley   Chairman

7th April 1909

* * *

[136] The 136th meeting of the Circle was held on 7th April 1909 at 33 Bloomsbury Square.

Present. 11 members out of 29, 3 visitors—Sir Richard Stapley in the chair.

Apologies for absence. (7) from Messrs: Bullock, Byles, Matheson, McKillop, Robertson, Rylett & Walker.

Also absent. (11) Messrs: Adams, Alden, Gridley, Hobson, Lilley, Murray Macdonald, Ramsay MacDonald, Morrison, Perris, Rea, & Samuel.

Minutes of the previous meeting were read & confirmed. Suggestions for the next session[']s programme were put forward and Messrs: Burrows Husband Walsh and the Secretary were appointed as a special committee to formulate proposals.

Mr. Brereton read his paper on 'Vocational education: the Future

[132] Enacted in 1908.

of the Higher Elementary School: Proposed Reforms and their bearing on the general question of Unemployment'.

Education should be for livelihood as well as for life. The present education of the masses and lower middle classes is too much a servile imitation of the old academic curriculum of our secondary schools. There shd be 3 stages (1) purely general including literature (2) general-professional in wh the curriculum is gradually fitted to the need of some group of cognate occupations (3) direct preparation for some definite profession or calling. Under such a system the acquisition of skill would be subordinated to the acquisition of scientific principles, the formation of character wd remain the paramount aim and the craftsmanship wd serve as an instrument of culture. In the majority of technical schools there shd be two sides, one commercial & the other technical with a preliminary undifferentiated year. To prevent excessive production of any particular type of workman there shd be created central local committees for the various groups of trades.

In the discussion the following opinions were expressed: (1) That the present system of education has produced the most stupid generation of adults for 30 years & that the hope of the future is to introduce into the curriculum a large element of active & manual work (2) That elementary teachers fail owing to their incapacity of dealing with children above the age of 12—an age at wh it wd be well to reclassify. (3) That at present our teachers are drawn too much from people who have failed at anything else.

Richard Stapley   Chairman

5th May 1909.

* * *

[137] The 137th meeting of the Circle was held on the 5th May 1909 at 33 Bloomsbury Square.

Present. (15) 3 visitors, Sir Richard Stapley in the chair.

Apologies for absence. (7) from Messrs: Alden, Lilley, Ramsay MacDonald, Matheson, McKillop, Rylett & Walker.

Also absent. (8) Messrs: Adams, Gridley, Millin, Morrison, Perris, Rea, Fox-Pitt, & Samuel.

Minutes of the previous meeting were read & confirmed. Mr. Gridley's name was removed from the list of members for non-attendance & non-payment of subscription.

Mr. J.E. Raphael, proposed by Mr. Walsh, and Mr. G.P. Gooch, proposed by Mr. Robertson, were unanimously elected to membership of the Circle.

The Committee appointed at the previous meeting to consider the programme for the next session submitted alternative schemes (1) on taxation, poor-law reform & local government (2) on the rise & decadence of States & civilisations. The first scheme was adopted by the Circle.

It was decided to put off the June meeting to the 9th June.

Mr. Walsh read his paper on 'Recent Developments & Tendencies in the Higher Education of Girls—with special reference to what has been accomplished by the Act of 1902'.[133]

The education of women suffered by the Renaissance & Reform movements of the 15th & 16th centuries. Towards the end of the 17th century the accomplishment theory set in, but the 19th century brought a new set of ideals of womanhood and the beginnings of emancipation. Girls began to share more and more the benefits of higher education on equal terms with boys. The Act of 1902, unifying & co-ordinating all educational work, the new regulations for the instruction of Pupil Teachers and the scholarship schemes arising out of the latter resulted in a great increase in the number of secondary schools & generally in enormous gain to the cause of the education of girls. The results we may look for from this awakening to the importance of higher standards & of enlightened teachers are that the schools will foster the development of healthy minds in healthy bodies & produce women capable of taking their due share in the real responsibilities of life, women worthy of that wider citizenship wh is generally opening up for the sex.

In the discussion the following opinions were expressed (1) that the educational work of pre-reformation convents, if it existed at all had been over-rated.

(2) that there was at present little sign of that widening of the whole mental outlook & discarding of class prejudices wh wd indicate real education as distinguished from the acquisition of culture

(3) that it was necessary to develope the imaginations of girls to make them realise their position in the social order

(4) that the influence of married women in girls' schools is very desirable.

Richard Stapley   Chairman

* * *

On the 22nd May Mr. & Mrs. Percy Alden very kindly invited the Circle to their house Mansfield Loughton. The Chairman and ten

---

[133] The Education Act.

members were able to accept the invitation and spent a very pleasant afternoon.

* * *

[138] The 138th meeting of the Circle was held on 9th June 1909 at 33 Bloomsbury Square.

Present. 12 members—Sir Richard Stapley in the chair.

Apologies for absence (14) from Messrs: Alden, Burrows, Byles, Husband, Ramsay MacDonald, McKillop, Morrison, Perris, Russell Rea, Robertson, Rylett, Samuel, Walker, & Murray Macdonald.

Also absent. (4) Messrs: Adams, Hobson, Lilley, & Millin.

The question of having a 'Ladies Night' was raised by Mr. Brereton, discussed & deferred to the Octr meeting.

Minutes of the previous meeting were read & confirmed.

In the absence of Mr. McKillop, his paper on 'Democracy & University Education' was read by the Secretary.

The paper outlined a complete scheme of education from infancy onwards in an ideal democracy under which all citizens wd so far as possible receive an equally high standard of education and be competent to perform equally high functions—a democracy wh wd be incompatible with the continued existence of the institutions of private property and marriage in their present imperfectly developed state. Children who at the age of 14 or 15 shewed the proper aptitude would, after a year or so more of general education, proceed to higher literacy or higher technical education in a college or polytechnic as the case might be. Those who then shewed sufficient promise wd go to the University or the scientific University. All education throughout wd be entirely free and in all its branches as open to girls as to boys. A degree in domestic science was advocated.

In the discussion the idea of universal manual & physical training met with general approval, but not the idea of universal military training.

Objection was expressed to the notion that only those who could attain a certain standard of knowledge shd go to the universities, and to the general pigeon-holing tendency of the scheme.

Richard Stapley   Chairman

6 October 1909

* * *

[139] At the Rainbow Circle Dinner held at the National Liberal Club on the 16th June 1909 there were present Sir Richard Stapley, in the chair, Messrs: Alden, Brereton, Bullock, Byles, Crook, Husband, Murray Macdonald, Ramsay MacDonald, Matheson, Millin, Parsons, Fox-Pitt, Rea, Robertson, Gooch & Walsh.

Richard Stapley

* * *

Sixteenth Session 1909–1910

[140] The 140th meeting of the Circle was held, at 33 Bloomsbury Square, on the 6th October 1909.

Present. 21 members out of 29, 1 visitor, Sir Richard Stapley in the chair.

Apology for absence. from Mr. Walker.

Also absent. Messrs: Alden, Harley, Ramsay MacDonald, Millin, Morrison, Perris & Samuel.

Minutes of the previous meeting were read & confirmed.

Accounts for the past session were presented & accepted.

Record of attendance during the past session was read as follows:

Out of a possible total of 9 meetings, not including the dinner,

Mr. Herdman, the Chairman & the Secretary attended	9
Messrs: Brereton, Crook & Husband	8
Messrs: Bullock & Walsh	7
Messrs: Burrows & Millin	6
Messrs: Harley Hobson & Matheson	5
Mr Byles:	4
Messrs: Lilley & McKillop	3
Messrs: Adams, Murray Macdonald, Robertson & Walker	2
Messrs: Alden, Ramsay MacDonald, Perris, Rea, Rylett & Samuel	1

Also out of a possible six meetings, Mr. Fox-Pitt attended 5: out of a possible two meetings Mr. Raphael attended two.

The average attendance was 13.8 as against 16.4 for the previous session.

Sir Richard Stapley was re-elected chairman.

Mr. Parsons was re-elected Secretary

Messrs: Bullock, Crook, Brereton, Harley, Herdman and Lilley were elected as the Committee.

Mr. Bullock conveyed to the Circle Mr. McKillop's regret that he was obliged to resign his membership owing to having taken up an appointment abroad. Mr. Brereton proposed that Ladies shd be admitted to one of the meetings. Mr. Burrows proposed that if so 1st June wd be a suitable meeting to wh they shd be admitted. Both proposals were carried by 8 votes against 2, the majority of the members present shewing a discreditable neutrality.

Mr. Robertson gave his address on Tariff Reform as it appears in 1909.

He traced the history of the movement as represented by Caillard[134] & Byng,[135] & then by Chamberlain. Chamberlain's first departure was imperialistic. He recognised that it wd be necessary to tax food and began by saying 'your food will cost you more'; then finding that this did not arouse enthusiasm—'your food will cost you the same', & later 'your food will cost you less'. His second departure was based on the notion of 'stagnant trade' and 'doomed industries' and led to the formation of the Tariff Reform League.[136] The cry of the Tariff Reformers in 1906–7 was 'to broaden the basis of taxation & to check emigration'[,] in 1908 'to provide employment by keeping out foreign goods'. The idea of Tariff Reform as a means of raising revenue was illusory and incompatible with its function of creating employment.

In the discussion some emphasis was laid on the fact that the most remarkable & mischievous thing about the Tariff Reform Movement as it appears today is that the imperial sentiment, which even if wrong-headed was at all events idealistic, has completely left it.

Richard Stapley   Chairman

3 Nov. 1909.

* * *

[141] The 141st meeting of the Circle was held on 3rd Nov 1909 at 33 Bloomsbury Square.

Present. 14 members out of 29 & one visitor, Sir Richard Stapley in the chair.

Apologies for absence. (6) from Messrs: Byles, Gooch, Hobson, Matheson, Murray Macdonald & Robertson.

Also absent. (9) Messrs: Adams, Alden, Lilley, Fox Pitt, Ramsay MacDonald, Morrison, Perris, Rea & Samuel.

The Minutes of the previous meeting were read & confirmed.

Mr. Husband read his paper on 'The Relations between Local & Imperial Taxation'.

Local rates are levied not only for local services ('beneficial' rates) but also for certain national services locally administered ('onerous' rates). The present basis of local rating viz: 'benefit received' is inadequate & inequitable so far as the class of onerous rates is concerned;

---

[134] Sir Vincent Henry Penalver Caillard (1856–1930), chairman of Tariff Commission 1904, author of *Imperial Fiscal Reform* (London, 1903).

[135] G. Byng, industrialist, author of a book on *Protection* (London, 1903).

[136] In 1903.

& the present system of dealing with the 'Assigned Revenues' has led to great confusion of accounts both in the National & Local Budgets.

The outstanding problem is to find an equitable basis for the distribution amongst local authorities of the grants from the Consolidated Fund in lieu of the basis of the 'fixed payment' grants-in-aid of 1887–8 & the basis of area of collection of the local taxation licences. The grants should be

(a) Only for National Services locally administered

(b) Strictly limited to a specified proportion of the aggregate cost of each assisted service.

(c) Allocated between different districts according to their ability & necessity—to be ascertained by the Central Govt: after investigation.

(d) Subject to suspension or reduction in cases of inefficiency.

In the discussion attention was directed to the lack of continuity of administration of local authorities under present conditions, & to the necessity of large areas of local govt. for such services as education.

Two cures were suggested for the chaos in the A/cs

(1) More local & less national control

(2) More national & less local control.

Richard Stapley   Chairman
1 Decr 1909.

* * *

[142] The 142nd meeting of the Circle was held on 1st Decr 1909 at 33 Bloomsbury Square.

Present. 16 members out of 29 and one visitor—Sir Richard Stapley in the chair.

Apologies for absence 4 from Messrs: Alden, Crook, Hobson & Rylett.

Also absent. Messrs: Adams, Lilley, Murray Macdonald, Ramsay MacDonald, Morrison, Perris, Fox Pitt, Rea & Samuel.

Minutes of the previous meeting were read & confirmed.

Mr. Raphael read his paper on the Minority Report of the Poor Law Commission.[137]

The dominant features of the Minority Report are (1) its insistence on the preventative aspect of the treatment of the poor and (2) its desire to follow the tendency of the times which is to concentrate the

---

[137] The Royal Commission on the Poor Laws (1905–9) published Majority and Minority Reports, the latter mainly prepared and promoted by Beatrice Webb, assisted by Sidney, through the Fabian Society.

whole of the provision for each service in any locality in the hands of the specialised local authority. The conditions of the problem demand not a division according to the presence or absence of destitution but according to the services to be provided. The community shd therefore cease to maintain a special organ for the mere relief of destitution, and get rid of the costly overlap of services resulting from the provision for each separate class being undertaken in the same district by 2 or more local authorities as well as by voluntary agencies.

Public provision for children of school age shd be under the education authority: for the sick, incapacitated, & aged needing institutional treatment—under the Health Committee, for the mentally defective—under the Asylums Committee, for the Aged to whom pensions are awarded—under the Pensions Committee.

There shd be a new officer—the Registrar of Public Assistance. Voluntary agencies shd be systematically organised in conjunction with the public bodies.

The able-bodied in distress shd be dealt with under a Government Department, comprising a National Labour Exchange, a Trade Insurance Division, a Maintenance & Training Division, an Industrial Regulation Division, an Emigration & Immigration Division and a Statistical Division.

In the discussion the following opinions were expressed[:]

It wd be necessary to organise voluntary charity if only to prevent the proposed Registrar of Public Assistance from being absolute, since statutory persons may easily become worse than statutory bodies unless closely supervised. The various new systems set up by the Minority Report would overlap. The Minority over-rate the value of the official & expert element and seem to strike against self-help & to encourage the reckless over-production of children.

On the other hand the Majority Report encourages over-lapping, & drives back under the Poor-Law the bona fide unemployed who have recently been emancipated from it. It wd set up everywhere glorified Charity Organisation Society Committees, & the Charity Organisation Society is even now more disliked than the Poor Law Guardians.

Richard Stapley   Chairman

2 Feby 1910.

* * *

[143] The 143rd meeting of the Circle was held on 2nd Feb. 1910 at 33 Bloomsbury Square.

Present. 13 members out of 29, & 3 visitors—Sir Richard Stapley in the chair.

Apologies for absence. (7) from Messrs: Bullock, Byles, Hobson, Murray Macdonald, Ramsay MacDonald, Matheson & Robertson.

Also absent. Messrs: Adams, Alden, Crook, Lilley, Morrison, Perris, Rea, Rylett & Samuel.

Minutes of the previous meeting were read & confirmed.

Mr. T. Hancock Nunn gave an address on 'Public Assistance & Social Welfare—a criticism of the methods of administration re-commended in the Majority & Minority Reports of the Poor Law Commission'.

The revolutionary point of Majority Report is that, instead of merely meeting by physical means destitution as it exists, it proposes that in every case the causes of distress shall be carefully enquired into. This fundamental principle leads to (1) abolition of guardians (2) co-operation of charitable societies wh are governed by motives quite different from those that have actuated relieving officer. Classi-fication of cases & of institutions leads to selection of larger admin-istrative area—the county area—where there are a sufficiently large number of different institutions. Fundamental error of Majority Report's proposals is in the composition of the Committee wh is not properly representative or elective. One of the main objections to Minority Report is that its administrative proposals depend largely on the Registrar whose task wd be impossible. Even if not impossible it wd be unworkable since elected committees who had to investigate cases wd object to having their recommendations subject to sanction or veto of autocratic registrar. Objection to proposals of both Reports is that they wd take the matter out of the hands of poor people's own neighbours. To examine into causes of distress is primarily the function of voluntary workers. There wd in many cases inevitably be two parallel bodies—the official & the voluntary—working on same lines & both drawing upon Rates. An alternative proposal is to constitute 'Councils of Social Welfare' on lines of Hampstead Council—by sel-ecting out of the electorate persons who shew an active interest in welfare of the poor. Such a council has a direct mandate to promote co-operation & co-ordination of effort.

In the discussion it was suggested (1) that County Councils wd not wish to take on additional work & wd find means of passive resistance (2) that the awakening of neighbourly feeling was the real solvent of the difficulty of dealing with destitution (3) that the suggested councils of social welfare would not be workable everywhere.

Richard Stapley   Chairman

2nd March 1910.

[144] The 144th meeting of the Circle was held on 2nd March 1910 at 33 Bloomsbury Square.

Present. 16 members out of 29 & one visitor—Sir Richard Stapley in the chair.

Apologies for absence (7) from Messrs: Hobson, Murray Macdonald, Perris, Rea, Robertson, Rylett & Samuel.

Also absent. Messrs: Adams, Crook, Harley, Lilley, Ramsay Mac-Donald, & Morrison.

Minutes of the previous meeting were read & confirmed.

Mr. Gooch gave an address on the Recommendations of the Majority & Minority Reports respecting Unemployment.

Under the proposals of the Majority Report unemployment wd be dealt with by the Public Assistance Committee. Objections to this are (1) it wd force the unemployed back into the Poor-Law (2) it wd lead to inequality of treatment & of standards in different districts. (3) it wd not be possible in localities like West Ham where there are congested masses of unemployed.—Under the proposals of the Minority Report unemployment wd be dealt with by a special national authority—or failing that by a new committee of the county council.

Mr. Gooch then dealt with recommendations of both Reports respecting (1) Labour Bureaux, (2) Insurance against Unemployment—in wh connection he described the Ghent system[138] & Mr. Churchill's scheme[139] (3) the attack on Casual Labour (a) by decreasing unskilled boy & girl labour, raising school-age & improving technical & physical education (b) by more systematic organisation of public works (c) by reduction of hours of labour (d) by state provision for widows & deserted wives with young children. He then dealt with specific suggestions respecting unemployed men classified according to efficiency (1) Home Assistance (2) Partial home assistance (Hollesley Bay system[140]) (3) Prolonged stay in Agricultural Colony (4) Detention Colonies for vagrants & loafers.

In the discussion a description was given of the working of certain penal colonies on the continent.

The following opinions were expressed:

1. Labour Exchanges cd not be compulsory until there was some means of dealing with unemployed as a whole: National system with powerful central clearing house therefore necessary.

---

[138] A Belgian voluntary insurance scheme by means of workmen's associations, with state subsidies.

[139] Winston Churchill had embarked in 1908 on a campaign to decasualize labour through labour exchanges [Labour Exchanges Act (1909)], and to assist the residual unemployed through state-created demand.

[140] A farm colony that retrained unemployed people for new occupations on the land.

2. Ghent system of Insurance the best: the difficulties cd be over-come: Trade Unions must act under State regulations.

3. Doubtful whether policy of adapting public works to seasons of unemployment wd be efficacious.

4. All the proposals were only palliatives & unemployment is inevitable until the adoption of Socialism.

                                    Richard Stapley   Chairman
6th April 1910.

* * *

[145] The 145th meeting of the Circle was held on the 6th April 1910 at 33, Bloomsbury Square.

Present. 15 members out of 29.

Apologies for absence (8) from Messrs. Alden, Burrows, Hobson, Murray Macdonald, Ramsay MacDonald, Rylett, Samuel and Walker.

Also absent Messrs. Adams, Crook, Gooch, Morrison, Rea, Robert-son.

Minutes of the previous meeting were read and confirmed.

Mr. Bullock suggested that the next session should be devoted to the consideration of Second Chambers. The proposal was referred to a special committee, consisting of the Chairman, Mr. Matheson, and the Secretary.

Mr. Harley read his paper on Local Government in its bearing on Citizenship and National Life. History of Local Government in England is almost co-extensive with Constitutional history during the period before the Norman Conquest and fills a very large space in Constitutional history until legislative power of Parliament became firmly established. In later days the Counties and Boroughs lost the vigorous individuality of their early life and their self-elected councils came to regard municipal office not as a trust but as a lucrative inheritance.

Between the Reformation and Reform Act of 1832, three factors exerted their influence on the spirit of Local Government:

(1) Foundation and abnormal growth of Poor Law.

(2) Progressive extension of magistrates' jurisdiction in counties.

(3) Decay of Municipal institution in boroughs.

The disadvantages of small area of administration are illustrated by modern history of Local Government in London prior to Act of

1899.[141] Innumerable District Boards and separate authorities for different services. Jobbery and poor type of citizen arise less from small area than from lack of sense of electoral responsibility. Better remuneration is mainly responsible for the more suitable type of person now available for positions in the Local Government service which is remarkably free from officialdom as compared with Imperial Civil Service.

In the discussion the following opinions were expressed:

(1) Salaries should be given to County and County Borough Councillors.

(2) Municipal work needs standardising. No means at present of comparing work of different municipalities.

(3) Electors should be fined for not voting.

(4) The real difficulty in Local Government is a general lack of interest in the matter. On the other hand, great development of provincial municipalities distinguished for enterprise and public spirit worthy of notice.

(5) The policy of local work for local men a bad one. It might be well to have local contracts arranged by one central authority.

Richard Stapley   Chairman

4th May 1910.

* * *

[146] The 146th meeting of the Circle was held on the 4th May 1910 at 33 Bloomsbury Square.

Present. 12 members out of 29.

Apologies for absence (15) from Messrs: Bullock, Byles, Crook, Gooch, Hobson, Lilley, Murray Macdonald, Ramsay MacDonald, Millin, Rea, Robertson, Rylett, Samuel, Raphael & Walker.

Also absent. (2) Messrs: Fox-Pitt & Morrison.

Minutes of the previous meeting were read & confirmed.

The proposed programme (for next session) drawn up by the committee appointed at the previous meeting was discussed at length, and—with considerable modifications—adopted.

Mr. Alden read his paper on 'Local Government. Present scope, with special reference to powers (adoptive Acts &c:) possessed, but not sufficiently used'.

Local government has enormously extended its powers in recent years. During last 30 years receipts from rates have more than doubled & total expenditure of local authorities now about £130.000.000 a

[141] London Government Act (1899).

year. Whole question of local taxation calls for revision since the burden falls with undue weight on poor districts. The Acts wh deal with local government need to be systematized & above all things simplified, & administration shd be made more economical by redistribution of powers and enlargement of area of local authority. Present scope of local government is shown by the number of adoptive & permissive Acts—such as Lighting & Watching Act, Baths & Washhouses Act, Burial Act, Public Health Improvement Act, Public Libraries Act, Notification of Births Act, Employment of Children Act, Provision of Meals Act, Museums & Gymnasiums Act &c:, and the activity & efficiency of particular local authorities may be gauged by extent to which they avail themselves of the powers conferred by these Acts. A wise & discriminating system of Grants-in-Aid wd tend to produce maximum of efficiency at minimum of cost.

In the discussion the following opinions were expressed:

1. License given to local authorities is too generally abused, & it is a question whether it wd not be better to make more services compulsory.

2. More services shd be made national rather than local e.g. Poor-Law & Education Services.

3. Local Government shd be taught in schools as a branch of civics.

Richard Stapley   Chairman

1st June 1910

* * *

[147] The 147th meeting of the Circle was held on 1st June 1910 at 33 Bloomsbury Square. It was the first 'Ladies' Night'.

Present. 13 members out of 29 and 11 visitors of whom 10 were ladies.

Apologies for absence (14) from Messrs: Alden, Brereton, Bullock, Byles, Crook, Gooch, Hobson, Murray Macdonald, Morrison, Rea, Raphael, Robertson, Rylett, & Samuel.

Also absent. Messrs: Lilley & Perris.

Minutes of the previous meeting were read & confirmed.

Mr. Burrows read his paper on the future scope of Local Government and the future relations between the Municipality & the National State. He dealt severely with individualists and 'so-called social reformers' and put in a general plea for communalism. He said that the future scope of local government should be everything wh the municipality can do better than the citizen & that this comprised most things. As examples he mentioned

(a) the sweeping of all chimneys 'at stated periods, with the best appliances, the best machinery and the best labour'
(b) the rendering of all building material non-inflammable (c) the erection of all buildings: and (d) the provision of municipal co-operative dwellings, 'beautiful, artistic, stately—with fountains, statues, flower-beds, pictures, library[,] recreation-rooms & common dining-hall'. He looked forward to the time when the municipality wd be the State and the State the municipality, when there wd be no more quarrels as to their limitations & functions & respective spheres.

The discussion turned mainly on Socialism and Individualism & was marked by violent differences of opinion as to what constituted (a) a Socialist (b) an Individualist (c) a 'spurious individualist'.

Richard Stapley   Chairman

5th October 1910.

* * *

[148] The Rainbow Circle Dinner was held on the 15th June 1910 at the National Liberal Club.

Present. Sir Richard Stapley in the chair, Messrs: Bullock, Burrows, Crook, Gooch, Hobson, Husband, Ramsay MacDonald, Matheson, Parsons, Perris, Rea, Robertson, Samuel, Walker & Walsh: also Messrs: Roskill & Trevelyan.

It was decided that in the ensuing session, the 'Ladies' night' should be a special night unconnected with the course, & that a lady should be asked to read a special paper.

Richard Stapley   Chairman

5 Oct. 1910

* * *

17th Session[142]

[149] The 149th meeting of the Circle was held on the 5th October 1910 at 33 Bloomsbury Square.

Present 16 members and 4 visitors. Sir Richard Stapley in the Chair.

[142] The full talks given in this session were published by the Circle as *Second Chambers in Practice* (London, 1911). Each chapter is preceded by a precis and followed by an outline of the discussion. These addenda reproduce the minutes almost verbatim.

Apologies for absence—7—from Messrs. Alden, Burrows, Murray Macdonald, Ramsay MacDonald, Matheson, Robertson and Samuel.

Also absent Messrs. Adams, Byles, Gooch, Lilley and Russell Rea.

The minutes of the previous meeting were read and confirmed. Accounts for the past session were presented and accepted. It was decided that the subscription for the current session should be 2/-.

The record of attendance during the past session was read, as follows:

Messrs. Herdman, Husband, Walsh, the Chairman and the Secretary attended	8
Messrs. Brereton and Burrows	7
Messrs. Harley, Matheson, Millin and Raphael	6
Messrs. Bullock, Fox-Pitt and Walker	5
Messrs. Byles and Gooch	4
Mr. Adams	3
Messrs. Alden, Crook, Lilley, Perris, Robertson and Rylett	2
Messrs. Hobson, Murray Macdonald, Ramsay MacDonald & Rea	1
Dr. Morrison and Mr. Samuel	0

Average attendance was 15 as against 13.8 last year.

Sir Richard Stapley was re-elected Chairman. Mr. Parsons was re-elected Secretary. Messrs. Bullock, Crook, Brereton, Harley, Herdman and Lilley were elected to the Committee.

The Secretary announced the resignation of Dr. Morrison, whose name was transferred to the visitors' list.

A letter was read from Mr. Matheson offering on behalf of Messrs. P.S. King & Co. to publish the papers of the current session without risk or expense to the Circle. The Circle decided to thank Mr. Matheson for the offer and to inform him that the Circle viewed the project favourably, subject to the consent of the writers, and to an opportunity being afforded for reconsidering the question later on.

Mr. Harley read his paper on the Second Chamber in France and Switzerland and the Referendum. The French Senate is now wholly an Elective Assembly, its members being elected from each Department or Colony by (1) Deputies (2) Members of the Conseil Général (3) Arondissement Councillors (4) Delegates elected by each Municipal Council. The Senators hold office for 9 years, and one third retire each year. The Senate is faulty in its composition: the age limit of 40 is in practice a defect and it is doubtful whether as a legislative body the Senate has any real function or serves any useful purpose. On the other hand the Second Chamber or Council of States in Switzerland is constructed on the only plan which can be theoretically justified— that of the interests of constitutive states of the Federation as contrasted with the interests of the Federation as a whole. If the two Houses disagree, they sit together, and the majority of the united assembly carries the day. The will of the people is further safeguarded by the Referendum. Mr. Harley gave a short account of the working of the Referendum, with particulars of recent cases in which it had been applied, including the rejection of the proposals for a State or Federal Bank and for a system of compulsory universal Insurance, proposals which he held to have been rejected by reason of the people's objection to officialism.

In the discussion the following opinions were expressed:

(1) That the writer had done scant justice to the French Senate, which in point of composition was the best the world had yet produced.

(2) That the functions of a Second Chamber ought to be to prevent reactionary as well as hasty and ill-considered legislation.

(3) That the Referendum does not act conservatively in Switzerland which is essentially a progressive country.

(4) That one of the main uses of the Referendum is its educative influence on voters to whom it tends to give a real and continuous interest in politics and that it is also an important reaction on the Party System.

Widely divergent views were expressed as to whether or not this last effect was a benefit to the body politic.

Chairman.

2 Nov: 1910.

* * *

[150] The 150th meeting of the Circle was held on the 2nd Novr. 1910 at 33 Bloomsbury Square.

Present. 17 members out of 28, Sir Richard Stapley in the chair.

Apologies for absence (7) from Messrs: Alden, Byles, Lilley, Robertson, Rylett, Samuel & Walsh.

Also absent. Messrs: Adams, Murray Macdonald, Raphael & Russell Rea.

Minutes of the previous meeting were read & confirmed.

Mr. McKillop, proposed by Mr. Matheson & seconded by Mr. Bullock, was unanimously re-elected to membership.

A letter from Mr. Lilley, asking to be relieved from undertaking his December paper was read. After some discussion Mr. Gooch kindly agreed to read the paper, and Mr. Matheson to read a paper on the Second Chamber in the U.S.A. on Jan. 11.

Mr. Walker read his paper on the Second Chamber in Canada, South Africa and Australasia. He gave a description of the Legislative systems in these colonies with some account of their evolution &

shewed that in the subordinate or Provincial Legislatures the uni-cameral system is gaining ground. In all three Constitutions (Canada, South Africa & Australia) there is a definite proportion between the numbers in the two Houses, there are arrangements for bringing any disputes between the two Houses to an early settlement, and the tendency in the development of the constitutions has been steadily to give greater power & advantage to the popular chamber. In the latest of the three—that of South Africa—all matters can be brought to an issue during the course of a single Parliament, and provided that a Ministry has a majority in the popular House greater than the hostile majority in the Senate it is practically independent of any action that may be taken by the Senate.

In the discussion the following opinions were expressed:

1. That where there is a Federation the utility of the Upper or Federal Chamber is obvious, but in a unitary state is the reverse of useful & many colonial states are finding this out.

2. That judging by colonial experience the Upper House is of little use as a safeguard, since it tends to become a reflex of the Lower House.

3. That the bicameral superstition is gradually dying.

Richard Stapley   Chairman

14 Dec. 1910.

* * *

[151] The 151th meeting of the Circle was held on the 14th Decr. 1910 at 33 Bloomsbury Sq:

Present: 14 members out of 29—Sir Richard Stapley in the chair—one visitor.

Apologies for absence from Messrs: Burrows, Murray Macdonald, Perris, Raphael & Samuel.

Also absent. Messrs: Adams, Alden, Bullock, Crook, Hobson, Lilley, McKillop, Rea, Robertson & Rylett.

Minutes of the previous meeting were read & confirmed.

Mr. Gooch gave an address on the Second Chamber in Germany & in Austria-Hungary.

Action of these chambers is largely determined, & power limited, by prerogatives & personal influence of Emperor. The German Bundesrath is by far strongest Upper Chamber in the world and acts to some extent as a Council of State. Prussia is dominant & though not necessarily able to secure accomplishment of all her desires can veto any proposal of wh. she disapproves. The Bundesrath can initiate bills of every kind & veto measures passed by Reichstag, & in co-operation with Kaiser, can dissolve Reichstag whenever it thinks fit. When a re-distribution of seats in Reichstag, already long overdue, takes place, serious conflicts between the two houses likely to be more frequent. The most original feature in Upper Chambers of component States of German Empire is to be found in practice of Würtemburg, Baden & Hesse, where in event of Upper Chamber rejecting budget, the issue is settled by majority of votes cast in the two chambers.

The Upper Chamber of Austria closely resembles that of Prussia. An important feature is that by a recent modification of the Constitution the life-peers may not be fewer than 150 nor more than 170. Thus Emperor has abandoned right to get his own way by swamping Upper House with new peers.

In Hungary the predominance of the Lower House is definitely established, & relations between the two Houses resemble in many respects those existing in Great Britain.

In the discussion the following opinions were expressed:
1. That notwithstanding militarism & bureaucracy, democracy does make advance.
2. That Germany is in a good many ways (unspecified) ahead of our own democratic country: this possibly due to wider powers of local government. Against this it was objected that local govt. in Germany is purely bureaucratic.
3. That unless we are careful we too may injure democracy & increase the power of the King.

Richard Stapley   Chairman
11 Jan. 1911

* * *

[152] The 152nd meeting of the Circle was held on the 11th Jan. 1911 at 33 Bloomsbury Square.

Present. 14 members & 2 visitors—Sir Richard Stapley in the chair.

Apologies for absence from Messrs: Alden, Byles, Crook, Hobson, Murray Macdonald, Ramsay MacDonald, Raphael, Rylett, Samuel, Walker & Walsh.

Also absent. Messrs: Adams, Brereton, Lilley & Fox-Pitt.

Minutes of the previous meeting were read & confirmed.

Mr. Matheson read his paper on the Second Chamber in the U.S.A. He sketched the composition & working of the Senate & the House of Representatives, and also of the Legislatures of the different states, giving some account of the experiments that were being made by the latter. He dwelt on the rigidity of the federal constitution. He emphasized the fact that although in theory the House & the Senate are equal in all matters of legislation, except in regard to treaties, in practice the Senate is the stronger. This is because of its practical permanence & because Senators, though of the same type as members of the House are for the most part the strongest & ablest men of that type. The Executive being independent of the legislative body, there is no party government in any such sense as in the United Kingdom.

In the discussion the following opinions were expressed:

1. That for practical purposes we can learn nothing from the American legislative system since a federated state cannot supply an example to a consolidated unitary state such as ours.
2. That the real legislative business of America is all done by Committees.
3. That the Senate is an anomaly: it has executive as well as legislative powers, and it is too small for a deliberative chamber & too big for an executive chamber.
4. That the Senate is the worst element in the American constitution because the system of having an equal number of Senators for each state cannot be altered.
5. That the Senate's power to revise treaties is one wh. in some form we might well adopt in this country.

Richard Stapley   Chairman

1 Feb. 1911

* * *

[153] The 153rd meeting of the Circle was held on the 1st Feb. 1911 at 33 Bloomsbury Square.

Present. 24 members & 4 visitors. Sir Richard Stapley in the chair. The largest meeting on record.

Apologies for absence. from Messrs: Ramsay MacDonald, Matheson, Raphael, Samuel and Walker.

Minutes of the previous meeting were read & confirmed.

Mr. Robertson read his paper on 'Bicameral versus Unicameral Legislative Systems considered in the light of the four preceding papers'.

There are no valid arguments for Second Chambers as apart from the special cases of federations like the U.S.A. and Switzerland, and the theoretic argument against them has never been met. If no single chamber is to be trusted for legislation in general, why is it to be wholly trusted in finance, the most vital form of legislation? If the Second Chamber is to be so small in numbers, so hedged about by checks & restrictions, that it could be either out-voted or over-ruled, where is its control?—Second Chambers are in practice constant sources of friction where they are not mere instruments of delay—and delay can be better provided for by other expedients. There is much to be said for some such system as that of Norway[143]—The prospect for this country is that we shall have a new Second Chamber. The country is not ready for single-chamber government, though if steady educative propaganda were kept up for 5 years, it might then be ready. The nation may someday learn that any required check upon a democratic legislature should be within it.

In the discussion the following opinions were expressed:

1. That Single-Chamber government is theoretically the best but impossible in this country in present state of public opinion.

2. That a Second Chamber, but smaller than House of Lords, is emphatically necessary: that we could hardly do better than form it by selection from that body as it stands: that what we want from it is sympathetic & serious criticism of the measures of the Lower House; and that the proposed limitation of powers wd tend to make House of Lords more sympathetic.

3. That House of Lords shd be abolished in its present form[;] its effective members shd stand for the Lower House wh shd then elect a 2nd Chamber on the Norwegian principle.

4. That the new 2nd Chamber shd be small & chiefly nominated (in part at least from present House of Lords): powers shd be limited to those of delay.

5. That the new 2nd Chamber shd be formed by allowing the present House of Lords to 'dwindle away' until only a small body left to criticise & advise [How it was to 'dwindle away' was not explicitly stated].

Richard Stapley   Chairman

1st March 1911

* * *

[154] The 154th meeting of the Circle was held on 1st March 1911 at 33 Bloomsbury Square

Present. 14 members & 3 visitors—Sir Richard Stapley in the chair.

Apologies for absence. from Messrs: Alden, Bullock, Ramsay Mac-Donald, Parsons, Raphael, Rea & Samuel.

Also absent. Messrs: Adams, Brereton, Harley, Hobson, Lilley, Murray Macdonald, Fox Pitt & Rylett.

Minutes of the previous meeting were read & confirmed.

[143] Incorporating delaying powers but involving the co-operation of lower and upper chambers, as described in *Second Chambers in Practice*, p. 95.

Mr. Perris read his paper on 'The British Cabinet & Executive in relation to Parliament'.

Cabinet Council, a consultative & irregular body whose decisions needed confirmation of Privy Council, first mentioned as suspicious innovation in reign of Charles I. It can hardly be regarded as forerunner of Cabinet as we know it. Definite party government under homogeneous cabinet dates from last years of XVIIth Century. Acknowledgement of chief of cabinet (or Prime Minister) came after death of William III. Public services were gradually rescued from privilege & peculation & subjected to public scrutiny & parliamentary control. Gradual increase in number of ministers afford rough measure of growth of State business. Present cabinet system is open to criticism in that policy of certain departments, notably Foreign Office Admiralty & War Office, not sufficiently open to scrutiny of House. The Imperial Defence Committee[144] & the Colonial Conference[145] are recent creations wh have not yet found their proper place in relation to cabinet system: the former is a questionable departure & both illustrate difficulty of extending cabinet system to a federation of the Empire. The creation of a really strong second chamber wd weaken whole of our State structure by sapping exclusive responsibility of executive ministry to House. The British Cabinet is the centre of a system of government actually & potentially best the world has to offer & we shd seek in its improvement—not in external checks & balances—means of giving weight to experience & wisdom in conduct of State affairs.

In the discussion the following opinions were expressed:

1. That the ideal wd be to get rid of the Cabinet by conducting affairs of each Department by a Committee.
2. That the Cabinet system might prove an instrument for encroachment by the Crown
3. That the Government was carried on to dangerous degree by permanent officials who possess undue power.
4. That though the author was unduly optimistic the British Constitution cd not with advantage be exchanged for any other in existence. Committees wd be unsuitable as substitutes for ministers, but desirable as a supplement to them—the need for a Committee on Estimates being specially obvious. A Committee for Foreign Affairs wd break down because success occasionally depended upon immediate action.

[144] Committee of Imperial Defence, formally established in 1904.

[145] Which began to meet periodically from 1887, initially comprising the colonial secretary and the prime ministers of the self-governing colonies, and from 1907 including a member of the Indian Council.

5. That Committees wd introduce danger that a Cabinet Minister might shield himself behind a committee & so diminish his responsibility.

Richard Stapley   Chairman

15th March 1911

* * *

[155] The 155th meeting of the Circle was held on 15th March 1911 at the Baptist Church House Southampton Row. Ladies' night.

Present. 12 members, and 17 visitors of whom 14 were ladies. Sir Richard Stapley in the chair.

Apologies for absence from Messrs: Alden, Bullock, Burrows, Herdman, Murray Macdonald, Ramsay MacDonald, Matheson, Raphael, Samuel & Walker.

Minutes of the previous meeting were read & confirmed.

Mrs Cloudesley Brereton gave an address on 'Motherhood, the Home & Medical Inspection of Schools'.

She dwelt upon the necessity for getting the parents to co-operate with the medical authorities in the care of the health of the children, & urged that without such co-operation medical inspection wd be to a large extent useless. Voluntary social workers such as managers of schools, members of Care Committees, of Poor Law & Local Government bodies could do much to secure this co-operation. One danger in connection with medical inspection of schools is that we may decrease our vigilance upon early years of infant life because the schools will over-haul the children when they come of school-age. The Teachers' Training Colleges should impress upon the young teachers the importance of medical inspection & of the inter-dependence of home & school and of body & mind.

In the discussion general agreement was expressed with the lecturer's views & particularly with the necessity for bringing school & home into correlation & of getting parents & children on the side of reform. There was some divergence of opinion as to the attitude of poor people towards the school doctor. Other questions considered were the use & abuse of the free-dinner system for necessitous children, the desirability of training scholars (boys especially) to some trade, & of compulsory continuation schools coupled with a half-time system.

Richard Stapley   Chairman

5th April 1911

* * *

[156] The 156th meeting of the Circle was held on the 5th Apr. 1911 at 33 Bloomsbury Square.

Present. 16 members & 3 visitors—Sir Richard Stapley in the chair.

Apologies for absence. (7) from Messrs: Burrows, Byles, Murray Macdonald, Raphael, Robertson, Rylett & Samuel.

Also absent (6) Messrs: Adams, Alden, Lilley, Perris, Fox Pitt & Russell Rea.

Minutes of the previous meeting were read & confirmed.

The following subjects were suggested tentatively for consideration in the next session:

1. Foreign Policies in different countries.
2. National Ideals in politics in different countries.
3. The different forces or movements that have contributed to modern progress.
4. Modern thinkers—especially political thinkers—& the movements associated with them.

This last was proposed by Mr. Gooch as a variant of the third & found most favour. He was asked to suggest names for consideration at the next meeting.

Mr. Ramsay MacDonald gave an address[146] on the British Parliament in relation to suggestions for the future, including Extension of Franchise, Elimination of Plural Vote, Proportional Representation, and the Referendum.

The discussion turned mainly on the last two points—Proportional Representation & the Referendum, neither of which were favoured by the Reader, and the following opinions were expressed:

1. That Proportional Representation secures a better reflection of the will of the people.
2. That the Reader had under-rated the educative effect of the Referendum, wh wd stimulate the will of the people to express itself more effectively. It was desirable to bring home to the people their sense of responsibility for the success or failure of legislative measures.
3. That Representative government acts along Resultant lines & the notion of a special mandate for separate measures was unsound. That the people ought to express their opinion on the great principles of things, but that the details of measures shd be hammered out by the representatives.
4. That the Referendum could only be reactionary in its working.

Richard Stapley   Chairman

3rd May 1911

* * *

[146] Summarized at the end of the minutes of 14th June 1911.

[157] The 157th meeting of the Circle was held on the 3rd May 1911 at 33 Bloomsbury Square.

Present. 15 members & 2 visitors—Sir Richard Stapley in the chair.

Apologies for absence (7) from Messrs: Burrows, Byles, Gooch, Raphael, Rea, Robertson & Samuel.

Also absent (7) Messrs: Adams, Alden, Brereton, Ramsay Mac-Donald, Fox-Pitt, Rylett, & McKillop.

Minutes of the previous meeting were read & confirmed.

The subjects, suggested by Mr. Gooch, for the next session were discussed and, with some amendments, agreed upon.

Mr. Murray Macdonald read his paper on The British Parliament in relation to proposals for Home Rule all round.

1. The only remedy adequate to meet congestion of business in House of Commons is a measure of devolution whereby control of strictly separate interests of each of the countries combined in United Kingdom wd be transferred from Imperial to Subordinate Parliaments. 2. Each country already has its own separate interests separately dealt with, and we have only to follow existing differences to determine nature & extent of powers to be assigned to the subordinate legislatures. Difficulties of the subject lie in question of distribution of taxing powers, & contribution of each country towards imperial expenditure. Customs & Excise must in any case remain under exclusive control of Imperial Parliament. 3. Home Rule all round would allow electors to distinguish between Imperial & domestic questions & it wd no longer be possible for power obtained by a government for a definite imperial purpose to be used in domestic legislation upon wh opinion of country had not been asked or expressed. 4. Home Rule all round wd facilitate a federation of Empire. 5. Measures of domestic legislation being removed from Imperial Parliament conflict between the two Houses wd be minimised.

In the discussion the following opinions were expressed:

1. Arguments in favour of separate legislation for England Ireland & Scotland are strong enough without any consideration of remote possibility of an Imperial Parliament in wh Dominions beyond the ɔeas shd be represented.

2. Legislation touching national economics—such as Factory Legislation, Nationalisation of Railways & Canals—shd not be dealt with separately for the different countries.

3. Measures proposed by the separate legislatures shd not be subject to Imperial Parliament, but shd be subject to veto of Crown—on advice, say, of a panel of 3 judges.

4. Progress of British Empire will be dependent upon the subordinate legislatures being given considerable power of experiment.

5. Different measures of devolution shd be given to the subordinate

legislatures according to their needs: they shd not all have the same powers. The delegated powers shd be specified, leaving the reserved powers unspecified.

Richard Stapley   Chairman

31 May 1911

* * *

[158] The 158th meeting of the Circle was held on 31st May 1911 at 33 Bloomsbury Square.

Present. 10 members & 2 visitors—Sir Richard Stapley in the chair.

Apologies for absence (12) from Messrs: Alden, Brereton, Byles, Crook, Husband, Murray Macdonald, Ramsay MacDonald, Raphael, Robertson, Samuel, Walsh & McKillop.

Also absent. Messrs: Adams, Bullock, Harley, Lilley, Fox Pitt, Rea & Rylett.

Minutes of the previous meeting were read & confirmed.

Mr Herdman read his paper on Representative Government. After briefly reviewing the Session's discussions, he laid stress on the fact that legislative systems in modern civilised countries are almost universally bicameral, and that the Second Chambers display great variety of form & function. He suggested that their useful functions were (1) to delay hasty legislation and (2) to exercise some sort of check on the popular house. The essence of good government is that it shd be directed to right objects & attained by justifiable means. The outward form, the machinery of government (though important) is of subsidiary importance. In our House of Commons we have now the form of popular representation, but the representation itself is much the same as it was before we had the form. As regards finance, in this country we object to interference by the Second Chamber, but it is well to remember that in certain other scarcely less vigorous countries this objection is not displayed.

In the discussion the following opinions were expressed:

(1) That the history of this country in modern times affords no instance of hasty legislation—wh need not really be feared.

(2) That the writer had too low an opinion of representative government & overestimated the capacity of the mass of the people for government. It is more practicable to choose men to carry on the business of government than for the mass of the people to give explicit directions.

(3) That the existence of the bicameral system in new countries is due to other causes than those mentioned—in some cases to the federal nature of the constitution.

(4) That the abolition of the veto of the House of Lords wd not stand durably unless some means of consulting the will of the people on important constitutional points is adopted.

(5) That the general feeling of the Circle seemed to be in favour of the Unicameral system as the most enlightened, though this country might not at present be ready for it.

Richard Stapley   Chairman

11 October 1911

* * *

[159] The Annual Dinner of the Rainbow Circle was held at the National Liberal Club on the 14th June 1911.

Present. Sir Richard Stapley (in the chair) Messrs: Alden, Bullock, Burrows, Byles, Crook, Gooch, Hobson, Ramsay MacDonald, Matheson, Millin, Parsons, Robertson, Samuel, & Walsh; also the following old members: Sir Sydney Olivier, Mr. Roskill & Mr. Trevelyan.

It was decided to hold the meetings in the ensuing session on the 2nd Wednesday instead of the 1st Wednesday in the month.

It was also decided to have a Ladies' night on the same times as before.

Richard Stapley   Chairman

11 October 1911

* * *

Précis of Mr. Ramsay MacDonald's paper read before the Circle at the 156th meeting.

Extension of Franchise in that it wd supply new experience of and outlook on life and new motives for legislation is necessary, and would make House of Commons more representative; but it would not affect necessity or otherwise of check on its authority by second chamber. The only important section of the community that would be enfranchised would be women, but their votes wd not be likely to make any great difference to the nature of our legislation. Present system of Plural Voting is neither sound in principle nor rational in practice. Property is no test of political ability or public virtue. Proportional Representation would not alter existing conditions for the better— indeed it wd lower practical efficiency of Parliament and lessen its representative character. Referendum would reduce responsibility of governments and remove effective authority of Parliament to disorganised mass of the people. It is reactionary in its working and its control over legislation is unreal. Only satisfactory check on Democracy is inward check of its own intelligence and vigilance.

* * *

Eighteenth Session

[160] The 160th meeting of the Circle was held on 11th Octr. 1911 at 33 Bloomsbury Square.

Present. 15 members—Sir Richard Stapley in the chair.

Apologies for absence (7) from Sir Wm Byles, Messrs: Gooch, Murray Macdonald, Ramsay MacDonald, Raphael, Rylett & Walker.

Also absent. (8) Messrs: Adams, Alden, Hobson, Millin, Fox Pitt, Russell Rea, Robertson & Samuel.

Minutes of the previous meeting were read & confirmed.

Accounts for the past session were presented & accepted.

The record of attendance during the past session was read, viz:

Out of a possible total of 9 meetings, not including the dinner & the ladies' night,

Sir Richard Stapley, Messrs: Herdman & Millin attended	9
Messrs: Husband & Parsons	8
" Gooch, Harley, Matheson, Perris & Walker	7
" Bullock, Crook, Hobson & Walsh	6
" Brereton & Burrows	5
" Fox Pitt & McKillop	4
Sir Wm Byles, Messrs: Ramsay MacDonald & Robertson	3
" Lilley, Murray Macdonald, Russell Rea & Rylett	2
" Adams, Alden & Raphael	1
Mr. Samuel	0

The average attendance was 15.5 as against 15 in the previous session.

Sir Richard Stapley was re-elected Chairman.

Mr. Parsons was re-elected Secretary.

Messrs: Crook, Brereton, Harley, Herdman & Lilley were re-elected to the Committee.

The Chairman announced the resignation of Mr. Bullock who has moved into the country. It was resolved to send Mr. Bullock a letter expressing the regret of the Circle at his resignation. His name was added to the Visitors' list.

Owing to Mr. Rylett's inability to attend his name also was removed to the Visitors' list.

Mr. H. Golding, proposed by the Secretary & seconded by Mr. Lilley was elected to membership. The Rev. R.P. Farley proposed by Mr. Lilley & seconded by Mr. Walsh was also elected.

It was resolved to send a letter of condolence to Mr. Ramsay MacDonald on the recent death of his wife.

Mr. Brereton regretted that he found himself unable to read the paper on Sorel & Syndicalism on Jan. 10th, and Mr. Farley undertook to fill his place.

Mr. Crook read his paper on Tolstoi.

Tolstoi, dominated by the religious Asiatic spirit, could only have been a product of Russia where the influences of both Western & Eastern civilisations meet. He was the greatest recent exponent of the teachings of Jesus, as he understood them. His treatment of the doctrine 'Resist not evil' was original & forceful, and from it he deduced certain definite rules of life, wh however are open to grave practical objection. It was characteristic of him that his line of thought should lead him to class together as equally objectionable, armies, juries, prisons, factories, disorderly houses & parliaments, and denounce the Church, the State, Culture, Art, Civilisation & all forms of Government. His political anarchy was based on the doctrine of universal love by wh this present life ought to be altered into something far holier & happier than is now dreamed of. Tolstoi was more a religious than a political, social or economic reformer & what he accomplished in every field was mainly due to his religious ideas. He was vehemently opposed to almost all the movements of his time—in politics, economics, industry, education & art. He sympathised profoundly with the objects of some of them but not with the methods. He gave impetus to the cause of international peace more by inspiring other men than by his own direct action. Like nearly all great religious reformers he was a fierce opponent of the Spirit of his Age. He stands out as a great force that makes for righteousness, as a great modern saint who preached as no one else did in our generation that God is Love.

In the discussion the following opinions were expressed: That the fundamental factor in considering Tolstoi is the action of external circumstances on the spirit of a genius. The Russian revolutionary movement is the greatest factor in modern history and the greatest factor in Tolstoi's development.

That Tolstoi cd not be logical because he had a perfect passion for truth & was in a constant condition of growth & development.

That he had a greater influence on ethics than any other man in the 19th century: he was the conscience not merely of Russia but of Europe.

Richard Stapley   Chairman

8th Nov. 1911

* * *

[161] The 161st meeting of the Circle was held on 8th Nov. 1911 at 33 Bloomsbury Sq.

Present. 19 members & 3 visitors—Sir Richard Stapley in the chair.

Apologies for absence (4) from Mr. Alden, Sir Wm Byles, Mr. Gooch & Mr. Raphael.

Also absent. Messrs: Lilley, Murray Macdonald, Ramsay Mac-Donald, Fox Pitt, Russell Rea, Robertson & Samuel.

Minutes of the previous meeting were read & confirmed.

A vote of thanks to Mr. Matheson was passed for the admirable way in which he carried through the publication of the papers read during the previous session.

A vote of congratulation to Mr. Robertson was passed on his appointment to office under the Government.[147]

Mr. F.W. Goodenough, introduced by Mr. Brereton, proposed by Mr. Perris & seconded by Mr. McKillop was elected to membership.

Mr. Golding read his paper on 'Bergson'.[148]

One of the greatest of the world powers is inertia (a) of rest (b) of motion. Its operation in human affairs to be seen in custom, convention, habit, fashion, imitation. We are not however completely abandoned to dead set of tendency. Man uniting creature & creator conquers inertia by dividing it against itself. In 19th century philosophy specially significant are (i) revolt against Panlogism expressed in increasing prominence accorded to alogical element in reality (ii) attempt made by pragmatists to reduce axioms to postulates or conventions (iii) emphasis of the quasidogmatic nature of value judgments. Bergson consummates & interprets revolt against doctrine that scientific law & order can ever swallow up the contingent & the incommensurable, that to a sufficiently vast intelligence past & future wd alike be present and known[,] a doctrine wh unwarrantedly assumes essential unreality of time & change. In 'The Immediate Data of Consciousness'[149] Bergson mainly concerned himself with establishing reality of duration, incessant change, novelty, & showed that determinist arguments are founded on spatial metaphors applied inadmissibly to mental phenomena: & on confusion of real duration with a homogeneous medium wh is termed time but on analysis proves to be only a bastard space. In 'Matter & Memory'[150] Bergson elaborates his theory of knowledge, deals with relation of perception to reality, with the role of consciousness & nature of connection of mind with brain. In 'Creative Evolution'[151] he demonstrates inadequacy alike of the mechanical & teleological hypotheses & holds that evolution is explicable only as manifestation of a vital impulse, an *élan*

[147] As Parliamentary secretary to the Board of Trade.
[148] Henri Louis Bergson (1859–1941). French philosopher.
[149] *Essai sur les données immédiates de la conscience* (Paris, 1879). Translated as *Time and Free Will* (London, 1910).
[150] Published in English, London, 1910.
[151] Published in English, New York, 1911.

de vie evidently closely akin to Schopenhauer's 'will to live'. Life appears as incessant effort to suspend the degradation of energy, to forge out of inert matter an instrument of freedom. Life is greater than all thought about life can be: intelligence is an instrument evolved primarily for the handling of matter, & is characterised by radical inability to comprehend life. Instinct & intelligence represent divergent solutions of same problem: intelligence is not developed instinct—nor instinct annulled intelligence. In man intuition though almost extinguished still survives, & if we are to seize life in its wealth of potentialities we must supplement intelligence with intuition. Mr. Golding's criticism of Bergson was mainly directed to his theory of knowledge, his doctrine of intuition, his claimed vindication of freedom, & his resort to Schopenhauerism on his proved inadequacy of the accidental variation theory.

In the discussion the following opinions were expressed:

1. Bergson must give up the abruptness of the distinction he draws between organic & inorganic, between instinct & intellect.

2. The alleged connexion between Schopenhauer & Bergson a mere coincidence. Bergson really started from an antagonism to Herbert Spencer with whom he was at one time in accord.

3. Idealism & Realism both fail to solve the problem of philosophy. Bergson's great discovery is that there is a way out of the dilemma namely in recognising that Life is something wider than Intellect.

4. Every portion of matter has memory in it. Consciousness is memory preserving the past in the present.

5. Though space & time may be inadequate for explanation of things in general they are not therefore untrue. The testing point of Bergsonism has yet to come.

John A. Hobson   Chairman

13 December 1911

* * *

[162] The 162nd meeting of the Circle was held on 13th Decr 1911 at 33 Bloomsbury Square.

Present. 20 members—Mr. Hobson in the chair, Sir Richard Stapley being absent through illness.

Apologies (5) from Messrs: Alden, Burrows, Ramsay MacDonald, Raphael & Sir Richard Stapley.

Also absent. Messrs: Murray Macdonald, Fox-Pitt, Russell Rea, Robertson & Samuel.

Minutes of the previous meeting were read & confirmed.

Mr. Adams read his paper on William James.

James approached philosophical questions from the standpoint of psychology. He held that concepts can be nothing else than designative their whole essence & value being to point us to perception, to enable us to predict the percepts we shall experience in the future and to organise our experience. Hence follows that theory of pragmatism according to wh truth is but a class name for definite working values in experience. On pragmatist principles we cannot reject any hypothesis if consequences useful to life flow from it. James was a Pluralist, claiming that Pluralism is more scientific than Monism, agrees more with the moral & dramatic expansiveness of life, & allows for genuine novelty & freedom of will.

In criticising James's views Mr Adams suggested that thought must be the sole judge both of its own concepts and of the perceptual flux, and must try to harmonise them in some wide view, that the pragmatic view of truth is superficial unsound & unsatisfactory, & still more so the Pluralistic view of the Universe. James's theories are, however, negatively of great value as sharp & piercing criticisms of current philosophical systems.

In the discussion the following opinions were expressed:

1. The Pluralist conception is justified in so far as it emphasises unique values of separate elements of reality: but these uniquenesses interpenetrate & their interpenetration is the key to reality & spiritual life.

2. James was right in so far as he denied absolute truth to any body of accumulated doctrine in any school of thought, but not in his loose conception of pragmatic truth.

3. The element of personality entered largely into James's thought & interpretation of the world. By his criticism of barren absolutism & his emphasis of warm reality of life he contributed valuably to modern philosophy.

4. James's chief significance lay in his popularising of philosophy & carrying to victory the revolt against Hegelianism.

Richard Stapley   Chairman

10th January 1912

* * *

[163] The 163rd meeting of the Circle was held on the 10th Jan: 1912 at 33 Bloomsbury Square.

Present 16 members and one visitor—Sir Richard Stapley in the chair.

214 MINUTES OF THE RAINBOW CIRCLE, 1894-1924

Apologies for absence (5) from Mr. Brereton, Sir Wm Byles, Mr. Husband, Mr. Matheson & Mr. Raphael.

Also absent. Messrs: Alden, Lilley, Murray Macdonald, Ramsay MacDonald, Fox Pitt, Russell Rea, Robertson, Samuel & Goodenough.

Minutes of the previous meeting were read & confirmed.

Mr. Farley read his paper on Sorel & Syndicalism.

Prevailing dissatisfaction with received ideas nowhere more ably stated than by Sorel, the implacable enemy & unsparing critic of modern society, the apostle of the Social Revolution in its sharpest form. Syndicalism relies on federation of trade unions & will have nothing to do with development along parliamentary & democratic lines. Its method, its weapon, is to be the general strike wh is to be quite independent of politics. Sorel maintains that proletarian violence can not only make the social revolution sure but is the only means left to European nations, besotted by humanitarianism, of getting back their old energy.

In the discussion the following opinions were expressed: 1. Sorel's theory is absolutely barren because he does not shew what can result from catastrophic action of general strike.

2. French democracy has great distrust of all associations formed within the State. Sorel's idea is that a general co-operation & cohesion of workers will constitute such a menace to society that it will enable the workers to extort more than can be obtained by representative methods.

3. Sorel is symptomatic of social movement of the day & so far valuable. The greatest need of the present moment is the excitation of the masses to do something for themselves, to take in hand their own redemption.

4. Syndicalism proper finds its origin in countries where an unsuccessful attempt has been made to achieve real reform by parliamentary socialism. French Syndicalists propose to establish suddenly & revolutionarily an entirely new & proletariate state. In this country the object of those who favour the general strike is rather to secure establishment of minimum rates of wages.

5. Anything that makes for disorganisation has no future in it. Sorel's system stands condemned by his lack of definite end as the result of the Napoleonic struggle he advocates.

Richard Stapley   Chairman

14 February 1912

* * *

[163a] The 163rd[152] Meeting of the Circle was held on the 14th Feby 1912 at 33 Bloomsbury Square.

Present. 15 members & 2 visitors—Sir Richard Stapley in the chair.

Apologies for absence from Sir Wm Byles, Messrs: Ramsay MacDonald, Matheson, Golding & Walker.

Also absent. Messrs: Alden, Adams, Hobson, Canon Lilley, Messrs: Murray Macdonald, McKillop, Fox Pitt, Russell Rea, Robertson, & Samuel.

Minutes of the previous meeting were read & confirmed.

Mr. Perris read his paper on Hervé[153] & the Peace Movement. He traced the growth of the Peace Movement from 1898 when the Tsar of Russia led the way, & he pointed out that although it has had small successes in the way of Conferences & arbitration treaties it has been quite ineffectual in stopping the growth of armaments or in removing the danger of war between European States. The attitude of continental socialists is favourable to the right of legitimate defence & conversion of permanent armies into citizen armies after the Swiss model. Gustave Hervé is not a great man but a great symptom—a revolutionary socialist who holds that it is necessary to open combat on military servitude & the whole range of ideas on wh it rests—patriotism in particular. He advocates the strike against war. Reformers ought to limit themselves to efforts wh directly & demonstrably reduce the evil of military establishments & the risk of war & shd endeavour to increase the faith of men & nations in pacific methods of settling disputes.

The discussion turned mainly on the questions of 'legitimate defence', arbitration courts—with or without executive power to enforce their decisions—, & the practicability or otherwise of stopping a war (a) by a general strike (b) by a military strike.

Richard Stapley   13 March 1912

* * *

[164] The 164th Meeting of the Circle was held on the 13th March 1912 at 33 Bloomsbury Square.

Present. 18 members & 4 visitors—Sir Richard Stapley in the chair.

Apologies for absence—from Messrs: Burrows, Gooch, Ramsay MacDonald, Matheson, McKillop, Robertson & Walker.

Also absent. Canon Lilley, Messrs: Murray Macdonald, Fox-Pitt, Russell Rea and Herbert Samuel.

[152] An error in enumeration—should be 164th.
[153] Gustave Hervé (1871–1944). French socialist, internationalist and pacifist.

Minutes of the previous meeting were read & confirmed.

Mr. Hobson read his paper on 'Olive Schreiner, Ellen Key and Feminism'.[154]

He dealt with the recent factors that have produced the feminist movement—notably education of women, large increase in the number of careers open to them, and the smaller families that generally prevail nowadays among the middle class—the class primarily affected. The chief demands of the movement are (1) for freedom of personality, (2) for equal share in shaping social life. The air of individualism & sex antagonism, the general disparagement of sex to be seen in the writings of Cicely Hamilton,[155] Olive Schreiner, Ellen Key and Mrs. Gilman,[156] indicate a protest against the domination of the male. Society seems to be moving to two conditions of change (1) Option of independent economic life for women (2) Stricter monogamy with greater facilities for divorce.

The discussion turned mainly on the questions of Equality of Opportunity for men & women in social & economic life, the sociological fallacies respecting matriarchy, increased facilities for divorce, equal payment for men & women doing the same work, payment for maternity, the sex-hostility displayed in and induced by the feminist movement, and comparison of the nature and extent of the movement in this country and other countries—particularly the United States of America.

Richard Stapley   Chairman

27th March 1912.

* * *

[165] The 165th meeting of the Circle was held on the 27th March, 1912, at the Baptist Church House, Southampton Row.

Present: 9 members, 5 ladies and 1 other visitor. Sir Richard Stapley in the chair.

Apologies for absence were received from Messrs. Alden, Byles, Farley, Herdman, Matheson, Parsons, Robertson, Adams, Crook, Gooch, Ramsay MacDonald, McKillop and Russell Rea.

The minutes of the previous meeting were read and confirmed.

Miss Constance Smith[157] gave an address on 'Women in sweated

---

[154] Olive Schreiner (1855–1920), South African writer and radical; Ellen Key (1849–1926), Swedish author and lecturer on the feminist movement and child welfare.

[155] Cicely Hamilton (1872–1952). Actress, playwright, feminist and suffragette.

[156] Charlotte Perkins Stetson Gilman (1860–1935). American feminist, socialist and social reformer.

[157] The original name on the programme was that of Gertrude Tuckwell, the President of the Women's Trade Union League.

and dangerous trades.' Those who thought that so far as women are concerned comparative peace reigned in the labour world were rudely undeceived by the Bermondsey Strike[158] last summer with its pitiful demand of a quarter of an hour for tea and 1/- a week additional pay. It is not, however, necessary to dwell upon the facts of the extreme cases. The condition of what may be called the middle army of women workers—e.g. of those engaged in one of the sixteen branches of the clothing trade, which is regarded as their special province, is sufficiently significant: of these, over 50% are working a full week for a wage of less than 15/- and over 20% for a wage of 10/-. How inadequate such wages are can be immediately realised by a moment's reflection upon the cost of living in any large town. The employer obviously assumes that his woman employee is living at home. This however is by no means invariably the case, and then her life is one of privation coupled with temptation.

Generally woman's position in the labour market is unsatisfactory for many reasons including:

1. The lack of organization in women's trades with the notable exception of the textile industries.

2. The seasonal character of many of such trades.

3. Difficulty of direct access to the employer.

4. The low age of entry and uncertainty as to continuance owing to the possibility of marriage.

5. The prevalent system of fines and deductions and of various forms of evasion of the Truck Act.[159]

It should be noted that the condition of the home worker is even worse than that of the factory hand as she is entirely outside the protection of the law.

As regards dangerous trades the general idea that workers receive good wages is not in accordance with fact.

The conditions of the work of women in the Pottery District are still highly unsatisfactory as evidenced by the enormous amount of sickness in certain branches, the effect on the birth rate and the general deterioration of vitality.

The special rules for Factory Workers in these trades seem to have but little effect and the only real remedy would be the removal of all women from the trade.

As against this however work in the Potteries is the only means of

---

[158] Up to 14,000 women went on strike for increased wages in the Bermondsey district of London in August 1911, organized by the National Federation of Women Workers. The Federation was represented among others by Herbert Burrows.

[159] The Truck Acts were a series of Acts from 1725 onwards to protect workers against substitution of goods, or truck, for wages. The latest of those was the Truck Act of 1896 protecting workers from harsh fines for infringements of rules or for damage.

livelihood in the district open to women. Still something might be done were the facts generally realised and were the use of none but leadless glaze encouraged. In the last resort the community as a whole is answerable for present conditions and the ultimate remedy is only to be found in the general enlightenment of public opinion and an increased sense of responsibility.

In the discussion the establishment of a Trade Board System and the raising of the school age were advocated, the latter partly on the ground that child labour proves a very real temptation to slackness on the part of the parent.

Attention was also called to the failure of 'white lists' and to the need for improvement in the conditions of Factory work. If factories were more beautiful and more wholesome places not only would the character of the work itself be improved but also the health and general well-being of the workers.

It was further suggested that the Insurance Act was to a certain extent a step in the direction of the organization of woman's labour and that thus perhaps the way would ultimately be made clear for the minimum wage—the only really effective solution of the problem.

Chairman

17 April, 1912

* * *

[166] The 166th meeting of the Circle was held on the 17th April 1912 at 33 Bloomsbury Square.

Present. 12 members and one visitor—Mr. Heaford, one of the executors of Ferrer's will—Sir Richard Stapley in the chair.

Apologies for absence. 10 from Messrs: Alden, Burrows, Farley, Gooch, Goodenough, Husband, Murray Macdonald, Matheson, McKillop & Roskill.

Also absent. Messrs: Adams, Hobson, Canon Lilley, Messrs: Ramsay MacDonald, Perris, Fox-Pitt, Russell Rea, Samuel & Walker.

Minutes of the previous meeting were read & confirmed. Members were asked for suggestions for the next session's discussions. Mr. Robertson thought it might be useful to consider proposed remedies for Labour Unrest and undertook to sketch out a programme.

Mr. Robertson read his paper on Ferrer[160] & the Anti-clerical Movement in Spain:

---

[160] Francisco Ferrer (1849–1909). Spanish free thinker and educationalist. Executed on spurious charges of having supported an Anarchist uprising, he became a cause célèbre for Rationalists such as Robertson. See W. Archer, *The Life, Trial and Death of Francisco Ferrer* (London, 1911).

Ferrer's innocence of complicity in the Barcelona outrages has been proved beyond all question. He is simply a martyred propagandist of militant rationalism in a priest-ridden Catholic country. His educational methods in so far as they sought to make children miniature free-thinkers & premature aeratists rather than to develope their thinking faculties were not so ideally scientific as he thought, but as a reformer he shd be judged in correlation with the education and the no-education he saw around him. The comparison is entirely favourable to Ferrer.

In the discussion Mr. Heaford contributed interesting particulars of the Escuela Moderna[161] & of its influence in towns other than Barcelona. He also mentioned the fact that the same court that had tried Ferrer had just ordered the restitution of his property to his heirs, thus practically admitting that he had been unjustly condemned.

The other chief points discussed were the didactic rationalism of Ferrer's educational methods, and the question of what constitutes religion.

Richard Stapley   Chairman

8 May 1912.

* * *

[167] The 167th meeting of the Circle was held on the 8th May 1912 at 33 Bloomsbury Square.

Present 16 members & 3 visitors, Sir Richard Stapley in the chair.

Apologies for absence from Sir Wm Byles, Messrs: Brereton, Matheson, Robertson & Walsh.

Also absent. Messrs: Alden, Gooch, Hobson, Murray Macdonald, Ramsay MacDonald, McKillop, Fox-Pitt, Russell Rea, & Samuel.

Minutes of the previous meeting were read & confirmed.

Mr. Robertson's proposals for the next session's programme were considered &, with some slight modification, adopted.

Canon Lilley read his paper on Murri[162] & Italian Modernism.

In the discussion the following opinions were expressed:

That no Church has been in the van of progress since history first began: that the task of the modernists—the reformation of the Church from within—is hopeless.

That any great reconstruction of the Church would disintegrate it, but that without a schism pure-spirited reformers like Murri would not have a following.

---

[161] Modern Schools were founded in Barcelona by the League of Free Thinkers to combat clericalism.

[162] Romolo Murri (1870–1944). Former priest, Italian Christian Democrat politician.

That the best hope of idealist movements is with the modernists & that it is possible that the next great religious movement may come from Italy.

That Kierkegaard anticipated Murri & liberal christians generally.

Richard Stapley

12th June 1912

* * *

[168] The 168th meeting of the Circle was held on the 12th June 1912 at 33 Bloomsbury Square.

Present. 15 members & 4 visitors—Sir Richard Stapley in the chair.

Apologies for absence (5) from Messrs: Burrows, Farley, Ramsay MacDonald, Raphael & Walsh.

Also absent. Messrs: Alden, Murray Macdonald, McKillop, Perris, Fox-Pitt, Russell Rea, Robertson, Samuel, Goodenough & Sir William Byles.

Minutes of the previous meeting were read & confirmed.

Mr Harley read his paper on Anatole France.[163]

He divided the French literature of the 19th century, in relation to social movements, into three periods (1) the period before 1850 (2) the scientific period represented by the Zola of the Rougon-Macquart series & (3) the period after 1880 represented by Anatole France. The first was troubled, anxious & conscience-stricken, inclined to take refuge in the past: the second was sober & scientific: the third combined the knowledge of the second with the anxiety & travail of the first. Anatole France did not, like Zola, aim at depicting social life in all its most sordid details. He recognised that some selection is necessary although at times he is pessimistic as to the possibility of making a really representative selection. Extracts were read from some of his works shewing how much he emphasized the materialistic side of history & it was shewn that he had a point of view for everybody from Pilate to ex-President Roosevelt. His difference from the characteristic attitude of Zola is due to the fact that not Biology but Sociology is the science of the 20th century. In his materialistic mood, however, Anatole France describes man as 'an animal that eats & drinks & makes love', & the whole seeming contradiction between the views of the Epicurean man of letters & the Socialist politician is due to the fact that in his speeches he proclaimed that 'thought is the most essential function of humanity'.

[163] For an earlier version see J.H. Harley, *The New Social Democracy* (London, 1911), chapter V.

The latter part of the paper was devoted to an attempt to explain how the two Frances—writer & socialist—could be explained & harmonised.

In the discussion the following opinions were expressed:

That Anatole France alone among the literary men of his country believes in the reality of the progressive movement in France: that his resolute stand for progress in a reactionary age is a great achievement: but that he has no faith in God or in any kind of religion & it is doubtful whether he has much in man, though he is sincere as far as he goes: that as an ironist, a mocker, a destructive critic, he is doing for this century what Voltaire did for his: that his most marked failing—as also Zola's—is his total lack of insight into the religious spirit.

Richard Stapley   Chairman

9th October 1912.

* * *

Memorandum.

[169] The 169th meeting was held at Tunbridge Wells from the 21st to the 23rd June 1912, when Sir Richard Stapley most kindly entertained the Circle at the Spa Hotel. Nearly all the members put in an appearance for at least a part of the time. The weather was ideal and the Circle gave itself up wholeheartedly to enjoyment. Where discussion was of a serious nature it was for the most part conducted by two's & three's somewhat surreptitiously. Some of the staidest members (it is better not to mention names) revealed unsuspected powers, & depths, of frivolity—especially on the last night of this most pleasant visit.

The Circle presented Sir Richard with an album containing the photographs of all the present members[164]—a little gift intended as a token of the honour & affection in wh he is held by them, & of their appreciation of all he has done for the Circle during so many years.

The only item of business transacted was the re-election of Mr. John Roskill in place of Mr. Fox-Pitt whose name was removed for non-attendance.

Ambrose Parsons   Hon: Secy.

* * *

[164] See British Library of Political and Economic Science, Coll. Misc., 575/5.

Nineteenth Session

[170] The 170th meeting of the Circle was held on the 9th Oct. 1912 at 33 Bloomsbury Square.

Present. 15 members out of 30—Sir Richard Stapley in the chair—one visitor.

Apologies for absence (10) from Sir Wm Byles, Messrs: Burrows, Brereton, Crook, Gooch, Goodenough, Husband, Murray Macdonald, Ramsay MacDonald, Robertson & Roskill.[165]

Also absent. (5) Messrs: Alden, Rea, Samuel, & Canon Lilley.

Minutes of the 168th meeting were read & confirmed.

The Accounts wh shewed a balance of 1s/8d were presented & accepted.

The Record of Attendance was read as follows:

Out of a possible 9 meetings—excluding the Ladies' night -

Messrs: Crook, Harley, Herdman & Parsons attended	9
” Golding, Millin, & Sir Richard Stapley	8
” Brereton, Farley, Husband, Perris & Walsh	7
Mr. Adams	6
Messrs: Burrows, Goodenough, Hobson & Walker	5
” Gooch, Matheson, McKillop, Raphael[166] & Canon Lilley	4
Sir Wm Byles	3
Messrs: Alden & Robertson	1
” Fox Pitt, Murray Macdonald, J.R. MacDonald, Russell Rea & Samuel	0

Average 16.2

In view of Mr. Samuel's non-attendance at the regular meetings during the past 3 years it was decided to remove his name to the Visitors' List.

Sir Richard Stapley was re-elected as Chairman
Mr. Parsons   ”   ”   ” Secretary
Messrs: Brereton, Crook, Harley, Herdman & Canon Lilley were re-elected to the Committee.

Mr. Perris read his paper on Compulsory Arbitration.

Compulsory Arbitration is almost universally suspect in the Labour world. The peaceful methods of settling disputes may be classified under 5 heads (i) Investigation of disputes & publication of reports thereon (ii) Direct Negotiation—the commonest & most successful method (iii) Mediation & Conciliation wh are even more successful in preventing disputes than in settling them (iv) Arbitration proper wh implies a voluntary submission but not necessarily acceptance of

---

[165] 11 apologies—Brereton transferred from 'also absent' list.
[166] Additional note for the first four names: 'out of possible 5'.

the award (v) Judicial or Administrative process enforced by State—such as settlement of wages by Wage Boards & Compulsory Arbitration.

The Canadian & Australasian experiments[167] are interesting but of little value to us owing to radical differences in circumstances. Legally enforceable arbitration is not properly arbitration but a branch of the law. The difficulties of imposing it upon the thousand & one complex trades & the many possible questions of industrial dispute are vast. But apart from that the point is that state prevention of strikes implies the State regulation of adult labour in all its branches & this implies a new judiciary & administration supported by national opinion, recognition of living minimum wage for all workers, & full organisation both of men & masters. There is no present prospect of any of these conditions being realised.

In the discussion the general sense of the Circle was against Compulsory Arbitration as ordinarily understood, but it was held that increased powers would be put into the hands of the State in the matter of conciliation, & that experiments would probably be tried following to some extent the lines of Canadian & Australasian legislation—especially since the Nation has a direct interest in intervening in strikes wh hold up the industry of the country. Opinions were expressed that the essential weakness of arbitration in industrial affairs is the absence of a standard to appeal to; & that the objection of the workers has its basis in the fact that they do not think justice wd be done to them by the arbitrators.

Richard Stapley   Chairman

13 Novr 1912

* * *

[171] The 171st Meeting of the Circle was held at 33 Bloomsbury Square on 13th Novr 1912.

Present. 20 members out of 29—Sir Richard Stapley in the chair.

Apologies for absence (3) from Sir Wm Byles, Messrs: Walker & Russell Rea.

Also absent. Messrs: Alden, Lilley, Murray Macdonald, Ramsay MacDonald, McKillop & Robertson.

Minutes of the previous meeting were read & confirmed.

---

[167] Of particular interest are the following: in Canada, the Arbitration Act of 1888 (Nova Scotia) and the Industrial Disputes Investigation Act (1907), known also as the Lemieux Act; in Australia, the Industrial Arbitration Act of New South Wales (1901) and the Law of Arbitration and Conciliation (1904); in New Zealand, the Industrial Conciliation and Arbitration Act (1894), discussed by Reeves in Meeting 30 and by Harley in Meeting 94.

Mr. Hobson gave an address on 'Causes of Social Unrest with special reference to the Cost of Living'.

Causes of discontent among all sections of workers in all grades of industry and commerce and in both sexes are chiefly Education in its widest sense and Rise of Prices. Under Education are included such influences as the cheap press, the Music Hall, Picture Palace, popular editions of books and the wide franchise. An increasingly intelligent interest in actual conditions of life has helped to change attitude towards the Rich, to increase sense of class consciousness, to foster feeling that great powers or potentialities possessed by the democracy are thwarted by forces it cannot grasp, and to make more vocal insistent desire for fuller life.

As long as the workers were conscious of gaining ground they were satisfied—too easily indeed. But after tangible progress for 50 years, there has been something like a stoppage. Since 1895 prices have risen without equivalent rise in wages. Expansion of gold supply is a factor, but not as sometimes assumed the predominant one. More important are rapid extension of 1. Banking 2. Joint Stock enterprise (enlarging forms of 'securities' which are main basis of credit); 3. Financing of over-seas investments which fructify but slowly.

If with accelerated supply of money, production of goods kept pace prices would not rise—but various causes are operating against this— e.g.—Growth of expense on Armaments, Trusts—restricting output, wasteful multiplication of distributing classes, and rapid spread of luxurious habits among classes endowed with power to save.

Price of labour, which is relatively more abundant than capital, less mobile and not so well organised, does not rise correspondingly.

In the discussion the following subjects among many others were touched upon: The historic rise in prices consequent upon discovery of Spanish silver mines: the recent rise due to action of Trusts and modern social legislation: discontent due to modern decay of Religion; the cosmic consciousness, bimetalism, the Insurance Act, the emancipation of Russian serfs, the French Revolution, the imperviousness of Lord Hugh Cecil; motor veils[sic] and the cost of boots.

Richard Stapley   Chairman

11 Dec. 1912

* * *

[172] The 172nd Meeting of the Circle was held at 33 Bloomsbury Square on 11th Dec. 1912.

Present. 20 members & 2 visitors—Sir Richard Stapley in the chair.

Apologies for absence (4) from Sir Wm Byles, Messrs: Ramsay MacDonald, Raphael & Robertson.

Also absent. (5) Messrs: Alden, Adams, Crook, Lilley & McKillop.
Minutes of the previous meeting were read & confirmed.

Mr. Russell Rea read his paper on the Nationalisation of Mines &
Railways.

The nationalisation of Railways is admitted to be well within range
of practical politics & is desirable from point of view of economy &
efficiency, but no important effects wd be likely to follow either to
national finances, our industries, or the condition of railway servants.
The nationalisation of Coal mines is a feasible proposition, the State
to be the universal coal landlord & to work as well as own all collieries.
It has to be remembered that coal is a wasting national asset & this
is one of the governing considerations in deciding whether it is wise
for State to assume control. Continental nations on State ownership
system get for the State little if any more in royalties than we get out
of our small tax on private royalties, but they have one great advantage in that they retain State control of concessions. One great argument in favour of nationalisation is that the letting, getting &
distributing of our coal on present system is extravagant, primitive &
chaotic. For the efficient & prudent development of the industry State
control & central direction are necessary. The argument that the
present system might be remedied by creation of one or more huge
coal trusts (as is being done in Germany) is answered by the fact that
such an issue wd introduce dangers of even greater evils than the
present & that the regular & scientific development of the mines wd
not be secured unless the Trusts were given   unthinkable coercive
powers over the surface owner.

In the discussion opinions were expressed that the means of transport & the supply of coal being prime national necessities national
control is peculiarly desirable in order that these important services
may not be held up by labour disputes, but that the difficulty of
the purchase proposition of the mines, containing as it does a large
speculative element, had perhaps been under-estimated by the writer.
On the general principle of state control of industries the administration & methods of certain Government Departments came under
criticism. 'I name no names' one speaker cryptically observed 'but
the member of this Circle who has the honour of representing the
Department that recently took over the National Telephone Company
will know to what Department I refer.'[168]

Richard Stapley   Chairman

8 Jan. 1913.

* * *

[168] A reference to Ambrose Parsons, the secretary.

[173] The 173rd meeting of the Circle was held at 33 Bloomsbury Square on the 8th January 1913.

Present. 17 members and 1 visitor—Sir Richard Stapley in the Chair.

Apologies for absence (6) from Mr Brereton, Sir William Byles, Messrs. Hobson, Ramsay MacDonald, Perris and Roskill.

Also absent. Messrs. Alden, Crook, Lilley, Murray Macdonald, Russell Rea and Robertson.

Minutes of the previous meeting were read and confirmed.

Mr Goodenough read his paper on Co-Partnership.

After explaining his own sympathetic attitude towards the working classes and to the principle of Trade Unionism and criticising trade union methods and policy as experienced and understood by him, he sketched the causes of the present acute stage of conflict between Capital and Labour, and commented upon certain proposed or attempted remedies—Conciliation Boards, Sliding Scales, Compulsory Arbitration, Co-operative production, Municipal trading, national ownership and Syndicalism. He said that Co-Partnership approached most nearly ideal system of uniting Capital, Ability and Labour to the one end of true economic production for mutual profit justly divided, but mere Profit Sharing was of little more value than any other Premium or Bonus system. He then gave a detailed account of the typical Co-Partnership system adopted by the Gas Light & Coke Company. He thought that broadly speaking a system of Co-Partnership which did not interfere with the rights of men to belong to their unions, might be generally adopted given the co-operation of labour organisations.

In the discussion, the following opinions were expressed:

That the writer's strictures on the mind and character of the working man and of Trade Unions were unduly severe.

That the principle of Co-Partnership depends on the steadiness of the business, and while the system is excellently adapted to a few industries, such as Gas, the difficulty of extending it lies in uncertainty of surplus for bonus, and also in the fact that two-thirds of working men work from job to job.

A description was also given of Zeiss's system of Co-Partnership.[169]

Richard Stapley   Chairman

5th March 1913.

* * *

---

[169] Carl Zeiss (1816–1888). German optician, who organized his industry on the basis of workers' participation in profits.

[174] The 174th meeting of the Circle was held at 33 Bloomsbury Square on the 5th March 1913.

Present. 20 members and 2 visitors—Sir Richard Stapley in the Chair.

Apologies for absence (5) from Sir William Byles, Messrs. Golding, Murray Macdonald, Ramsay MacDonald and Walker.

Also absent. Messrs Adams, Alden, Crook and Russell Rea.

Sir Sydney Olivier was unanimously re-elected to membership.

Mr. Robertson read his paper on Minimum Wage Boards.

Theory of the system is that in certain low-paid industries, mostly employing women, in which trade unions are either impossible or incapable of efficient strike-pressure, the Trade Board on which both employers and employed are represented, undertakes to bring about higher minima of wages. The system has been on the whole successful in the Chain-making and Lace-finishing trades—in the Cardboard box-making trade and the Tailoring trade it is in the experimental stage. There are many difficulties and complications in the application of the system owing to (1) different cost of living in different parts of the country (2) differentiations of trade product and consequent questions as to what is or is not properly within the scope of a particular board.

Difficulties of application to Agriculture, apart from question of whether the industry could afford to pay higher wages, in its enormous extent and in fact that wage-rates vary from county to county and even from parish to parish. On the whole Mr Robertson did not think extension to agriculture practicable.

In the discussion the following opinions were expressed.

That the principle of Trade Boards had proved to be sound: that they had given an impetus to organisation of both workers and employers: that an umpire should be appointed to decide the margin of various branches of different trades.

That Trade Boards tend to level up the bad employer to the good and sometimes to raise standard of good employer.

That they inevitably lead to speeding-up of work, and in this connection it is to be remembered that while there is frequently much inefficiency in factory and business management, there is a danger and an evil in the appalling efficiency of certain modern factories.

That the writer was unduly pessimistic as regards difficulty of establishing a Trade Board for agriculture: system might first be tried in one county.

Richard Stapley   Chairman

12th March 1913.

* * *

[175] The 175th meeting of the Circle was held on 12th March 1913 at 33 Bloomsbury Square.

Present. 17 members—Sir Richard Stapley in the chair

Apologies for absence (4) from Messrs: Gooch & Ramsay Mac-Donald, Sir Sydney Olivier, & Sir Wm Byles

Also absent. Messrs: Adams, Alden, Crook, Goodenough, Hobson, Lilley, Murray Macdonald, Rea & Robertson.

Minutes of the previous meeting were read & confirmed.

Mr. Burrows read his paper on 'the General Strike'.

The General Strike is not in itself a remedy for Labour unrest but behind it is the idea of radical reconstruction of the social organism. The workers, among whom Labour unrest is fast spreading, feel that ultimately they must rely on their own efforts & organisation to improve their lot. The basis of all Labour unrest is the class war under wh the employer is 'out for' as much work as he can get out of the labourer for as little wages as he can give, & the labourer is 'out for' as much wages as he can get for as little labour as he can give. Labour combinations were at first content with mere improvement of conditions: they now aim at socialisation of land & capital. They have learned that sectional strikes are of comparatively little use. But a general strike, i.e. a strike of all workers in every trade, skilled or unskilled, has never taken place & probably never will. Partial general strikes, i.e. complete strikes in one big trade, or perhaps in two simultaneously, are not only possible but will probably take place before long. They will not be really successful unless they result in fundamental transformation of the social system—a transformation wh will need the patient co-operation of all the best men & women.

In the discussion the following opinions were expressed:

That a general strike was an impossibility, because the workers wd be the first to suffer, & it wd involve race suicide. That the whole idea implies distrust of all rational reconstruction by constitutional, political or moral means. On the other hand, that it was possible & desirable to organise not only big strikes in large industries, but a real general strike; & that a general strike against war was quite feasible. That it was desirable to appoint a Minister of Labour, definitely on the side of labour. Arguments were also adduced against socialist schemes & ideals in general.

Richard Stapley

9th April 1913.

* * *

[176] The 176th meeting of the Circle was held on 9th April 1913 at 33 Bloomsbury Square.

Present. 17 members and one visitor (Mr. Cohen)—Sir Richard Stapley in the chair.

Apologies for absence (6) from Messrs: Alden, Burrows, Farley, Murray Macdonald, Ramsay MacDonald & Robertson.

Also absent. Messrs: Adams, Gooch, Lilley, Perris, Raphael, Rea, & Sir Sydney Olivier.

Minutes of the previous meeting were read & confirmed.

Suggestions for next session's papers were tentatively discussed.

Mr. Harley read his paper on the 'Right to Work'.

The Right to Work is only the obverse of the Duty incumbent on society to organise its work. Elizabethan administration by the 'Act for the Relief of the Poor'[170] admitted, in theory at all events, duty of organising industry in a time of dislocation and stress, but there is no evidence that in practice the Act ever became an assertion of the Right to Work.

The Right to Work may mean either (1) the right of the workless to any kind of work: or (2) to his own kind of work. The Poor Law Report of 1834 grudgingly admitted the former only, and made the work provided as repellent and distasteful as possible. The Unemployment Act of 1905 enacted that work might be found for the workless without disfranchising them, but gave no proper facilities for seeking out and scheduling schemes of work, which as a matter of fact have been few and far between. Only a small percentage of applicants received any work at all and that work was largely of a kind for which they were in no degree fitted. The Right to Work Bill,[171] as it stands, is so impracticable as to be of speculative interest only, imposing almost impossible tasks on local authorities without indicating how they are to be performed. In this respect it is much inferior to the Minority Report of the Poor Law Commission, the proposals of which, however, even if carried out in their entirety, would hardly cure the disease of unemployment. The real importance of consideration of the Right to Work with its correlated Duty, is that it brings us face to face with the fundamental problem of industrial society, and raises the question whether the claim can possibly be met so long as our business system is constituted on the basis of vendible values.

In the discussion the following opinions were expressed:

That it is the duty of Society in its own interest to see to the welfare of the workers and in a certain sense this confers on the individual the

---

[170] Act of 1598.

[171] The Labour party had repeatedly attempted, through the introduction of Bills in 1907 and 1908 and amendments to the Address, to secure the right to work.

right to work. The crux of the problem is how to modify or reconstitute Society to enable it to perform this duty.

That if the right to work be admitted, irrespective of character and ability, morality and discipline in Society would be undermined.

Richard Stapley   Chairman

7th May, 1913.

* * *

[177] The 177th meeting of the Circle was held on the 7th May 1913 at 33 Bloomsbury Sq.

Present. 13 members & 2 visitors—Sir Richard Stapley in the chair.

Apologies for absence from Messrs: Alden, Brereton, Burrows, Farley, Gooch, Goodenough, Ramsay MacDonald, Matheson, Robertson, Roskill, Archdeacon Lilley & Sir Wm Byles.

Also absent. Messrs: Adams, Murray Macdonald, Perris & Rea.

Minutes of the previous meeting were read & confirmed.

The subjects for next session were discussed & provisionally settled.

Mr. Walsh read his paper on Education in relation to Social Unrest. So far as there is a connection between Unrest & a quickening intelligence of the workers considerable credit is due to fact of compulsory education for more than a generation. Incompleteness of the education given is partially responsible for some of the uglier symptoms of unrest. Comparatively recent extension of educational franchise to girls on equal terms with boys is a factor in the feminist movement. The education given to Public school boys is largely to blame for aloofness or patronising attitude of the governing classes. As regards system of education in the national schools it is to be noted that real progress has been made: the vicious system of payment by results has been abolished & more attention is given to 'hand & eye' work. In girls' schools the spinster influence is still too predominant. As regards remedial possibilities of education, Society seems to be split into 2 camps—the rich & the poor—each suspicious of the other & not having learnt to understand each other or the necessity for general co-operation to secure a free full life for all. Much may be done to inspire a spirit of goodwill in the body politic through the medium of an education as complete on the spiritual & ethical as on the material & intellectual side.

In the discussion, Trade Schools were criticised & also the curriculum of the ordinary schools. It was suggested that the elements of physiology, psychology, eugenics & civics—not necessarily taught as such—might be imparted with advantage: also that more use might be made of sports as a medium of education in citizenship. The question of transferring cost in part or whole, from local rates to Exchequer was also dealt with.

Richard Stapley   Chairman

11 June 1913

* * *

[178] The 178th meeting of the Circle was held on the 11th June 1913 at 33 Bloomsbury Sq.

Present. 19 members & 5 visitors—Sir Richard Stapley in the chair.

Apologies for absence—from Messrs: Alden, Ramsay MacDonald, Millin, Perris, Robertson, Walker, Sir Wm Byles & Archdeacon Lilley.

Also absent. Mr. Murray Macdonald & Mr. Russell Rea.

The programme for the next session was finally settled.

Mr. Herdman read his paper 'Audi Alteram Partem'.[172]

He questioned the existence of Labour or social unrest as a phenomenon peculiar in kind to our own age, & thought the signs of movement (essential to vitality) in things intellectual, moral & social—but particularly social—a matter for congratulation. The very complexity of our own times which enables any new cause to produce a vastly more important effect than in preceding ages, insures also that society will be able to meet the new situation with a resource born of that complexity. As regards recent strikes, two causes not hitherto mentioned in the Circle's discussions were the abnormal heat of 1911 and the instinct of mimicry. The main cause was no doubt economic and due at least in part to the expenditure of wealth on the S. African war, on increased armaments, & on recent social legislation. For the ills arising from war & militarism some help is to be looked for from the Hague tribunal, wh, though feeble at present, is a step in the right direction. The cost of social reform ought to be brought home to the working classes by extension of direct taxation. The tendency of trade unions on the one hand to repudiate bargains, & on the other to be led by a small but insistent minority, ought to be remedied by an extension of the democratic spirit—present *representative* system being unsatisfactory & not truly democratic. We should recognise once for all that waste in human society is inevitable & that all we can do is

---

[172] Hear the Other Side.

to reduce (not abolish it). We should concentrate on the ills that *can* be cured & our endeavours to find the right method shd be guided by reason rather than by emotion or enthusiasm.

In the discussion the following opinions were expressed:

1. Expenditure on armaments & expenditure on social legislation designed to improve efficiency & conditions of workers are totally different in their economic effects. Increased efficiency of workers leads to increase of wealth.

2. There is in economic rent of land & profits due to monopoly &c: a large surplus that might be devoted to improving conditions of labouring classes—through their organisation or through instrumentality of State. No remedy could be worse than that of direct taxation of workers.

3. The rigid & logical application of doctrine of evolution to human life in all its developments is hardly sound. It results in a scientific Calvinism wh leaves out of account the factor of Freewill & of that benevolence wh leads to care of defective & inefficient. Those states that most display this benevolence make most progress. The attitude of cool rationalism, though interesting & stimulating, understates claims of emotion.

Richard Stapley   Chairman

8 Oct. 1913.

* * *

[179] At the Rainbow Circle Dinner held at the National Liberal Club on 18th June 1913, the following were present:

Sir Richard Stapley, (in the chair) Sir Sydney Olivier, Messrs: Alden, Gooch, Walker, Perris, Matheson, Walsh, Raphael, Parsons, Herdman, Husband, Farley, Roskill, & Hobson, and Dr. Morrison (an old member).

* * *

[Twentieth Session: 1913–1914]

[180] The 180th meeting of the Circle was held on 8th Oct. 1913 at 33 Bloomsbury Square.

Present. 20 members & 1 visitor—Sir Richard Stapley in the chair.

Apologies for absence—from Sir Wm Byles, & Messrs: Murray Macdonald, Golding & Ramsay MacDonald.

Also absent. Sir Sydney Olivier, Archdeacon Lilley, & Messrs: Adams, Goodenough, Perris & Russell Rea.

Minutes of the 178th & 179th meetings were read & confirmed.

The Accounts which shewed a deficit of 8/- were presented & accepted.

The Record of Attendance was read as follows:

Out of a possible nine meetings, excluding the dinner,

Sir Richard Stapley & Messrs: Harley, Herdman, Parsons & Walsh attended	9
Messrs: Golding, Husband, Matheson & Millin	8
Messrs: Farley, Hobson, McKillop & Raphael	7
Messrs: Brereton, Burrows, Goodenough, Roskill & Walker	6
Messrs: Gooch & Perris	5
Messrs: Adams & Crook	4
Sir Wm Byles, Archdeacon Lilley, & Messrs: Murray Macdonald, Russell Rea, & Robertson	1
Sir Sydney Olivier, & Messrs: Alden & Ramsay MacDonald	0

Average attendance 17.5 as against 16.2 for the previous year.

Sir Richard Stapley was re-elected as Chairman

Mr. Parsons   ”   ”   ” Secretary

Messrs: Brereton, Crook, Harley, Herdman & Archdeacon Lilley were re-elected as the Committee.

Sir Richard Stapley, on behalf of the Circle, presented Mr. Parsons with a beautiful mahogany bureau. Sir Richard stated that it was the desire of the Circle that the following letter, which accompanied the gift, should be entered in the minutes:

8 October 1913

Rainbow Circle

Dear Mr. Parsons,

The Members of the Rainbow Circle beg your acceptance of the accompanying Bureau as a small token of their most cordial appreciation of the admirable services you have rendered to the Circle during the time you have been its Secretary.

The untiring energy and kindly zeal you have so consistently shown, and the personal kindness you have always manifested to every member have endeared you to all. We hope, that when you use the Bureau you will be reminded of our very warm wishes for your continued happiness and welfare.

Signed on behalf of the members

Most sincerely yours

Richard Stapley.’

Mr. Parsons, in returning thanks, did his best to explain that the testimonial was, in the words of the liturgy, ‘more than either he desired or deserved’ inasmuch as he had for many years received from the Circle far more than he could ever give to it. He said he would always treasure the gift as a permanent reminder of the goodwill & kindly feeling of the Circle towards him.

Mr. Alden read his paper on Rural Housing.

Board of Agriculture in recent Report on decline in agricultural population regards as one of most important causes of discontent the deficiency of adequate or satisfactory housing accommodation. Repair of cottages under Housing & Town Planning Act 1909 has already been considerable & resulted in improvement, but the greater the energy of Local Authorities in issuing Closing orders the more difficult does situation become & the more insistent the call for immediate action in providing new cottages—particularly since the Act has so far been a failure as regards compulsory building, & number of new cottages erected in last 2 years is only 1/10th number closed or demolished. Private enterprise is baulked by fact that only the benevolent landlord will build cottages that will not return an economic rent—4/- or 5/- a week—wh the agricultural labourer by reason of his low wages is unable to pay. Suggested Remedy: Institution of minimum wage and Govt Grant towards cost of building. The latter is open to serious objections wh are, however outweighed by fact that its effect wd be immediate & that judicious grants-in-aid to local authorities are the most effective lever that can be used by a central Department. The grant required for erection of 120.000 cottages to be let at 3/- would be not more than £275.000 a year.

The discussion turned mainly on the success of the Irish Housing Act, the desirability of the Agricultural Labourer's reducing his family, the unsuitability of building byelaws for rural districts, the advantages & disadvantages of wooden cottages, & cheap building by the Rural Co-operative Society. The opinion was expressed that if building be subsidised it shd only be for a short time till wages are brought up to a proper level.

Richard Stapley   Chairman

12 Nov. 1913.

* * *

[181] The 181st Meeting of the Circle was held on 12th November 1913 at 33, Bloomsbury Square.

Present. 21 members and 5 visitors, Sir Richard Stapley in the Chair.

Apologies for Absence—from Sir William Byles, and Messrs. Murray Macdonald and Ramsay MacDonald.

Also absent—Messrs. Alden, Gooch, Harley and Rea, and Archdeacon Lilley.

Minutes of the previous meeting were read and confirmed.

Mr. Hobson gave his address on Rural Wages. Among causes of low wages are custom, immobility, low efficiency, bad farming, bad commercial management, and high rents. In the new attitude towards labour, there is general acceptance of principle of living wage and practical application of this principle in Trade Boards and Miners' Wage Boards. Question is how to secure it also in case of Agriculture. There ought to be a levelling-up of bad employers to good, and bad districts to good. If agriculture in the North can yield living wage with reasonable profit, why not elsewhere? The wide discrepancies in the same district argue in favour of economic feasibility. If minimum wage enforced by law, certain difficulties would no doubt arise from fact that efficiency could hardly be expected to rise at once. Low rented lands on margin of cultivation would go out of cultivation, certain of the arable land would be converted to pasture. More efficient labour might mean fewer labourers with consequent unemployment. Unemployment might be met by small holdings, afforestation schemes, assisted emigration, and training colonies for other work. In short, the question of rural wages cannot properly be considered without considering also the related problems of Rural Housing and Gardens, Small Holdings, Development of Crown Lands, credit for farmers and small-holders, security of tenure, transport co-operation, and improvement in science and business of Agriculture.

In the discussion the following opinions were expressed.

Institution of Wage Boards for Agriculture would involve meeting together of labourers to discuss their wages, an unparalleled event which would give Trade Union organiser his opportunity. The minimum might be fixed on the low side to start with. When organisation was accomplished it would almost certainly rise. Fixing of minimum wage is accompanied not only by healthy co-operation among workers but by increased efficiency on part of employers. Two great difficulties from point of view of Trade boards are prevalence of inefficiency and sub-normal labour, and prevalence of time work system. Time work necessary in our country where labourer has to be kept employed all the year round, but in other countries there is often a schedule of piece-work prices for different operations. It will be necessary to move slowly. Probably best to begin in under-rated district and recognise necessity of grading labour.

Richard Stapley   Chairman

10th December, 1913.

[182] The 182nd Meeting of the Circle was held on 10 Dec. 1913 at 33 Bloomsbury Sq:

Present. 18 members & 2 visitors—Sir Richard Stapley in the chair.

Apologies for absence from Messrs: Alden, Brereton, Gooch, Ramsay MacDonald, Roskill & Walker, Sir Wm Byles & Archdeacon Lilley.

Also absent. Messrs: Adams, Murray Macdonald, Russell Rea & Sir Sydney Olivier.

Minutes of the previous meeting were read & confirmed.

Mr. Crook read his paper on Migration.

He gave statistics of migration to towns & emigration abroad shewing among other things that decline in number of agricultural labourers between 1881 & 1901 was in England 30%, Scotland 31%, Wales 24%, coincidently with increase in population of 25%. He also gave particulars of interesting research work of his own regarding movement of agricultural population in 70 rural parishes of Mid Kent. This, to certain members not gifted with capacity for sudden assimilation of detail, vaguely & inconsequently reminiscent of biblical chronologies—indeed at conclusion of 70th item, one member in anticipation of familiar words 'here endeth the first lesson' visibly braced himself to sing 'Magnificat'. Causes of migration & emigration ascribed to low wages, want of house accommodation, want of prospects, want of amusements, want of holidays, want of work, turning of arable land into pasture, labour-saving machinery, dislike of agricultural work brought about by education, & enterprise of individuals. These were considered in detail & various suggestions made, but with cautionary note that the progressive who sets out to stay decay of rural population may really be a reactionary in disguise.

In the discussion the following opinions were expressed:

That the general drift to towns may be part of a general degeneration: That the largest cities do not tend to grow as they did: That decentralisation of trade is going on to some extent & factories tend to move out to rural districts. That our agriculture is relatively unproductive: production in Denmark e.g., under worse circumstances much greater per head. That our agricultural labour ought to be more mobile.

But the discussion turned mainly on dulness[sic] of village life. One speaker gave his desolating experience of 2 years' residence in remote village, where there was not even a public house—an institution wh in his view wd have been cheaply purchased at cost of a little drunkenness.

Richard Stapley   Chairman.

14 Jan 1914

[183] The 183rd Meeting of the Circle was held on 14 Jan 1914 at 33 Bloomsbury Square.

Present. 19 members & 3 Visitors—Sir Richard Stapley in the chair.

Apologies for absence (6) from Messrs: Gooch, Hobson, Ramsay MacDonald, Matheson & Goodenough & Archdeacon Lilley.

Also absent. Messrs: Harley, Murray Macdonald, Perris, Rea & Robertson.

Minutes of the previous meeting were read & confirmed.

Mr. Cloudesley Brereton announced that Mr. Christopher Turner[173] was willing to read the paper set down in Mr. Brereton's name for 11th March, & the Circle approved the substitution.

Sir Sydney Olivier read his paper on Agricultural Co-operation & Land Banks.

England is not a country of peasant proprietors or *small* farmers & Agricultural Co-operation is on that account less developed than in most Continental countries & in Ireland. First stimulus to Agricultural Co-operation is generally some new need or economic pressure—e.g. exclusion of Danish cattle & pigs from Germany, wh. forced Danish farmers to improve their produce & develope trade with England. Co-operation usually starts in form of organisations for supply & distribution on advantageous terms of such things as chemical manures, insecticides, feeding stuffs, & later of implements & livestock. Co-operative societies for assembling & grading produce for market have been successful—e.g. in Denmark & Ireland. Much might be done by fruit growers in same methods that have proved of advantage in egg & poultry farming.

As regards Agricultural Banks, the reader gave interesting details of what had been done in Jamaica, India & Ireland.

In the discussion the Circle generally endorsed the view that the relatively small number & the isolation of small or peasant farmers in this country made co-operation difficult. Opinions were expressed that the good moral effects of co-operation are even greater than the economic effects, & that one important factor in readier co-operation among peasants of certain other countries—e.g. Italy, Russia, Ireland—is that they are accustomed to communal ideas from birth & by tradition.

Richard Stapley   Chairman

11 Feb. 1914

* * *

---

[173] Should be Turnor.

[184] The 184th Meeting of the Circle was held on 11th Feb. 1914 at 33 Bloomsbury Square

Present 22 members & 5 visitors—Sir Richard Stapley in the chair.

Apologies for absence (4) from Messrs: Ramsay MacDonald, Rea, & Walker, & Archdeacon Lilley

Also absent. Messrs: Alden, Hobson, Murray Macdonald, & Sir Sydney Olivier.

Minutes of the previous meeting were read & confirmed.

Mr. Robertson read his paper on the Taxation of Land Values.[174] The present plan whereby rates are levied on building values & improvements & even on machinery is obviously bad & inexpedient. Recognition of necessity for rationalising our rating basis & revising our land system in interest of an increased production is the strongest support for proposal to revise national taxation on similar lines. Simplest & fairest plan appears to be the rating & taxing of all land on its capital site value as officially determined, & combining this principle with that of rating an income on basis of existing income tax assessment, in order to secure observation of the general principle of 'equality of sacrifice'. Objection may be raised on the ground that a man who invests his money in land wd pay more than one who invests solely in stocks & shares, but it has to be remembered that land is an important monopoly, & on the enjoyment of that luxury a man is properly taxable in the national interest.

The discussion was unusually discursive & but rarely came to grips with taxation of land-values. 1001 different questions were raised, including those of Infected cattle, the Repudiation of the National Debt, the Nationalisation of Land (with special reference to the model of William the Conqueror) & the finding of 'gold, silver, sturgeon & great whales'.

Richard Stapley   Chairman

11 March 1914

* * *

[185] The 185th Meeting of the Circle was held on 11th March 1914 at 33 Bloomsbury Sq:

Present. 15 members & 3 visitors, Sir Richard Stapley in the chair.

Apologies for absence from Messrs: Alden, Burrows, Crook, Gooch, Golding, Hobson, Ramsay MacDonald, McKillop, Perris & Robertson.

---

[174] The talk was published in May as 'a paper read to a Discussion Circle.' Cp. J.M. Robertson, 'The Taxation of Land Values', *Contemporary Review*, vol. cv (1914), 624–630.

Also absent. Messrs: Adams, Murray Macdonald, Matheson, Russell Rea & Archdeacon Lilley.

Minutes of the previous meeting were read & confirmed.

Mr. Christopher Turner[175] read his paper on 'Tenure of Agricultural Land'.

Primary test of any system of tenure is 2-fold, vizt: whether the land is carrying as many people as it should & whether the cultivators are producing as much food for the nation as potential value of the land warrants. The system in this country fails the test on both points. The landowner does not get the rate of interest on his capital that he should: the farmer does not get the profit that he should. Selling value of agricultural land is low & appears still lower if considered in relation to its potential value. Low rental is not the advantage to the farmer that it ought theoretically to be, as it tends to make him take more land than he can master & to farm *ex*tensively when he wd do better both for himself & nation with smaller area farmed *in*tensively. Only 12% of occupiers own their own holdings—a lower percentage than in any other country. It shd be raised to at least 60%. Great developments & organisation have taken place in other countries under wh ownership is more predominant than tenancy. Development, however, not impossible under tenancy. Greater co-operation, increased banking facilities, organised markets, improved transport, improved rural education, all urgently needed—and if there is to be Protection, the first industry to be protected shd be Agriculture.

In the discussion the opinion was expressed that the system of tenure is not of supreme importance, organisation, co-operation, & education being the things most wanted. There is a genuine feeling or conviction on the part of most farmers in England that the landlord & tenant system is the best for them.

Richard Stapley   Chairman

8 April 1914.

* * *

[186] The 186th Meeting of the Circle was held on 8 April 1914 at 33 Bloomsbury Square

Present. 11 members & one visitor—Sir Richard Stapley in the chair.

Apologies for absence from Messrs: Brereton, Byles, Crook, Golding, Goodenough, Ramsay MacDonald, Murray Macdonald, Matheson, Russell Rea, Robertson, Roskill & Walker.

[175] Should be Turnor.

Also absent (7) Messrs: Adams, Gooch, Harley, Hobson, Perris, Sir Sydney Olivier, & Archdeacon Lilley.

Suggestions for next session were put forward & a small committee was asked to consider them.

Mr. Husband read his paper on Transport to Markets.

He touched on the question of facilities for export of agricultural produce, but dealt more particularly with Transport to Home-Markets by Rail (including light-railways) waterways & roads. The State might well do something to improve matters—particularly under powers conferred by Development & Road Improvement Act 1909. But even more may be expected from organised self-help on following lines:

a. Bulking of Consignments by neighbouring farmers

b. Insistence on enlarged limit of weight in parcel post, & adoption of C.O.D. system.

c. Utilisation of Rural Party Line Telephone facilities.

d. Establishment of milk collecting depots.

e. Direct trading between organised producers & organised consumers.

In the discussion the following opinions were expressed:

Our people are far behind foreigners in the application of science to their needs—e.g. we have hardly any light railways.

Motor traffic may be better than extension of light railways.

Nationalisation of transport is essential.

If canals were more useable they wd be more used.

Richard Stapley

13 May 1914.

* * *

[187] The 187th meeting of the Circle was held on 13 May 1914 at 33 Bloomsbury Square.

Present. 15 members & 1 visitor—Sir Richard Stapley in the chair.

Apologies from Messrs: Alden, Brereton, Gooch, Goodenough, Husband, Ramsay MacDonald, Millin, Roskill, Raphael, & Sir Wm Byles.

Also absent. Messrs: Adams, Murray Macdonald, Russell Rea, Robertson, & Archdeacon Lilley.

Minutes of the previous meeting were read & adopted.

It was decided that the subject for next session shd be a consideration of the various factors taken into account in foreign policy.

Mr Walsh read his paper on 'Technical Education in Agriculture'.

Agriculture is the one great national industry to wh scientific method has not yet been applied with any degree of system or thoroughness. Want of education & of the proper kind of education is largely responsible. Elementary education & elementary teachers are not so good in rural as in town areas. More attention ought to be given to practical activities, such as wood-work, school gardens, beehives &c: But the fundamental weakness of our present system is absence of effective linking up of Preparatory with Technical work proper. The present scheme of Board of Agriculture, with its arrangements for research, its division of the country into 12 districts each associated with a central University Institute or College, & its Farm Institute grants, is most promising.[176] Again certain County Councils have appointed special committees with an 'Agricultural Organiser' as adviser & as director of the county staff of teachers. The present gap between the Elementary school & the Technical Instruction is but poorly bridged by voluntary Evening Classes. What is wanted to begin with is extended school-age, extended curriculum, & well-staffed central schools for older scholars.

The discussion turned mainly on the Scheme of the Board of Agriculture, Farm Institutes, an interesting educational experiment at Top Hill, described by an Agricultural Organiser, & the causes that make rural education inherently more difficult than urban.

Richard Stapley   Chairman

10 June 1914

* * *

[188] The 188th meeting of the Circle was held on 10 June 1914 at 33 Bloomsbury Square

Present. 13 members & 2 visitors—Sir Richard Stapley in the chair.

Apologies from Messrs: Alden, Burrows, Farley, Goodenough, Golding, Ramsay MacDonald, Matheson, Millin, Raphael, & Sir Wm Byles.

Also absent. Messrs: Adams, Murray Macdonald, Perris, Russell Rea, & Robertson, Sir Sydney Olivier, & Archdeacon Lilley.

Minutes of the previous meeting were read & confirmed.

Mr. Harley read his paper on Land Nationalisation.

While not supporting the doctrine as usually expounded by collectivists he held that in the future the State should as far as possible be the sole ground landlord. The State need not at once take over all

---

[176] Cp. Departmental Committee Report on Agricultural Training in England and Wales, 1908 (Cd. 4206), and Memos in 1909 (Cd. 4886) and in 1912–13 (Cd. 6039).

the site values in the centre or in the precincts of big cities or boroughs. These can be dealt with by restrictive provisions in Acts of Parliament with a view to preventing the lease-holder from being exploited. But some central department might earmark the sites in developing areas & prevent all possibility of their unearned increment being removed from the hands of the community. In all cases the community shd insist on having some voice, some measure of control, supervision & right of intervention.

In the discussion the following opinions were expressed:
That the real issue is whether the best results are to be obtained by public ownership or by a measure of public control by taxation or otherwise. That the terms of holding & using land shd be such as to evoke the best output. That the process of valuation shd be a single central system, applied with all local knowledge obtainable. That the aggregation of private property on a large scale is detrimental to the national welfare.

Richard Stapley   Chairman

14 Oct. 1914

* * *

[189] The 189th meeting of the Circle was held at the Swan Hotel, Streatley, from Sat: 20th to Mon: 22nd June 1913,[177] when the Circle had the great pleasure of entertaining their Chairman. They could not attempt to vie with him in hospitality, but they felt it a privilege to turn the tables on him for once—even in a modest kind of way.

There were present Sir Richard Stapley, Sir Wm Byles, Messrs: Adams, Brereton, Crook, Golding, Husband, Parsons, Perris, Raphael, Roskill, Samuel & Walker. The weather was good & the Circle made the most of it. Social & philosophical questions, though not officially barred, gave way to the more primitive problems connected with boating, swimming & fishing. Mr. Perris managing a Canadian canoe with the sure touch of a Red Indian, & Mr. Raphael performing circular evolutions in a punt in wh he paid rapid visits to Berkshire & Oxfordshire alternately, were sights to remember. A chub successfully landed was understood to be worth £5—to the Thames Conservancy.

Richard Stapley   Chairman

14 Oct. 1914

[177] Should be 1914.

Twenty-first Session 1914–15

[190] The 190th Meeting of the Circle was held on 14th Octr 1914 at 33 Bloomsbury Square.

Present. 19 members & 1 visitor. Sir Richard Stapley in the chair.

Apologies (5) from Messrs: Alden, Burrows, McKillop, Raphael & Ramsay MacDonald.

Also absent Messrs: Gooch, Murray Macdonald, Perris, Russell Rea, Archdeacon Lilley & Sir Sydney Olivier.

Minutes of the 188th & 189th meetings were read & confirmed.

The Accounts which shewed a balance in hand of 18s/6d were presented & accepted.

Sir Richard Stapley was re-elected as Chairman.

Mr. Parsons   ”   ”   ” Secretary.

Messrs: Brereton, Crook, Harley, Herdman & Hobson were elected to the Committee.

The record of attendance during the previous session was read as follows:

Out of a possible nine meetings, excluding the week-end up the River,

Sir Richard Stapley & Messrs: Herdman, Parsons & Walsh attended	9
Messrs: Farley, Husband & McKillop	8
” Burrows, Crook, Millin & Raphael	7
” Brereton, Harley, Roskill & Walker	6
” Golding, Hobson & Matheson	5
” Goodenough, Perris, Robertson & Sir Sydney Olivier	4
” Alden, Gooch & Sir Wm Byles	3
Mr. Adams	2
Messrs: Murray Macdonald, Ramsay MacDonald, Russell Rea, & Archdeacon Lilley	0

The average attendance was 17.1 as against 17.5 for the previous year.

Mr. Crook read his paper on 'Foreign Policy & Sentiment'.

He contended that Sentiment is not merely *a* controlling force in all foreign policy, but that no influence can compare with it in power save the very kindred influence of race. He supported his thesis by reference to the widely differing sentiments that have actuated all modern wars & the appeal to sentiment made by all successful foreign ministers. Among many examples he mentioned the following: The sentiment inherent in the Munroe[sic] Doctrine, the sentiment of liberty for themselves & for others respectively that animated the two sides in the American Slave War: the superman idealism represented by the Bernhardi[178] school of German thought; the Habsburg tradition that the Austrian Emperor shd leave his empire larger than he found it: the Turks' memory of their former greatness.

In the discussion the following opinions were expressed:

That since Sentiment is one of the mainsprings of all human action the really important thing is the analysis of the particular motive underlying the particular sentiment. In all cases there is a concrete motive—often economic—around wh sentiment works: e.g. the mine motive in the Boer War: the desire of the Southern states to retain slave labour in the American Slave War. Again, that in considering German sentiment, it has to be remembered that behind the whole German policy is intense desire to rival England in colonial possessions.

Richard Stapley   Chairman.

11 Nov. 1914

* * *

[191] The 191th Meeting of the Circle was held on 11 Nov. 1914 at 33 Bloomsbury Square

Present 19 members & 1 visitor, Sir Richard Stapley in the chair.

Apologies (5) from Messrs: Alden, Brereton, Burrows, Gooch & Raphael.

Also absent. Messrs: Adams, McKillop, Millin, Perris, Walker & Archdeacon Lilley.

Minutes of the previous meeting were read & confirmed.

Mr. Robertson read his paper on 'Foreign Policy in relation to Parliamentary Government'.

In considering the ideal of publicity wh is bound up with the principle of parliamentary control he traced the policy preceding the Afghan war & dealt with various other modern crises—notably that of 1911.[179] He maintained that Parliament does in fact control foreign policy in the same sense in wh it controls war: that in point of fact the present methods have frequently averted war where a method of regular public discussion wd probably not have done so: & that even in cases in wh Governments can be seen on retrospect to have entered upon wars either stupidly or criminally, it is very doubtful whether the fullest democratic control wd have averted these courses. He pointed out the practical difficulty, if not impossibility, of adoption of

[178] Friedrich Adam J. von Bernhardi (1849–1930). German general, author of militarist-nationalist books publicised by the British press, including *Germany and the Next War* (published in English, 1912) and *Britain as Germany's Vassal* (published in English, 1914).

[179] Presumably the Agadir crisis in Morocco between France and Germany.

open diplomacy by one state, the others retaining present methods. He suggested tentatively, but admittedly without conviction, that it might theoretically be an improvement to have a Committee of Control of Foreign Affairs to act with the Foreign minister or to take his place.

In the discussion the following opinions were expressed:

That though the great obstacle is the nature of the press, yet if open diplomacy were carried on, public opinion cd be brought to bear before too late: the people are more peaceable than the ministers: that open diplomacy even in one state wd lead to a better general diplomacy.

That we do not discuss sufficiently in Parliament the relation between domestic & foreign policy, or the general principles of foreign policy.

That there is no real parliamentary control of foreign policy in this country, & that until treaties & understandings are negotiated & controlled by the representatives of the people it is idle to talk of our having self-government.

Richard Stapley   Chairman.

9 Dec. 1914

* * *

[192] The 192nd Meeting of the Circle was held on 9 Decr 1914 at 33 Bloomsbury Square.

Present. 20 members & 1 visitor—Sir Richard Stapley in the chair.

Apologies from Messrs: Farley, Gooch, Ramsay MacDonald, Raphael, Roskill & Archdeacon Lilley.

Also absent. Messrs: Goodenough, Murray Macdonald, Perris & Robertson.

Mr. Harley kindly undertook to read his paper in January to meet the convenience of Archdeacon Lilley.

Mr. Hobson read his paper on 'Foreign Policy & Trade'.

In modern times the economic factor is normally the chief directive influence in Foreign Policy. The early sense of co-operation when foreign trade meant exchange of 'unlikes' gives way to a sense of rivalry when nations exchange likes & compete with those 'likes' in neutral markets. States often use Trade for political or territorial aggrandisement. In a poorly developed country their first claim may be a sphere of legitimate aspiration, then a sphere of interest, a sphere of influence, a protectorate & finally a colony. Trade in earlier forms did not necessitate political possession as modern Capitalism, with systematic exploitation of all valuable resources, now does. As ordinary markets give place to markets for Concessions & Investments, the investors seek to use their governments to support their investments. But State assistance to Concession Mongers or financial groups is to be condemned because (1) fraught with damage to the economic development of the country wh practises it, (2) a constant danger to peace & (3) a form of spurious socialism using public money & power for private gains. Free Trade as a basis of pacific relations is as sound a principle as ever.

In the discussion the following opinions were expressed:
(1) That a distinction shd be drawn between relations of undeveloped countries & relations between a developed & an undeveloped country.
(2) That pressure of population is disappearing as a practical factor in the economy of European states.
(3) That a distinction shd be made between Trade wh is essentially the business of the merchant & the skipper & the process of developing a country by railways, mining & engineering.
(4) That Protectionist countries are far more influenced in their foreign policy by trading considerations than Free Trade countries.

Richard Stapley   Chairman
13 Jan. 1915.

* * *

[193] The 193rd Meeting of the Circle was held on 13 Jan. 1915 at 33 Bloomsbury Square.

Present. 14 members—Sir Richard Stapley in the Chair.

Apologies for absence (8) from Messrs: Burrows, Golding, Gooch, Goodenough, Matheson, Raphael, Walker & Archdeacon Lilley.

Also absent. Messrs: Adams, Alden, Hobson, McKillop, Millin, Robertson, Murray Macdonald & Russell Rea.

Mr. Harley read his paper on 'Foreign Policy & Industrial Solidarity'.

Karl Marx & others once held the view that one result of the great industrial revolution would be such a community of interests between the wage-slaves of every occupation throughout the world that the whole course of the world's future wd be materially modified[;] that though nations were at war the soldiers would fraternise in the trenches & the proletariat wd have to be convinced that nationality was worth fighting for. In point of fact the proletariat & its various societies of workers had no effect on the course of the Franco-Prussian War of 1870, the Russo-Turkish war of 1876, the Russo-Japanese war, the Balkan wars or the present European war. It is to be noted however that on the eve of war certain public anti-war protests have been made by socialistic organisations. Industrial considerations are not specially fitted to make men fraternal or solid. It is very difficult to keep even a number of amalgamated groups of workers true to each other in the face of the common enemy. Industrial Solidarity can only be regarded as a very prospective influence on foreign affairs.

In the discussion the following opinions[180] were expressed: Industrial Solidarity is a continually increasing & progressive force. The wage earner will get more share in effective govt & more control of the things that make for peace & war. Only in so far as Industrial Solidarity finds political expression will it have influence on foreign policy. Because up to now it has not been instrumental in preventing a war that does not shew that it is without effect on foreign policy & that its effect is not potentially far greater than at present appears. The fact that the French Govt just before the present war was afraid of a split owing to the socialists & syndicalists is significant of the reality of the power & still more of the potentiality of Industrial Solidarity as something to be reckoned with.

Richard Stapley

10. Feb. 1915

* * *

[194] The 194th Meeting of the Circle was held on 10 Febr. 1915 at 33 Bloomsbury Square.

Present. 18 members & 3 visitors, Sir Richard Stapley in the Chair.

Apologies for absence from Messrs: Alden, Farley, Gooch & Raphael.

Also absent. Messrs: Goodenough, Hobson, Murray Macdonald, Ramsay MacDonald, Perris, Robertson, Russell Rea, & Sir Sydney Olivier.

Minutes of the previous meeting were read & confirmed.

It was announced that Mr. Harold Wright had kindly consented to read a paper on 'Foreign Policy & Pacifism' in place of Mr. Norman Angell.

Archdeacon Lilley read his paper on 'Foreign Policy & Religion'.

Christianity came into existence not only with a definite social conception but as a society embodying that conception. The claim was that the great social ideals of justice, peace & human brotherhood belonged to the reality of the eternal order & that it existed to mediate that order in history. It has been the only considerable force in Europe

---

[180] This is inaccurate. Unusually, the discussion does not reflect a plethora of views but a coherent polemic against the speaker, possibly indicating the reaction of the majority of those present.

to do anything towards converting those ideals into fact. For first 300 years Christianity preserved the purity of its ideals by seclusion from life of the world state. Then, coming into contact with secular policy its work as an instrument of civilisation really began. For a long time afterwards Europe was still in some sense one state, with Emperor as secular head & Pope as spiritual head. The Renascence brought about disruption of the Christian Republic & disintegration of Christendom as a spiritual authority. In every powerful state the Church became identified with State policy. It no longer spoke with one voice but with as many voices as there were states, & this involved abolition of the Christian conscience in all international controversies. So far as Lutheranism is concerned, the Church abdicated also on principle, relating religion almost wholly to the inner life. In certain matters of the highest moral moment Christian conscience no longer exists. We can however detect in the present the promise of a new form & activity of the same conscience. Democracy has long been developing an organ of authority within the unit of the national life, & since the chief functions of modern civilisation are largely international, international units will also be formed. Hence will grow a super-federal & in time a simply human lay conscience wh will find its chief inspiration in the ideals of justice, brotherhood & pity. Then there will once more be a power & authority in the world to shape nations & societies to a fuller justice, a larger intelligence & a more trustworthy goodwill.

In the discussion the following opinions were expressed:

That justice, righteousness & peace are not purely Christian virtues. They will sway humanity in the future, because they are human virtues.

That religion is still an effective force in foreign policy of S.E. Europe, but that there are signs that Mohammedanism is going to cease, as Roman Catholicism & Protestantism, have ceased to be effective.

That universal powers are always retrogressive, human progress depending upon the detachment & individual development of different units.

That nations shd organise for peace as they have hitherto organised for war.

Richard Stapley   Chairman

14 April 1915.

* * *

[195] The 195th meeting of the Circle was held on 10th March 1915, at 33 Bloomsbury Square.

Present. 18 members & Mr. Harold Wright, Sir Richard Stapley in the chair.

Apologies for absence (8) from Messrs: Burrows, Farley, Gooch, Hobson, McKillop, Raphael, Roskill, Russell Rea & Archdeacon Lilley.

Also absent (4) Messrs: Goodenough, Murray Macdonald, Robertson & Sir Sydney Olivier.

Mr. Perris kindly agreed to read his paper in April to meet the convenience of Mr. Gooch who is prevented by illness.

Mr. Harold Wright read his paper on 'Foreign Policy & Pacifism'.

The idea of pacifism is progress through ever-widening co-operation of the whole of mankind in a struggle for mastery over Nature. It looks to creation of a society of nations, based on conception of equal rights & mutual protection, as the natural expression of human progress. The traditions of diplomacy are vicious & pacifists set a higher value on maintenance of peace & a lower value on the prizes (often little more than the power to bully & dominate) for wh diplomatists struggle. Cobden & Bright with their principles of non-intervention save in defence of the nation's own honour or interests & their belief in commerce & the practical example of peaceful living as regenerating & unifying influences among nations, are examples of pacifists whose effect, on foreign policy, was considerable & on the right side. Question for pacifists now is whether policy of non-intervention profoundly right in Cobden's day, is any longer adapted to present necessities, or whether the nations shd not rather organise for mutual protection & advantage—including chastisement of the nation that breaks the international compact.

In the discussion the following opinions were expressed: That the official relations of nations are entirely out of the hands of the people & their representatives, & that in any reconstitution of the Concert of Europe the fundamental change must be the democratisation of foreign policy.

That the threat of excommunication from trade wd be effective with a recalcitrant nation.

On the other hand that the peaceful influence of trade is perhaps something of a delusion & that trade has in fact been one cause of the present war.

Richard Stapley   Chairman

14 April 1915

* * *

[196] The 196th meeting of the Circle was held on 14th April 1915 at 33 Bloomsbury Square.

Present. 16 members—Sir Richard Stapley in the chair.

Apologies for absence (7) from Messrs: Golding, Gooch, Hobson, McKillop, Raphael, Roskill & Walker.

Also absent. (7) Messrs: Alden, Murray Macdonald, Ramsay MacDonald, Millin, Robertson, Rea, & Archdeacon Lilley.

Mr. A.G. Gardiner was elected a member on the motion of Mr. Perris. The Committee, with the addition of Sir Sydney Olivier & Mr. Farley, were instructed to draft a programme for next session.

Mr. Perris read his paper on 'Foreign Policy & Financiers'.

He dealt with the Cobdenite & the Bismarckian views of the influence of money on foreign policy. He then shewed how the competition of financial syndicates operating in undeveloped or ill-organised countries leads to international troubles & that there is a correspondence between the increase of private financial adventure & the increase of the machinery of war in every national State. He dealt especially with the influence on foreign policy of (1) foreign investments wh are for the most part employed fruitfully (2) foreign loans—wh involve State policy on one side or both & wh shd not as a rule be made to countries at war or about to go to war (3) the finance of the Armament firms, wh is almost wholly maleficent. The State ought to take the whole field of high finance under its control & direct surplus capital into fruitful channels.

In the discussion the following opinions were expressed:

That financiers, except perhaps in small & undeveloped countries, are generally in favour of peace, but that their activities by calling in the aid of diplomacy & patriotism in defence of their operations in foreign countries, tend to create difficult & dangerous international situations. That the conflicting financial interests of Germany & Russia were an important factor in bringing about the present war.

Richard Stapley   Chairman

12 May 1915

* * *

[197] The 197th meeting of the Circle was held on 12 May 1915 at 33 Bloomsbury Sq.

Present. 17 members & 3 visitors. Sir Richard Stapley in the chair.

Apologies. (6) from Messrs: Alden, Gooch, Hobson, Raphael, Robertson, & Ramsay MacDonald.

Also absent Messrs: Adams, Goodenough, Gardiner, Murray Macdonald, Lilley, Millin, Perris & Russell Rea.

Minutes of the previous meeting were read & confirmed.

The Committee presented their scheme for the ensuing session & it was adopted.

Sir Sydney Olivier read his paper on Foreign Policy & Race.

Race in the sense of breed is only found in uncivilised parts of the earth & has little to do with foreign policy. All civilised states are hybridised. The active impulses wh lead to foreign policy are not characteristically & differentially racial, but rather human or vital. States may be classified as (1) States whose population is or has come to regard itself as of one race (2) States of mixed races politically recognised as equal & more or less in equilibrium in their mutual relations (3) States containing a conquered people of different race. In the first class race has nothing to do with foreign policy. In the second the mixture may affect foreign relations as it did relations with the Transvaal. The generalised antagonism between Slav & Teuton is little more than a rallying cry. If the Balkan slavonic peoples cd get their freedom & Austrians & Magyars wd respect it, race wd not make them more hostile to Germans than to Russians.

In the discussion the following opinions were expressed:

That similarity of race & blood goes for little as compared with similarity of govt, language, or general civilisation.

That different ways of looking at things react to produce characteristics of race: that there is a distinct difference between Orient & Occident wh will eventually produce a conflict in acute form.

That race as a question of breed only accounts for unconscious elements of action. That sometimes when there has been a tendency to war, race sympathy & relationship have promoted it.

Differences of opinion arose through some members speaking of race as though it were synonymous with nationality. The discussion was also remarkable in that it strayed around a large number of subjects the relevancy of wh was not immediately apparent—e.g. War babies, the land system in Ireland, the Lost Tribes of Israel & the marriage customs of Kaffirs.

Richard Stapley   Chairman

9 June 1915.

* * *

[198] The 198th meeting of the Circle was held on 9 June 1915 at 33 Bloomsbury Square.

Present 17 members & 4 visitors—Sir Richard Stapley in the chair.

Apologies (4) from Messrs: Crook, Golding, Matheson & Raphael

Also absent Messrs: Adams, Alden, Gardiner, Goodenough, Lilley, Murray Macdonald, Millin, Olivier, Robertson, & Russell Rea.

Minutes of the previous meeting were read & confirmed.

Mr. Gooch read his paper on 'Foreign Policy & the Press'.

He passed in review all the more important newspapers in England, France, Germany, Austria, Italy & Russia, with comments on their standing & influence in their own country & in other countries. He regarded Foreign Affairs as the most difficult & responsible part of the work of a paper. In home affairs the reader can usually test & criticise, but in foreign affairs he cannot do so. The growth of syndicates makes it easier to manufacture opinion & the student of foreign affairs must know enough to check what he reads. The Press is a good servant but a bad master.

The discussion turned largely on the merits of various editors of foreign news, & on the foreign correspondents, of the English papers. The opinion was expressed that there is little hope for the regeneration of the Press so long as it is run by capitalist syndicates which crush out the sense of personal & individual responsibility.

Richard Stapley   Chairman

13 October 1915

* * *

Twenty-Second Session 1915–16

[199] The 199th meeting of the Circle was held on 13 Oct. 1915 at 33 Bloomsbury Square

Present. 14 members & 1 visitor—Sir Richard Stapley in the chair.

Apologies for absence were notified from Messrs: Alden, Byles, Gooch, Gardiner, Golding, McKillop, Millin & Robertson.

Also absent Messrs: Adams, Hobson, Lilley, Murray Macdonald, Ramsay MacDonald, Perris & Russell Rea.

Minutes of the previous meeting were read & confirmed.

The Accounts were presented & accepted. In view of the balance £1–17- no levy was made for the current session.

The Record of Attendance was read as follows:

Out of a possible 9 meetings

Messrs: Byles, Harley, Herdman, Walsh, the Chairman & Secy attended	9
" Brereton & Crook	8
Mr. Matheson	7
Messrs: Farley, Golding, Roskill & Walker	6

,,	Adams, Burrows & Olivier	5
,,	Hobson, McKillop, Millin, Perris & J.R. MacDonald	4
Mr. Goodenough		3
Messrs:	Alden, Robertson & Russell Rea	2
,,	Gooch, Lilley & Murray Macdonald	1
Mr. Raphael (on active service)		0

Average attendance 17.4 as against 17.1 for the previous year.

Sir Richard Stapley was re-elected as Chairman

Mr. Parsons   ,,   ,,   ,, Secretary

Messrs: Brereton, Crook, Harley, Herdman & Hobson were re-elected to the Committee.

Mr. Burrows gave an address on 'Labour & the War—now & after'.

While not discussing the rights or wrongs of the war, the subject of labour in connexion with it is in some respects even more important than the war itself. That is only temporary but the Labour question as affected by it will largely shape the welfare of this & other nations for generations to come. For many years before the war Trade Unionism worked within the four corners of the present capitalistic system as part of it. Since the advent of the Labour Party an attempt has been made by Labour to break away from this with varying success, that success as yet not having been very large. The war forced the Govt. into an entirely new set of relations with Labour at large. The Govt. set up large experiments in mock Socialism—mock because it was State Control without the actual association of the workers in it. One of the results was the accentuation of labour troubles & strikes. The Defence of the Realm Act[181] & the Munitions Act[182] went far on the road to the 'servile state'.[183] The Trade Unions wh after all represent only about 1/4 of the whole body of workers delivered themselves body & soul into the hands of the Govt. with but little corresponding advantage to themselves. After the war it will be most difficult to restore the old Trade Union conditions wh had been fought for so strenuously, & the hopes of those who think there will be an era of true socialism will be disappointed. If the Conscriptionists get their way there will be a great recrudescence of militarism wh will be used by the exploiting classes to repress democratic aspirations & working class movements. Yet our keynote shd be optimism for eventually mankind will know & appreciate the universal scientific law that neither in physics, mentality nor morality can the individual live to himself alone.

[181] Enacted in 1915.
[182] Munitions of War Act (1914).
[183] A term popularized by Hilaire Belloc's book of that title.

Just as Mr. Burrows was approaching his peroration his sentences were punctuated by the explosion of Zeppelin bombs hard by. Lady Stapley kindly sent in a message suggesting that the Circle might be well-advised to withdraw from its exposed position to the comparative security of a more protected room. The Circle acted on this thoughtful suggestion & soon after separated without discussing the address—& indeed without hearing Mr. Burrows' peroration, a loss wh shd be set in the general account that is being piled up against the Kaiser.

Richard Stapley   Chairman

10 November 1915

* * *

[200] The 200th[184] meeting of the Circle was held on 10 Nov 1915, at 33 Bloomsbury Square.

Present. 14 members, Mr. Samuel and 2 other visitors. Sir Richard Stapley in the chair.

Apologies for absence and congratulations. Numerous letters of apologies for absence and congratulations to the Chairman on the occasion of the bi-centenary were read. It was decided that these letters should be recorded in the minutes. The letters, etc. were as follows:

To the Chairman
From Mr. Russell Rea.

'A rather painful indisposition confines me to this house, and prevents me being present at the 200th meeting of the Rainbow Circle—of which you are the centre.

I think you may look back with some satisfaction on the 20 years career of this little society, which you have held together in such complete harmony.

One after another you have seen young men with ideas and convictions, which they have expressed, and perhaps even formed, in the 'Circle', go out into the world to endeavour to give effect to them. And it must also be a satisfaction to you to see, that when they have become engaged in public life and duty, they have for the most part, remained faithful to the 'Circle'.

Tomorrow you will be surrounded by some new, but by many old friends.'

To the Chairman
From Mr. Ramsay MacDonald.

'I fully intended to be with you to-night, but I can see that I may

---

[184] A miscount: in effect the 201st meeting (see meeting 163a above).

not be able, in view of the debate that is on to-day. If I possibly can, however, I shall attend the Rainbow Meeting. If I am not there pray convey to the members my regrets and apologies.

What a long time it seems since we had that first dinner in the Rainbow Tavern, and yet I remember quite distinctly that the leading item in the bill of fare was a specially liberal helping of cod-fish!'

From Mr. Goodenough (telegram).

'Much regret indisposition prevents my being present on bicentenary meeting heartily wish you and Circle many happy returns.'

From Lieutenant Raphael (telegram).

'Greatly regret military duties prevent my being present tonight.'

To the Secretary

From Mr. Trevelyan.

'I am so sorry that I shall be unable to come to the Rainbow Circle dinner on Wednesday. Please remember me to Sir Richard Stapley and say how much we all owe to him for his continuous interest in the Circle.'

From Dr. Morrison.

'I am exceedingly sorry I shall not be able to attend the meeting of the Circle on Wednesday next as I have an imperative engagement that evening.

It would have been a great pleasure to me to have been present at the two-hundredth meeting to show my appreciation of the admirable work of my friend Sir Richard Stapley in keeping the Circle together for more than 20 years. With all good wishes for the success of the meeting.'

From Mr. Bullock.

'Please join my cordial congratulations, and the expression of my gratitude, and my best wishes for the future, to the chorus of hearty affection which will greet the Chairman of the Rainbow Circle tomorrow evening.'

From Mr. Murray Macdonald.

'I agree most warmly with what you say about the debt the Circle owes to Stapley, and if I could I should be with you on Wednesday. But I cannot: Please make my apologies to Sir Richard and the Circle.'

From Mr. Byles.

'I shall do my best to attend the R.C. on Wed. if only because I strongly desire to pay homage to Stapley to whom the Circle owes so much. But I am very doubtful, as we have an important War Debate (Vote of Credit) at the House of Commons that night.'

From Mr. McKillop.

'If this reach you in time—which I doubt—please add mine to the volume of appreciation raised by the occasion and offered to our chief on the 200th meeting of the Rainbow.'

Apologies for absence, and congratulations, were also received by word of mouth from Messrs. Alden, Crook, Hobson, & and Sir Sydney Olivier.

Mr. Burrows on behalf of the Circle offered the Circle's congratulations to the Chairman and expressed the appreciation of his [word(s) illegible] & gratitude for his kindness & hospitality.

Mr. Golding read his paper on 'Compulsory Service.'

If the War represents a struggle between nationality and imperialism between democracy and absolutism, then the triumph of right by voluntary effort of the freest of the peoples engaged would possess a moral lustre which would be obscured if compulsion were adopted. Compulsion in destroying spontaneity of superb spirit of self-sacrifice for great issues would kill the spirit also. Between compulsion and moral suasion—even tho' that be backed by final alternative of conscription—there remains psychologically a deep gulf and the element of freedom is well worth the effort represented by the canvass. Liberty of choice as to taking up arms constitutes one of our most effective checks on foreign policy. Faced with prospect of triumph of German militarism we should experience no difficulty in obtaining practically all the available manhood of the country. If the voluntary system breaks down and conscription be adopted in order to carry the war to a successful issue, it must be adopted for the period of the War only: the sacrifices made to break down militarism must not be used to fasten militarism permanently upon the country.

In the discussion the following opinions were expressed:

A vast standing army maintained by compulsion is a terrific danger to a nation's future.

The present voluntary enlistment of 3 or 4 million men is the most splendid exhibition of patriotism.

Compulsion is a bad thing in itself.

It is desirable to have some means of compelling physically-fit slackers to enlist. Conscription might take a democratic form and tribunals might be set up to consider cases for exemption.

Richard Stapley   Chairman

8 Dec: 1915

* * *

[201] The 201st meeting of the Circle was held on 8 Dec. 1915 at 33 Bloomsbury Sq:—Sir Richard Stapley in the chair, succeeded later in the evening by Sir Sydney Olivier.

Present. 16 members & 1 visitor.

Apologies for absence from Messrs: Alden, Brereton, Burrows, Gooch, Ramsay MacDonald, McKillop & Millin.

Minutes of the previous meeting were read & confirmed.

Mr. Husband read his paper on 'Approaches to Peace—Mr. Hobson's letter to Nation of 16 Oct. & subsequent correspondence.'[185]

He first gave extracts from the correspondence. He described the real issues at stake as those of pseudo-imperialism v. Democracy, national egotism v. international good faith. Germany has sinned against human brotherhood & international duty. Mr. Hobson suggests that the objects of the Allies can be achieved by something short of a complete victory at arms. In this he is influenced by general ideas of humanitarianism & the brotherhood of peoples. But man has a moral claim to punishment for offences against his kind. In the present stage of human development, States for their own liberty & protection must take into their own hands the work of Judge & Executioner. The Allies' objects cannot be attained by peace proposals when the domination of German arms has not yet been reduced. Peace proposals are therefore premature & our physical arm must achieve unmistakable superiority before we can terminate the physical conflict.

In the discussion the following opinions were expressed:

That the main thing to consider is the future security of Europe— Punishment of the vanquished by the victor is indistinguishable from vengeance & not likely to be just.

That if Germany retired voluntarily from the invaded territory she wd thereby admit to her own people the failure of her aggressive policy.

On the other hand

That a spectacular defeat is necessary to impress & disillusion the German people.

That we must not dismiss as illusory the idea that punishment may bring about a change of view & even a change of heart.

That any discussion of peace in press or parliament is detrimental at the present time.

Richard Stapley   Chairman

12 Jan. 1916

* * *

[185] J.A. Hobson, 'Approaches to Peace', *Nation*, 16.10.1915, in which Hobson proposed negotiations to encourage Germans to assume that the total destruction of Germany was not an allied war aim. The letter triggered off a lengthy correspondence and included letters by G.K. Chesterton (critical), C.R. Buxton (supportive) [both on 30.10.1915]; G.H. Perris (supportive) [20.11.1915]; C.F.G. Masterman (critical), G. Lowes Dickinson (supportive) [both 27.11.1915]; and responses by Hobson (6.11.1915, 20.11.1915, 11.12.1915).

[202] The 202nd meeting of the Circle was held on 12 Jan 1916 at 33 Bloomsbury Square.

Present. 11 members & 2 visitors—Sir Richard Stapley in the chair.

Apologies for absence from Messrs: Brereton, Burrows, Byles, Farley, Gooch, Golding, Hobson, Ramsay MacDonald, McKillop & Millin.

Minutes of the previous paper[186] were read & confirmed.

Mr. Goodenough read his paper on 'Labour & the War', dwelling mainly on the relations between Capital & Labour just before the war broke out. He deplored the general want of mutual confidence between employers & employed & shewed how the men act against their own interests in restricting output & opposing scientific management. He urged that in view of the great industrial difficulties that may be expected after the war everything possible shd be done now to improve relations & to do away with the scarcely veiled hostility wh was fatal to the well-being of the industrial state.

In the discussion the following opinions were expressed:

That the only means by wh the workers have been enabled to improve their position & to get a larger share of the surplus value has been by organisation, by contest with capital & by restriction of output, wh last is an admitted evil. There has been no voluntary move to improve matters on part of employing classes.

That a greater cause of antagonism between Capital & Labour than restriction of output is that Labour is beginning to realise that it is being exploited & to resent lavish display of wealth by profit-earning class.

That the war has caused a redistribution of wealth such as 100 years of ordinary life wd not have produced.

That the condition of permanent hostility between employers & employed is a great detriment to the nation. The soullessness of the relations is due largely to work becoming more & more mechanical owing to development of machinery & to increase of limited liability companies.

Richard Stapley   Chairman

9 Feb. 1916

* * *

[203] The 203rd meeting of the Circle was held on 9 Feb. 1916 at 33 Bloomsbury Square.

Present 12 members & 1 visitor—Sir Richard Stapley in the chair.

---

[186] Should be 'meeting'.

Apologies for absence were notified from Messrs: Brereton, Burrows, Gooch, Golding, Ramsay MacDonald, McKillop, Millin, Roskill & Walker.

The chairman said a few words on the loss the Circle had sustained by the death of Mr. Russell Rea, the Circle passed a vote of sympathy with Mrs. Rea & the family & instructed the Secretary to write a letter of condolence.

The Secretary read his paper on 'The Blockade'.

He commented on some of the figures recently published in the Daily Mail & the Morning Post to shew that what Germany lacked through stoppage of direct imports from America was made good to a large extent by the re-export of supplies received in abnormal quantities by neighbouring countries. He regarded the figures as practically worthless from a statistical point of view. He then dealt with the demand for a regular blockade in the technical sense & mentioned some of the reasons why such a blockade was not applicable in present circumstances & conditions. His view was that the present blockade, regular or irregular, was a common-sense development of the old principles & was probably the most effective that had ever been known. No doubt there was some leakage, but enemy trade both inwards & outwards was broadly speaking stopped.

The discussion turned mainly on the difference between our present method & a technical blockade, & on the question of the commodities (luxuries) that were of express purpose allowed to go through. The question was raised whether (since it was impossible to starve a country so largely self-supporting as Germany) the policy of keeping out food supplies might not be a mistaken one.

Richard Stapley   Chairman

8 March 1916

* * *

[204] The 204th meeting of the Circle was held on 8 Mch. 1916 at 33 Bloomsbury Square.

Present 11 members—Sir Richard Stapley in the chair.

Apologies for absence were notified from Messrs: Burrows, Golding & Matheson.

Mr. Roskill read his paper entitled 'Some thoughts on recent war literature'. He commented on the high sense of duty & the splendid spirit shewn in the writings of certain young English & French soldiers who have fallen in battle—Rupert Brooke, Oxland, Butler Wright,

Grenfell, Camille Violand & René Decluy[187]—& then going back a century mentioned the great influence the poems of Körner[188] & Arndt[189] had in effecting the liberation of Germany from the French. He then went on to shew how badly England as a whole needed the awakening & purifying influence of the spirit of such men in her ordinary affairs—particularly in her want of foresight as evidenced in (1) the lack of legal obligation on the head of an English family to provide for his widow & children (2) the management of the Gallipoli campaign (3) the slow development of the application of science to industry (4) the infirmities of the Acts relating to electric light & traction & telephony. In all such matters he contrasted our country unfavourably with Germany whose advance in commercial progress & production has astonished the world. On the other hand he admitted in the settlement of South African affairs the foresight of Sir Henry Campbell-Bannerman[190] to wh was due among other things the possibility of our being able to make use of the services of so capable a man as General Smuts[191] of whom Mr. Roskill gave a most interesting account.

In the discussion attention was drawn to the fact that Germany is a collection of large self-governing towns wh have never given up the self-govt. they have developed through the centuries, whereas in this country the policy has been to have a strong central govt. The opinion was expressed that notwithstanding Germany's foresight in the matter of education, & in application of science to industry & commerce, the intellectual & metaphysical life of Germany has largely disappeared. She is given up to the crudest & most degraded materialism & contributes nothing to the highest progress of the human race, & nothing immortal either in Art or Letters.

Richard Stapley   Chairman

12 April 1916

* * *

[205] The 205th meeting of the Circle was held on 12 Apl. 1916 at 33 Bloomsbury Sq:

[187] Rupert Brooke (1887–1915), Nowell Oxland, d. 1915, Julian Grenfell (1888–1915), Camille Violand (1892–1915), René Decluy (1892–1914).

[188] Karl Theodor Körner (1791–1813), German lyric patriotic poet.

[189] Ernst Moritz Arndt (1769–1860), German historian, politician and patriotic poet.

[190] Henry Campbell-Bannerman (1836–1908). Liberal politician, prime minister 1905–08.

[191] Jan Christiaan Smuts (1870–1950). South African statesman and premier.

Present 15 members & 2 visitors—Sir Richard Stapley in the chair.

Apologies for absence were notified from Messrs: McKillop & Ramsay MacDonald.

Minutes of the previous meeting were read & confirmed.

A preliminary discussion took place on the subjects for the next session & the Committee were instructed to draw up a programme for submission at the next meeting.

Mr. Farley read his paper on 'Recent proposals for a social & industrial policy after the War'.

Proposals more or less definite had been made for capturing German trade & for Tariff Reform, for putting women & crippled soldiers to work on the land, for a Peace policy, & for Educational reforms, after the War. We are not only behind Germany in technical & scientific education, but behind Switzerland, Denmark, Holland & Belgium in so important a matter as rural education. The reconstruction of our educational, industrial & social systems ought to engage our earnest consideration now. Our future industrial policy shd include state control of railways & canals, of the drink traffic, & of key industries. Our social policy shd include abolition of the causes of poverty, co-ordination of all philanthropic & religious agencies in any area, & the combatting of venereal disease. Our land policy shd include reform in the matter of wages, housing, co-operation & credit banks. Our most formidable enemy after the War will be on this side of the German Ocean—our own national inertia & short-sightedness. All experience since August 1914 has added weight to educational & social policies advocated for years by disinterested reformers.

The discussion turned mainly on education—with due regard to its defects & shortcomings in this country. The danger of cutting down expenditure on so vital a service was enlarged upon: on the other hand it was pointed out that after the War there wd be need for the most stringent economy in every direction.

Richard Stapley   Chairman

10 May 1916.

* * *

[206] The 206th meeting of the Circle was held on 10 May 1916 at 33 Bloomsbury Square.

Present. 20 members & 1 visitor—Sir Richard Stapley at first & afterwards Mr. Hobson in the chair.

Apologies were notified from Sir Wm. Byles, Mr. Ramsay Mac-Donald & Mr. McKillop.

Minutes of the previous meeting were read & confirmed.

The programme for next session, drawn up provisionally by the Committee was presented & adopted.

Sir Richard Stapley read his paper on 'Some hopeful spiritual results of the War'.

In the comradeship experienced in the struggle, both in the preparation for war & in the field, we can see a unity wh will operate in the reconstructive activities immediately confronting us. Traditions, worn-out idols & set formulas must make way for something better suited to the growing needs of individuals & communities. We shall realise that the strength & security of a nation come through moral & spiritual growth. Some sort of spiritual explosive generated by war experiences will undermine the doleful doctrines of evangelical Christianity on immortality: we may look not merely for co-operation one with another, on this plane of being, but for co-operation with human entities on planes beyond the boundary line of earth.[192] A bigger earth & a greater self will be linked together in the perception of the one-ness of God & Man: of Spirit & Matter: of Life here & Life yonder.

In the discussion the following opinions were expressed:

War is a retrogression & a disruptive influence. The present war is making a great separation between the Central Empires & ourselves & allies. The gravest damage of war is in the turning back of orderly processes of thought & feeling. The longer the war goes on the more do reactionary theories embody themselves in our policy. Possibly the admitted liberating process of war in scrapping old prejudices & barriers will enable us to grapple better with the immediate problems but this is not certain. The evils of war are certain; the good uncertain.

Richard Stapley   Chairman

7 June 1916

* * *

[207] The 207th meeting of the Circle was held on 7 June 1916 at 33 Bloomsbury Sq:

Present. 16 members 1 visitor. Sir Richard Stapley in the chair.

Apologies were notified from Sir Wm. Byles, Messrs: Golding, & Ramsay MacDonald.

Minutes of the previous meeting were read & confirmed.

Mr. Herdman read his paper on 'Martial Law'.[193]

Martial law is a phrase of many meanings. Originally it was the

---

[192] Stapley also played host to the mystical Christo-Theosophical society.

[193] For the full version of the paper see J.O. Herdman, 'Martial Law', *Contemporary Review*, vol. cx (1916), 364–72.

law administered in the Court of the Constable & Marshal: the Constable was the General of the King's armies: the Marshal was responsible for the discipline of the hosts in the field. Together they formed a court partly judicial partly executive: the jurisdiction was both criminal & civil, the criminal comprising wrongs committed by soldiers beyond the seas, appeals of felony & injuries to honour; the civil, contracts respecting deeds of arms at home & beyond seas. The executive functions embraced war at home & abroad, heraldry, coat-armour & funerals. After the attainder of Buckingham in 1521 the office of Constable fell into abeyance, but it was held that the Marshal could in all matters act alone. In 1533 the office of Marshal became hereditary in the house of Howard & so remains. The Court was voted a grievance by the House of Commons in 1640 but it has never been abolished. Notwithstanding the existence of this Court the King used from time to time to issue special Commissions giving the Commissioners power to exercise control over soldiers on active service in accordance with Articles of War. Out of this practice grew martial law in its second sense, namely military law. This body of rules is now wholly statutory: it applies only to persons subject to military law— a technical phrase practically synonymous with soldiers: it is contained in the Army Act 1881 as amended by later statutes, & this code is put in force each year for one year only by virtue of an Army Annual Act. All these Acts are directly derived from the Mutiny Acts of which the first was passed in 1689, the object in the earlier Acts being to subject soldiers to special law in time of peace & within the four seas. The Army Act applies both at home & abroad, in peace & in war. Different from both of these meanings is the third & quite incorrect use of the phrase when it is applied to the right & the duty of all good citizens, whether soldiers or civilians, to prevent a breach of the King's peace & to help in restoring the peace if & when broken, even if necessary to the extent of taking life. When an army is in possession of foreign territory & when an enemy is in possession of British territory, necessarily control devolves on the general. These are the two cases in which the Duke of Wellington said that martial law was only the will of the general in command. In this country it is impossible to declare a state of siege, & there is no power to try rioters or rebels (unless they be soldiers) otherwise than by the common law. This is proved by the necessity of passing an Act of Indemnity whenever there has been any exercise of martial law in the popular but wholly intangible acceptation. The Defence of the Realm Acts make no reference to martial law: they do but authorize in certain circumstances the trial by court-martial of certain new offences created by regulations made under them: these regulations do not mention rebellion & probably the trials in Ireland were therefore wholly illegal, unless they be justified by the very loose vague & general language of regulation 50.[194] Probably also the deportation of persons to England was the crime of praemunire under the Habeas Corpus Act.

In the discussion the following opinions were expressed:

An Act of Indemnity was necessary in past cases of the exercise of martial law because the facts were in dispute.

Martial law is, on the whole, as likely as ordinary law to result in justice being done & probably leads to less bloodshed than a strict application of ordinary law.

Martial law in Ireland may reopen the historical quarrel between England & Ireland.

Recent shooting of civilians in Ireland was inexpedient whether illegal or not.

Underneath the acquiescence of British working men in their work of making munitions &c. there lies a deep resentment against the administration of the Defence of the Realm Regulations.

Richard Stapley   Chairman

11 Oct. 1916

* * *

[208] The 208th meeting of the Circle was held on 21st June 1916 at 7.30 p.m. around a great hospitable round table at the National Liberal Club by the kind invitation of the Chairman.

Present: Sir Richard Stapley (in the chair), Messrs: Brereton, Burrows, Sir Wm. Byles, Messrs: Bullock, Crook, Gooch, Golding, Gardiner, Goodenough, Husband, Hobson, Harley, Herdman, J.R. MacDonald, Matheson, Sir Sydney Olivier, Messrs: Parsons, Roskill, Robertson, Wallas, Walker & Walsh.

Sir Richard Stapley said a few words with regard to the work of the Circle, its aims & ideals. Mr. Burrows, proposing the health of the Chairman, assured him of the esteem & affection felt for him by every member.

The readers of the papers for the next Session were settled & conversation then became general & informal.

Mr. Roskill sent letter.

Richard Stapley   Chairman

11 Oct. 1916

* * *

---

[194] In the aftermath of the Easter Rising of 1916 martial law was imposed, although not directly provided for by the Defence of the Realm Act of 1916.

Twenty-third Session: October 1916—June 1917.

[209] The 209th Meeting of the Circle was held on 11th Oct. 1916 at 33 Bloomsbury Square.

Present 19 members, the Rt. Hon. T. Lough[195] & 2 other visitors— Sir Richard Stapley in the chair.

Apologies for absence (3) from Messrs: Farley, Golding & Parsons.

Minutes of the 207th & 208th meetings were read & confirmed.

Record of Attendance for the last Session was read as follows:
Out of 9 meetings,

Messrs: Harley, Herdman, Husband, Walsh, the Chairman & the Secretary attended	9
Messrs: Crook, Farley, Matheson & Roskill	8
” Goodenough & Walker	7
Sir Sydney Olivier & Mr. Burrows	5
Mr. Hobson	4
Messrs: Adams, Brereton & Golding	3
” Alden, Gardiner, Millin, & Robertson & Sir Wm. Byles	1
” Raphael (on active service) McKillop (on munitions) Perris (on war correspondence) Gooch, Murray Macdonald, Ramsay MacDonald & Archdeacon Lilley	0

Average attendance 14.2 as against 17.4 for the previous year.

Resignation. Mr. Murray Macdonald's resignation was announced.

The Accounts, which shewed a deficit of 17s/9d, were presented & accepted. A subscription of 3/- per head was agreed to.

Sir Richard Stapley was re-elected as Chairman
Mr Parsons   ”   ”   ” Secretary
Messrs: Brereton, Crook, Harley, Herdman & Hobson were re-elected to the Committee.

Mr. Hobson gave an address on Finance.

The revenue before the War might be put at £200,000,000, & present revenue at £500,000,000. If the War ended in a year's time, probable revenue required would be £450,000,000. To find the money Protection under the guise of 'widening the Basis of Taxation' would doubtless be suggested. Tax on incomes and inheritances shd be differentiated according to their source & origin & the degree of utility to which income was put. Unearned surplus beyond the amount of income necessary to stimulate the individual to work should be absorbed by the State. After the war Capital & Labour will probably not be greatly impaired, but the distribution of wealth may be worsened. The problem will be to maintain high interest, high wages & high revenue. Effective co-operation of Capital & Labour will be

---

[195] Thomas Lough (1850–1922). Liberal M.P. for West Islington 1892–1918.

necessary. The claims of Labour must be satisfied & a high rate of consumption must be maintained if the miracle of production is to continue in a modified form. There will be great need for national-isation of monetary machinery. Agricultural & working class credit must be extended. Before the war there were violent fluctuations of Prices & of Rates of Exchange. There shd be international com-missions of experts for securing reliable cheap finance of international commerce & for regulating amounts of currency & credit so as to keep world-prices steady & enable business calculations to be con-ducted safely with the object of utilising to best advantage the real productive powers of the different nations.

In the discussion the following opinions were expressed:

That one item of Capital to be returned to us after the War was the equal tonnage of ships destroyed by Germany: that there shd be international arrangement of wages no less than of prices: that the State has become a new capitalist & that there will be a jar when State capital is dissolved into individual capital: that the question of finance turns on how the war will end: that disarmament is a field for economy: that excess profits tax should be continued after the War: that high wages have already caused a great redistribution of wealth.

Richard Stapley   Chairman
8 Nov. 1916

* * *

[210] The 210th meeting of the Circle was held on 8th Nov. 1916 at 33 Bloomsbury Square.

Present. 19 members, the Rt. Hon. F.A. Acland[196] & two other visitors—Sir Richard Stapley in the chair.

Apologies for absence were notified from Sir Wm. Byles & Messrs: Farley, MacDonald & Raphael.

Minutes of the previous meeting were read & confirmed.

Mr. A.G. Gardiner read his paper on 'Imperial Defence'. What our policy of Imperial Defence will be after the War will depend on success or otherwise of proposed League to enforce Peace, on kind of Peace achieved, on attitude we are called upon to adopt towards those who have been our enemies & our friends, & on nature of Imperial relationships that will be required as result of present experience. The Navy must still be our main defence. The development of submarine

[196] F.A. Acland (1861–1950). Canadian politician and journalist.

warfare has changed ideas of naval defence & naval power—& not in our favour since it has modified disparity between the stronger & the weaker naval power. There will be a greater tendency to regard Imperial Navy as a unit, but in matter of military forces the Dominions will provide for their own security. The defence of India, involving maintenance of professional army, will be a governing consideration of our military system. The constitution of the Army will have to be overhauled & the officering must be more intellectual & competent & inspired by a new spirit representing general temper & outlook of nation. Conscription is not desirable since we cannot maintain a supreme Navy, a continental Army, & our credit at the same time. The true lesson of national defence for us is necessity of increasing the value of our human material both physically & nationally for the purposes of citizenship.

In the discussion the following opinions were expressed:

That the writer had exaggerated the value of the submarine.

That some form not of conscription but of compulsory military training shd be adopted.

That more attention shd be devoted to scientific artillery & machine gunnery.

That the great task of the Allies was to form a League of Nations against War & get Germany to join it. Such a League must involve limitation of armaments on some formula to be agreed upon.

That we must have compulsory continuation education for boys of 14 to 18, physical training leading up to 1 or 2 months' camp being an important & compulsory part.

Richard Stapley   Chairman

13 Dec. 1916

* * *

[211] The 211th meeting of the Circle was held on 13 Dec. 1916 at 33 Bloomsbury Square.

Present 13 members, Mr. A. Ponsonby M.P., Mr. Graham Wallas & 3 other guests—Sir Richard Stapley in the chair.

Apologies for absence were notified from Messrs: Burrows, Byles, Gooch, Parsons & Roskill.

Mr. J.R. MacDonald gave an address on Representative Govt.

Committees. There are ten French Parliamentary Committees. The Reporter of the Committee sees the bill through the house. The Committee system gives a greater number of men a chance of shewing what they can do, but is of no value as regards quality of legislation. In England anyone interested in a bill can get on the Committee but this is impossible in France owing to the selection being by lot. In Finance the objection to the system is definite; in France the budget is a political & not a financial measure. In England more committees might be useful for administrative purposes, but 2 changes wd be necessary (1) bills wd have to go over from session to session (2) drastic changes with a view to less obstruction & bargaining wd have to be made in the Report stage.

A 2nd Chamber—might be valuable (1) as a check (2) as a Court of Revision (3) as a real 2nd chamber. As to (1) this is pretty well given up: such a chamber must have either different interests or different opinions: the latter wd mean alteration of constituencies or of votes. As to (2) we must have some such court of appeal, a body charged with putting bills into proper legal form so as to carry out the ideas of their authors. As to (3) a real 2nd Chamber wd only lead to conflict.

Party system. It is difficult to see how we can do without it. But in the country party works to produce not opinions but votes: so H. of C. gets filled up with inferior partisans: hence obstruction wh when effective strengthens the hands of the Govt. as it prevents Govt. supporters from speaking & leads to the closure.

Foreign policy. We must get the people interested in it. All treaties & commitments shd be disclosed but the discussion preliminary thereto shd be secret.

Franchise. All adults shd have it. The woman-vote in Australia has made no practical difference in political results.

In the discussion the following opinions were expressed:
Administrative Committees are improved by having officials among their members. Ministers shd be able to speak in both Houses. There has been a great increase in the power of the executive. The Foreign office debate in the House shd be made a reality: there shd. be a day for policy & a day for details—but no publicity of negotiations. Treaties shd. be periodically revised. With greater publicity the press wd be less liable to stir up strife.

Richard Stapley   Chairman

10 Jan 1917.

* * *

[212] The 212th meeting of the Rainbow Circle was held on 10 Jan. 1917 at 33 Bloomsbury Square.

Present. 16 members, 3 visitors, Sir Richard Stapley in the chair.

Apologies for absence were notified from Sir Wm Byles & Messrs: Golding & MacDonald.

Mr. Robertson read his paper on 'Trade Policy'.

If the proposed Trade-war is to consist simply in *not* trading with Germany & in trading with other people instead it shd be called a trade boycott, but the Allies cd not boycott German trade so as to keep it depressed without at the same time injuring their own. Moreover Germany wd simply seek trade by all means in her power in neutral markets where she wd undersell the Allies who wd in the process be likely to suffer more than Germany. Trade is not war and cannot be turned to warlike ends without ceasing to be trade wh is a matter of reciprocal advantage. The ideal of a perpetual processus of trade aiming at perpetual injury of an enemy is a chimera. The one thing deserving the name of a purposive trade war is a tariff-war—a procedure of retaliatory increases of tariffs, wh is not a war by trade, but financial war by curtailment of trade. Every fiscal procedure wh thinks to inflict ruin without incurring it, to promote trade by injuring other people's trade is but an attempt to outwit the law of death.

In the discussion the following opinions were expressed:

That the proposed policy of a definite trade alliance between the Central Powers, in so far as it wd involve a breaking down of international barriers in a large area wd be a step towards international free-trade & wd be good.

That the number of industries that claim to be key industries & deserving of help by the State increases daily. Such claims might diminish if the industries were continued under State control, the state taking a large proportion of the profits.

That the 5-ply[197] tariff now being seriously considered wd lead to endless friction & harm both politically & commercially.

That the attitude of other countries might be entirely different to us if to our command of the sea we added a protectionist policy.

Richard Stapley   Chairman

14 Feb 1917

* * *

[213] The 213th meeting of the Circle was held on 14 Feb 1917 at 33 Bloomsbury Sq:

Present. 17 members, Mr. Graham Wallas & Mr. Herbert Samuel—Sir Richard Stapley in the chair.

An apology was notified from Sir Wm Byles.

---

[197] A reference to the five propositions of the Balfour Committee (1916–17) on post-war trade and Imperial economic relations, debarring—among others—future trade with present enemy countries. Cp. J.M. Robertson, *The New Tariffism* (London, 1918), pp. 23–4.

Minutes of the previous meeting were read & confirmed.

Mr. Graham Wallas gave an address on 'Imperial Relations'. An empire cannot exist under modern conditions without close federation. In this connexion many questions arise—e.g. the voting power of the respective constituents—whether the Army & Navy shd be fused or remain under separate control—whether the trend shd be in the direction of more monarchy or less monarchy. There is a real danger in existence of enormous armed force centred in a personal monarch. Then again constructive imagination is needed to decide where capital towns, railways, & centres of scientific industry & investigation shd be established.

Break-up of our first empire in 1776 was due to development of colonial policy such as is now advocated in certain quarters. Our plans for the govt. of South Africa shd be formulated jointly with those of the French. In India our position becomes every year more unsafe. We have obligations in India but cannot afford to stake everything on defending our position. Responsibility for her defence must be transferred—at least in part—by recognising that the government of India must be carried out for the benefit of India itself. A system of International control of the Tropics seems to be indicated— a system in wh our empire may fade into a larger unity.

In the discussion the following opinions were expressed:
Unless unity of British Empire is preserved any wider federation is hopeless. The dominions think it essential that they shd have a voice in foreign policy. An Imperial Executive & an Imperial Assembly quite possible. India & Egypt shd be represented but not on population basis. Some international arrangement shd be got to work in regard to all parts of the world that are weak or backward.

Richard Stapley   Chairman

14 March 1917

* * *

[214] The 214th meeting of the Circle was held on 14 Mch. 1917 at 33 Bloomsbury Sq.

Present. 14 members & Mr. H.J. Mundella—Sir Richard Stapley in the chair.

Apologies were notified from Messrs: Alden, Burrows, Hobson & Walker.

Minutes of the previous meeting were read & confirmed.

Sir Richard Stapley made reference to the recent death of Lady Stapley who had for so many years taken so kindly & so lively an interest in the Circle, & the Circle expressed their deep sympathy with him in his sorrow. A memorial notice from the Christian Commonwealth was read & also Mr. Cloudesley Brereton's memorial verses which were published later in the Contemporary Review.[198]

Mr. Brereton read his paper on 'Education'.

He dealt with the need of increased expenditure on education & of altering system of taxation to meet it: the need of improving the teachers' position & prospects without making them civil servants: the question of building accommodation wh might to large extent be of temporary character with advantage: the question of smaller classes wh help a child to think for himself & tend to develope individuality: the question of self-govt. of scholars: the prolonging of school-life: the more direct preparation for livelihood: part-time education: organisation of secondary education: the grading of all education: university reform: & the question of bigger educational areas.

Of the 3 forms of humanism, viz. Language-culture (including literature & history): Nature-culture (including mathematics) & Craft-culture, insufficient attention is given to the last. Yet the hope of the future especially lies in its proper development since for the bulk of the children this is the particular type of culture that will fit them best for their life-work.

In the discussion the following opinions were expressed:
The school buildings—with spacious rooms & corridors—have great effect on both children & teachers. Education is hampered at every turn for want of proper buildings & when we can get plenty of elbow room educational experts will increase.

There is a great danger in turning education of a child into vocational directions too early.

Children whose brain-power is far below the average are turned out with less education than they might have owing to attempt to teach them all too many subjects. Capacity for learning ought to be more taken into account.

There was a general consensus of opinion that the pay & status of the teachers must be improved & be more in relation to their social utility: also that the whole system of local taxation must be revised on income tax basis.

Richard Stapley   Chairman

18 Apl. 1917

* * *

[215] The 215th meeting of the Circle was held on 18 Apl. 1917 at 33 Bloomsbury Square.

[198] Cloudesley Brereton, 'Here is no Room for Tears', *Contemporary Review*, vol. cxi (April 1917), 544.

Present. 15 members Sir Rider Haggard[199] & another visitor.

Apologies for absence were notified from Sir Wm Byles, Mr. Gooch & Mr. Roskill.

Minutes of the previous meeting were read & confirmed.

Mr. Alden read his paper on Land Policy.

Whatever our present emergency measures may be we must go on to deal with whole agricultural problem in broad & generous fashion. The average English farmer is conservative & narrow-minded & afraid of any change even in his manures. Rich men pay high prices for land not put to agricultural or economic uses. The State must discountenance old principles of private property & feudalism & do for agriculture what has been done for the production of munitions. After the war in addition to 300.000 agricultural labourers now on active service there may be another 300.000 who will desire to cultivate the soil either here or in the Dominions, but they must have larger opportunities & a fuller life than obtains here at present. The State can help by acquiring land for settlement of discharged sailors & soldiers in State colonies of small holdings on tenancy basis, disused military hutments & expert guidance being provided at State expense. Light railway plant & motor lorries set free after the war shd be used for development purposes & to foster co-operation. Nothing the Govt. has yet suggested ensures that the Back to the Land movement will arouse much enthusiasm. The agricultural question must be regarded from standpoint of national health & well-being as well as from that of independence as regards food supplies.

In the discussion the following opinions were expressed:

Through submarines & air ships we are losing our position as an island & becoming a continental power. Either we must store food against a condition of war or cut down our population to a number for wh we can grow supplies. Feudal ideas in agricultural industry still survive & are an evil—but tenant farmers really like them. The land must be freed from its burdens & made more remunerative. Artificial small-holdings are a doubtful success & only answer where the small-holding spirit exists: there is much to be said for actual ownership wh arouses more personal interest. The State must have more control over the land whether owned by State or by individuals. Prejudice against co-operation will probably be less after the war.

Richard Stapley   Chairman

9 May 1917

* * *

[199] Henry Rider Haggard (1856–1925). Novelist, interested in rural reform.

[216] The 216th meeting of the Circle was held on 9th May 1917 at 33 Bloomsbury Square.

Present. 19 members & Mr. A.E. Zimmern who had kindly undertaken, at very short notice, to read a paper.[200] Sir Richard Stapley in the chair.

Minutes of the previous meeting were read & confirmed.

Apologies for absence were notified from Sir Wm Byles & Mr. Ramsay MacDonald.

The circumstances that prevented Sir Wm Lever from being present were explained & a letter was read in wh he kindly accepted the Circle's proposal that he should give his paper at a special meeting on the 23rd May.

Reference was made to the serious illness of Mr. Herbert Burrows & it was agreed to send him a letter expressing the Circle's sympathy.

The Committee's draft programme for next session was presented & accepted with one amendment.

Mr. Zimmern read his paper on the British Working Man.

His chief points were 1. the importance of capturing the sensibility of the working classes between the ages of 14 & 18
2. that Socialism is a red-herring across the path of development 3. that we shall never get close association between English & Continental working classes until they understand one another better.

The working class is the most English of the English people who on the whole are characteristically stupid in the sense of being impervious to ideas & of having an excessive dislike to using what minds they have. The Labour movement is nominally committed to Socialism, but it is not socialism as understood on the continent that the working man really wants. He has other qualities besides stupidity—notably a strong sense of personal dignity & self-respect, with which are bound up his constitutionalism & his understanding of the necessity of give & take in self-government. He wants responsibility & to be treated like a gentleman & to have a measure of control over his own life &, collectively, over the common life. One fundamental difference between the Continental & the British working class movements is that the continental working man thinks of political problems in terms of economics while the British working man thinks of economic problems in terms of politics.

In the discussion the following opinions among many others[201] were expressed:
That the real strength & weakness of man are common to all classes

---

[200] The original speaker on the programme was to have been Philip Snowden on Labour from the Workmen's point of view.

[201] An obvious indication of an expectedly passionate discussion of a provocative paper!

& that stupidity, as defined, was common to men of all races, nations & classes.

That the Socialist, the syndicalist & the Co-operator are all actuated by the same motive—to eliminate profiteering from industry.

Richard Stapley   Chairman 23 May 1917

* * *

[217] The 217th meeting of the Circle was held on 23rd May 1917 at 33 Bloomsbury Square.

Present 12 members & 8 visitors including Sir Wm Lever, Sir Richard Stapley in the chair.

Minutes of the previous meeting were read & confirmed.

Apologies for absence were notified from Messrs: J.R. MacDonald, Parsons & Roskill.

Sir Wm Lever gave an address on Labour Policy from the employer's point of view.

The real problem is to see that Capital, Management & Labour each gets a fair share in the profits of an industry & to settle what that share should be. A better understanding of each other, employer & employee, & of the principles that make for national wealth is essential if the shares of either are to be increased. At present there is too much suspicion & distrust on both sides. For the real betterment of industry Co-partnership (not profit-sharing) is necessary, inducing the employee's interest in making the industry successful. Factory hours shd be reduced to six a day & education & physical training of the employee shd be continued even to the age of 30 in time thus set free. Enormous Trades Unions, Co-operative Societies & Combinations of employers indicate growth & development, & any combination that depends on anything other than right & justice is doomed to failure. No combination of employers can be justified unless the economies effected by combining are shared with the consumer.

A discussion followed.

Richard Stapley   Chairman

10 Oct. 1917

* * *

Twenty-fourth Session.

[218] The 218th meeting of the Circle was held on 10 Oct. 1917 at 33 Bloomsbury Square.

Present. 17 members—Sir Richard Stapley in the chair.

Apologies for absence were notified from Messrs: Perris & Burrows & Sir Sydney Olivier.

Minutes of the previous meeting were read & confirmed.

Record of Attendance for the previous session was read as follows:
Out of 9 meetings

Messrs:	Crook, Herdman, Husband & Sir Richard Stapley attended	9
”	Brereton, Goodenough & Matheson	8
”	Gooch, Harley, Walker & Walsh	7
”	Adams, Golding, Parsons & Sir Sydney Olivier	6
”	Alden, Burrows & Roskill	5
”	Hobson, McKillop & Millin	4
”	Gardiner & Robertson	2
Mr. MacDonald		1
Messrs:	Farley, Perris, Sir Wm Byles & Archdeacon Lilley	0

Average attendance 16 as against 14.2 for the previous year.

The Accounts wh shewed a deficiency of 17/- were presented & accepted. A subscription of 3/- per head was agreed to.

Sir Richard Stapley was re-elected as Chairman
Mr. Parsons   ”   ”   ” Secretary
Messrs: Brereton, Crook, Harley, Herdman & Hobson were re-elected to the Committee.

Mr. Matheson read his paper on 'The New Russia'.

He dealt with the past history of Russia & of how her development had suffered from her commercial isolation, the bureaucracy, the police system, & the repressive measures of succeeding Tsars. The Crimean war marked the real starting point of her continuous though intermittent struggle for liberty. Enormous social changes were wrought by the establishment of County & Town Councils under Alexander II. The 'nihilism' of the 60's born of despair at the apathetic ignorance of the peasants & the hollowness of the Govt.'s reforms was only a passing phase & was soon replaced by the Social Revolutionary Movement wh developed into the 'Will of the People' party in the 70's. The repressive policy of Alexander III & Nicholas II increased the general unrest. The Japanese War threw into clearer relief the domestic evils wh had found their natural manifestation in its disasters. Right up to the eve of the present war, when there were barricades in Petrograd & all was ripe for a revolutionary outbreak, strikes recurred with increasing frequency & extent. The war, wh was very popular, seemed at first a solvent for all political differences, but the Govt. by maladministration threw away a great opportunity. Eventually, partly owing to actual hunger & impending starvation in the capital, the revolution took place. It was not organised: it happened. The revolution shd not be regarded merely from the point of view of its probable immediate effect on the war, but rather as potentially the greatest triumph yet won for the causes for wh the Allies are supposed to be fighting.[202]

In the discussion the following opinions were expressed:

The Revolution was delayed by the war: not due to the war, wh was generally accepted as a liberating influence by the socialists & revolutionists. The weakness of the revolution is that the people are mainly anxious about sound theories of politics & administration— more interested in theoretical than in practical questions.

Unsuccessful wars in wh Russia has engaged have given the greatest impetus to liberation.

There will be a phase when Russia will not be a Republic but possibly a constitutional monarchy, though this will not last—Eventually she will probably become a Federal Republic.

The great development of the co-operative movement in Russia seems to argue that there is no necessity for her to learn organisation from Germany.

Richard Stapley   Chairman

14 Nov. 1917

* * *

Committee meeting

A Committee meeting was held on 4th Decr. 1917 at 33 Bloomsbury Square to nominate candidates for vacancies in the Circle. Present. Messrs: Brereton, Crook, Harley, the Chairman & the Secretary. The Secretary reported that 4 names had been sent in, namely

Mr. De Lisle Burns[203] proposed by Mr. Brereton
Mr. A. Wigglesworth   ”   ”   ” Husband
Mr. T.L. Gilmour   ”   ”   ” Matheson
Mr. Cyril Hurcomb   ”   ” the Secretary

Mr. Burns & Mr. Hurcomb were known to wish to join & to be able to attend the meetings. The Secretary had written to Mr. Wigglesworth & Mr. Gilmour asking them whether they wished their names to be put forward, whether they wd be able to attend with reasonable regularity, & if so whether they wd be good enough to give a brief account of themselves for the information of the Committee. Mr. Gilmour had replied to the effect that in normal circumstances he wd much like to join the Circle but that at present

---

[202] The reference is to the March 1917 Kerenski revolution. Many British liberals hailed it as a triumph for liberalism and democracy.

[203] Read 'Delisle Burns'.

there was no chance of his attending at all. Mr. Wigglesworth replied affirmatively & sent the particulars desired.

Mr. Gilmour being ruled out, the biographical particulars of the other candidates were given as follows:

Mr. De Lisle Burns. 2nd Class Classical Tripos 1900. At Rome for 4 years doing archaeology & scholastic philosophy. Lecturer on Philosophy at R.C. College, St. Edmunds, until the attack of Pius X on the Modernists. Extension Lecturer for Cambridge, Oxford & London Universities. War Office Intelligence Staff 1916–17. Ministry of Reconstruction 1917. Author of 'The Growth of Modern Philosophy', 'Political Ideals' 'Greek Ideals' 'The Morality of Nations' 'The World of States' & of the following: in the Aristotelian Society Papers 'William of Ockham on Universals' 'The State in its external relations' 'Ethical Principles of Reconstruction'. Personally known to Messrs: Brereton, Lilley, Gooch, Hobson, Matheson & Crook.

Mr. A Wigglesworth. Lived in Italy & in this country in business connexions until 3 years ago when he joined Ministry of Munitions. Delegate to U.S.A. last spring & Delegate on recent mission to Paris. Now in Inter-Allied Munitions Bureau. Has contributed to the Contemporary Review, Light of Reason, & Light. Has lectured to Imperial Institute on Fibres in East Africa (wh he visited in 1913) & author of various technical treatises. Personally known to Sir Richard Stapley, Mr. Husband & some other members.

Mr. Cyril Hurcomb. Scholar of St. John's Oxford 1901. 1st in Mods. 1903 2nd in Greats 1905. Civil Service (G.P.O.) 1905. Private Secretary to Sir Mat[t]hew Nathan[204] 1910/11. Private Secretary to Mr. Herbert Samuel & later to Sir Charles Hobhouse 1911–14. Admiralty Transport Dept. 1915. Ministry of Shipping 1916. Personally known to Mr. Herbert Samuel, Mr. Golding & Mr. Parsons.

The Committee had regard to the facts that these 3 candidates had all attended one or more meetings of the Circle, that they were all keen to join & wd be able to attend, & that they were all men who wd be likely to be acquisitions. The Committee considered that the candidates were in every way suitable for election & unanimously agreed to nominate them.

The name of Mr. Percy Nunn[205] was mentioned as a possible candidate, but the Committee thought it desirable at present to leave one vacancy open.

The Committee recommended that the method of procedure

[204] Sir Matthew Nathan (1862–1939). Governor of Natal, later of Queensland. Career in public service. Secretary to the Post Office 1909–11.

[205] (Sir) Percy Nunn (1870–1944), educationalist. At the time he was vice-principal of the London Day Training College.

adopted in the nomination of candidates on this occasion shd be taken as a precedent.

Richard Stapley   Chairman

* * *

[219] The 219th meeting of the Circle was held on 14 Nov 1917 at 33 Bloomsbury Square.

Present. 17 members & 8 visitors—Sir Richard Stapley in the chair.

Apologies for absence were notified from Mr. Gardiner & Mr. Roskill.

Minutes of the previous meeting were read & confirmed.

The Chairman made a sympathetic reference to the loss the Circle had sustained by the death of Sir William Pollard Byles.

Mr. Gooch gave an address on the Problem of Constantinople.

The near Eastern question is the problem of filling up the vacuum created by gradual disappearance of Turkey from Europe. Acquisition of Constantinople one of Russia's deep-rooted ambitions from time of Peter the Great. In recent times there has been a certain conflict between Russia's aim for path from North to South & Germany's similar aim for path from West to East. Mr. Gooch dealt with diplomatic negotiations between Ae[h]renthal & Izvolsky[206] 1907–8, Austria to annex Bosnia & Russia to have right to send fleet through the Straits. England not wishing to wound or damage Young Turks opposed opening up of Straits. In 1913 Young Turks asked England for money & men to reform Asia Minor, offering full executive powers, but did not get what they wanted & so turned to Germany. Liman von Sanders'[207] mission clinched dominance of German power in Turkey. As regards future of Constantinople & Straits many solutions have been suggested. Russia has no claim from point of view of nationality & cd not hold Constantinople without a land approach wh wd involve domination of Balkans. Constantinople might be internationalized or remain independent with international or American control of Straits.

The discussion was marked by unusual reticence, each member being generously loth to 'take up the time of the Circle' so that the others might have opportunity of speaking. Mention was, however, made of the great force of nationality & passion for freedom on part of the various Balkan peoples; & of the fact that there must be some deep-lying reason—quite apart from diplomatic transactions—why

[206] Count Alois Aehrenthal (1854–1912), Austrian foreign minister; and Alexander Petrovich Izvolski (1856–1919), Russian foreign minister.
[207] Liman von Sanders (1855–1929). German general.

Turkish empire has constantly receded. Kerenski was quoted as repudiating any notion on part of Russian people of annexing Constantinople—a course totally opposed to their belief in people having freedom to govern themselves. Gladstone was referred to as the man who broke with the old policy & made us anti-Turk on account of Turkish faults & mismanagement.

Richard Stapley   Chairman

12 Decr. 1917

* * *

[220] The 220th meeting of the Circle was held on 12 Decr. 1917 at 33 Bloomsbury Square.

Present. 16 members & 2 visitors—Sir Richard Stapley in the chair.

Apologies for absence were notified from Mr. Roskill.

Minutes of the previous meeting were read & confirmed.

The Report of the Committee nominating Mr. DeLisle Burns, Mr. A. Wigglesworth & Mr. Cyril Hurcomb to vacancies in the Circle was read & adopted & these candidates were unanimously elected.

Mr. Crook read his paper on 'The Irish Question'.

Dealing first with the race question (wh he traced from palaeolithic times) he emphasised the fact that the British invasion of Great Britain was the last complete conquest & never reached Ireland, & that in any large anthropological sense there is no British blood in Ireland. Similarly there is no Latin & no Teutonic blood. The settlement in Eastern Ulster has not been absorbed into the Irish race but remains an enclave. Differences, racial, religious, economic, agrarian, political & social have prevented its absorption.

Ireland's geographic position, cutting her off from western European life & thought, except as filtered through England, has made her more interested in America than England is.

The agrarian troubles in Ireland are due to the forcing of the feudal system of land tenure on to a country wh had a much older & deeply-rooted system basally different.

The economic disparity between England & Ireland is largely artificial—the deliberate creation of a powerful despot wh was also a jealous trade rival.

Mr. Crook reviewed the political mismanagement of Ireland, the crippling & abolition of her parliament, & the growth & inwardness of the Sinn Fein movement, & concluded by saying that any real settlement of the Irish question must leave unhampered in the hands of the Irish people executive power & financial control.

The discussion was generally favourable to Mr. Crook, though his views on race, archaeology, the feudal system & education came in for some criticism. The opinion was expressed that the history of Irish institutions is the history of arrested developments: also that Ireland is not being & has not·been treated on an equality with England & is thus not getting the benefit of the union.

Richard Stapley   Chairman

9 Jan. 1918

* * *

[221] The 221st meeting of the Circle was held on 9 Jan: 1918 at 33 Bloomsbury Square.

Present. 15 members & 5 visitors, Sir Richard Stapley in the chair.

Apologies for absence were notified from Messrs: Burrows, Alden, Matheson, Roskill & Walker.

Minutes of the previous meeting were read & confirmed.

Mr. Robertson read his paper on the Novels of Joseph Conrad.

The art of Conrad is less popular in its appeal than that of any of the imaginative literary geniuses of last century—except the novels of Meredith & Clough. Meredith & Conrad may be bracketed in that they both handle great & arresting problems of character, personality & conduct. Conrad besides being a great master of language has in supreme degree the faculties of perception & conception, vision & reproduction, in a spontaneous union. His very artistic faults are excesses of the creative faculty. The provision of atmosphere is with him a matter of course: his slight episodes introduced as background are themselves backgrounded but this idiosyncracy never curtails the ultimate aim of presenting character. The final impression left by his art is that of greatness, of tragic intensity, of vivid realisation of life & circumstance, of invincible patience in his artistic reproduction. He is sombrely ironied but has no humour.

In the discussion the following opinions were expressed:
That though Conrad is the most effective writer of the present day his method is rather vexatious:
That Wells is superior to him in style & magnitude.
That Conrad is unique in that he belongs to no country.
That his power is very largely descriptive power & that may not be enough to give his books permanence.

Richard Stapley   13 Feb. 1918.

* * *

[222] The 222nd meeting of the Circle was held on 13 Feb. 1918 at 33 Bloomsbury Square.

Present. 20 members—Sir Richard Stapley in the chair.

Apology was notified from Mr. Husband.

Minutes of the previous meeting were read & confirmed.

Mr. Harley read his paper on the Novels of Arnold Bennett.

He regarded the Fantasies or shockers as standing in intimate relation to Arnold Bennett's whole art, but devoted most of his criticism to the more serious novels. Bennett set out to write an epic of modern industry based on all that was most typical in the Five Towns, but from innate cynicism failed to enter into the heart of his characters or to make us realise their pathos. His most important work is contained in the 'Old Wives' Tale' & the trilogy—'Clayhanger', 'Hilda Lessways', & 'These Twain'. His comments on life are clever, but cold & external. Nowhere does he let down the roots of his philosophy deep enough, but tries to explain everything in term of materialism.

In the discussion opinions were somewhat divided, but for the most part it was held that the writer had hardly done full justice to Bennett's merits as an artist. On the one hand Bennett was compared to a kinematograph, but on the other hand it was urged that his characters were convincing & skilfully delineated: that Bennett was wise in confining himself to objective treatment: & that even apart from his artistic achievements he had produced documents wh are interesting & humanly valuable.

Richard Stapley   Chairman 13 Mch '18

* * *

[223] The 223rd meeting of the Circle was held on 13 Mch 1918 at 33 Bloomsbury Square.

Present. 17 members—Sir Richard Stapley in the chair.

Apologies for absence were notified from Messrs: Alden, MacDonald, Robertson & Roskill.

Minutes of the previous meeting were read & confirmed.

Mr. Golding read his paper on 'the Novels of Mr. H.G. Wells'.

Mr. Wells is the modern, the contemporaneous, writer *par excellence*. His sphere of influence dwarfs that of any other living English writer. He strikes from innumerable points at the blind vulgarity of our social values, satirizes our smugness, rages at the levity of our statesmanship, assails everything in life that is vegetative, blatant & supine. He is intensely alive & intensely interested in life in all its aspects. He sometimes sullies the purity of his art by didacticism & propaganda & frequently stages personalities wh represent rather than embody types. His sympathy with the victims of the social drift, like Kipps & Mr. Polly, lacks Dostoievsky's passionate apprehension of souls. He does not possess in any eminent degree the power of creating personalities. He is a gifted psychologist of the subtle & intricate rather than of the profound. He lacks the genius of the inner life—the gift of a creative intensity of sympathy. It is noteworthy that his characters possess little magnanimity or disinterestedness.

As a writer of prose it wd be difficult to overpraise him. He possesses in a singular degree the gift of the creative & illuminating phrase. His prose is adequate to anything demanded of it but lacks the supreme charm of poetic splendour, such as we get for instance in Joseph Conrad.

In the discussion the following opinions were expressed:

The great interest of Mr. Wells lies in his intense sincerity, his supreme sense of the uncanny, & his truthful presentation of the life of our times.

He is incapable of touching the soul of man, missing all that is highest & noblest & is hence a rather repellent figure in English literature.

He has a sincere passion for disentangling the muddle of the world.

Opinions on the merits of his style varied considerably.

Richard Stapley   10 April 1918.

* * *

[224] The 224th Meeting of the Circle was held on 10 April 1918 at 33 Bloomsbury Square.

Present. 15 members & 2 visitors—Sir Richard Stapley in the chair.

Apologies were notified from Messrs: Burrows, Gooch, Hobson & Walsh.

Minutes of the previous meeting were read & confirmed.

The Committee, with the addition of Mr. Wigglesworth, were instructed to draft a programme for the next session.

Mr. Goodenough read his paper on the proposition 'That the Power of the Executive has increased, is increasing & ought to be diminished'.

George III was the cause of Dunning's[208] famous resolution: Lloyd George, by undermining Cabinet government & control of Parliament,[209] is paving the way for the present resolution—though we

---

[208] John Dunning (1731–1783). Barrister and politician. In 1780 carried a resolution in the House of Commons that 'the influence of the crown has increased, is increasing, and ought to be diminished.'

[209] A reference to the changes in the nature of prime ministerial government introduced by Lloyd George after 1916.

really need to consider the matter not in its present abnormal setting but from the point of view of more normal times to come. The problem is to bring about closer control of Government by the people governed—a wider & deeper interest in political affairs leading to more vital relationship between electorate & Executive. It is a question not only of Parliamentary control of Executive but of control of Parliament by informed public opinion. Effective criticism & control of Executive—ministers & civil servants alike—loses none of its importance when the holders of power are regularly accountable to the community. We want to relieve the Govt. of all but governing work: to get away from Govt. by 'Orders in Council', from Govt. interference with trade, & from Govt. control of industry. We want Home Rule all round to free Parliament from local legislation & we want a return to the normal system of a Cabinet collectively responsible for all the acts of the Executive.

In the discussion the following opinions were expressed:
The House of Commons must recover full financial control & also control of foreign policy. There will have to be a breaking up of cabinet functions & some extended system of Parliamentary committees. The whole tendency of politics is in the direction of a demand for extension of State activity. Parliamentary vigilance, democratisation of Civil Service itself, & Decentralisation, are remedies for evils—actual or potential—of bureaucracy.

Richard Stapley   Chairman

8 May 1918

* * *

[225] The 225th meeting of the Circle was held on 8 May 1918 at 33 Bloomsbury Sq:

Present. 20 members & 1 visitor—Sir Richard Stapley in the chair.

Apologies for absence were notified from Messrs: Hurcomb, Parsons & Roskill.

Minutes of the previous meeting were read & confirmed.

The Committee's draft programme for the next session was submitted & adopted with one or two modifications. It was decided that the hour of meeting for next session shd be 7.45 pm.

Mr. Hobson read his paper on 'The Newspaper'.

The 3 chief uses of the Newspaper are (1) to communicate News (2) to interpret News (3) to promote discussion & judgment. The conditions under wh the journalist writes—particularly those of immediacy & supposed infallibility—make satisfactory performance of these tasks difficult even granting that he has high standards of integrity & impartiality. But within last generation journalism has passed from status of a profession into that of a trade & the modern newspaper is marred by economic & class bias, subject to various business, political & social pressures & to advertising interests. The greatest peril lies in the systematic usurpation of public opinion by men who are skilled wholesale exploiters of the public mind for the satisfaction of their lust for personal power, & journalism is the most dangerous of trades because its most expert practitioner can exert the most poisonous influence on the soul of man. The growth of a Business Trust wh reaches out on the one side into public sentiment & on the other into the secret plans of Govts. is a grave danger to Democracy. If Democracy is to be saved the directing motive power of the Press must be transformed. Sound public opinion demands a Press wh is operated as a disinterested social service, & wh will both inform & reflect it. The superstition of anonymity shd disappear in articles containing critical judgments. Correspondence shd be honestly & fairly dealt with. It is possible that the new broadening & deepening of political interest in the general mind due to the intense importance of new issues may make feasible a free newspaper run on co-operative lines as an organ for the new democratic movement.

In the discussion the following opinions were expressed:
the indictment of the Press, though severe, was not exaggerated. We now see that the Press may be one of the great dangers of democracy. The appeal to the mass has been made by the wrong people. The new principle is the poisoning of the news columns. The paper is run on an uneconomic basis & the real power is placed in the hands of the advertiser.
Remedies. smaller papers: signed articles: education. Past experience has shewn that a collectively owned newspaper is not practicable.

The worst fault of the Harmsworth press[210] is not the poisoning of the news columns. Anonymity is dying. The desire for pure straight scientific truth is not common. There can be no regeneration of the world by a new journalism. Labour papers are as bad as others.

Richard Stapley   Chairman

12 June 1918.

* * *

[226] The 226th meeting of the Circle was held on 12 June 1918 at 33 Bloomsbury Sq:

[210] Alfred Charles William Harmsworth (1865–1922), journalist and newspaper proprietor. Founded the *Daily Mail* and *Daily Mirror*, proprietor of *The Times*.

Present. 18 members & 3 visitors—Sir Richard Stapley in the chair.

Apologies for absence were notified from Messrs: Burrows, Golding, MacDonald & Millin.

Minutes of the previous meeting were read & confirmed.

Mr. Herdman read his paper on 'the proposed League of Nations'.

It is desirable that there be set up with what speed be possible an International Court of Justice to perform for nations functions akin to those performed by Courts of Municipal Law & that such Court be armed with an adequate sanction. This wd be the last & greatest step in the evolution of the reign of Law. There is nothing illogical or absurd in applying to Nations the same rule that each of them has succeeded in applying to its own people. The first pre-requisite to its creation is the will to create it among those who will be partakers in its benefits. The impulse already exists, born of the unspeakable sufferings of the human race in the present War, & there is a growing conviction that something new must be done to prevent repetition of present experience. We have a rough idea of what such a Court might be in the Hague Tribunal & the existing body of rules for regulation of international affairs wd form a nucleus of the Law to be administered. An international police must be set up to enforce the judgments of the Court & there must be total, universal & final disarmament of the Nations. The Court wd deal not only with wrongs akin to criminal wrongs—to wh besides ordinary acts of national aggression must be added such things as land-grabbing from backward nations—but with wrongs analogous to civil wrongs such as tariffs, cartels & bounties. It wd also regulate such matters as international transport, copyright, coinage, weights & measures &c.

In the discussion the following opinions were expressed:

The spirit of nationalism has been so fostered by the present war that it has almost wiped out the spirit of cosmopolitanism. Community of ideas among the nations is necessary to the realisation of an International Court of Justice. The feasibility of such a Court wd depend on extent to wh nations are prepared to surrender the conception of unfettered national sovereignty wh has been the curse of the modern world.

That 4 pieces of machinery wd be necessary (1) a Court to deal with legal questions (2) a Conciliation Court (3) some form of international parliament (4) an international executive.

The question was also raised whether we are to have several Leagues of Nations or whether the present opposing alliances are to be admitted into one League.

Richard Stapley   Chairman

9 Oct. 1918.

Twenty-fifth Session.

[227] The 227th meeting of the Circle was held on 9 Oct. 1918 at 33 Bloomsbury Square.

Present. 16 members & 1 visitor—Sir Richard Stapley in the chair.

Apologies for absence were notified from Messrs: Burrows, Golding & Roskill.

Minutes of the previous meeting were read & confirmed.

Record of Attendance for the previous session was read as follows:

Out of 9 meetings

Messrs:	Brereton, Crook, Harley, Herdman & Stapley attended	9
"	Goodenough, Golding, Husband, & Matheson & Sir Sydney Olivier	8
"	Gooch, Walker & Walsh	7
Mr. Hobson		5
Messrs:	Alden, McKillop & Roskill	4
Mr. Robertson		3
Messrs:	Gardiner & MacDonald	2
"	Adams & Millin	1
"	Burrows, Farley & Perris	0

Out of a possible 6 meetings

Mr.	Wigglesworth	6
"	Hurcomb	5
"	Burns	3

Average 17.2 as against 16 for previous session.

Mr. Millin's resignation on account of age & ill-health was announced.

The accounts, wh shewed a balance in hand of 1/-, were presented & accepted.

Sir Richard Stapley was re-elected as Chairman
Mr. Parsons   "   "   " Secretary
Messrs: Brereton, Crook, Harley, Herdman & Hobson were re-elected to the Committee.

Sir Sydney Olivier read his paper on the British Bureaucracy.

A true bureaucracy exists only where the permanent official acts without reference to a Minister or without his authority & the Minister is not responsible to Parliament & the electorate. This was not the case in this country before the war, & the popular notion of Ministers' subserviency to permanent officials is fallacious. When critics of the public service speak of Bureaucracy they have in mind stodgy & bad methods of doing business wh tend to become stereotyped in Govt. Departments, but this is a very different matter from irresponsible rule by permanent officials—who as a fact are inclined to err on the side of safety.

Suddenly during the war immense responsibilities of new public duties have been assumed by the State & vast new Departments have been extemporised: the activities of pre-existing offices have been increased 10-fold & 20-fold. Ministerial responsibility has been practically suspended & superseded by ministerial subordination to a self-directing War Closet. The new Departments have necessarily been staffed by persons not trained in the public service & have been run almost regardless of cost. Some of them will probably be abolished soon after the War, some will survive during the period of international reconstruction & some have come to stay. No one however imagines that the present style of public administration can be continued. The incursion of men accustomed to brisk methods of office business has done a great deal of good to the old civil service Departments, but the business men & the casuals, dug-outs & flappers who have accompanied them, have imported much that, compared with old civil service standards, is slipshod, insufficient & dangerous, & that any responsible minister in peace time wd have to eliminate. To deal with internal administrative defects a new Department shd be established, a Board of Efficiency & Economy charged with the continuous supervision & improvement of administrative method & taking over from the Treasury the control of the staffing & recruiting of the Service in co-operation with the C[ivil] S[ervice] Commissioners. Furthermore the House of Commons might, through standing committees, organise a general oversight of ministries & departments.

In the discussion the suggestions for yet another Govt. Department (the Efficiency Department) & for greater Parliamentary control of ministers met with general approval.[211] The discussion tended to develope into a description of the virtues of civil servants & the shortcomings of business men as seen by the civil servant—& a description of the virtues of business men & the shortcomings of civil servants as seen by the business man. One business man, however, championed the Civil Service on grounds which caused visible consternation among the civil servants present, who seemed to prefer being attacked.

Richard Stapley   Chairman

13 Nov. 1918.

* * *

[228] The 228th meeting of the Circle was held on 13 Nov. 1918[212] at 33 Bloomsbury Square.

Present. 17 members—Sir Richard Stapley in the chair.

---

[211] The civil servant Parsons obviously felt otherwise.

[212] Curiously, it was not felt necessary to refer to the armistice only two days after it had come into effect.

An apology was notified from Mr. Robertson.

Minutes of the previous meeting were read & confirmed.

Mr. Gooch read his paper on Extension of Self Govt for India.

He traced the 4 stages of Govt. in India (1) by the E[ast] I[ndia] Co: (2) by E[ast] I[ndia] Co: & Crown (3) by the Crown (4) now starting by Crown & people. The Councils Act of 1861 set up Provincial Councils on wh a few Indians sat in advisory capacity. The Councils Act of 1892 increased the number of Indians & allowed native bodies to select & recommend them. Under the Morley-Minto reforms[213] Indians were appointed to the Viceroy's Executive Council, the Executive Councils of the Provinces & the Council of the Secretary of State. The Montagu-Chelmsford[214] scheme will for the first time give responsibility to the people & arrange for certain functions of govt: to be transferred at once to the Provincial Govts. & for certain other functions to be reserved to the control of the Govt: of India— more of the latter functions to be transferred as the Provincial Govts. shew themselves capable of dealing with them.

The discussion turned mainly on the question of the reserved functions, & on the general attitude of the Indian Civil Service to reform.

Richard Stapley   Chairman

8 Jan: 1919

Note: The meeting fixed for 11 Decr. 1918 was cancelled owing to the illness of Sir Harry Johnston.[215]

* * *

[229] The 229th meeting of the Circle was held on 8 Jan 1919 at 33 Bloomsbury Square.

Present. 16 members & 4 Polish visitors introduced by Mr. Harley— Sir Richard Stapley in the chair.

Minutes of the previous meeting were read & confirmed.

Apologies were notified from Messrs: Burrows, Robertson & Roskill.

Mr. Harley read his paper on the Future of Poland.

He dealt with Poland's geographical situation & considered whether a land devoid of natural boundaries & a people pressed in on every side by other nations could become a rounded whole & retain a distinct nationality. He pointed out that as a matter of fact Poland had manifested her sense of individuality in spite of all. A

---

[213] Of 1909, which gave Indians greater legislative and executive power.

[214] Of 1918, proposing constitutional reforms and precursor to the Government of India Act, 1919.

[215] Sir Harry Johnston (1858–1927). Explorer and ethicist. Unable to speak on 'How can Tropical Africa best be developed?'

paramount task of the Peace Conference is to redress the outrageous wrong & injustice done by the Partition of Poland. A reconstituted Poland can be trusted to stand as a barrier against Prussianism, but her future is an international future & must be safeguarded by the League of Nations. Poland's outlet to the sea must involve possession of the port of Dantzig, though this wd drive a wedge between Pomerania & East Prussia & expose Europe to the increasing Prussian ambition to bridge the gap & restore an unbroken unity of its lands.

The discussion to wh the Polish visitors made valuable contributions turned largely on the proposed frontiers. It was argued that Poland shd include Upper Silesia, wh is ethnographically Polish, West Prussia, East Prussia, & Eastern Galicia, Lithuania being an independent State. On the other hand it was urged that the Polish claim to Dantzig was not valid, that there ought to be a system of internationalising certain rivers, such as the Vistula, & that Poland ought to have access to the sea without absorbing territory largely occupied by Germans & the possession of wh wd cause future trouble.

Richard Stapley   Chairman

12 Feb 1919

* * *

[230] The 230th meeting of the Circle was held on 12 Feb 1919 at 33 Bloomsbury Square.

Present. 14 members & 3 visitors, Sir Richard Stapley in the chair.

Minutes of the previous meeting were read & confirmed.

Apologies were notified from Messrs: Golding, Gooch, Walker, Walsh & Burrows.

Sir George Paish gave an address on the effect of the War on the Finance of the belligerent countries.

There was never any doubt about Great Britain's ability to finance the War, though at first we were too optimistic in thinking it cd be financed cheaply. The productive power of Great Britain has actually increased. The money we have lent to our friends is not all good— Russia, for instance, has defaulted. Whether France & Italy can pay what they owe us is doubtful. France will owe abroad 1500 millions, Italy 600 millions, in both cases mostly to us & U.S.A. & their productive power has been impaired. The situation in Russia is deplorable. Food production is about $\frac{1}{2}$ what it was. The wealth of U.S.A. has grown & she is likely to gain in consequence of the rise in prices. Her wheat crop sprang up from 700 million bushels to 1000 million in the first 2 years, & last year to 900 million, the surplus of wh she is selling at high prices. Net effect is to make U.S.A. the world's banker now—& potentially for many years, displacing Great Britain in this respect. She will probably ask us to redeem our debt wh means that the rest of the world will have an unprecedented call on our savings. Order must be maintained so as to make the rest of the world believe in ability of Great Britain to meet her liabilities, wh as foreign debt, amount to £2000 million. The foreign debts of the Entente powers shd be converted into Bonds to a total of £5000 million—League of Nations Bonds guarantied by practically the whole world: 4% free of taxation in all countries so that they may circulate freely. Great Britain, U.S.A., & Germany shd guarantee £1000 million each. France is in a very dangerous situation: she owes abroad 1500 millions. She shd be forgiven that debt & shd guarantee 500 million. Italy shd similarly be forgiven her debt of 600 million & guarantee 200 million. All the world shd contribute to the loan in some measure since the welfare of the whole world is at stake.

Great Britain has a home debt of 6000 millions wh has come out of current income. Hence the nation has been able to invest 1200 million a year as against 200 million in normal times. The persons who have made vast profits shd contribute voluntarily out of their accumulations—otherwise there shd be a levy.

The discussion turned on the pros & cons for a capital levy & on the possibility or otherwise of preparing a national balance sheet. Opinion was expressed that the first thing of all is to increase supply of food & raw material.

Richard Stapley   Chairman

12 March 1919.

* * *

[231] The 231st meeting of the Circle was held on 12 Mch. 1919 at 33 Bloomsbury Sq:

Present. 15 members & 1 visitor—Sir Richard Stapley in the chair.

Apologies were notified from Messrs: Burrows, MacDonald, Roskill & Walsh.

Minutes of the previous meeting were read & confirmed.

Mr. Wigglesworth read his paper on State control of Trade after the War.

He gave an account (1) of the pre-war activities of the German govt., acting through vast ramification of Consulates, Banks, Brokers, Merchants & Shipping Companies, conquering the world by peaceful penetration & becoming sole possessor of certain key industries—such as Tungsten, essential for manufacture of shells: & (2) of the special war-measures taken by British Govt: to control industry especially in manufacture of munitions. He criticised the Govt: for alleged tendency to appoint to certain positions business men unconnected with particular trades concerned. As regards future he advocated strengthening of trade organisations & associations wh shd keep in touch with Trade Intelligence Department. Industrial Councils composed of best elements amongst employers & workmen shd be created & shd organise a Trade Parliament with object of preparing legislation in trade matters for ratification by Imperial Parliament. The real duty of govt: as regards control of trade is to undertake

1. Research & exploration.
2. Management of communal enterprise & exploitation of national resources.
3. Opening up & improving fresh tracts of land.
4. Protection of trade interests.
5. Maintenance of discipline in commerce, industry & agriculture.

The discussion turned mainly on whether & if so to what extent Germany's industrial enterprise was fostered & guided by the State for military purposes.

Richard Stapley   Chairman

9 April 1919.

* * *

[232] The 232nd meeting of the Circle was held on 9 Apl: 1919 at 33 Bloomsbury Sq:

Present. 12 members & 1 visitor, Sir Richard Stapley in the chair.

Apologies were notified from Messrs: Burrows, MacDonald, Parsons, Matheson & Wigglesworth.

Minutes of the previous meeting were read & confirmed.

The Committee were instructed to draft a programme for the next session.

Mr. Walker read his paper on 'Housing & Town-Planning after the War'.

The demolition of slums & improvement of insanitary dwellings appertain to Local authorities: the construction of new houses, save those put up in place of slums, has been practically confined to private enterprise. Before the war the rate of such construction had fallen off, during the war building was virtually stopped, & now for various causes (including high cost of materials) it is no longer remunerative. Local authorities are being invited to build. In L[ondon] C[ounty] C[ouncil] area full particulars have been obtained of the unsatisfactory housing & the problem is a very big one, the difficulty of it being intensified by the fact that the powers for dealing with it are divided between L.C.C. & the Borough Councils. Arrangements have been made for co-operation between those bodies & also for co-operation with the local authorities of Greater London. The L[ondon] G[overnment] B[oard] proposes that the Govt. shd bear any loss incurred by local authorities over the proceeds of a penny rate. Probably it will also be necessary to call in & to subsidize private enterprise. Reasonable town-planning in London & Greater London is unnecessarily difficult owing to the fact that 80 to 90 different authorities are possessed of Town-planning powers & the schemes of contiguous authorities are often prepared without relation to each other. This shd be altered & the whole question considered also in relation to improved methods of transit.

Questions & discussion followed.

Richard Stapley   Chairman
14 May 1919.

* * *

[233] The 233rd meeting of the Circle was held on 14 May 1919 at 33 Bloomsbury Sq:

Present. 20 members & 1 visitor—Sir Richard Stapley in the chair.

An apology was notified from Mr. Roskill.

Minutes of the previous meeting were read & confirmed.

The Committee's proposals for the programme for next session were explained & adopted with slight modification.

Mr. McKillop read his paper on 'The future of Trade Unionism'.

The first thing needed is a systematic organisation of employers & employed covering the whole of industry. We must discover the means of securing that every working-man is a member of his appropriate union, possibly making it illegal for an employer to employ a person who cannot produce his Trade Union card. We must provide also for freedom of movement from one Union to another. The various unions must join together on a national basis so that any particular trade can be dealt with as a whole. The Unions must alter their machinery so that members of Councils are representatives & not merely delegates. The employing or directing class must be organised also, & the creation of a permanent joint body for the regulation of Industry will then be fairly simple. The Unions being in a position to negotiate on level terms with the employers there will be an inducement to increase output to the utmost. It is possible that the new Industrial body suggested wd come into conflict with Parliament—& even that Parliament might gradually wither until its functions have been completely absorbed by the new body.

In the discussion various opinions were expressed as to extent of ca'
canny policy & methods of dealing with it.

Opinion was also expressed that some means must be devised
whereby bargains entered into by Union officials shd be loyally
observed by the members: and that inefficiency of employing class is
largely responsible for our relatively low productivity.

Richard Stapley   Chairman 4 June 1919

* * *

[234] The 234th meeting of the Circle was held on 4 June 1919 at
33 Bloomsbury Square.

Present. 16 members & 2 visitors, Sir Richard Stapley in the chair.

Apologies for absence were notified from Mr. Burrows & Mr.
Husband.

Minutes of the previous meeting were read & confirmed.

Mr. Herdman read his paper on 'the Passing of the Judiciary'.

In the middle of the 19th century the judicial bench in this country
had attained eminence by virtue of its own good qualities, confidence
by reason of the impartiality & sanity of its judgments, & commanded
respect at home & abroad. A change has come firstly by natural
development, secondly by legislative interference, thirdly by the decay
of a great ideal. Legislative interference has been of two sorts, direct
& indirect. Of the former the Emergency Act[216] & the Town Planning
Act 1909 are examples—under wh arbitrators appointed by Govt.
Departments are empowered to give final decisions on disputed points.
This is a fatal flaw in that the arbiter is, or belongs to a Department wh
is, a party to the issue. The legislature actively, directly, & definitely
excludes whole ranges of important topics from the purview of the
Courts of Justice. The public begin to doubt if they ever had any
rights or if they had whether they are worth bothering about. The
Arbitration Act[217] is an example of indirect interference, inclusion of
the arbitration clause in an agreement preventing appeal to the Courts
of Justice.

The discussion turned mainly on the practical merits of arbitration.

Richard Stapley   Chairman

8 Oct. 1919

* * *

[216] Possibly a reference to part I of the Munitions of War Act (1915), according to
which the government could refer disputes to binding arbitration.

[217] There existed no such Act. This was presumably a reference to the Conciliation
Act of 1896.

Twenty-sixth Session

[235] The 235th meeting of the Circle was held on 8th Octr. 1919 at 33 Bloomsbury Sq.

Present. 17 members & 1 visitor, Sir Richard Stapley in the chair.

Apologies for absence were notified from Messrs: Golding & Hobson.

Minutes of the previous meeting were read & confirmed.

Record of Attendance for previous session was read as follows:

Out of 8 meetings

Messrs:	Crook, Herdman & Hurcomb & Sir R. Stapley attended	8
"	Brereton, Matheson & Parsons	7
"	Gooch, Golding, Goodenough, Harley, Wigglesworth & Sir Sydney Olivier	6
"	Alden McKillop & Walsh	5
"	Husband, Roskill & Walker	4
"	Hobson & Robertson	3
Mr. Burns		2
Messrs:	Adams & MacDonald	1
"	Gardiner & Perris	0

Average 15.75 as against 17.2 for the previous session.

The A/cs wh shewed a deficit of £1-1-11 were presented & accepted.

Sir Richard Stapley was re-elected as Chairman.

Mr. Parsons   "   "   " Secretary.

Messrs: Brereton, Crook, Harley, Herdman & Sir Sydney Olivier were elected to the Committee.

Mr. Gooch gave his address on the Peace Terms as they affect the conquered nations.

The peace is essentially a French peace—a Clemenceau peace. As regards Germany the terms are on the whole unnecessarily hard. While there is nothing to criticize in some of the provisions, e.g. respecting Posen & Schleswig, those relating to the Saar Valley arrangement are very questionable, as also those relating to the Dantzig 'corridor', wh is really a wide block of land 30 to 70 miles wide & including some $2\frac{1}{2}$ million Germans. It was inevitable that Germany shd lose all her colonies. The provision most bitterly resented by the Germans is the session of 140.000 milch cows.

Austria Austria is beaten & destroyed & if ever there was a case for magnanimity it was here: but the terms of the treaty are more severe than those on Germany & are a monument of cruelty & unwisdom. Austria is reduced to a country smaller than Belgium, cut off from Adriatic by 100 miles of territory, cut off from coal supplies wh used to come from Bohemia, cut off from Hungary the source of meat & corn. Her position is desperate. The cruellest thing is the French determination that Austria shall not join with the German republic.

Bulgaria has been let off lightly: she loses Dobrudja, Strumnitza, & the N.W. corner & is also cut off from the Aegean.

Turkey What remains of Turkish Thrace will be taken away. Constantinople will probably remain Turkish but whether the administration will be taken over by the L[eague] of N[ations] is not certain. In Syria France will take Lebanon & the Beyrout littoral.

In the discussion opinion was expressed that there was no practicable alternative to the protection by England & other European countries of large territories in Asia Minor. It was suggested that the plebiscite in connexion with the Saar arrangement might not be acted upon.

Richard Stapley   Chairman

12 Nov. 1919

* * *

[236] The 236th meeting of the Circle was held at 33 Bloomsbury Sq: on 12 Nov. 1919.

Present 17 members & 2 visitors. Sir Richard Stapley in the chair.

Apologies for absence were notified from Messrs: Golding, Matheson & Wigglesworth.

The Circle tendered its good wishes to Sir Richard on his forthcoming visit to Jamaica: and in this connexion a letter from Mr. Burrows was read.

A notice was read of the erection of a tablet in the Church of St. Jude-on-the-Hill Hampstead to the memory of the late Lieut. John E. Raphael.

Sir Sydney Olivier read his paper on The Mandatory System of the League of Nations.

He pointed out that the covenant is very vague in many of its terms wh appear to require highly expert interpretation; & that there is no provision for enabling any people to decide by its own pronouncement whether it will or will not remain under the sovereignty of the State which formerly governed it: further that the content of a Mandate is not required to be framed by, or on behalf of, the Council of the League if the 'Members of the League'—a term itself not clearly defined—have previously made an agreement upon the subject. He made special reference to Africa & to the draft mandates prepared by the Anti-Slavery Society.

In the discussion opinion was expressed that unless we develope the Mandatory System the League of Nations will be merely a scrap of paper

that the idea of mandates is noble & enlightened but not generally believed in

that France will not take seriously the idea of responsibility for native races—on the other hand that we need not despair even of France.

A.L. Lilley   Chairman

10 Dec. 1919.

* * *

[237] The 237th meeting of the Circle was held at 33 Bloomsbury Square on 10 Dec 1919.

Present 13 members & Archdeacon Lilley (a former member) who consented to preside.

Apologies for absence were notified from Messrs: Gooch, Goodenough, Matheson & Roskill.

It was decided to change the hour of meeting to 8 o'c.

Minutes of the previous meeting were read & confirmed.

Mr. Hurcomb read his paper on 'The Limits of Government control in times of peace.'

It is difficult to limit Govt. interference by any rule save that of expediency. To argue from any success of the war controls may easily lead to false inferences as to what can be done in peace: for the aim of the controls was to maximise war effort: they rested largely on temporary emergency powers: & they had unlimited command of personnel. Mr. Hurcomb then examined four main spheres of control, vizt:, over (1) foodstuffs, raw materials & commodities in general (2) Shipping (3) Transport & (4) Mining.

He concluded that the State will not buy, import, & distribute so cheaply as the whole body of merchants & that the conduct of internal trade & industry shd not be a function of the State: that Free Shipping & Free Commerce are vital to each other: that the development of State control can proceed with advantage when the industry is monopolistic not as a result of organisation but from its own nature: & that in public utility services the State can extend its functions with least fear of mistake.

In the discussion opinion was expressed that war experience has created a general prejudice against nationalisation of industries, but that no importance need be attached to this as the experience was under abnormal conditions: that the attempt of the State to control prices was wrong, but that it was sound to allow Govt: or municipality to compete on level terms with private enterprise: that nothing will remedy high prices except production & the workers are exhausted: that control of Exchange Rates wd have been very valuable: that the control of Exchange Rates wd have been most pernicious.

J.M. Robertson   Chairman

14 Jan: 1920.

* * *

[238] The 238th meeting of the Circle was held on 14 Jan. 1920 at 33 Bloomsbury Square.

Present. 15 members & 2 visitors, Mr. Robertson in the chair.

Apologies were notified from Messrs: Crook, Golding & Mac-Donald.

Minutes of the previous meeting were read & confirmed.

Mr. Wigglesworth read his paper on the New Industrialism.

He drew attention to the evils current during the pre-war régime of peace—slums, ca'canny, bad workmanship, antagonism between employer & employed: then to the dislocation of the wages system brought about by the war. He urged that now everyone ought to be trained for his trade or profession to a minimum degree of efficiency, & suggested 3 rates of pay in each, dependent on highest, medium & lowest efficiency. He suggested a new Ministry of Industry to settle rates between employers & Trade Unions & to fix standards of efficiency. He advocated more scrupulous attention to the needs of the workman, as in America, co-operative production, profit-sharing, & international credits.

In the discussion doubts were expressed as to practicability of grades of efficiency & as to desirability of the proposed new Ministry. The question was raised whether there is any possible principle for regulating rates of wages in an industry, & for regulating rates paid in one industry as compared with those in another. The Ford Motor works, Bolshevism, the Land Values Act,[218] the Gattie[219] scheme of Transport,

---

[218] Though there had been frequent proposals on land valuation, no such Act was in existence at the time.

[219] The proposals of Alfred Warwick Gattie (1856–1925) for improving the handling of goods and transport were examined by a departmental committee of the Ministry of Transport in 1919–20.

Strap-hanging, Depreciation of the Currency, an admirable translation of Lucian & other topics of current interest were also discussed.

J.M. Robertson   Chairman

11 Feb: 1920.

* * *

[239] The 239th meeting of the Circle was held on 11 Feb. 1920 at
33 Bloomsbury Square.

Present. 15 members & 3 visitors, Mr. Robertson in the chair.

Apologies were notified from Messrs: Burrows, Crook, Golding &
McKillop.

Minutes of the previous meeting were read & confirmed.

Mr. Robert Lynd read his paper on Sinn Fein.

It has been said that Ireland is not a nation: but few things are
more difficult to define than a nation. A nation is a compromise, a
tradition, an affection, and Ireland is as homogeneous as any other
nation that has undergone a period of subjection. The Gaelic League
is to be noted in the development of the Sinn Fein movement. It
spread among serious-minded young men who felt for the first time
their kinship with the old saints & scholars. Sinn Fein policy was
first formulated in the 'United Irishman'.[220] The policy is distinctly
towards separatism. It is to give not only a political policy to Ireland
but to enunciate a philosophy of nationalism. By 1910 Mr.
Redmond[221] had got guarantees that a Home Rule bill wd be introduced & the majority of Irishmen put their faith in this & Sinn Fein
largely died. When Carson[222] began to arm Ulster a body of volunteers
was formed to oppose the Carson volunteers. The Fenian element (the
Fenian organisation had never died) was predominant. During the
war the more extreme element desired defeat of England & chance
of insurrection. Sinn Feiners generally regarded the actual insurrection as a mistake & though some joined in more or less reluctantly
they looked on it as a demonstration. At present time the S.F. leaders'
trouble is not to incite their followers to acts of violence but to keep
them from such. The crimes are not the work of the S.F. organisation.
The movement, wh is frankly republican, is based on passion for
nationality & ideal of distinctiveness. No measure of subordinate
Home Rule will ever again be acceptable. The alternatives for
England are (1) to persuade Ulster to accept a form of Dominion

---

[220] A periodical founded in 1899 by Arthur Griffith. Renamed *Sinn Fein* in 1905.

[221] John Edward Redmond (1856–1918). Irish politician, home ruler and M.P.

[222] Edward Henry Carson (1854–1935). Q.C., Conservative M.P. Organized Ulster
Volunteers against Home Rule.

Home Rule or (2) to withdraw British troops & leave Ireland to work out her own problems in her own way.

In the discussion opinion was expressed that the Sinn Fein party is closing its eyes to the Ulster problem & that the best solution was Dominion Home Rule with 2 parliaments for the time being, with the hope that real union may come later.

W.M. Crook   Chairman

14 April 1920.

Note. The March meeting was cancelled at the last moment owing to illness of Mr. G.D.H. Cole[223] who was to have given a paper on Guild Socialism.

* * *

[240] The 240th meeting of the Circle was held on 14 Apl. 1920 at 33 Bloomsbury Sq:

Present 13 members & 1 visitor. Mr. Crook in the chair.

Apologies for absence were notified from Messrs: Golding, Gooch, Burrows, MacDonald & Roskill.

Minutes of the previous meeting were read & confirmed.

The Secretary reported that the Committee had considered the candidature of Capt. H.B. Usher, proposed by Mr. Robertson & seconded by the Secretary, & recommended his election. He was then unanimously elected.

Mr. Robertson read his paper on Egyptian Unrest.

The spirit of Egyptian nationalism is nothing new & is now more pervading than ever. British control has been faced by the special dilemma that the more the people are educated the more surely does the race consciousness evolve. That dilemma determined the repressive policy of Cromer.[224] Professing to be opposed to permanent occupation he was in principle committed to a policy wh shd fit the people for self-govt., but he instinctively sought to keep Egypt uneducated, just as he also set his face against giving the people some degree of representation & of employment in the public service. Of course to have left Egypt as it stood to native management wd have meant return to financial corruption & political coercion. He had established strict financial control, & accepted a constructive economic policy, & he had abolished the lash, the labour corvée & the salt monopoly. These things are greatly to his credit but beyond them he had no constructive policy. The immediate difficulty will be to

---

[223] George Douglas Howard Cole (1889–1958). Socialist, historian and economist.

[224] Evelyn Baring, Earl Cromer (1841–1917). Agent and consul- general in Egypt, 1883–1907.

reconcile the nationalist aspirations to a progressive as against an instantaneous acquisition of independence. We must secure abolition of the Capitulations & return to the principle of employing Egyptians in the public service. We have to face the alternatives of giving Egypt her chance & of having her develope into an Eastern Ireland.

In the discussion the following opinions were expressed: Education is the real problem: if we cd give a right education we shd be preparing the way for self-govt. The agitating class mainly consists of students & young journalists: the agitation is not a religious but a political movement on ordinary logical liberal grounds. British officers are not in direct touch with the Egyptians—as they are with natives in India. The proclamation of a protectorate is felt as a step in exploiting the country for benefit of capitalists. Egyptian landowners are solid with the revolutionaries to get us out. The movement for independence is irresistible.

Percy Alden   Chairman

12 May 1920.

* * *

[241] The 241st meeting of the Circle was held on 12 May 1920 at 33 Bloomsbury Square.

Present. 14 members & 2 visitors. Mr. Alden in the chair.

Apologies for absence were notified from Messrs: Adams, Golding & Walker.

Mr. Alden communicated grave news of the state of Sir Richard Stapley's health.

Minutes of the previous meeting were read & confirmed.

The programme for the ensuing session was discussed & settled.

Mr. Bhupendranath Basu gave an address on Indian Unrest.

With the consolidation of British rule, there came about a tendency to consolidation of the Indian peoples into a common nation. In the last century there have been great developments in religion, & in social usages. There is for instance a great difference in observances respecting caste & even a movement for validating inter-caste marriages. India is not so immobile as people outside think. Unofficial Europeans have no sense of responsibility towards India. Indians feel that they are not only subject to bureaucracy but to irresponsible European opinion. Every retrograde step the Govt. has taken has been supported by unofficial Europeans. The Indians became more & more hopeless of influencing the Govt. Lord Morley tried to reform the councils, enlarging them but placing the elected members in permanent minority. The Indians began to think constitutional agitation useless: but nevertheless they believed in the English people, & in the war hoped that their support & loyalty wd be recognized. This hope was to some extent realized by Declaration of 1917. Then came the Punjab incident[225] & what has gone down deep into the hearts of Indians has been the humiliating treatment of their leading men under martial law. What answer is England going to make? Is English civilisation only skin-deep? It stands arraigned before the bar of humanity.

In the discussion opinion was expressed that some emphatic expression of condemnation of the Punjab incident was called for: and also that under no circumstances (except such as might apply to British subjects) shd an Indian subject be arrested & deported without trial.

Percy Alden   Chairman

9 June 1920.

* * *

[242] The 242nd meeting of the Rainbow Circle was held on the 9th June 1920 at 33 Bloomsbury Square.

Present—20 members and one visitor. Mr. Alden in the Chair.

Apologies were notified from Messrs. Golding and Matheson.

Mr. Alden spoke of the great loss the Circle had sustained by the death on the 20th May of Sir Richard Stapley, who had been President for 26 years, and whose personality had meant so much to the Circle. Mr. Alden introduced Miss Dunn who, for 25 years, had been the companion of Sir Richard and Lady Stapley, and who accompanied him to Jamaica. Miss Dunn gave the Circle an account that no one else could have given of the few months Sir Richard spent in Jamaica and of his last illness. She spoke of his patience and gentleness and consideration for others, during the whole period when his physical powers were failing; of his peace of mind and his quiet enjoyment of the sunshine and of the beauty of his surroundings, notwithstanding that his sight was failing. She said that the fact that he saw more clearly when the brightness of the day was passed brought home to her with fresh force the words 'At evening time there shall be light'— words which in their symbolic sense were so wholly appropriate in the case of Sir Richard. She said that in his last illness on the voyage home he seemed to suffer little actual pain and was calm and conscious almost to his last hour. He died at sea while still one day's journey from home. Miss Dunn also said how much Sir Richard had always

---

[225] The massacre perpetrated at Amritsar by British troops in 1919.

thought of the Circle and how keen he had always been not to miss a meeting. Among all his many and varied interests, the Rainbow Circle was nearest to his heart.[226] She read the following short obituary notice which appeared in 'The Nation'. (29 May 1920)[:]

A friend of Sir Richard Stapley, who died the other day at sea, writes me:

'Stapley was astonishingly different from any type of London merchant one hears about. Yet he belonged, undeniably, to the City—as Common Councillor and as joint architect of a business which has been something of a legend in the textile trades. In the 'seventies of last century, Richard Stapley left the firm of Samuel Morley and started in London Wall as manufacturers and wholesalers, mainly of women's and children's outfitting. The house achieved a great record, and the average City man did not hesitate to ascribe its swift ascent to the adoption of a higher standard of ethics than the accepted code. But it was in his wide intellectual interests that Richard Stapley was most remarkable. He had no great gift for public life, though he stood twice as a Liberal candidate in London. But his range of acquaintance was immense. You got the impression that there was no man or woman belonging to the advanced guard in social and religious thought whom he did not know, or for whom, if he deserved it, Stapley failed to provide a room and an audience. For twenty years or so a society called the Christo-theosophical, formed of people interested in mystical thought, met in his Bloomsbury Square house; and for at least an equal period he gave more than intellectual hospitality to a circle of radical thinkers who had originally met for discussion in the less congenial air of a Fleet Street tavern. He was one of the company of intimates who gathered around the late William Clarke, and he was for long a faithful hearer and supporter of Stopford Brooke at Bedford Chapel.[227] When, later, Mr. R.J. Campbell (companion of his last voyage) entered upon the exiting stages of his spiritual pilgrimage, there was nothing strange to anyone who knows Richard Stapley, then a deacon of the City Temple, in seeing him stand by the side of his friend.'

She said she was giving to the Circle the Silver Bowl which the Circle had presented to Sir Richard on the occasion of the 100th meeting, some 15 years ago, at his country house at Horeham, and which had been on the table at every meeting since. She also said that she wished Mr. Herbert Burrows to have the chair in which Sir Richard had presided for so many years.

When Miss Dunn had withdrawn it was decided to write to her

[226] Cp. Percy Alden's obituary of Stapley in *Progress*, no 53 (1920), 43–7.
[227] Stopford William Wentworth Brooke (1859–1938). Liberal M.P. 1906–10, Unitarian minister and lecturer.

expressing the Circle's deep sympathy with her in her sorrow and thanking her for the gift of the Bowl.

The following letter from Mr. Herbert Burrows was read.

'My health will not allow me to write much but I must send you some words of sorrowful greeting for next Wednesday night.

Mere words cannot of course express what we are all feeling and nothing can make up for the grievous loss we have sustained. But nothing would be further from his wish than that we should waste words in vain regrets. If he could speak to us again he would tell us to look to the future of humanity generally rather than dwell on the past. If I read his life aright the keynote of that life was the constant effort for the harmonious future of all Mankind. For over a quarter of a century that was what he strove to make the binding force in the Rainbow.

We have each of us in our day belonged to many societies but never to one, I take it, like the Rainbow. For a score or more of men, differing from each other so widely as we do in politics, in thought, in theology and in views of life to meet together for twenty five years and, while differing, frankly and freely, hardly two of us agreeing, yet without a jarring word or a cross note, is as far as I know a unique experience. We shall all agree that this was largely due to his wise and brotherly influence. Personally, and I am sure we all felt this, I never left a Rainbow meeting without feeling in the widest sense that there was a common bond in humanity which only needed fostering to make life fuller, richer and more worth living. What we owed to him no tongue can tell, we can only feel it in our hearts and be thankful.

Wednesday night's gathering will be a somewhat fateful one as certain decisions will have to be arrived at which will have a large influence on our future as a Society. I feel above all things that we must continue and not think for a moment of discontinuing our meetings. To do that would be a virtual treason to his memory. I know that the best decision will be arrived at by all of you and that the one aim will be to make the Rainbow in the future what it has been in the past, a centre of brotherly influence and light.

I wish I could be with you but as you know it is impossible. I send the best and kindest greetings to you all and I shall look for news that your decisions will be arrived at in the brotherly spirit which was his chief aim and joy.

Ever sincerely yours
Herbert Burrows.'

It was decided to write to Mr. Burrows, thanking him for the letter and acquainting him with Miss Dunn's kind wish that he should have Sir Richard's Chair.

The minutes of the previous meeting were read and confirmed. Mr. Crook read his paper on the 'League of Nations'.

He reviewed the ideals from which the League has sprung, commented on the Covenant clause by clause, & considered its actual working—including its inactivities—up to the present. His opinion was that it is still possible in spite of the defects of the Covenant to make the League not only a real power but the most real power in the world. The steps necessary to attain this end are:

(1) The disappearance, as soon as the last treaty is ratified, of the Supreme Council

(2) The early meeting of the Assembly of the League

(3) The early establishment of the Permanent Court of International Justice

(4) Disarmament of the victors in the recent great war.

(5) Enrolment in the League of our late enemies.

(6) Enlargement of the Council so as to include our late enemies & many more of the neutral States.

(7) An absolute veto on the private manufacture of the munitions of war.

In the discussion Mr. Crook's views met with general agreement but some members thought that his view of the objects of the League was too limited & that the more international activities added to the League the better. Opinion was expressed that the fundamental weakness of the League of Nations arose from the fact that international Democracy has not yet asserted itself.

John A. Hobson   Chairman

27 Oct. 1920.

* * *

Twenty-seventh Session

[243] The 243rd meeting of the Circle was held [on 27th October 1920] at Stapley House 33 Bloomsbury Sq: now the Headquarters of the Stapley Trust & of the British Institute of Social Service—Mr. Hobson in the chair.

Present. 16 members

Apologies for absence were notified from Messrs: Burns, Golding, MacDonald, & Wigglesworth—& a letter was read from Mr. Herbert Burrows.

Minutes of the previous meeting were read & confirmed.

Mr. Hobson proposed & Mr. Alden seconded the election of Mr. Roskill as president for the year & he was thereupon unanimously elected. Mr. Hobson then vacated the chair.

Mr. Hobson was elected as Vice-president
Mr. Parsons   ”   ”   ” Secretary
Messrs: Alden, Brereton, Crook, Herdman & Harley were elected as the Committee with the President, Vicepresident & Secretary ex officio.

The Record of attendance for the previous session was read as follows:

Out of eight meetings,

Messrs:	Alden, Brereton, Herdman, Hurcomb, Harley, Husband & Parsons attended	8
”	Walsh & Wigglesworth	7
”	Crook, Gooch, Olivier & Roskill	6
”	Matheson & Robertson	5
Mr. Walker		4
Messrs:	Burns & Goodenough	3
”	MacDonald, Perris (& the late Sir R. Stapley)	2
”	Gardiner & Golding	1
”	Adams, Hobson & McKillop	0
Out of a possible 2 meetings Capt. Usher		2

Average attendance 15.5 as against 15.75 for the previous year.

The Accounts, shewing a deficit of 19/-, were presented & accepted. The subscription for the session was fixed at 7s/6d.

Mr. Gooch gave his address on 'the present political situation in Germany'.

He dealt first with the typical moderate German's view of the causes & origins of the war & referred to the German White Book presented at Versailles.[228]

The Revolution in Germany at the end of 1918 spread from Kiel to Berlin with surprising rapidity & with very little bloodshed. No one regretted the Kaiser whose flight had the effect of breaking up the monarchical party into 3. From the armistice to June 1919 Germany was in the mood to accept her place in a peaceful democratic unarmed Europe. When the terms of the Treaty were made known there was an extraordinary revulsion & hardening of feeling & many felt that there was nothing to do but to plan & prepare for a future war. The new Constitution is more centralised than that drawn up by Bismarck in 1867. The separate States remain but their special privileges are much reduced. There is complete adult suffrage & a most elaborate system of Proportional Representation. The present politicians are a very poor lot & have done nothing to give the Govt. authority among the people. Mr. Gooch then dealt with the 6 political parties & their representative men: the problems of territory

---

[228] *Is Germany Guilty? German White-Book concerning the Responsibility of the Authors of the War* (English translation, Berlin, 1919).

(especially southern Silesia): the economic problems of the indemnity, of the capital levy: & of credit & exchange: the morale of the country—weakened by the paralysis of the bourgeoisie & their fear of Bolshevism: & the intellectual life—wh shews signs of being freer than since the time of Bismarck. Mr. Gooch thought that in 10–20 years' time Germany wd be relatively steady again.

Questions were asked concerning Oswald Spengler's book,[229] on the lengths to wh nationalism had carried Germany & other countries, on the Kautsky documents,[230] the pre-war penetration of Turkey by Germany, & of Germany's fear of losing the Rohr [Ruhr] district.

Percy Alden   Chairman

10 Nov. 1920.

* * *

[244] The 244th meeting of the Circle was held [on 10 November 1920] at Stapley House, Mr. Alden in the chair.

Present 14 members & 2 visitors.

Apologies were notified from Mr. Roskill & Sir Sydney Olivier.

Minutes of the previous meeting were read & confirmed.

Mr. Hobson gave an address on the present political situation in the United States.

As regards America's attitude to the League of Nations neither Democrats nor Republicans are prepared to commit their country to the League as it stands. There is a widespread feeling of resentment against 'Wilsonism'. While many Americans are favourable to America being a member of some League they feel that the present League is too English. The ordinary American has little feeling for individual liberty: he consents to being standardized & thinks everyone shd conform to the habits & wishes of the majority. The Labour question presents peculiar features in that nearly all the hard manual work is performed by negroes or recent immigrants. Capital is better organized & more autocratic than here. There is a great deal of idealism in America—in business as in other relations of life—& if the business & emotional urges can work together America will have a great work to do in helping to restore broken Europe.

In the discussion the following opinions were expressed:

---

[229] A reference to *The Decline of the West*, which brought Spengler (1880–1936) fame and censure.

[230] A collection of documents first published in Germany in 1919, and later translated into English under the title *Outbreak of the World War. German Documents Collected by Karl Kautsky and edited by Max Montgelas and Walther Schücking* (O.U.P., New York, 1924).

We shd put our whole strength behind the League of Nations & hope that America will come in later, with reservations.

The unskilled worker immigrating into America from Italy or Central Europe never really learns the language, & the task of organizing the workers is thus rendered difficult.

America is likely in the next few years to have labour troubles which will cripple her industry & so absorb her attention that she will have little energy free for helping Europe.

Development towards Free-trade, the Colour question, Prohibition, & the Freedom of the Seas, were also discussed.

John Roskill   Chairman

8. xii. 20

* * *

[245] The 245th meeting of the Circle was held on 8th Decr. 1920 at Stapley House.

Present 9 members & 3 visitors Mr. Roskill in the chair.

Apologies were notified from Messrs: Gooch & Parsons.

Minutes of the previous meeting were read & confirmed.

Mr. Wigglesworth read his paper on the present political situation in Italy.

D'Annunzio's filibustering expedition[231] fanned flame of ill-will against Jugo Slavs & necessitated maintenance of a large army wh Italy cannot afford & cost of wh has aggravated her bad financial situation. Domestically extremists have stirred up strife in industrial & agricultural worlds & the tyranny of Labour is being felt more acutely in Italy than in other European countries: but the Cooperative movement is unusually strong & active. Mr. Wigglesworth gave a brief account of the political parties—including the new clerical party—the partito popolare—& the socialist party wh lacks unity. Bolshevism has gained no real footing & is not likely to. In social legislation Italy is at the head of civilized nations & is the first country to introduce compulsory profit-sharing. Italy is handicapped by not having any coal-fields & is developing her abundant water-power. Former thrift & simple living have disappeared since the war & output has been decreased by the 8-hour day. The Govt. realizes that production is the chief remedy for economic difficulties & is seeking every means to increase it. On the whole there is every reason for optimism with regard to the future of Italy.

[231] Gabriele D'Annunzio (1863–1938), Italian poet and journalist. He organized the seizure of Fiume in 1919, in connection with the dispute over the town between Italy and Yugoslavia.

The discussion turned mainly on
1. How Italy was to recover from her present economic difficulties &
in particular the depreciation of her Foreign Exchange.
2. How the experiments of giving workers a share in management
were likely to proceed & succeed.
3. The future relations with Jugo-Slavia.
4. The rivalry between the clerical & other co-operative schemes—
wh it was considered might promote efficiency of both.
5. The relative merits of Vitamins & Calories.

John Roskill   12 Jan 1921   Chairman

* * *

[246] The 246th meeting of the Circle was held on 12th January
1921 at Stapley House.
    Present 18 members & 3 visitors—Mr. Roskill in the chair.
    The President in opening the proceedings expressed the sorrow of
the Circle at the untimely death of Mr. G.H. Perris who had been a
member for over 25 years & was to have given the paper that evening.
The Secretary intimated that he had, on behalf of the Circle, sent a
letter of condolence to Mrs. Perris. He also gave a list of the papers
contributed by Mr. Perris to the Circle since 1895, vizt:
Oct. '95 The evolutionary standpoint in Social Theory.
Mch. '97 Home Rule[232]
Mch. '99 The Weak
Feb. '00 Imperialism in relation to Trade & Finance[233]
Feb. '03 Militarism in Germany
Dec. '03 Egypt
Mch. '05[234] National Financial Problems & Readjustment.
Mch. '06[235] International relationship.
    "   '11 The British Cabinet & Executive in relation to Parliament.
Feb. '12 Hervé & the Peace Movement
Oct. '12 Compulsory Arbitration.[236]
The paper he was to have given that evening wd have been his twelfth.
    The following extract was read from a letter from Mr. Burrows:
    'Our dear friend Perris's death was a very great blow to me. For
many years he & Wm Clarke & I were friends & fellow-workers. We

---

[232] More accurately: 'Nationalism, Federalism and Home Rule.'
[233] This paper was never given. Parsons was relying on the printed programme when
compiling the list.
[234] Postponed to April 1905.
[235] Postponed to April 1906.
[236] Parsons left out Perris' paper on Foreign Policy and Finances in April 1915.

went to Constantinople & South Eastern Europe together & with him I also went to the Peace Congress in America, where we addressed many meetings. He was a true man & a faithful worker in the cause of true Democracy. We shall all mourn his loss & the gap it leaves in the ranks of the workers for humanity'.

Minutes of the previous meeting were read & confirmed.

Apologies were notified from Messrs: Golding Hurcomb & Mac-Donald.

Mr. Harley, who at short notice & considerable inconvenience had kindly consented to read his paper that evening instead of in March, read his paper on the present political situation in Poland.

He dealt at length with Poland's claim to Upper Silesia—wh he considered valid—& with German & Bolshevist propaganda directed against that claim. He discussed the Polish offensive at Kiev & set forth the reasons for it—though for his own part he regarded it as a military & political mistake. He controverted the idea that Poland is a nation of Imperialists with reactionary traditions & represented her as trying experiments & making constitutions to the very eve of the Partition. He described Poland as a land of contrasts & a meeting place of peoples fitted by the clash & contact of varied races & cultures to form a starting point of forward development in the world's history. As regards Poland's outlet to the sea he regarded the Peace Conference device in respect to Dantzig as unsatisfactory. In conclusion he drew attention to the signs of emergence of a stable political system, the National Democrats & the Socialists being the only 2 parties definitely & distinctly opposed to one another & forming the nuclei of a 2-party system.

In the discussion the following opinions were expressed:

The Upper Silesian question ought to be settled solely on its merits & with reference to wishes of the population.

The cause of the Russo-Polish war was desire of Russia to carry the social revolution further to the west & was unconnected with territorial questions. That that war had done infinite harm & that the question who started it was a difficult one to answer.

That Lloyd George acted wisely in keeping Dantzig from being swallowed up by Poland & insisting on plebiscite for Upper Silesia.

John Roskill   9 Feb. 1921   Chairman

* * *

[247] The 247th meeting of the Circle was held on 9th Feb. 1921 at Stapley House.

Present. 14 members & 6 visitors—Mr. Roskill in the chair.

The President in opening the proceedings expressed the sorrow of the Circle at the death of Mr. T.F. Husband who had died after a very short illness within 12 days of the January meeting at wh he was present. Sir Sydney Olivier paid a tribute to Mr. Husband as a man & as a liberal-minded public servant. The Secretary gave a brief account of Mr. Husband's connexion with the Circle, wh dated back to 1895, & read a letter from Mrs. Husband stating that the cause of death was myoclonic encephalitis. It was decided to send a letter of sympathy to Mrs. Husband.

Dr. Seton-Watson read his paper on 'the present political situation in Austria.' He dealt with the new states that have arisen from the dismemberment of the Austrian Empire & said that a great step forward had been made by the Peace Treaty towards disentanglement of the races.

Czecho-Slovakia is the strongest & most flourishing of all the new states & has made most progress since the Armistice. She has a highly-educated class & a strong intellectual movement & tradition, but a bad legacy of bureaucracy from Austria. The country is nearly self-sufficing in food. She has done more to order her finances than any other continental state. The German problem is her weak point & nothing is happening to bring about reconciliation.

Jugo-Slavia has made an amazing recovery after the war. The people have shown remarkable resilience. Administratively they are behind-hand & decentralization is essential. The movement for unity has made real strides & is strongly supported by the younger generation. Roumania has suffered from complete breakdown in transport due to loss of personnel & plant in the war to sabotage & corruption. The plunder by Germans & Hungarians was on an enormous scale. Roumania in turn plundered Hungary later, removing much plant wh is lying derelict. Agrarian reform & education have made great headway. The Church has been reorganized & united with absolutely democratic government.

Better economic intercourse & removal of artificial trade barriers are needed for all these countries.

In the discussion attention was directed to the subsistence question, enormous populations literally starving owing to sectional spirit of the secessional states. Other points dealt with were treatment of Jews, Education, & the strike of doctors & officials.

John Roskill   Chairman

9 March 1921.

* * *

[248] The 248th meeting of the Circle was held on 9 March 1921 at Stapley House.

Present. 14 members & 4 visitors, Mr. Roskill in the chair.

Apologies for absence were notified from Messrs: Gardiner, Golding & Herdman.

Minutes of the previous meeting were read & confirmed.

M. Maurice Andra gave an address on the present political situation in France.

The French people resent the idea not uncommonly expressed in this country that they are a militarist or imperialist nation or that they are reactionary. The Republic has thoroughly proved its worth & there is no possibility of the return of a king. The last elections shewed that the people had lost faith in the radical party & that they wanted something practical done. The attitude towards education is entirely democratic. There is no danger from anything like Bolshevism—on the contrary there is a movement in the direction of co-operation between capital & labour. The economic question dominates the whole political situation. There is an enormous war-debt & finance is completely disorganized. France had great wealth invested in Russia, Roumania & Germany, all of wh is lost. She is really going fast towards bankruptcy.

In the discussion the following opinions were expressed:

It is practically impossible to increase taxation in France without disastrous results.

The population will probably decrease for a time.

France will, in Asia Minor, probably have to give up Syria & keep to the coast.

The French people have not much confidence in the League of Nations.

The question of reconstruction of the devastated areas by German labour was also discussed.

John Roskill   13 April 1921.   Chairman

* * *

[249] The 249th meeting of the Circle was held on 13th April 1921 at Stapley House.

Present. 11 members & 3 visitors, Mr. Roskill in the chair.

An apology for absence was notified from Mr. Brereton.

Minutes of the previous meeting were read & confirmed.

Members were asked to communicate to the Secretary any suggestions they might have for the programme for next session.

Mr. Noel Buxton, proposed by Mr. Crook, was elected a member.

Mr. Noel Buxton read his paper on the present political situation in the Balkan States. He pointed out that those who had studied the Balkan States were right in their warning that the trouble to Europe wd come from that quarter. He gave a comprehensive account of the political position in each of the States, of their mixed population, of their economic relation with other countries, of their commerce & trade, imports & exports. He also dealt with the extent of the war on these States & of their grievances arising from the Paris settlement.

In the discussion the following opinions were expressed[:]

That the removal of imperialistic ambitions & domination of Austria & Turkey will have an enormous effect on the development of the Balkan peoples.

That there were already patent signs of recovery in these countries— in wh connexion the amount of new building going on was mentioned.

That Bessarabia was in danger of being reconquered by Bolshevist army.

That Greece was overstraining her finances & man-power.

That the L[eague] of N[ations] ought to forbid the lending of money for armaments to small states.

John Roskill   Chairman

11 May 1921.

* * *

[250] The 250th meeting of the Circle was held on 11 May 1921 at Stapley House.

Present 15 members & 2 visitors, Mr. Roskill in the chair.

An apology for absence was notified from Mr. Wigglesworth.

Minutes of the previous meeting were read & confirmed.

The Committee's recommendations for the programme for next session were communicated & with slight modification adopted.

Sir Fisher Dilke & Mr. T.L. Gilmour were elected members.

Capt. Usher read his paper on the present political situation in Mesopotamia.

He gave a description of Mesopotamia, indicating its vastness, the varied character of the country, its vague & arbitrary frontiers, & the varying races by wh it is sparsely populated. The problem of Mesopotamia is part of the problem of the Arab world as a whole. Whatever happens in Persia reacts on Mesopotamia. Under Turkey the administration of Mesopotamia was a mere inefficient & corrupt muddle. Our own difficulties in administering the country are many & varied. We are fostering as well as we can the growth of self-governing institutions but Mesopotamia is not ripe for self-govt. We have reorganized the administration of justice, proceedings being conducted in Arabic: we have elaborated a penal code: & we have established railways & irrigation schemes.

In the discussion the following opinions were expressed:

That it is doubtful whether our occupation of Mesopotamia will benefit the Empire in view of the heavy costs & remote prospects of profit: that we are in for something like the occupation of Egypt & that the breakdown of that occupation is a warning: that the Empire is taking on more than it can carry: On the other hand that we are there as mandatories & that we cannot sacrifice our prestige & bring about chaos in the East.

John Roskill   8 June 1921

* * *

[251] The 251st meeting of the Circle was held on 8 June 1921 at Stapley House.

Present. 11 members 2 visitors—Mr. Roskill in the chair.

Apologies were received from Messrs: Alden, Hobson, Hurcomb, MacDonald & Wigglesworth.

Minutes of the previous meeting were read & confirmed.

The Circle then waited for Mr. Chrouschoff[237] who was to have read the paper on the present political situation in Russia. Before long a message was received from him regretting his inability to attend owing to illness. Shortly afterwards the Circle dispersed, deriving what consolation it could from the reflection that 'God loves an idle Rainbow no less than labouring seas' [Ralph Hodgson][237]

John Roskill   Chairman

12 Oct. 1921

* * *

28th Session: 1921–22.

[252] The 252nd meeting of the Circle was held on 12 Oct 1921 at Stapley House

Present. 14 members & 2 visitors. Mr. Roskill in the chair.

Minutes of the previous meeting were read & confirmed.

---

[237] Matheson's second wife was Helen Chrouschoff, a lecturer on Russian history and a translator of Russian books; Ivan Chrouschoff was presumably a relation.

[238] Ralph Hodgson (1871–1962), English poet. The poem appears in *Eve and Other Poems* (London, 1913).

Apologies for absence were notified from Messrs: Alden, Golding, Herdman & MacDonald.

A letter from Mr. Burrows conveying greetings & good wishes was read.

A letter was read from Mr. Delisle Burns regretting that inability to attend the meetings necessitated his resignation.

Mr. Roskill was re-elected as president

Mr. Hobson   ”   ”   vice president

Messrs: Alden, Brereton, Crook, Harley & Herdman were re-elected as the Committee with the President Vice-president & Secretary ex officio.

The Accounts shewing a balance of 5s/3d on the right side were presented & accepted.

The Record of Attendance was read as follows:

Out of 9 meetings:

Mr. Crook attended	9
Messrs: Alden, Matheson, Parsons & Roskill	8
” Gooch, Hurcomb & Walker	7
” Goodenough Harley & Herdman	6
[Mr. Husband]	[4]
Messrs: Golding, McKillop, Robertson & Usher	3
Sir Sydney Olivier	2
Messrs: Adams, MacDonald, [Perris] & Buxton	1
[Mr. Gilmour]	1
Messrs: Burns & Gardiner	0

Average 13.5 as against 15.5 for previous year.

Mr. Felix W. Crosse, proposed by Mr. Robertson, seconded by Mr. Crook, was unanimously elected.

Mr. Robertson read his paper on the attitude of the Allies towards Germany.

A demand for punitive indemnities is ethically incontestable so long as punitive theory underlies treatment of individual criminals. A nation is as properly punishable for its collective actions as is a man. Germany is morally liable for the whole cost of the war—& the way to teach electorates of England & France to give up the idea of her paying anything like that cost is not to tell them that it is immoral but to shew them that it is absurd & that permanent impoverishment of any nation means not only that it cannot pay large indemnities but that its poverty will tend to keep *them* poor. The most scientific way of making Germany pay wd. be to extract from her as regular tribute for given period those raw materials wh she produces & wh the Allies require. But even that wd be very difficult without curtailing the German industry upon wh all further payment must depend. And the amount of indemnity receivable is determined by the degree of recovery of our normal power of consumption.

The discussion turned more on the moral than on the economic aspect of indemnities. The question was debated whether to receive an indemnity was ever an advantage—even a material advantage—to the victorious country.

Opinion was also expressed that if the German indemnity had been fixed that wd have tended to clear up the economic & political future & to stabilize trade: also that the steps our Govt. had taken to improve our position in relation to that of Germany had had precisely the reverse effect.

John Roskill   Chairman

9.xi.21

* * *

[253] The 253rd meeting of the Circle was held at Stapley House on 9 Novr. 1921.

Present. 16 members & 1 visitor.

Minutes of the previous meeting were read & confirmed.

Apologies were notified from Mr. Herdman & Mr. Robertson.

Mr. G.F. Reid[239] proposed by Mr. Matheson & seconded by Mr. Gilmour, was unanimously elected as a member.

Mr. Alden read his paper on the attitude of America towards the Allies & Germany.

The present condition of things in Europe is not such as to incline America to interfere. Our enemies in the States (& they are legion) wage unwearying warfare against the idea that America's interests are in any way involved in saving the situation for France or for Great Britain. About 1/3rd of America is friendlily disposed to Great Britain & perhaps 10 to 15% more to the Allies as a whole. This minority possesses real power: but half the people are Anglophobes. America is not a country but a continent: 35% of the people are of foreign born parents & 13.000.000 are actually foreign born. Every politician who thinks he has something to gain by attacking the Allies is willing to use the Germans & Irish in his campaign. Part of the attempt to curry favour with France is due to desire of many Americans to injure England. By America's attitude to the Allies we mean the attitude of the President, the Govt:, & the Anglo-Saxon minority. There is still a hope that with modifications a League of Nations may eventually win American support. America does wish for a League of Peace: she does not wish for membership of the Supreme Council or a share in

---

[239] Should be G.T. Reid.

its decisions. She dreads the idea of being a party to all the secret wrangling of European Foreign Offices. She has shewn herself disinterested in her Far Eastern policy & will press for the open door in China. One of the immediate advantages of America's Treaty of Peace with Germany is that U.S. can take the lead & approach the Allies with requests for modification in the Treaty of Versailles wh, as it stands, is likely to destroy Germany economically. America's position as the creditor nation of the world is becoming more & more embarrassing to herself. The situation generally wd be eased if there were a cancellation of all claims—a matter in wh Great Britain might take the first step.

In the discussion the following opinions were expressed:

That America may see that the chaotic state of Europe demands her interference & she may desire alliance with this country.

That American economic development will compel her to take a hand in politics as well as economics in all parts of the world.

That the anti-British feeling in America is on the whole a diminishing quantity.

That in the proposed general cancellation of indebtedness the debts owing to us are on the whole bad debts whilst the debt we owe to America is a good debt.

John Roskill   Chairman 14.xii.21

* * *

[254] The 254th meeting of the Circle was held at Stapley House on 14th Decr. 1921.

Present. 18 members, Sir Wm. Joynson-Hicks & another visitor, Mr. Roskill in the chair.

Apologies were notified from Mr. Herdman, Sir Sydney Olivier, Mr. Robertson, Mr. Walsh & Mr. Wigglesworth.

Minutes of the previous meeting were read & confirmed.

Sir Wm. Joynson-Hicks had very kindly, & in true sporting spirit, accepted the Circle's invitation to speak on 'the Conservative Outlook'. His acceptance was particularly appreciated by the Circle since he came in full knowledge that his rôle wd be that of Daniel in Den of Lions, & the Circle felt honoured by the trouble he had taken in preparing for their consideration a carefully written paper.

He said that Conservative principles may still be expressed in Disraelian formula as maintenance of our institutions, preservation of the Empire, & improvement of the conditions of the people. He deprecated coalition of parties wh at best cd be but a temporary arrangement. The present Coalition is always compromising & has ceased to govern. The poor character of all recent legislation is due in part to the Acts not having encountered any opposition or proper criticism. The Safeguarding of Industries Act,[240] for instance, endeavours to embody two divergent principles. The Statute Book is congested with ill-digested legislation wh does not work & much of wh has been repealed.

The break-up of the coalition & return to clear-cut Conservative & Liberal parties will not lead to Bolshevism as some fear. Working men are not communists: they are either conservatives or liberals. More than 40% of the men voters & 50% of the women are always wholly conservative & a conservative government is a likely possibility in near future. The main objects for wh the Coalition was formed have been attained as far as they are likely to be. The present-day Conservative policy differs very strongly from Liberal policy in foreign & imperial affairs—especially on such questions as those of Egypt & India. The conservative idea with regard to all coloured nations is the old Roman idea—that they shd be governed by benevolent autocracy of the whites.

In the discussion the Lions, with gentle insistence, dismembered Daniel under local anaesthetic (Rainbow mixture) of goodwill & genuine admiration for the frankness & sincerity & kindliness with which he had expounded his somewhat Babylonian views. It remains in doubt whether he did not enjoy the process as much as the Lions did—indeed he seemed unconscious of his spiritual demolition. The following opinions, among many others, were expressed:

The conservative instinct shrinks from change: the liberal instinct looks out for ways in wh to change things for the better. In that sense there will always be men who are essentially conservative & men who are essentially liberal, & soundest form of democratic govt. is the 2-party system.

The general conservative attitude of mind is that some shd govern & some obey: the liberal attitude is that all shd govern & all obey: the Labour party believe that in time working men will be capable of taking a share in management & control of industry.

The conservative party is not a national party but a class party—more so than the Labour party. It is not a constitutional party except when in power: it is a revolutionary party & ready to go against will of majority. The fundamental weakness of conservatism today is that its supporters do not believe in Democracy but merely exploit & use it.

John Roskill   Chairman

11 Jan: 1922

* * *

[240] Enacted in 1921.

[255] The 255th meeting of the Circle was held at Stapley House on 11 Jan: 1922.

Present. 13 members & 1 visitor Mr. Roskill in the chair.

Apologies were notified from Messrs: Brereton, Gardiner, Gilmour, Sir Fisher Dilke, Golding, Herdman & MacDonald.

Minutes of the previous meeting were read & confirmed.

It was announced that Mr. Hobson had kindly agreed to change dates with Mr. MacDonald & wd thus read the paper at the next meeting.

It was decided that the April meeting shd be on the 1st Wedn. (5th April) instead of the second.

Mr. W.M. Crook read his paper on the Liberal Outlook.

He described the attitude & the trend of thought to wh the word liberal is properly applicable. War in countries wh have a considerable amount of liberty always makes for reaction: in despotically governed countries it generally makes for liberty. The country wh is beaten almost invariably gains more in liberty than the country wh wins. This is illustrated by results of Franco-German war. Germany emerged with extended forms of liberty, but they were only forms & Bismarck in smashing the liberal party broke down liberalism. The trinity of Imperialism, Socialism & Protection led steadily to 'World power or downfall'. British inherent faith in freedom shd prevent England suffering Germany's fate.

Since unorganized liberal opinion is powerless there is in practice no liberal outlook apart from the liberal party. The Labour party is essentially a class party with no political ideals or spiritual vision. On almost all but economic questions it does not differ essentially from the liberal party & it will probably disappear leaving the field to the Conservative & Liberal parties. Liberal principles (e.g. on Foreign policy, Imperial policy, education, finance & trade) are already definite: but in Industrial policy the position is not yet fully evolved.

In the discussion the following opinions were expressed:

The likely future of the Liberal party is that it will be the 3rd party in the State, the Conservatives coming first & the Labour second.

Liberalism hits the happy mean between undue centralization (whether Conservative or Socialist) & utter banishment of State as in Guild Socialism. It tries to use the State for what the State alone can do & leaves a very free hand to self-realization otherwise. It is the saving political force, not being absolutely dominated by class ideals.

The maintenance of Free trade is largely bound up with the maintenance of the Liberal party.

The country is ripe for an appeal to principle & good govt.: but the appeal must include an industrial policy founded on sound economics.

John Roskill   Chairman

8 Feb. 1922

* * *

[256] The 256th meeting of the Circle was held at Stapley House on 8 Feb. 1922

Present. 13 members 1 visitor, Mr. Roskill in the chair.

Apologies were notified from Messrs: Crook, Gardiner, Gooch, Herdman (letter preserved in archives of Circle) MacDonald, Robertson, Walsh & Sir Fisher Dilke.

Minutes of previous meeting were read & confirmed.

Mr. Hobson gave an address on 'Taxation—the burden of'.

We must not tax in a way that will reduce supply of any of the factors of production. Tax beyond a certain point takes away incentive to work or power to save. Progressive income tax & progressive inheritance tax are the soundest methods. There is room for improvement in our present system of exemptions & abatements—improvements wh might result for instance in less hardship on families of considerable size. There is something to be said for present differentiation between incomes that are called earned & unearned—though the differentiation is not altogether sound. It might be possible to rely on individual assessments instead of deducting at source: but Treasury dead against it & the point is not one to be pressed. The ideal is a single tax wisely based on income & abolition of all taxes of indirect nature.

The Revised Budget about balances for this year & may shew small surplus of say 20m. But next year revenue will be decreased somewhat as follows:

In respect of E.P.D.[241] & disposal of war stores   200m.
    "   "   " Income Tax: Super Tax, Customs & Excise   50m.
Revenue thus becomes 960m. & expenditure must be cut by 180m. Expenses wh will not recur = say 70m. But interest on American debt will equal 50m. We must therefore cut by 160m. in order to balance next year. Irreducible expenditure (interest on debt & pensions including O.A.P.) = 345 + 130m. Hence the 160m. must come off

---

[241] Excess Profits Duty, imposed on all businesses in 1915.

the remaining 655m. for supply services. A tax revenue of 964m. must be obtained—& this is so high as to prevent recovery of trade. A Capital levy might have been a good (& fair) thing immediately after the war, but it has now passed out of range of practical politics if it was ever in it. There must be no attempt to reduce taxation this year. A revival of trade plus no further fall in prices wd save the situation.

In the discussion the following opinions were expressed:

That no improvement in trade is in sight.

That Govt: inflation & creation of fresh debt wd be preferable to retention of present crippling tax.

That if we have a single tax there wd be no bridle on expenditure.

That 1/3rd of our pre-war customers are not able to buy from us at all.

That capitalization of pensions wd be unsound & a bad precedent.

John Roskill   Chairman 8. iii. 22

* * *

[257] The 257th meeting of the Circle was held at Stapley House on 8th March 1922.

Present 15 members & 1 visitor, Mr. Roskill in the chair.

Apologies were notified from Messrs: Gardiner, Golding, Herdman, Hobson, McKillop, Matheson & Sir Sydney Olivier.

Minutes of the previous meeting were read & confirmed.

Mr. Gooch gave his address on 'the European Situation'.

The various parts of old Russia are nearly all united again under Moscow—excepting Finland & Poland wh are separated with Russia's goodwill. Finland has settled down fairly well, but Karelia is still a bone of contention between her & Russia. Livonia & Courland, amalgamated as Latvia, will probably be driven into economic union with Russia. The Russo-polish frontier is a very temporary affair—200 miles too far to the east. The fortunes of Lithuania are bound up with those of Poland: but there is at present no firm political agreement between the two. They will go on quarrelling about Vilna for some time. Eastern Galicia is not yet settled. It has been conquered by the Poles but the whole of the peasant population is Ruthene. In the next 10 or 20 years Poland will be smaller, Russia bigger.

Turkey. The treaty of Sèvres gave Thrace to Venizelist[242] Greece: but now Turkey will probably get Eastern Thrace. Bulgaria ought to have Western Thrace. She is absolutely certain to become a powerful state & nothing can stop her from getting to the sea. Roumania, the

---

[242] Eleutherios Venizelos (1864–1936). Greek statesman and prime minister.

rottenest state in Europe, has emerged much too big—frontier too far west. Great Serbia or Jugo-Slavia is torn asunder by struggle between centralizers & Home-Rulers. Montenegro Croatia & the Slovenes desire autonomy.

Of all the new states Bohemia has best chance of surviving. Her most difficult problem is that of granting autonomy to Slovakia. Economic unity combined with political autonomy should be the ideal for Austria, Hungary, Bohemia, & Serbia. Italy's one great problem is to keep on good terms with her neighbours across the Adriatic.

England, France & Germany. England shd forgive France her debt & renounce claim to any reparation in favour of France & Belgium. This wd create a better atmosphere & make possible a sounder general settlement. The proposed English guarantee of the Franco-German frontier wd be deplorable. It wd be followed by secret military conventions & in effect by an alliance—& by similar arrangements between Germany & Russia. It wd be utterly destructive to the Unity of Europe & to the effectiveness of the League of Nations. Sufficient guarantee cd be given in two ways (1), & preferably, by going back to Belgian precedent of 1870 & making a similar treaty with both France & Germany or (2) by a collective guarantee of the existing frontiers of any nations that liked to come into the arrangement.

In the discussion the following opinions were expressed:

That there was still some danger of a Serbo-Italian war. That the central feature in the European problem is the development of the great resources of Russia, wh will be undertaken by Germany with or without England. That the penetration of Germany into Russia may relieve the pressure of Germany westwards.

J.A. Hobson   5 April 1922.   Chairman

* * *

[258] The 258th meeting of the Circle was held at Stapley House on 5th April 1922.

Present. 14 members & 3 visitors, Mr. Hobson, Vice-President, in the chair.

Apologies for absence were notified from Messrs: Gilmour, Gooch & Herdman.

Minutes of the previous meeting were read & confirmed.

Mr. Roskill, President, read his paper on 'Problems of Currency & Exchange'.

Before the war England was the chief creditor nation & a bill on London (the most economical instrument of foreign exchange) the usual means of settling international trade indebtedness. The convertibility of the bills into gold was the cause of the confidence that attached to them, gold being the only important legal tender. As the value of each country's currency cd be compared with gold, the various currencies cd be compared with each other & a rate of exchange was established. The 'specie point' constituted an automatic limit to the fluctuations of exchange. Now our paper currency is no longer convertible into gold at face value. The U.S.A. is the only country on a gold basis & no other country can get back to a gold basis until the exchange value of its currency has risen to a par with that of the United States. Under the Federal Reserve Banking system in U.S. the currency not covered by gold is secured against commercial bills of exchange, whereas 85% of our currency is secured against unfunded Govt: debt. It wd be a good thing if we adopted the same system. There is no direct means of restoring the exchanges. Trade, international & unrestricted, must be revived before we can re-establish currencies. Finance is only the handmaid of trade & chaotic exchanges are the effect & not the cause of chaotic national & international conditions. Production is the only means by wh real as distinct from artificial deflation can be effected.

The discussion turned largely on the effect on America of our proceeding to pay our debt: on the possibility & the wisdom or otherwise of cancellation of European war debts: & on the Federal Reserve Banking system. On other aspects of the question the following opinions were expressed: that American unemployment will drive America to Free-trade: that the only way to economic salvation is by reduction of colossal Governmental expenditure: that the only way to economic salvation is by increased production: & that the only way to economic salvation is by getting back to a gold basis of currency.

John Roskill   Chairman

10 May 1922.

* * *

[259] The 259th meeting of the Circle was held at Stapley House on 10 May 1922.

Present. 13 members, Mr. Roskill in the chair.

Apologies for absence were notified from Messrs: Gardiner, Herdman, MacDonald, Reid & Walker.

Minutes of the previous meeting were read & confirmed.

The Committee's recommendations in connexion with the programme for the next session were discussed & adopted.

The Circle, on the recommendation of the Committee, decided to drop the practice of inviting questions before starting the discussion, in the hope that the time thereby saved wd enable meetings to close by 10.0 pm.

Mr. Goodenough read his paper on 'Industrial Prospects'.

There is no general active revolt against working for capitalists: the workers do not consciously recognise that they are out for anything except wages, hours & security against unemployment. But that is no reason why we shd be content with the Old Order if we can see practical ways of reforming it or replacing it by a better New Order. Public ownership & operation of industry wd fail to produce as good results as the present system in 95% of the industrial field. Salvation does not that way lie. The general situation is already better & will improve: the cause of our industrial instability & weakness lies primarily in Persons, not Systems. The failure so far of Trade Union-ism, Socialism, Communism, to put industry on a permanent foun-dation of prosperity results from *substitution* of co-operation for individual effort, initiative & responsibility. Considering the great advance in education & intellectual capacity of the workers the fall in their sense of personal responsibility duty & honour in relation to industry is the more deplorable though inevitable through misguided policy of the Unions & the too-common attitude of employers. The root weakness is want of confidence due to Ignorance, Cowardice & Selfishness on all sides—& Industrial Prosperity is a question of human relationships with confidence as the prime essential. Trade Unions shd leave politics to politicians only seeking to influence politics so far as they affect industrial conditions & shd concentrate on industrial efficiency, discipline, & relations with employers. Employers shd be animated by the spirit of Service & shd consider the welfare & safety of their workers, & the ways in wh they can share in the industry, as by profit-sharing & co-partnership.

In the discussion the following opinions were expressed:

That there is a new industrial order emerging & certain industries that have to be put into hands of State or under State control, the public being confronted with alternative between public & private monopoly.

That the question of the relation between different businesses in one industry & between different industries needs consideration.

That we want more & more to see employers & employed making experts in management, in councils & so on.

That the ideal is the preservation of the principle of private own-ership tempered by co-operation & state supervision.

John Roskill   Chairman

14 June 1922

* * *

[260] The 260th meeting of the Circle was held at Stapley House on 14th June 1922.

Present. 13 members & 2 visitors, Mr. Roskill in the chair.

Apologies for absence were notified from Messrs: Gilmour, Golding, Gooch, Crosse, Herdman & Hobson.

Minutes of the previous meeting were read & confirmed.

Sir George Paish, proposed by Mr. Roskill & seconded by Mr. Matheson was elected a member of the Circle.

Mr. J.R. MacDonald read his paper on the Labour Outlook. The real meaning of the Labour Party was a revolt against the materialism of Capitalism. The Trade Union movement was a counter-revolution against the industrial revolution in favour of human freedom. All the talk about co-operation between capital & labour is illusory. The appeal of the Labour Party is a catholic one: it has never appealed to labour except through Trade unions, but it has always taken its stand on social well-being. It is not & never has been a mere class party. It made its appeal to the Trade Unions because they were nearest to the material forces against wh it opposed spiritual forces. Socialism valued the efficiency of a bureaucracy with a great amount of control & responsibility but always had suspicions of it. Then came the Guild Socialism movement—with a curious reversion to mediaevalism. The Labour Party did not accept Guild Socialism but took some of its ideas, notably that of workshop control. The Labour Party desires the union of industrial & political advance.

An effect of the war has been to throw the control of the Party more & more into the hands of Trade Unions, wh unfortunately results in struggle between Labour & Capital to get as much as possible out of the community. Another difficulty the Party has to contend with is the rise of Communism.

The Labour Party holds that we cannot continue to pay the burdens wh war has imposed, & proposes a capital levy to reduce the debt. In internal economic reconstruction the Labour Party is an unrepentant nationaliser & wd start with Railways & Mines. In the workshop, experiments with extended Whitley Councils[243] are in contemplation with a view to industrial peace & participation in control of industry.

In the discussion the following opinions were expressed:

That the Labour Party is essentially a socialist party & not entitled to represent the workers: that the Trade Union does not & cannot represent them politically.

---

[243] Joint standing industrial councils were proposed in 1917 by a subcommittee of the Committee on Reconstruction, chaired by the Liberal M.P. J. Whitley. The councils that were formed consisted of representatives of employers and of trade unions and submitted recommendations on issues such as terms of employment and the prevention of differences between the two sides of industry.

That the Labour Party is poorly represented in the House of Commons & seems to reject its intellectual men.

That nationalisation is not an end in itself, & may make against human liberty rather than for it.

John Roskill   Chairman

11 Oct: 1922.

* * *

29th Session: 1922–23

[261] The 261st meeting of the Circle was held at Stapley House on 11th Octr. 1922.

Present. 15 members 1 visitor, Mr. Roskill in the chair.

Apologies for absence were notified from Messrs: Crosse, Herdman, Hobson, Matheson, Sir Geo Paish, Sir Fisher Dilke & Wigglesworth.

Minutes of the previous meeting were read & confirmed.

Mr. Roskill was re-elected President
" Hobson   "   Vice-President
" Parsons   "   Secretary

Messrs: Alden, Brereton, Crook, Harley & Hurcomb were elected as the Committee with the President, Vice-president & Secretary ex officio.

The Accounts shewing a balance of £5-1-1 were presented & accepted. The subscription was reduced from 7s/6d to 4s/-

The record of attendance was read as follows:

Out of 9 meetings

Messrs: Goodenough Hurcomb Parsons & Roskill attend[ed]	9
" Alden Crook & Matheson	8
" Brereton & Wigglesworth	7
" Gilmour Gooch Reid & Walker	6
" Golding Harley & Hobson	5
Mr. Crosse attended	4
" Robertson	3
Messrs: Buxton Gardiner & MacDonald	2
Sir Fisher Dilke & Sir Sydney Olivier	1
Messrs: Adams, Herdman, McKillop Usher & Walsh	0

Average 14.2 as against 13.5 for previous session.

Mr. Gardiner gave an address on Public Opinion & the Press.

The press is more powerful in its influence on public opinion than parliament the church & the school. Weekly press alone issues not less than 10 million newspapers every week—almost 1 to every household in the country. The press is the greatest force for creating public opinion: it is also out to make money & these things are not harmonious. A public spirited newspaper may find itself at variance with the interests of property & cannot afford to come into conflict with the people who have the power of giving out valuable advertisements. In that half the cost of journalism has to come from advertisements the very basis of journalism is unsound. To get great advertising great circulation is necessary & this is secured by popularising & sensationalism. The contribution that Northcliffe[244] made to the press was the manipulation of news—carried out with ruthlessness & audacity: even foreign correspondents had to write to order to support Northcliffe's own point of view. Another sinister consideration that emerges from the modern development of the commercialised press is the concentration of this power in the hands of a few men who are not publicists at all but who approach the subject as they wd a soap-factory or a brewery. The conscionable journalist who cannot be moulded tends to get squeezed out. The business of a newspaper is to be guardian of the public interests—but action & reaction between politicians & newspaper monopolists have many strange developments. Politicians give titles: newspaper men give support.

The way to cure the disease is not clear. Public discussion of it might create widespread distrust of the present press, wh wd be all to the good. It might be possible—though it is a debatable matter—to have an official newspaper wh wd be a check on the criminalities of the press. The only real remedy ultimately is an educated public.

The discussion turned mainly on the future & the financial position of the Times & on the ways of the late Lord Northcliffe.

John Roskill   Chairman

8.xi.22

* * *

[262] The 262nd meeting of the Circle was held on 8th Nov. 1922 at Stapley House.

Present. 8 members, Mr. Roskill in the chair.

Apologies for absence were notified from Messrs: Crook, Crosse, Gardiner, Golding, Gooch, Herdman, & MacDonald.

Minutes of the previous meeting were read & confirmed.

The resignation of Mr. Maurice Adams & of Mr. McKillop was announced. As so few members were present the meeting decided to

[244] Alfred Harmsworth. See meeting 225.

postpone Mr. Brereton's paper to the 10th January—Mr. Herdman having intimated that he could not read a paper on that date.

John Roskill   Chairman

13.xii.22

* * *

[263] The 263rd meeting of the Circle was held on 13 Decr. 1922 at Stapley House.

Present 13 members & 3 visitors—Mr. Roskill in the chair.

Apologies for absence were notified from Messrs: Golding, Gooch, MacDonald & Sir Sydney Olivier.

Minutes of the previous meeting were read & confirmed.

Mr. Reid read his paper on Modern Developments in Industrial Conciliation & Arbitration.

He sketched rapidly the course of legislation on the subject from the Act of 1800 'for settling disputes that may arise between masters & workmen engaged in the cotton manufacture' to the Act of 1896[245] which resulted from the findings of the Royal Commission on Labour 1894. The merit of that Act was that it gave the Board of Trade a definite official duty towards the parties concerned in industrial disputes. It became someone's 'job' to take a hand, from an industrial standpoint & with governmental authority, in a dispute: the public became not only accustomed to intervention but expectant of it. During the war the rights of both workmen & employers were curtailed & rates of wages were largely fixed departmentally or by compulsory arbitration. The 'Committee on Production' heard nearly 4000 cases & from it sprang the standing Arbitration Court[246] (set up on the recommendation of the Whitley Committee) to wh the Joint Industrial Councils (also a Whitley product) can appeal in the last resort. In recommending the institution of J.I.C.'s, wh have a much wider range of interest than the old conciliation Boards, the Whitley Committee were guided by actual experience of the working of the Trade Boards. The Arbitration Court has already given 750 decisions on every kind of difference likely to arise between employer & employed & has made a beginning of the task of laying down a corpus of industrial common law. The award of the Court is dependent for its observance upon the sense of honour & spirit of fair play of the parties. Trade Unionists generally are opposed to the idea of attaching legal sanction to an award.

---

[245] The Conciliation Act of 1896.
[246] Established on the basis of the Industrial Courts Act (1919).

In the discussion opinion was general that the time had not come for compulsion: that it wd tend to prevent the coming together of employers & employed & that the important thing is to create good-will & the habit of consulting together & that the objection of the workers to compulsory arbitration is the fear that if they surrender the right to strike they will deliver themselves over to the employer.

John Roskill   Chairman

10 Jan 1923

* * *

[264] The 264th meeting of the Circle was held on 10 Jan: 1923 at Stapley House.

Present 12 members & 2 visitors, Mr. Roskill in the chair.

Apologies for absence were notified from Messrs: Gardiner, Herdman, Hurcomb & MacDonald.

Minutes of the previous meeting were read & confirmed.

The President referred to the death on 13th Decr. of Mr. Herbert Burrows (in his 77th year) who was one of the original members of the Circle & who had taken an active part in its proceedings from 1894 to 1917 when he was struck down by illness. The President expressed the sorrow of the Circle at losing so old a friend, honoured & loved by all. He mentioned that Sir Richard Stapley's presidential chair which had been given to Mr. Burrows on Sir Richard's death had been kindly given back to the Circle & said that he felt it a true honour to occupy a chair that had been used by two such men.

Other members also paid tribute to the memory of Mr. Burrows, mentioning his abounding energy, his enthusiasms which he retained to the end, his work in social reform, his unfailing championship of the poor & the oppressed, his faith in humanity, his simplicity of soul & personal loveableness. A summary was given of the papers he had read before the Rainbow Circle: also a brief account of his funeral at which the Circle was represented by Mr. Hobson, Mr. Alden & the Secretary, Mr. Hobson giving the funeral address.

The following letter from his daughter, Mrs. Melvin, was read:

'... Your sympathy with us & your deep appreciation of my dear father, so thoughtfully expressed, have touched us deeply, & on behalf of my brother & myself I can only say a very heartfelt 'thankyou' in wh Mrs. Kindelan joins. Though we cannot regret that our dear one has at last won freedom from his inactivity, the blank in our lives is hard to bear; but we have an imperishable memory of his lovely & loving spirit in our hearts to comfort us. We have had many kind letters from members of the Rainbow Circle, & we shall be obliged if you will be kind enough, at your next meeting, to express to them on our behalf our very grateful thanks for their sympathy in our loss, & our thanks also to the whole Circle for the very beautiful flowers they so kindly sent ...'

Mr. Brereton read his paper on 'The need of Speech-training & a National Conservatoire'.

The mistaken cult of uncultured nature is to be seen in the realm of Art in revolt against technique. Technique is the generalised experience of the Art—not a substitute for but ancillary to creative work. In the art of Diction technique may be divided under the 4 headings of gesture, pronunciation, intonation & rhythm. The need for training in this technique concerns not only actors, politicians, barristers, clergymen & teachers, but the entire population. Our general methods of speech are so defective that the whole matter needs to be dealt with in the schools themselves. We ought to recover that joy in the spoken word wh is only second to the joy in song. The children shd be taught as soon as they enter the schools just as they are already taught the elements of drawing & music wh after all enter only incidentally into daily life. In addition to this there shd be an institution of higher education where speech in all its developments can be systematically studied. The few schools that already exist for this purpose (e.g. the Central School of Dramatic Art & the R.A. of Dramatic Art) shd be recognised as an integral part of a national system & a special faculty shd be created in the University.

In the discussion members, many of whom openly deplored their own lack of specific training, made a brave display of their respective & individual joy in the spoken word. General agreement was expressed with the writer's ideals & particularly with his eulogy of French methods—under wh a Frenchman is brought up to realise the glories & beauties of his own tongue. Discussion also took place on the desirability of encouraging reading aloud, on the effect of climate on tone of voice & pronunciation (very noticeable in 'God's own country'), on class slang & on the peculiar difficulties of dealing with the debased speech we call 'cockney'.

John Roskill   Chairman

14 Feb. 1923

* * *

[265] The 265th meeting of the Circle was held on 14 Feb. 1923 at Stapley House.

Present. 13 members & 3 visitors—Mr. Roskill in the chair.

Apologies for absence were notified from Messrs: Crook, Gardiner MacDonald & Walker.

Minutes of the previous meeting were read & confirmed.

Sir Geo: Paish gave an address on the subject 'Can Poverty be abolished?'.[247]

Only 25 per cent of the world's population is above the poverty line: but America with population of 110 million has only a small percentage below. The world has not a fraction of the population it cd maintain. Europe, India & China are congested but the rest of the world is underpopulated. The wealth produced by the world is only a fraction of what it might be. The power to produce wealth, to increase income, is almost unlimited: but it is necessary to spread out the population to sparsely peopled areas & to increase the use of labour-saving appliances. It is also necessary that the poor people shd demand more & more things. Trade depression is due to under-consumption, not to over-production: it is essential to economic development in that it brings about a redistribution of population, people being forced into doing things that are needed.

In England the great expansion of well-being in recent years (2/3rds of the population have been pushed above the poverty line in 2 generations) is due largely to the Education Act of 1870 wh has raised standards & made people want more. The modern system of Joint Stock Companies makes it possible for an increasing number of people to have capital interests. We want the mass of the people to be capitalists in that sense. We shd look to expansion of income rather than to redistribution of present income. It shd be possible to bring about great increase of wealth by promoting prosperity of other nations, finding capital for Russia, financing railways in India & China & working generally in co-operation with other nations—not building a wall round the British Empire.

In the discussion the following opinions were expressed:

1. That the accumulation & use of capital is, in combination with invention, the greatest power in increasing wealth.

2. That there is a danger in unifying the world too much for the purposes of generalisation. Local over-production & local over-population are very real difficulties.

3. That the idea that the working classes could get real control of

---

[247] The annual programme announced a talk by H. Golding for this meeting entitled 'The Ethics of Insurance'. Golding never gave that address to the Rainbow Circle, but delivered what presumably was the same talk to the Pearl Office Guild, a discussion group of the Pearl Insurance Company (cp. *The Pearl Gazette*, vol. ii, no. 11 (September 1923). It was published as 'The Social Value of Insurance' in *The Insurance Gem* (September, 1923), 4-5.

capital is too hopeful: that large gains under the present system go to people who are manipulators in industry—not pioneers.

John Roskill   14 March 1923.   Chairman

* * *

[266] The 266th meeting of the Circle was held on 14 Mch. 1923 at Stapley House.

Present 13 members & 1 visitor—Mr. Roskill in the chair.

Apologies for absence were notified from Messrs: Gardiner, Golding, MacDonald, Reid & Sir Geo: Paish.

Minutes of the previous meeting were read & confirmed.

Mr. Crosse read his paper on 'China & Japan'.[248]

The efforts of the Washington Conference[249] cannot rightly be regarded as altruistic or actuated by a new desire for the betterment of humanity, but as a practical business deal they have been fruitful in eliminating much confusion & in advancing the chances of a successful utilization of China's resources for the general benefit. For the next few decades there is every indication that China will provide ample trade & dividends for Britain & U.S.A.: that Japan will find enough scope in Manchuria & Mongolia, with perhaps Siberia, to keep her industries going & feed her population. She will also get her share of Chinese raw materials & trade. Barring possibility of friction between Japan & Russia, or Japan & a German influenced Russia, there is every sign of peace in the Far East. The ultimate development of the Far East is a matter of speculation, Among possibilities are (1) Overthrow of autocratic rule in Japan by a huge proletariat oppressed by sweating system (2) Revival of China under German-Russian influence & revival of Russo-Japanese conflicting policies in Siberia (3) A Sino-Japanese hegemony (4) An awakened China, massacring resident foreigners & strong enough to exclude all others as in the past.

In the discussion the following opinions were expressed:

1. Japanese authorities are doing their best to prevent proletariat from gaining control. Legislation against Trade Unions is in operation & no labour organisation will be tolerated.

2. The 4-Power agreement[250] has warned off exploitation of China by Japan.

[248] Cp. the detailed published version of the talk: F.W. Crosse, 'International Policy in the Far East', *Contemporary Review*, vol. cxxiv (1923), 34–43.

[249] Convened by the U.S.A. in 1921 in order to limit armaments, and included discussion of Pacific and Far Eastern issues.

[250] Between the U.S.A., Great Britain, France and Japan, to consult and respect each other's rights in the Pacific.

3. The Samurai have entered industry & are bringing their high ethical principles into play therein.

4. War between America & Japan is less & less likely.

5. The Washington Conference enabled us to get out of the entanglement of the Anglo-Japanese[251] alliance.

John Roskill   11.4.23   Chairman

* * *

[267] The 267th meeting of the Circle was held on 11 April 1923 at Stapley House.

Present 12 members & 2 visitors, Mr. Roskill in the chair.

Apologies for absence were notified from Messrs: Brereton, Crook, Gardiner, Golding, Goodenough, Harley, MacDonald, Reid & Sir Geo: Paish.

A letter was read from Mr. Herdman resigning. It was decided to ask him to reconsider his decision.

Minutes of the previous meeting were read & confirmed.

Mr. Gilmour read his paper on 'the Oil of the World'.

The world's present consumption of petroleum is about 100 million tons of wh 88% comes from North American continent. On data at present available it is not possible to form reliable estimate of potential supply of natural oil available, & pessimistic forecasts shd not be taken too tragically. It is reasonable to suppose that there exist large sources in many parts of the world wh have not yet been located or utilised. The world demand will tend to go on increasing & will be met to some extent by liquefaction of coal, tar-sand &c: & by discovery of processes for more economical utilisation of the supplies available. In this connexion account must be taken of the Bergin process, invented by the German chemist Dr. Bergius,[252] wh is already being operated on a commercial scale at Rheinau near Mannheim.

The commercial utilisation of oil is a business speculative in its nature, requiring the highest technical skill & organising ability as well a the provision of a very large amount of capital, & is best left to private enterprise.

The proper function of Govts: is to maintain 'the open door' both as regards the utilisation of the raw materials of the industry & the marketing of the products, & to prevent creation of a monopoly in either.

In the discussion the following opinions were expressed:

[251] Drawn up in 1902, and imposing neutrality, under certain conditions, on either side in the case of war with a third party.

[252] Friedrich Bergius (1884–1949). Industrial chemist, Nobel prize winner, 1931.

That the supply of crude oil is virtually inexhaustible: that it may pay later on to tap deeper wells in preference to extracting oil from coal, shale, & tar-sand: & that the economic value of extracting oil from coal may have to be compared with the value of turning coal into power—e.g. electric power—at the pithead.

That the anxiety of the U.S.A. as regards future resources depends on estimates of the world's reserves wh are largely guess-work, but wh shew that those reserves are situated outside U.S.A. in countries where govts: are relatively unstable. The policy of the open-door, observed by U.S.A. up to the war, is very desirable. We have not observed that policy in India & Burmah. Britain & U.S.A. ought to do everything possible to maintain the policy of the open-door & the govts: ought not to have any direct interest or control in the industry.

Percy Alden

* * *

[268] The 268th meeting of the Circle was held on 9 May 1923 at Stapley House.

Present. 12 members & 2 visitors, Mr. Alden in the chair.

Apologies for absence were notified from Messrs: Roskill, Brereton, Crook, Crosse, Gooch, Hobson, Walker & Sir Sydney Olivier.

A letter was read from Mr. Herdman withdrawing his resignation.

The Secretary explained that Mr. Walker who was to have read his paper much regretted that he was unable to be present owing to illness & that Mr. Robertson had at short notice kindly consented to take his place—with a different subject.

On the recommendation of the Committee Mr. S. Russell Cooke, proposed by the Secretary & seconded by Mr. Matheson, & Mr. Aylmer Vallance, proposed by Mr. Matheson & seconded by Mr. Gilmour were elected as members of the Circle.

The programme for next session drafted by the Committee was submitted & adopted.

Minutes of the previous meeting were read & confirmed.

Mr. Robertson read his paper on the Causation of the French Revolution. He made a powerful plea for accuracy of statement & scientific induction in historical criticism & research, & with over-whelming erudition demolished the proposition (endorsed by the late Professor Sidgwick) that it was the destructive work of Voltaire that made the Revolution possible. Religious motives had many times led to revolutions & the Catholic Church had constantly affirmed the removability of Kings obnoxious to her. Peasants who had never heard of free-thought rebelled because they suffered. The example of

English constitutionalism & freedom & the example of the American revolution counted for more than all Rousseau's teaching or Voltaire's influence. The clergy & noblesse who resisted every reform did more to precipitate the Revolution than all the propagandists put together. A great political revolution must have had a great political causation, & the catastrophic & distinctive character of the French Revolution resulted directly neither from religious nor anti-religious ways of thinking but from the fact that a general push for reform, under a weak government, coinciding with a season of acute distress, produced a crash wh went from bad to worse because the nation that sought to govern itself had had no practical preparation for the task & no adequate police system.

In the discussion the following opinions were expressed:

That the Russian revolution is a parallel case: we have to look to political & economic factors & no explanation of any great sociological upheaval can be true if it is simple.

That the 2 main causes were the conditions created during the whole of 17th century & the enormous effect of the American revolution.

That the primary cause of the Revolution was bad finance & the feudal system.

John Roskill   Chairman

13 June 1923.

* * *

[269] The 269th meeting of the Circle was held at Stapley House on 13 June 1923.

Present. 19 members & 2 visitors, Mr. Roskill in the chair.

Apologies for absence were notified from Mr. MacDonald, Sir George Paish & Mr. Wigglesworth. Mr. MacDonald tendered his resignation but it was decided to ask him to retain his membership.

Mr. G.C. Dougherty proposed by the President was unanimously elected as a member.

Minutes of the previous meeting were read & confirmed.

Sir Sydney Olivier read his paper on the Colour Question,[253] & a discussion followed in wh the following opinions were expressed:

That colour & race prejudice does not exist in France as in England, France having inherited the traditions of the Roman Empire. On the other hand the question was raised whether the toleration in France is not of recent growth & due to the great need for population.

[253] An indication of its contents may be gleaned from S. Olivier, 'Colour Prejudice', *Contemporary Review*, vol. cxxiv (1923), 448–57.

that the doctrine of racial superiority founded by Gobineau[254] has had bad moral & spiritual results, but that we must recognize that there are very marked differences between the various races.

that it is by no means clear that the dominant types are on an equality & that in the last resort we have to aggregate excellences.

that black races wd hardly agree that the English treat them less justly than do mediterranean races, though we may treat them with less sympathy.

that there is a dangerous fallacy in all attempts to size up races. Good qualities are in all but more developed in some than in others.

that races that remain pure as also extreme mongrels do not rise. The two extremes produce stagnation, but intermarrying in moderation makes for development.

that the solution of the race question by intermarriage is illusory & uncalled for. We want rather to look forward to a state of balance based in principles of international law & justice.

John Roskill   Chairman

10 Oct. 1923

* * *

Thirtieth Session. [1923–24]

[270] The 270th meeting of the Rainbow Circle was held at Stapley House on 10 Oct. 1923.

Present 13 members, Mr. Roskill in the chair.

Apologies for absence were notified from Messrs: Reid & Wigglesworth.

Minutes of the previous meeting were read & confirmed.

Mr. Roskill referred to the loss the Circle had suffered by the death of Mr. H. de R. Walker. He died suddenly on 31st July. Mr. Walker was elected to the Circle in July 1903: he resigned owing to pressure of parliamentary duties in 1906 (he was then member for Melton), but was re-elected in 1907. He had wide knowledge of colonial affairs & also of local government, & had read to the Circle papers on 'New Zealand' (1904) 'The Second Chamber in Canada, South Africa & Australasia' (1910) 'Housing & Town Planning after the War' (1919), & was going to read a paper on 'The Problem of Greater London' during the present session. Mr. Roskill paid a tribute to Mr. Walker's public service & also to his personality wh was distinguished by his

[254] Joseph-Arthur Comte de Gobineau (1816–1882). French philosopher who influenced race-thinking.

kindliness & modesty, his public spirit & his single-minded devotion to the cause of humanity. The Circle decided to send a letter of sympathy & condolence to Mrs. Walker.

Mr. Roskill was re-elected President
" Hobson   "   "Vice-President
" Parsons   "   Secretary

Messrs: Alden, Brereton, Crook, Harley & Hurcomb were re-elected as the Committee with the President, Vice-President & Secretary ex officio.

The Accounts were presented & accepted.

The Record of Attendance was read as follows:

Out of 9 meetings

Mr. Parsons attended		9
Messrs:	Alden, Gilmour, Hurcomb, Matheson & Roskill	8
"	Reid & Wigglesworth	7
"	Brereton, Gooch, Goodenough & Harley	6
"	Crook, Gardiner, Golding & Robertson	4
"	Crosse, Hobson, Sir Sydney Olivier, Sir Geo: Paish & the late Mr. Walker	2
Mr. Walsh		1
Messrs:	Buxton, Herdman, MacDonald, Usher & Sir Fisher Dilke	0

Out of 2 meetings Mr. Vallance attended 2 & Russell Cooke 1 Average attendance 13 as against 14.2 for the previous session.

Mr. Alden read his paper on 'Unemployment'.

The Percentage of unemployed last year was greater than for the last 50 years—15.4 as against 15.3 in 1921, 2.4 in 1920, 7.8 in 1908, 10.2 in 1886 & 11.4 in 1879. It looks as though there will be little or no improvement this winter. Local authorities have carried out almost as much work as their funds will allow. Non-revenue producing schemes wh wd indirectly assist trade—especially road development, bridge building, extension of docks wharves & harbours, will probably have to be set on Govt. The restoration of stable political & economic conditions is essential to the solution of the problem & the Govt: must be aroused to the supreme importance of settlement of reparations & inter-allied debt questions. Unemployment is a national question with an international bearing. A large amount of unemployment in one country mirrors some corresponding suffering in all other countries that have either exports or imports. Possible remedies are 1. Govt: aided by employers shd obtain all possible information as to probable trend of trade, so that Govt: may prepare well ahead for relief measures. 2. Employers shd be encouraged to adopt new & better methods of production & management. 3. Transport facilities shd be improved, enabling town-workers to live in country & use the land as an alternative source of income, at the same time increasing mobility of labour. 4. Relief works shd be designed with special reference to increasing industrial efficiency.

In the discussion the theory of cyclical depression of trade due to world harvest failure was discussed & the reasons for the extent of unemployment differing in various countries at the same time. Opinion was expressed that the root of the trouble in England is that we are an industrial country, dependent largely on supplying other countries with things they are now learning to make for themselves.

John Roskill   Chairman

14 Nov. 1923.

* * *

[271] The 271st meeting of the Circle was held at Stapley House on 14 Nov. 1923.

Present 17 members, an old member Archdeacon Lilley, & 3 visitors— Mr. Roskill in the chair.

Apology for absence was notified from Mr. Alden.

Minutes of the previous meeting were read & confirmed.

A letter was read from Mrs. Walker expressing her thanks to the Circle for their sympathy.

A letter was read from Mr. Felix Crosse tendering his resignation on account of ill-health. His resignation was accepted with regret & the hope that he wd rejoin if & when his health was restored.

Mr. Hobson gave an address on the subject of a Capital Levy.

The passive resistance of wealth during the war prevented conscription of wealth wh wd have been a not impossible political proposition. After the war there was a desire to make a special levy on war wealth. A committee sat & reported that it wd not be impracticable, but for certain reasons—including the smallness of the anticipated yield—no action was taken. Many people thought a capital levy wd have been a good thing then: it wd obviously be more difficult now. But the idea still receives considerable support: it is in the forefront of the Labour Party's programme & is endorsed by several distinguished economists. 3000 million could, it is said, be raised by a progressive tax of $5\frac{1}{2}\%$ to 50% on capitals over £5.000 up to £1.000.000, enabling taxation to be reduced by 162.000.000 gross.

The first objection raised against a capital levy is the danger that it might be repeated in another Emergency. The main thing to be considered is its reaction on trade & industry. Although there wd be no loss of material capital there wd be loss of trading capital. The capital of joint stock companies wd be exempt, as the levy wd be on individuals: but men whose own capital is in their private businesses wd be hit. Though the individual might thus be injured it is not so clear that society as a whole wd be injured. There is also some truth in the objection that considerable disturbance wd be caused by the transfer of money from one set of people to another. The value of investments wd oscillate in the market, but this wd be only temporary: the real value of the investments being the productivity of the businesses they represent. Against these objections must be set the lightening of taxation & the improvement of national credit. Other difficulties more substantial than those already mentioned are the large possibilities of evasion—as by transfer of property abroad & by false returns. It is also a question whether it is not bad tactics for a Labour party to press a capital levy at the present time, owing to misrepresentation for election purposes.

In the discussion the following opinions were expressed:

1. A consensus of favourable opinion on the part of people who have capital is necessary to success of a capital levy.

2. The issue is between 2 forms of taxation & if we can get through by our machinery of income tax it is doubtful whether we shd be wise to institute new machinery.

3. If we are dealing with capital levy as a fiscal question we ought not to find it put forward as an instrument for some ulterior object such as socialisation of industry.

4. Death duties are already an effective form of capital levy.

5. Capital levy now wd bring about nothing short of catastrophe. It is opposed by capitalists not because it wd hurt them but because they are convinced that it wd shake the whole fabric of trade & increase unemployment.

John Roskill   Chairman

12. xii. 23

* * *

[272] The 272nd meeting of the Circle was held at Stapley House on 12 Decr. 1923.

Present 14 members & 2 visitors, Mr. Roskill in the chair.

Apologies for absence were notified from Messrs: Brereton, Crook, Gardiner, Herdman, Robertson & Wigglesworth.

A letter of resignation was read from Mr. Golding who has taken an appointment in the ethical movement in the United States. His resignation was accepted with regret & the Secretary was desired to convey to Mr. Golding the Circle's good wishes & the hope that shd he return to England he wd seek re-election.

Mr. Gooch gave an address on the European Situation, passing in review the internal & external conditions of each of the European countries separately.

Russia Economically the corner has been turned—witness withdrawal of American Relief Commission[255] last summer. We are on the eve of recognition of the Soviet Govt. Relations between Russia & her succession states are improving.

Turkey has driven Greeks out of Asia Minor & the Powers out of Constantinople, dictating terms to her victors. It is to be noticed that the intimacy between Angora & Moscow is cooling.

Greece The 1.000.000 Greeks driven from Eastern Thrace are a strain on Greece at present but will become an asset. In internal politics Greece is still distracted. She may shortly move her king to abdicate (He did abdicate 6 days later).[256]

Bulgaria Stambouliski[257] did good work for his country, improving relations with Serbia & obtaining reduction of reparations from 88 million to 22 million. He became extremely autocratic & the revolt was a personal revolt against an intolerable tyrant. It is to be hoped that Greece will arrange an economic outlet for Bulgaria on the Aegean.

Roumania still the rottenest state in Europe—with corrupt & insufficient ruling caste. External relations with Russia not in immediate danger but Bessarabia remains a bone of contention. Relations with Hungary very bad.

Jugo-Slavia not developing well & dominated by old Serbs.

Hungary is just reaching the turning point: her recovery will be more rapid than that of Austria.

Austria on the up-grade. Relations with her neighbours very friendly. Dr. Seipel[258] has a way of establishing confidence.

Bohemia (Czecho-Slovakia) the most hopeful of all the new states, but too big. There is great dissatisfaction in Slovakia.

Italy is now a great power in fact, thanks to Mussolini & one of the only 3 remaining in Europe.

Germany. Bavaria wants to remain within Germany, but with full autonomy. Any separation of the Rhineland or the Ruhr will be but temporary. *France* will stick to her pledges knowing that she will not get much in the way of reparations & there will be difficulty in getting her out.

[255] The American Relief Administration was active in Russia on famine relief between 1921 and 1923.

[256] Note added by Parsons.

[257] Alexander Stambo[u]liski (1879–1923), premier of Bulgaria 1921–23.

[258] Dr Ignaz Seipel (1876–1932), Austrian Christian Social leader and Chancellor after world war one.

The discussion dealt mainly with the effect of the exploitation & organisation of Senegal by France: the depopulation of Armenia as weakening the economic resources of Turkey: the chronic instability of the Balkans: the regrouping of the European powers: & the growth of relations between Germany & Russia.

John Roskill   Chairman

9 Jan: 1924.

* * *

[273] The 273rd meeting of the Circle was held on 9 Jan 1924 at Stapley House.

Present 11 members, Mr. Christopher Turnor & another visitor, Mr. Roskill in the chair.

Apologies for absence were notified from Mr. Herdman & Sir Sydney Olivier.

Minutes of the previous meeting were read & confirmed.

Mr. Christopher Turnor read his paper on 'Agriculture'.

Agriculture in this country is in a bad situation particularly as regards arable land wh is the most important because it employs more labour & produces more food. The farmer does not pay an economic rent, does not pay an economic wage, & very often has never done an economic day's work. One result is undercapitalisation of the industry & another that the land does not produce what it might.

Agriculture has not been recognised by the Govt: as an industry vital to the welfare of the country. In Denmark the industry is highly organised & can weather periods of depression wh may & do result in reduced profits but not in working at a loss. Organisation applied to the farm itself wd do a great deal here, but wd not overcome the lack of organisation of the industry. The small man in Denmark gets the advantage of co-operation. We ought to face the squeezing out of the uneconomical farmer, & the necessity for forcing organisation of the industry. A sympathetic govt. is necessary but not omnipotent. Organisation can hardly come from above: a sound co-operative policy must be devised by agriculturists themselves. Co-operative flour mills ought to be started with co-operative bakery attached. The principles of co-operation ought to be taught in the schools. The agricultural labourer must be paid at least 30/- a week. A big agricultural credit bank ought to be set going at once to enable the farmer to buy his land: & this is a govt. affair. At present 80% of our farmers are tenants as against 10% in Denmark. In every country where there is a highly developed agriculture, the system is that of occupying ownership.

The discussion took the form of questions on the subject generally & dealt with Danish methods, railway rates, wages, education, Govt. control of wheat, the mentality of the farmer, & the alleged inefficiency of the Ministry of Agriculture wh was admitted however to have done & to be doing good research work.

John Roskill   Chairman

13 Feb. 1924

* * *

[274] The 274th meeting of the Circle was held on 13 Feb. 1924 at Stapley House.

Present 15 members & 1 visitor, Mr. Roskill in the chair.

Apologies for absence were notified from Messrs: Gooch & Herdman.

Minutes of the previous meeting were read & confirmed.

It was decided to hold the June meeting on the 4th instead of 11th June.

A letter was read conveying the Circle's congratulations to the Prime Minister & asking him & the other Rainbow members of the Government (Lord Olivier—India: Mr. Buxton—Agriculture: & Mr. Trevelyan—Education) to meet the Circle at Mr. Roskill's house on some convenient evening: & it was announced that the Prime Minister in reply had intimated that he wd try to fix a date shortly. The Secretary was directed to send a copy of the congratulatory letter to each member of the Circle.[259]

---

[259] Copies of Parsons' accompanying letter as well as the letter to MacDonald exist in the files of the Sir Richard Stapley Educational Trust and read as follows:

18 Feb. 1924.

RAINBOW CIRCLE.

Dear

By direction of the Circle I send you herewith a copy of a letter recently addressed to the Prime Minister, who has expressed his pleasure in accepting the invitation. Will you be so good as to note that the date fixed is Wednesday 27th February.*

Yrs: sincerely,
Ambrose Parsons
Hon. Sec.

* The meeting in fact took place a week later.

26 January, 1924

RAINBOW CIRCLE

My dear MacDonald,

On behalf of the Rainbow Circle I send you our most sincere and cordial congratulations and our earnest good wishes for that kind of success you and the Circle have always and consistently thought worth striving for. For right from the beginning— now some 30 years ago—when Stapley, William Clarke, yourself, Samuel, Burrows and a few others laid our foundations, we have held steadily to our basic idea of endeavouring, however humbly, to further the cause of righteousness and of freedom of spirit. In our early days the practical application of the apparently simple principies of justice, pity and brotherhood no doubt seemed an easier and more obvious thing than it does now when, partly through the inevitable process of growing older, we have learnt rather more of the complex nature of our raw material, man, (and at times he strikes us as very raw!) and of the difficulties thereby inherent in all schemes for his betterment. I think none of us will ever forget how the wise and kindly influence of Stapley—a really beautiful influence—kept us together and united in common aims however divergent our views as to appropriate means. The very clash of our views in the atmosphere of sincerity and goodwill he did much to create helped us to broader and clearer vision. We may well find ourselves thinking of him and of others of us whose course has been run but whose influence still remains. I mention only Clarke, Russell Rea, Byles, and dear old Burrows (whose faith in humanity and youthfulness of spirit persisted even through the enforced inactivity of the five years of his last illness). How stirred they, like us who survive, would have been now that to one of ourselves has fallen the high and heavy responsibility of governing the country! How anxiously and sympathetically they, like us, would have hoped that you may have the best of all human satisfactions—some measure of achievement in the direction we all hold best.

We want to give you and Olivier, Buxton and Trevelyan, our good wishes in person. If you can manage to meet us, Mr. and Mrs. Roskill have most kindly offered to call the Circle together at their own house one evening, in order that we may have a quite informal and simple gathering with a 'stand-up' supper. I am therefore to ask you whether you will be so good as to name any date convenient to yourself (preferably not a Sunday) on which you could all four come at 9.0 p.m. We imagine that some date before the House sits may suit you best: but if not, the weeks are open to you, the only date which is impossible for Roskill being the 14th February. He has not told me why he bars St. Valentine!

With very earnest and cordial good wishes.

Sincerely yours,
Ambrose Parsons,
Hon. Sec.

Mr. Harley read his paper on the future of the State.

The conception of the State dominant in the latter part of the 19th Century was of a society in wh everyone submits to be organized, subordinated & disciplined for the sake of a common end. This conception has been challenged successively by Syndicalism, Guild Socialism, & the Soviet system. A tendency has arisen to regard the State as one out of many forms of association & not necessarily as the dominating influence of the future. As society progresses the citizen becomes involved in all kinds of social combinations, such as trade, professional, co-operative, religious, scientific & literary: & much that has previously been enacted by parliament is now hammered out in other associations based on mutual interests. But though recognition of this fact modifies the old & narrow conception of the State, the State must still remain the biggest & most effectively co-ordinating form of association. Again objection is raised to the State's assumption of sovereignty, & there can be no doubt that states founded on locality will have to foreswear their ancient sovereignties & work together for the future of civilisation within some larger combination.

In the discussion the following opinions were expressed:

That some definite abatement of the idea of sovereignty is necessary— with submission to some impartial body, or super-state, on certain points. Within its own territory the state must have power to over-ride individual wills—by force if necessary. The State will have to devise means of a better form of bureaucratic control with an adequate sense of service within the bureaucracy & some expert check on it. [By some members the term Civil Service was preferred to Bureaucracy]. That voluntary associations will probably have to play a much larger part than heretofore. The National Savings Committee[260] is an interesting example of voluntary association assisted by the State.

That Russia has abandoned the territorial idea of the State & will endeavour to extend throughout Europe the idea of Union of Soviet Republics: that Italy by giving an autocratic turn to democracy is shewing the way to a new form of government.

That some kind of super-court, rather than super-state is a primary need of civilisation.

John Roskill   Chairman

* * *

[275] The 275th meeting of the Circle was held on 5th March 1924. By the kindness of Mr. & Mrs. Roskill it took the form of an 'At Home' at their private house. Of the Circle there were present Messrs: Brereton, Cooke, Crook, Sir Fisher Dilke, Messrs: Dougherty, Gardiner, Gilmour, Gooch, Goodenough, Harley, Hurcomb, Matheson, Sir Geo: Paish, Messrs: Parsons Reid Roskill Vallance & Wigglesworth and the Prime Minister also Mr. Trevelyan & Mr. Graham

---

[260] The National Savings Committee was formed in 1916 as part of the National Savings Movement, to encourage wise saving and spending, to undertake propaganda work on behalf of thrift and to advise on and approve financial details of schemes for the investment societies. It launched national savings certificates. T.L. Gilmour was on the committee from the outset. Cp. *The National Savings Movement. Its Origins, Aims and Development* (London, 1931).

Wallas, old members. It was the first ladies' night since 1912. The following account by Mr. Gardiner is extracted from the Nation of 8th March.[261]

'There was a pleasant gathering of the Rainbow Circle on Wednesday night in honour of the Prime Minister, Lord Olivier, Mr. Noel Buxton, and Mr. C.P. Trevelyan, all of them members of the Government, and all of them are also members of the Circle. That body is one of the oldest and most distinguished discussion societies in the metropolis. It is thirty years or so since it was formed, and for many years it has held its monthly discussions at the house of the late Sir Richard Stapley, in Bloomsbury Square. The membership of the Society is limited to twenty-five, and, although mainly Liberal in tone, it has included men of various opinions, among them Sir Herbert Samuel, Archdeacon Lilley, Mr. J.M. Robertson, Mr. Graham Wallas, Mr. J.A. Hobson, Sir Fisher Dilke, and the members of the government I have mentioned. It is no slight distinction for so small a body to have contributed so large a proportion of the membership of a single Government. The gathering in their honour took place at the house of the President, Mr. John Roskill, K.C., in Montagu Square.

A.G.G[ardiner].'

In the course of the evening Mr. Roskill spoke a few words to the following effect: [262]

Mr. Prime Minister, and other members of the Rainbow Circle, Ladies and Gentlemen,

We meet to celebrate a great occasion. The Rainbow Circle has about 25 members. Four of them are members of the Cabinet. I doubt whether any Society, so small in its numbers, has ever achieved so great a distinction.

Mr. Ramsay MacDonald is an original member of the Circle, and was its first Honorary Secretary, a position he held for six years, ending in 1900. Lord Olivier and Mr. Trevelyan are also old members. Lord Olivier read his first paper in 1895, and Mr. Trevelyan in 1897. Mr. Noel Buxton is a recent member. He read a paper on the Balkan States in April 1921, and we captured him then and there. He did not and could not then know that the golden road to Cabinet rank led from the Rainbow Circle.

There is only one note of regret tonight, and that is that our founder Sir Richard Stapley has not been spared to see it. The Circle owes

---

[261] The reproduced newspaper cutting, from the *Nation*, 8.3.1924, is attached to the minutes.

[262] A blank page was left in the diary. Roskill's speech, however, may be found in the files of the Sir Richard Stapley Educational Trust and is hence reproduced.

everything to Stapley. He had what John Donne in his sermon on a London Merchant calls a 'publique heart'. There were big strands of idealism in his nature, but he never allowed them to weave a veil between himself and reality. Through the kindness of his trustees, Percy Alden and George Gooch, both members of the Circle, we still meet at Stapley House, and as long as the Circle continues, it will be identified with his name, and with his aims.

Sir, you are the 39th Prime Minister of this country. If I could collect the other 38, and ask them: Which of you all has had the greatest difficulties to encounter and surmount? Which of you all has had to defy the greatest limitations, that poverty and meagre opportunity had placed upon an unconquerable will? Everyone of them would point to you. We are now in the 6th year since the end of the War. In that period you have had 3 predecessors. One of them is dead; peace be to his ashes. Of the other two, the improvisations of one, and the inertia of the other, can hardly be said to have contributed to European peace.[263] Since you have attained office, a brighter sky has dawned, a better outlook prevailed. You, Sir, who have throughout your political life been the target for abuse from so many quarters, a St. Sebastian of the minor newspapers, suddenly find yourself the darling of the stern, but not unbending, 'Times'. In the 'Times' of Monday, their Paris Correspondent, after deploring the bad feeling between France and England, brought about by your predecessors, writes that 'the more adroit and friendly methods of Mr. MacDonald have created an intense reaction'; and in the adjoining column there are these headlines in big type: 'Prime Minister's Letter'; 'Creating Confidence'.

Your friends of the Rainbow Circle, everyone in this room, and everyone outside it, wish you Godspeed on your pathway to Peace, and to getting us back to the integrity of things. May it be said of you that where the others have failed, you could reconcile. May this be your victory. Seeing you standing there, with that expression so familiar to us at the Circle, I think of what Bossuet said of Condé: 'He carried victory in his eyes'. Mr. Prime Minister, we thank you for coming amongst us tonight, and for giving us this opportunity of doing you honour.

Mr. MacDonald in reply thanked Mr. & Mrs. Roskill & the Circle for their good wishes: He spoke of some of the old members Sir Richard Stapley, William Clarke & Herbert Burrows now dead, & Sir Herbert Samuel, & of the short-lived Progressive Review wh they started. He spoke of the aims & method of the Circle & of the great value in larger

---

[263] The three prime ministers are, in sequence, Andrew Bonar Law (1858–1923), David Lloyd George (1863–1945) and Stanley Baldwin (1867–1947).

spheres of action of the frank exchange of views in an atmosphere of friendship & goodwill—the sort of thing we have been practising in the Circle for 30 years past, kicking at times if necessary 'but with the head & not with the heels'. He also recalled a historical fact unknown to most of the Circle that the change of meeting place from the Rainbow Tavern to the hospitable house of the late Sir Richard Stapley—a change wh proved so much to the Circle's advantage— was directly due to the Tavern having produced at dinner one evening a boiled cod so poor & watery that even philosophers turned against it.

John Roskill   Chairman

12-iii-24

* * *

[276] The 276th meeting of the Circle was held on 12 March 1924 at Stapley House.

Present 13 members & 3 visitors, Mr. Roskill in the chair.

Apologies were notified from Messrs: Alden, Goodenough, Harley Hurcomb MacDonald, Matheson & Lord Olivier.

Minutes of the previous meetings were read & confirmed.

A vote of thanks to Mr. & Mrs. Roskill was passed for their kindness in entertaining the Circle on 5th March.

Mr. Wigglesworth read his paper on 'New Views on Colonial Government.' He took a not unflattering view of the way in wh the British Empire had come into existence & of the British genius for colonization, maintaining that the essential difference between the British empire & previous empires that have fallen is that the latter were dominated by the idea of exploitation whereas the British empire is animated by the ideal of service. He toyed with the idea of unification by means of an Imperial Zollverein, or alternatively by a system of Colonial preference, but was alive to the difficulties that any scheme to such end wd present having regard to the fact that the Empire consists of self-governing dominions wh have their own views on fiscal questions, & of Crown colonies, Dependencies, Protectorates & Mandated Territories, & that the conditions & interests not only of each class but often of each colony within the class need separate consideration. As regards the mandated territories he held that to inspire confidence in the future the guarantee of the British government shd be granted to the title of all property acquired.

In the discussion it was suggested that the British Empire had grown up in 2 ways—one part founded in liberal ideas, the other acquired & held by conquest. To this it was objected that no such clear division was possible the growth having been hugger-mugger & multifarious in kind. It was generally held that no progress was to be looked for along so mechanical a line as that of a Zollverein—indeed that anything of the kind wd tend to disruption: & that it is a healthy thing that the relationship between the Dominions & the Mother country shd not be stereotyped. Opinion was expressed that if we get a new Europe, demilitarised, it wd be desirable eventually to give back G[erman] E[ast] Africa to Germany under mandate.

John Roskill   Chairman

9-iv-24

* * *

[277] The 277th meeting of the Circle was held on 9 April 1924 at Stapley House.

Present 10 members, Mr. Roskill in the chair.

Apologies for absence were notified from Messrs: Gooch, Herdman, Robertson & Wigglesworth.

Minutes of the previous meeting were read & confirmed.

Mr. Matheson read his paper on 'Gambling as a source of revenue'.

He toyed with the thesis that as life is a gamble there can be no other source of revenue than gambling & that the best way of getting it wd be by a fierce system of income tax. Dealing with the suggestion to tax betting, he dealt at length with the Report of the recent Select Committee[264] & summarised the Report on the practicability of such a tax, the Chairman's unadopted draft on its desirability & Mr. Foot's unadopted draft on its undesirability. Mr. Matheson's own conclusion was that there was no reason why on the analogy of the entertainment tax we shd not institute a tax on betting on the lines suggested to the Committee by the Board of Customs & Excise. Such a tax wd he considered provide statistics as to the extent of betting & diminish the evil of maintaining on the statute books a law wh cannot be enforced & is habitually violated without any sense of wrong-doing.

In the discussion, wh was without form but not void, the Circle shewed a personal ignorance of the subject wh might perhaps be accounted unto them for righteousness. Thus no one except Mr. Matheson seemed to know the meaning of a Starting Price, & even he had apparently acquired his knowledge by study of the Select Committee's proceedings rather than by experience. Opinion, though

[264] The Select Committee on a Betting Duty (1923, [139]).

not unanimous, inclined in favour of a tax—in the pious but uncertain hope that it wd lead to the diminution of betting the evils of wh were admitted by all.

John Roskill   Chairman

14.v.24.

* * *

[278] The 278th meeting of the Circle was held on 14 May 1924 at Stapley House.

Present 15 members 3 visitors, Mr. Roskill in the chair.

Apologies for absence were notified from Messrs: Crook Goodenough & Wigglesworth.

The Minutes of the previous meeting were read & confirmed.

The Committee's recommendations respecting the programme for next session were communicated & approved.

Mr. W.G. Constable, recommended by the Committee & proposed by Mr. Roskill was unanimously elected as a member.

Mr. Robert Lynd gave an address on The Situation in Ireland.

Ireland is still in a state of suppressed revolution. Northern Ireland has quite an efficient government, as shewn in maintenance of law & order & the recent passing of a good education act: but has done badly in its treatment of the minority. Tyrone & Fermanagh are, contrary to their material interests, anxious to leave Northern Ireland & to join the Free State, because, owing to the gerrymandering of electoral constituencies, Nationalists & Catholics have been largely disfranchised. Northern Ireland has also been unfair in its treatment of Sinn Fein prisoners, the wrong men being imprisoned as often as not.

Southern Ireland is apparently quiet. The Republicans have called off all physical force for the moment & have not the money to revive civil war. The Govt. has little hope of Ireland as an industrial country & is concentrating on agriculture. There is a deficit on budget of about 8 millions; but there is reason to hope that the country will soon be solvent with a very small national debt. The boundary question is extremely difficult. Pressure might be brought to bear by Great Britain to induce Ulster to make concessions.

After the address a number of questions were asked on such points as the reality of religious belief, the political influence of the Roman Catholic church, the Civic Guard, Agricultural Co-operation, Railway Grouping, the Labour Movement, the Boundary Question, & the prospects of any real union between North & South.

John Roskill   Chairman

4 June 1924.

* * *

[279] The 279th meeting of the Circle was held on 4 June 1924 at Stapley House.

Present. 13 members & 4 visitors (including Sir Sankaran Nair), Mr. Roskill in the chair.

Apologies for absence were notified from Messrs: Gardiner Gooch & Goodenough.

Minutes of the previous meeting were read & confirmed.

The programme for the coming session was read & adopted.

Mr. Vallance read his paper on the Political Significance of Bolshevism.

He identified Bolshevism with Communism & held that it finds formal shape with Marx & the manifesto of 1847[265]—the shape wh the Bolsheviks of today acknowledge as that of their own programme. He made a spirited defence of the Bolshevik thesis, stated as follows:

Hegelian views of progress are soporific bunkum, the history of mankind being merely the record of successive enslavements: True liberty can only be attained with the establishment of a voluntarily classless co-operative commonwealth where the means of production are socially owned: In Capitalist Society there are only 2 classes of political a[266] economic importance—the bourgeoisie & the proletariat; whose interests are irreconcilable: Communism can only be realised through force—i.e. by the dictatorship of the proletariat wh implies the seizure of political power & its maintenance if need be by the Terror: The dictatorship of the proletariat will be temporary. When Communism is fully established the State, wh by its nature is the expression of a ruling class will wholly disappear & mankind will at last be free.

He held Bolshevism to be a tendency in progressive thought in all countries sufficiently potent to have real significance in that it focussed into one integral policy many pre-existing ways of thought. He was convinced of the coming spread of Bolshevism in Western Europe & only feared that attempts at Revolution wd be premature & therefore detrimental to success.

In the discussion the general sense of the Circle was against the views of the paper. Opinion was expressed that the argument made no appeal to pure reason: that Bolshevism in practice in Russia does not make for freedom at all: that it tends to retrogression & creates conditions which destroy mental development: that it is fatal to throw away the evolutionary idea & idle to believe that catastrophic means can bring about change for the better.

John Roskill   Chairman

8 Oct. 1924.

[265] Read '1848'.   [266] Read '&'.

Thirty-first Session: 1924–25.

[280] The 280th meeting of the Circle was held at Stapley House on 8 Oct. 1924.

Present. 15 members & 1 visitor, Mr. Roskill in the chair.

Apologies for absence were notified from Messrs: Alden, Hobson & Wigglesworth & Herdman.

Minutes of the previous meeting were read & confirmed.

Mr. Roskill was re-elected President
"   Hobson   "   Vice-President
"   Parsons   "   Secretary

Messrs: Alden, Brereton, Crook, Harley & Hurcomb were re-elected as the Committee with the President, Vice-President & Secretary ex officio.

The Accounts were presented & accepted & the subscription was raised from 4/- to 5/-.

The Record of Attendance was read as follows:
Out of a possible 9 meetings,

Messrs: Dougherty, Gilmour, Parsons & Roskill	9
" Hurcomb, Matheson & Vallance	8
" Hobson & Reid	7
" Gooch & Harley	6
" Crook & Wigglesworth	5
" Alden, Brereton & Sir Geo: Paish	4
" Gardiner & Goodenough	3
" Cooke & Sir Fisher Dilke	2
Lord Olivier & Mr. Robertson	1
Messrs: Buxton, Herdman, MacDonald, Usher & Walsh	0

Out of a possible 2 meetings
Mr. Constable attended 2
Average attendance 13.5 as against 13 for the previous session.

It was decided to transfer Messrs: Herdman, Usher & Walsh to the list of honorary members.

Mr. William C. Keay, proposed by Mr. Brereton was elected a member.

Mr. Hurcomb read his paper on 'Recent Legislation on Transport'.

The Railway Act of 1921 ended the Government's control (assumed in the war) & inaugurated a new scheme of railway organisation & development. The various companies were invited to agree the terms on wh they shd amalgamate with one another in specified groups & a special Tribunal was created to settle schemes for them if they failed to agree by 1 Jan 1923. The economy in operation effected by grouping comes mainly through such things as mass production & standardisation of rolling stock, & the enhancement of credit through the great financial strength of the groups. The settlement of wages & conditions of service was a further contribution to stability. The system adopted is that of a Central Wages Board with a National Wages Board as an appellate body. The complicated & inelastic system of fares & freight charges has been substituted by a scheme under wh a Rates Tribunal fixes & revises standard charges designed to yield an annual standard revenue equivalent to the revenue in 1913 of the constituent companies. The actual level of rates & fares is now about 50% above pre-war. Where the rates yield a surplus on the standard Revenue 1/5th goes to the Standard revenue of the Company & 4/5th to reduction of rates. The Ministry of Transport is empowered to obtain returns & operating statistics with a view to seeing that the working & management of companies are efficient & economical.

As regards roads an important new power was conferred when the Ministry of Transport was enabled to classify roads for the purpose of grants & to defray half the salary & establishment charges of engineers or surveyors of Local Authorities. The Roads Act of 1920 transferred to the Ministry the functions of the old Road Board & administration of the Road Fund.

In the discussion the following points, among others, came up for consideration:

1. The saving made by not running half-empty trains in competition.
2. Whether amalgamation was leading to the pooling of wagons.
3. Whether the Ministry had any control in the internal arrangements of the different groups.
4. Whether there is undue delay in electrification.
5. The potentialities of oil as fuel.
6. The advantages (or otherwise) of a unified & possibly nationalised system as compared with the present system of several independent groups.
7. The alleged deteriorated service on the Southern railway as compared with the departed glories & efficiency of the old South Eastern.

John Roskill   Chairman

12.xi.24.

* * *

APPENDIX I

Limited evidence concerning the history of the Rainbow Circle after October 1924 exists in the British Library of Political and Economic Science, Coll. Misc. 575/6, deposited together with the minute books. The following are some of the more interesting documents.

1924–1925

8 Oct.	Recent Legislation on Transport	
		C.W. Hurcomb
12 Nov.	The Ideals of Labour	
		J. Ramsay MacDonald
10 Dec.	Dante as a Political Thinker	
		A. Parsons
14 Jan.	India	
		S. Olivier
11 Feb.	Some Aspects of Banking	
		G.C. Dougherty
11 Mar.	Agriculture	
		N. Buxton
8 Apr.	Education	
		C.P. Trevelyan
13 May.	Art and the State	
		W.G. Constable
10 June.	The Politics of Oil	
		S. Russell Cooke

* * *

[In the Ramsay MacDonald Papers there is reference to a Rainbow Circle debate on 8.12.1926 on The Revival of Free Trade, and a dinner on the occasion of the 300th meeting of the Circle on Wednesday, 12th January 1927, at Pagani's, Great Portland Street. Roskill replied to the toast of the Rainbow Circle, Herbert Samuel (who must have resumed contact with the Circle upon his return to Britain in 1925) proposed the guests and Anthony Hope Hopkins replied. Cp. Parsons to MacDonald, P.R.O. 30/69, 883–7, 8.12.1926 and 18.12.1926.]

* * *

1929–1930

9 Oct.	Television (with practical demonstration).	
		William C. Keay
13 Nov.	Politics and Scientific Method.	
		Graham Wallas
11 Dec.	Stock Exchange Reform.	
		Oscar Hobson
8 Jan.	World Financial Situation.	
		Sir George Paish
12 Feb.	The Second Labour Government.	
		H.B. Usher
12 Mar.	American Individualism	
		Stephen S. Wilson
30 Apl.	Italian Art and the Italian Exhibition.	
		W.G. Constable
14 May.	Electricity and National Life.	
		T.H. Minshall
11 June.	The European Situation.	
		G.P. Gooch

* * *

1930–1931

8 Oct.	The Financial Situation.	
		Sir George Paish
12 Nov.	Education—A Retrospect.	
		Cloudseley Brereton
10 Dec.	The Political Situation.	
		W.M. Crook
14 Jan.	The Newer Despotism.	
		J.H. Harley
11 Feb.	The Constitution of Andorra.	
		J.H. Craig
11 Mar.	Thrillers	
		J.M. Robertson
15 Apl.	The Outlook for British Commerce and Industry.	
		Sir Francis Goodenough
13 May.	The European Situation.	
		G.P. Gooch
10 June.	?	
		Lord Olivier

* * *

Text of a letter from Percy Alden to S.S. Wilson:

July 1st 1931

Dear Wilson,

The senior members of the Rainbow Circle met at an informal meeting held at the Reform Club last night and decided after a long discussion that it might be better to discontinue the Rainbow Circle before it weakened so much as to render it necessary. Some of the older members are now unable to come out at night or find it very difficult to come to town for the meetings and as these members have contributed very much to the interest of the discussion it would be very difficult to replace them. Then again some other members owing to political work have practically become honorary members, like Samuel, Usher and MacDonald. Roskill has had to resign owing to ill-health & so a new President would have to be found. Recently both Dougherty and Burns have resigned. Robertson can scarcely ever come. All this makes it more difficult to get papers from members that will attract an attendance and the last thing that we really want is that it should be regarded as a duty to attend and not as a pleasure. Taking into account all the circumstances it was felt that it would be wise to discontinue our meetings and leave it to those members who wish to keep in touch with one another to arrange for occasional dinners. If there is fairly general agreement on this question the Minute Books and the Stapley bowl can be left in the charge of the Stapley Educational Trust in case there should ever be any wish to revive in some form or other the Circle which has now been in existence for over forty years.[267] Would you be good enough to communicate the feeling of the older members to the rest of the Circle.

With kind regards,
Yours faithfully,
Percy Alden

P.S. Do not forget the cheque for the last two sessions.

* * *

Wilson consequently circulated the following in September 1931:

8, Erskine Hill, N.W. 11
September 1931

Dear Sir,

Rainbow Circle

In July I received a letter from Alden from which excerpts follow:
[excerpts from the previous letter]
During July and August it was impossible to summon a meeting of

[267] This was incorrect.

the Committee that would have been fully attended; but several of the members agreed that it would not be fair, in view of the letter quoted above, to ask any member to prepare a paper for the forthcoming session. No programme has been arranged.

It was felt however, that it would only be right to give members of the Circle an opportunity of discussing the decision of the Senior members, and therefore a meeting of all members will be held at 32 Gordon Square, W.C.1 at 8 p.m. on Wednesday, Oct. 14th to consider the future of the Circle, which would appear to be either immediate dissolution, or a revival based on an influx of a considerable number of new members. It is hoped that this meeting may be well attended.

Yours sincerely,
S.S. WILSON

* * *

The last meeting of the Circle took place on Oct. 14 1931. The following typescript records the event:

'The following are extracts from the draft minutes:

The 341st Meeting of the Circle was held at 32 Gordon Sq. on Wed. 14 Oct. 1931. There were present Messrs. Alden, Crook, Gilmour, Hurcomb, Harley, Keay, Reid, Wigglesworth and Wilson. Mr. Alden was in the Chair.

Apologies for absence were notified from Messrs. Brereton, Constable, Craig, Gardiner, Goodenough, J.A. Hobson, Minshall, Olivier, Roskill and Wallas. Letters from several of the foregoing were read.

A full discussion took place on the letter sent by Alden to the Secretary on 1 July to the effect that certain members felt that it might be desirable to discontinue the meetings of the Circle before it weakened so much by the dropping out of older members as to render that step necessary. It was explained that no programme had been arranged for this Winter.

It was generally agreed that apart from special occasions meetings recently have not been so well supported either in numbers or by the quality of the subsequent discussions as heretofore. Among the reasons mentioned for the decline in attendance were the increasing age of some members, the increased responsibilities on the part of others, the lack of cohesion in the programmes for each session, and the failure to introduce new members.

It was, however, felt by the members present that there is a need for a group of men of diverse interests with a liberal outlook to explore and discuss some of the current social, economic and political problems. The members present felt that the Circle had fulfilled this function in the past, and hoped that the general tradition might be carried on. Continuance, however, must involve the introduction of a number of new members; to maintain an effective membership of about 30, and an average attendance of 15–20, it appeared that the number should be at least 15.

A Committee composed of Alden, Harley, Hurcomb, Keay and Wilson, together with Constable, O. Hobson and Wallas (subject to their consent) was appointed to consider the names of possible new members and arrange a meeting in Dec. 1931 or Jan. 1932 at which members and selected entrants could jointly plan a future policy.

The members present at the meeting felt that all members, whether they would be able to take an active part in the future or not, would be willing to give loyal support to the attempt of the Committee to revive the Circle.

It will be realised that success depends upon the right type of new member being forthcoming, and the Committee hopes that every member will be good enough to send to the Secretary before Nov. 7. the names and qualifications of a few men who would in his opinion be suitable to assist in carrying on the broadest traditions of the Circle.

The Committee will consider the names sent in and will ask the nominators of the most suitable candidates to introduce them at the next meeting, of which notice will be sent to all members.

S.S. WILSON
8 Erskine Hill, N.W. 11.

The initiative of the Circle failed, but there was a special meeting of the 'survivors of the Circle' on 1 Feb 1933, in which G.P. Gooch spoke on The European Situation (no ladies).

The following members attended: Brereton, Wigglesworth, Constable, Reid, Keay, Alden, Hurcomb, Craig, Gilmour, Crook, Gardiner, Roskill, Harley, Wilson.

Notes of Gooch's talk include: 'Glad Hitler has come in as unquestioned leader of the largest political party ... Has a claim to a share of power—not dictatorship. Has criticised Governments cruelly in past. He will show himself either a windbag or a statesman.'

APPENDIX II

List of Members of the Rainbow Circle

Maurice Adams (1850–1935). *Member 1902–1922*. Founder-member of the Fellowship of the New Life, the precursor of the Fabian Society. Resigned from Fabians together with Ramsay MacDonald in 1900 over Fabian reluctance to take a stand on the Boer war. Editor of the *Sower*, then *Seedtime*; ethicist, member of Humanitarian League, writer and lecturer on social and ethical issues. Insurance broker at John B. Adams & Son.

Percy Alden (1865–1944). *Member 1903–1931*. Liberal M.P. for Tottenham 1906–18; Labour M.P. for South Tottenham 1923–24. Educated Balliol College, Mansfield College. First Warden of Mansfield House Settlement at Canning Town in 1891 (for 10 years). Edited *Echo* 1901–2. For several years member of West Ham Borough Council. Writer & lecturer on social, educational, economic & labour questions. Member of London School Board in 1903. Especially interested in unemployment. Knighted 1933. Bursar, Sir Richard Stapley educational trust. Chairman of the British Institute of Social Service. Honorary treasurer & secretary of Sulgrave Manor Board.

Rev. John Henry Belcher (1862–1912). *Member 1894*. Ordained in Endington 1887 as Congregational minister. Served as minister of St. Thomas' Square Congregational Church, Hackney; later became unitarian. Secretary of Christian Socialist League 1894–8. Member Fabian Society 1893–97, 1909–10. Labour Church supporter. Elected for Hackney School Board 1894. Involved in founding ILP branch in Hackney in 1895. Later militant I.L.P.-er in the provinces (Plymouth?).

Oscar William Bowen. *Member 1894*. County Member, National Liberal Club, 1894–1914. Listed as without occupation.

Victor Verasis Branford (1864–1931). *Member 1905*, did not take up his place. Banker and Chartered accountant, writer on social affairs, Honorary Secretary of the Sociological Society.

Cloudesley Shovell Henry Brereton (1863–1937). *Member 1906–1931*. Educationalist. Educated St. John's College, Cambridge. Erstwhile schoolmaster. Specialized in modern languages, especially in French, and on the French educational system. Unofficial liaison officer between French and British educational systems. Occasional lecturer at L.S.E. Member of the Permanent Council of the International Moral Education Congress. Agriculturist in later life. In 1904 married widow of Principal John Charles Horobin of Homerton College, Cambridge.

Rev. John Bullock (1850–1931). *Member 1898–1911. Circle Secretary 1900–1906.* Educated Pembroke College, Oxford. Deacon 1874. Priest 1875. Vice-Principal St. Kenelm's, 1878–81. Rector of Tubney, Berks., 1881–4. Headmaster St. Oswald's College, Ellesmere 1884–1889. Curate of St. Paul's Parsonage, Bow Common 1890–95. Member Universities' Settlement Association 1893. Resident Toynbee Hall 1896–98. Member Fabian Society 1898–1900 and author of Tract 89: *Old Age Pensions.* Manager of the Harrow Road group of Day Schools and the Harrow Road group of Evening Continuation Schools in the Marylebone Division of the London School Board from 1899. Retired to Hastings.

Cecil Delisle Burns (1879–1942). *Member 1917–1921 and again in late 1920s.* Lecturer and writer. Former catholic (excommunicated). Extension lecturer for Cambridge, Oxford and London universities. War Office Intelligence Staff 1916–17. Civil servant, Ministry of Reconstruction, 1917. Research department, Labour party. Lecturer in philosophy, London. Stephenson Lecturer in Citizenship, Glasgow University. Lecturer, South Place Ethical Society.

Herbert Burrows (1845–1922). *Member 1894–1903; 1904–5; 1905–22.* Co-founder, with H.M. Hyndman, of the Social Democratic Federation. Employed in Inland Revenue. Helped organize Bryant and May strike of women match-makers in 1889. In 1908 and 1910 unsuccessfully contested Haggerston. Member of the Committee of the International Arbitration and Peace Association and of the International Arbitration League. Theosophist. Lecturer, South Place Ethical Society.

Noel Buxton (1869–1948). *Member 1921-late 1920s.* Liberal M.P. 1905–18, Labour M.P. 1922–30. Minister of Agriculture 1924, 1929–30. Philanthropist. Baron 1930.

William Pollard Byles (1839–1917). *Member 1899–1917.* Proprietor of *Bradford Observer.* Liberal M.P. 1892–5, (Shipley division of Yorkshire), 1906–17 (North Salford). Member, International Interparliamentary Union for Peace and Arbitration.

William Clarke (1852–1901). *Member 1894–1901.* Journalist, radical liberal. Member, Fellowship of the New Life. Member Fabian Society 1886–1897. Fabian Essayist. Ethicist and Positivist. Leader writer *Daily Chronicle* 1890–99. Editor *Progressive Review.*

William Constable (1887–1976). *Member 1924–1931.* Art historian and critic, barrister. Director, Courtauld Institute of Art. Slade

Professor of Fine Art, Cambridge University 1935–7. Curator, Boston Museum of Fine Arts 1938–57.

Sidney Russell Cooke (1892–1930). *Member 1923-late 1920s.* Stockbroker, student at King's College, Cambridge 1911–14. Unsuccessful Liberal candidate. Career in City, adviser on financial pages of *Nation & Athenaeum.* Found shot dead, verdict accidental. Wife Helen Melville Smith, daughter of captain of Titanic.

Benjamin Francis Cowan Costelloe (1855–1899). *Member 1895–1898.* Barrister, member L.C.C. 1891–99.

William Montgomery Crook (1860–1945). *Member 1894–1898, and 1900–1931.* Schoolmaster, lawyer and journalist. Educated Trinity College, Dublin. Unsuccessful Liberal candidate 1892. Joined staff of *Methodist Recorder.* Editor *Echo* 1898–1900. Secretary Home Counties Liberal Federation 1902–1931. Ornithologist.

Felix Warren Crosse (1892–1974). *Member 1921–1923.* Undergraduate at Balliol College, Oxford. Civil servant, Ministry of Munitions, 1915; War Office Intelligence 1918; attached to Foreign Office 1919–23, 1949–52. Member Fabian Society 1913. In 1922 researcher for the Webbs' *English Prisons under Local Government 1689–1894.* Literary worker and translator.

Rev. Percy Dearmer (1867–1936). *Member 1894.* Anglican High Churchman, liturgicologist and hymnologist. Secretary of the Christian Social Union 1891–1912. In 1919 appointed Professor of Ecclesiastical Art, King's College, London; later Canon of Westminster.

Fisher Wentworth Dilke (Sir) (1877–1944). *Member from 1921.* Fourth Baronet. Nephew of Sir Charles W. Dilke and brother-in-law of John Roskill.

Geoffrey C. Dougherty. *Member 1923–1931.* Manager, Chancery Lane Branch, National Provincial & Union Bank.

Rev. Robert P. Farley. *Member 1911–1918* (effectively till 1916). Lecturer for the I.L.P. Member Fabian Society 1907–1917. Member British Institute for Social Service in 1913 and contributor to its journal *Progress.* Translator and writer.

St. George Lane Fox-Pitt (1856–1932). *Member 1908–1912.* Writer and inventor. Pioneer of electric lighting, invented carbon filament lamp and Lane Fox system of electric lighting and distribution. One of the first active members of the Society for Psychical Research, author of *Free Will and Destiny* (1920). Vice-President and Treasurer of the Moral Education League (offshoot of the Ethical Movement), in which connection he wrote *The Purpose of Education* (various edns., 1913–1925). Organizer of the first International Moral Education Congress, London 1908, and member of its Permanent Executive Council, together with Brereton. Unsuccessful Liberal candidate in three elections.

Alfred George Gardiner (1865–1946). *Member 1915–1931.* Journalist, writer and biographer. Editor *Daily News* 1902–19. Asquithian Liberal.

Thomas Lennox Gilmour (1859–1936). *Member 1921–1931.* Barrister and journalist. Reporter for *Nottingham Guardian*, then educated at Edinburgh University, journalist for the *Scotsman*. Called to the Bar, 1892, Middle Temple. In 1904 became general manager of the Mozambique Company. Worked with E.D. Morel on the Congo reforms. Expert on Finland. Temporary Secretary to the Rhodes Trust during the first world war.

Henry John Golding (1874–1931). *Member 1911–1923.* Born Sunderland. Initially Civil Servant in Secretary for Scotland's Department and General Post Office. Then became employee of Pearl Assurance Company (London head office), rising to Joint Assistant Manager. Ethicist, member Bayswater Ethical Church, lecturer on social, moral and philosophical issues for Fabian Society, ILP and Ethical Movement. Member Fabian Society from 1899, struck off 1930. Moved in 1923 to U.S.A. and joined Society of the Ethical Culture of New York, becoming one of its staff of Leaders in 1925.

George Peabody Gooch (1873–1968). *Member 1909-late 1920s.* Historian and writer. Educated Trinity College, Cambridge. Taught at Toynbee Hall. Liberal M.P. for Bath 1906–10. Editor *Contemporary Review* 1911–60.

Francis William Goodenough (1872–1940). *Member 1911–1931.* Controller of gas sales, Gas, Light and Coke Co. 1903–31. Later joint honorary secretary, National Gas Council. Chairman, member and adviser on numerous committees. Knighted 1930.

J. Corrie Brighton Grant (1850–1924). Radical M.P. for South-East (Rugby) division of Warwick from 1900. Barrister, Middle Temple.

Arthur Robert Gridley (185?- ?). *Member 1907–1909.* Scholar of Wadham College, Oxford, 1874–8. B.A. & M.A. 1881. Of Inner Temple 1877. Member Fabian Society 1891 for a short period. Unsuccessful Progressive candidate, Lewisham, 1910.

John Hunter Harley (1865–1947). *Member 1902–1931.* Journalist and expert on Poland. Born at Stirling, first class honours in mental and moral philosophy, Glasgow University. Ordained at Mansfield College, Oxford (1891–4) as Congregationalist Minister. Pastor, St. Neots, Hunts. (1894–7). Joined the staff of the *Echo*. Represented *Labour Leader* and *Daily Chronicle* in Press Gallery of House of Commons. President, National Union of Journalists, 1911.

Member, Fabian Society. Alderman, St. Pancras, active in London local government.

John Octavius Herdman (1862–1927). *Member 1905–1924.* B.A. (Dub.) in history and political science, 1884. Barrister at Law, Inner Temple, since 1892; on South Wales circuit from late 1890s till 1908. Occasional contributor to the *Contemporary Review*.

Leonard Trelawny Hobhouse (1865–1929). *Member 1903, resigned 1904,* did not take up his place. Social philosopher, liberal theorist and journalist. First Martin White Professor of Sociology at the L.S.E. Leader-writer, *Manchester Guardian*.

John Atkinson Hobson (1858–1940). *Member 1894–1931.* Journalist and writer, economist, social and political thinker, liberal theorist. Lecturer, Oxford University Extension courses; South Place Ethical Society. On staff of *Nation*; contributor, *Manchester Guardian* and other progressive newspapers and periodicals.

Cyril William Hurcomb (1883–1975). *Member 1917–1931.* Civil servant. Permanent Secretary, Ministry of Transport 1927–37. Director General: Ministry of Shipping 1939–41; Ministry of War Transport, 1941–7. Chairman, British Transport Commission 1948–53. Baron 1950.

Thomas Fair Husband (1862–1921). *Member 1895–1899 and 1907–1921.* Civil servant at the Board of Agriculture, ethicist.

William C. Keay. *Member 1924–1931.* General Secretary of the National Federation of Professional, Technical, Administrative and Supervisory Workers. Early supporter of Baird's work in developing television. Unsuccessful Labour candidate, Harwich, 1931.

Rev. Alfred Leslie Lilley (1860–1948). *Member 1895–1917.* Theologian and writer. Canon of Hereford Cathedral 1911–36. Archdeacon of Ludlow 1913–28.

James Ramsay MacDonald (1866–1937). *Member 1894–1920s. Circle Secretary 1894–1900.* Politician, Labour leader, Prime Minister 1924, 1929–35. Writer and journalist. Early member of Social Democratic Federation and of Fabian Society. M.P. 1906–18, 1922–35, 1936–7. Secretary, Labour Representation Committee and Labour Party 1900–12; Treasurer, 1912–24. Chairman, Independent Labour Party, 1906–9. Chairman, Parliamentary Labour Party in 1912.

John Archibald Murray Macdonald (1854–1939). *Member 1894–1916.* Educated Glasgow and Edinburgh Universities. Liberal M.P. for Bow and Bromley, 1892–5; for Falkirk Burghs 1906–18; for Falkirk 1918–1922. Member of London School Board 1897–1902. Before 1914 honorary secretary of the Cobden Club. Privy Councillor 1916. Contributor to *Nineteenth Century*, etc.

John McKillop (–1925). *Member 1902–1909 and 1910–1922.* First Secretary (from 1897) and Librarian of London School of Economics. Member Fabian Society 1894–1921, organised correspondence classes for them in the 1890s. Member Executive Committee of British Institute for Social Service. Occasional lecturer for Fabians, reviewer of books on sociology. Worked in first world war for Ministry of Munitions. Reputedly became a tramp and died abroad in a workhouse.

Frederick James Matheson (1868–1936). *Member 1903–1929.* Journalist; London Inspector for the Department of National Insurance, promoter of the National Insurance scheme. Spent some years in the U.S.A. as civil engineer in Pittsburgh and St. Louis. As correspondent of the *New York Herald* was one of the first to enter Havana after the U.S.-Cuban war. Returned to England as agent for New York publishers Messrs. Ginn & Co. Secretary of the British Institute for Social Service 1906–1909 (and on its Executive till 1929) and the editor of its journal, *Progress*; then superintendent at publishers P.S. King & Sons of works on civic, economic, political and social problems. Member Fabian Society 1906–1913. Failed to be elected to its Executive 1911.

George Francis Millin (1840–1921). *Member 1894–1918.* Author and journalist. Writer on social and land questions, Special Commissioner to the *Daily News*.

Rev. William Douglas Morrison (1852–1943). *Member 1897–1910.* Prison chaplain, then Rector of St. Marylebone 1908–41. Expert on penal reform.

Joseph Francis Oakeshott (1860–1945). *Member 1895.* Member and organiser of the Fellowship of the New Life; executive member, Fabian Society 1890–1902, poor law reformer. Civil servant, Inland Revenue Department, Somerset House. Trustee, London School of Economics.

Sydney Haldane Olivier (1859–1943). *Member 1894–1899 and 1913–1931.* Civil servant. Secretary, Fabian Society 1886–9, Fabian Essayist. Colonial Secretary, Jamaica 1900–4, Governor 1907–13. Permanent Secretary, Board of Agriculture 1913–17. Assistant Comptroller and Auditor of Exchequer, 1917–20; Secretary for India. Baron 1924.

George Paish (Sir) (1867–1957). *Member 1922–1930.* Statistician and Journalist. Joint Editor, *Statist* 1900–16. Adviser to Treasury 1916–18.

(Arthur) Ambrose Parsons (1872–1929) *Member 1903–1929, Circle Secretary 1906–1929.* Civil servant since 1893, mostly at the Stores Department of the G.P.O., rising to Senior Staff Officer. Member Fabian Society 1901–1926. Member, Executive Committee of British Institute for Social Service, 1928–9. Awarded M.B.E.

George Herbert Perris (1866–1920). *Member 1895–1920.* Journalist and author. Editor of *Hull Express*, 1885. For ten years on editorial staff of the Speaker. Foreign editor of the *Tribune* and of the *Daily News*. Editor of Concord, 1898–1906. Secretary of the Cobden Club, worker in the cause of peace. Member of the Ethical Movement. Founded what later became the International Arbitration Association.

John Edward Raphael (1882–1917). *Member 1909–1917.* Born in Brussels. Graduated in History from St. John's College, Oxford. Cricketer, footballer and all-round sportsman. Barrister, unsuccessful Liberal candidate for Croydon, 1909. Supporter of women's suffrage. Killed in France, June 1917.

Russell Rea (1846–1916). *Member 1895–1916.* Shipowner and merchant. Liberal M.P. for Gloucester 1900–10; for South Shields 1901–16. Junior Lord of the Treasury 1915–16.

William Pember Reeves (1857–1932). *Member 1896–1908.* New Zealand barrister, journalist and politician. Agent General, then High Commissioner for New Zealand 1905–8. Director, London School of Economics 1908–19.

George Thomas Reid (Sir) (1881–1966). *Member 1921–1931.* Student at London School of Economics, B.Sc. (econ.), First Class Hons. Secretary of Trades Boards 1912–19; Secretary of Industrial Court 1919–23; Assistant Secretary, Ministry of Labour; Secretary, Assistance Board 1938–44.

John MacKinnon Robertson (1856–1933). *Member 1899–1931.* Writer, freethinker, social and economic theorist, literary scholar and critic. Collaborator with Charles Bradlaugh on *National Reformer*; founder and editor of *Free Review*. Liberal M.P. 1906–18. Parliamentary Secretary to the Board of Trade 1911–15. Free trader. Lecturer, South Place Ethical Society.

John Roskill (1860–1940). *Member 1897–1899, 1900–1901 and 1912–1931. President and Chairman of the Circle 1920–31.* First Class Hons. Oxford 1880. Contested Stockport unsuccessfully for Liberal Party 1895. Barrister, judge of Salford Hundred Court of Record 1909–1937. Death of his wife in fire at his home precipitated break-up of Circle.

Rev. Harold Rylett (1851–1936). *Member 1896–1905 and 1906–1911.* Unitarian minister, journalist. Worked on staffs of *New Age* (editor and proprietor 1899–1907) and *Tribune*. Unsuccessful Liberal candidate, 1881 and 1910. Honorary secretary of the Stop the War Committee during the South African war.

Herbert Louis Samuel (1870–1963). *Member 1895–1912.* Liberal politician, writer and philosopher. M.P. 1902–18, 1929–35. Postmaster General, 1910. President, Local Government Board, 1914.

Home Secretary, 1916. High Commissioner for Palestine, 1920–5. Leader, Liberal party, 1931. Viscount, 1937.

Henry Cary Shuttleworth (1850–1900). *Member 1894–1895.* Undergraduate at Christ Church, Oxford 1874–6. Canon. Lecturer in theology at King's College, London, from 1883. Christian Socialist.

Richard Stapley (Sir) (1842–1920). *Member and Chairman of the Circle, 1894–1920.* Head of a London firm of warehousemen, philanthropist, worker in cause of technical education. Member of Council of City of London. Unsuccessful Liberal candidate Brixton Division 1892, Holborn Division 1910. Chairman Port of London Sanitary Authority, J.P. for Sussex. Left over £300,000 to found the Sir Richard Stapley Educational Trust.

Charles Philips Trevelyan (1870–1958). *Member 1895–1901.* Liberal M.P. 1899–1918. Joined Labour party 1918, M.P. 1922–31. Founder member, Union of Democratic Control. President of the Board of Education, 1924, 1929–31.

Herbert Brough Usher (1892–1969). *Member 1920 until late 1920s.* Journalist, civil servant. Assistant editor, *Westminster Gazette*, 1919. Unsuccessful Labour candidate, 1924, 1929. Personal Private Secretary to Prime Minister MacDonald, 1929–35.

Aylmer Vallance (1892–1955). *Member 1923–1929.* Journalist and editor. Assistant editor: *New Statesman, Economist*. Editor, *News Chronicle*. General Staff, War Office 1930–45.

Henry de Rosenbach Walker (1867–1923). *Member 1903–1906 and 1907–1923.* Liberal M.P. 1906–10. Elected member London County Council, 1913. Alderman of County of London, 1919. Writer.

Graham Wallas (1858–1932). *Member 1899–1901, and from late 1920s–1931.* Educationalist and social theorist. Early Fabian 1886–1904. Fabian Essayist. Writer on historical and social subjects. Lecturer at London School of Economics, 1895–1923. Professor of Political Science 1914–23. Member London County Council 1904–7.

William Trevor Hayne Walsh (1866–1938). *Member 1902–1924.* Undergraduate at St. John's, Oxford 1885–9, B.A. 1889. Schoolmaster. Resident Toynbee Hall 1898–1905. From 1903 Assistant Secretary, (Secondary Schools Department) Kent Education Committee. From 1923 worked in Rome under the Institut International d'Agriculture.

Alfred Wigglesworth (1865–1951). *Member 1917–1931.* Founder of Wigglesworth & Co., fibre merchants. In Ministry of Munitions 1914–18. Director of many sisal companies. In 1942 president, Fibre Trade Federation. Author of technical treatises.

Members who joined after 1924:

John Herbert McCutcheon Craig (Sir) (1885–1977). Principal Assistant Secretary, Treasury 1931; Deputy Master and Comptroller, Royal Mint 1938–49.

Oscar Rudolf Hobson (Sir) (1886–1961). Banker, financial editor of *Manchester Guardian*, 1920–29; Editor-in-Chief, *Financial News*, 1929–34; City Editor, *News Chronicle*, 1935–59. Nephew of J.A. Hobson.

Percy (Richard) Morley Horder (1870–1961). Architect, designer of educational and commercial buildings.

Thomas Herbert Minshall (1873–195?). Consultant engineer; Member, Institution of Electrical Engineers. Distinguished Service Order 1917.

George Sampson (1873–1950). Inspector of Schools (L.C.C.). Educationalist and writer. Hon. General Secretary of the English Association.

Lawrence Weaver (Sir) (1876–1930). Architect, journalist and author. Civil Servant, Director, London Press Exchange.

Stephen Shipley Wilson (b. 1904). Civil servant. Ministry of Transport 1929–47. Actively involved in nationalization and denationalization of steel 1947–60. Keeper of Public Records 1960–66. Cabinet Office historical section 1967–77.

Speakers who were not members:

Maurice Andra

Bupendranath Basu (1859–1924). Member, Council of Secretary of State for India 1917–1923. Vice-Chancellor, Calcutta University.

Henry Richard Fox Bourne (1837–1909). Journalist, writer and social reformer. Expert on Africa, secretary of the Aborigines Protection Society.

Maud Adeline Cloudesley Brereton (1871–1946). Educationalist, headmistress. Principal, then Bursar, Homerton Training College, Cambridge. Public health expert. Consultant, editor of publications, British Commercial Gas Association.

Arthur John Butler (1844–1910). Writer on Dante, professor of Italian language and literature, University College, London.

Allen Clement (Clem) Edwards (1869–1938). Barrister, Trade Union organiser, member of Fabian Society, Labour editor of the *Echo*, special commissioner on staff of *Daily News* 1894. Lib-Lab M.P.

Richard Burdon Haldane (Viscount) (1856–1928). Liberal politician, lawyer and philosopher. M.P., Secretary of State for War (1905–12), Lord Chancellor for the first Labour Ministry 1924.

William Joynson-Hicks (Viscount) (1865–1932). Conservative politician. M.P., Postmaster General, Minister of Health and (1924–9) Home Secretary.

William Hesketh Lever (Viscount Leverhulme) (1851–1925). Soapmaker, manufacturer and philanthropist.

Robert Lynd (1879–1949). Essayist, critic and journalist. On staff of the *New Statesman* (signing Y.Y.), Literary Editor of the *News Chronicle*.

Thomas Hancock Nunn (1859–1937). Original Resident of Toynbee Hall, 1885–94. Poor Law Guardian of Stepney. Voluntarist social welfare organiser in Hampstead. Member, Royal Commission on the Poor Laws, 1905–09; signed Majority Report. Assisted in establishing the London Council of Social Service in 1910 and the National Council of Social Service in 1919.

Edward Reynolds Pease (1857–1955). Founding member of Fabian Society, and its first secretary 1890–1913.

Robert William Seton-Watson (1879–1951). Professor of Central European History at the University of London, 1922–45; Professor of Czechoslovak Studies, Oxford University 1945–9. Expert on central European and Balkan history and politics.

Constance Isabella Stuart Smith (1859–1930). Writer for National Anti-Sweating League, and on international labour law and other industrial subjects; member of Christian Social Union Research Committee; H.M. Lady Inspector of Factories 1913–1921; H.M. Deputy Chief Inspector of Factories, 1921–1925.

Christopher Hatton Turnor (1873–1940). Writer on land and agricultural subjects.

(Henry) Spenser Wilkinson (1853–1937). Barrister at Lincoln's Inn. Journalist on the *Manchester Guardian* (1882–92), *Morning Post* (1895–1914). Fellow of All Souls, Chichele Professor of Military History 1909–1923.

Harold Wright (1883–1934). Liberal activist and journalist. Assistant editor of the *Nation & Athenaeum* 1923–30; editor 1930–31.

Alfred Eckhard Zimmern (1879–1957). Classicist and historian, Fellow of New College, Oxford. Supporter of League of Nations. Montague Burton Professor of International Relations at Oxford 1930–44.

INDEX OF PAPERS LISTED BY AUTHOR

Numbers refer to the numbered meetings.

DATE DUE
